Taste of Home.

The
Ultimate
Cookie
Collection

499 scrumptious cookie recipes—
from classic cookies, brownies and bars to holiday favorites.

Taste of Home

A Taste of Home/Reader's Digest Book

Editor: Janet Briggs
Art Director: Lori Arndt
Layout Designers: Emma Acevedo, Catherine Fletcher,
 Julie Wagner
Proofreader: Linne Bruskewitz
Editorial Assistant: Barb Czysz
Food Editor: Janaan Cunningham
Senior Recipe Editor: Sue A. Jurack
Recipe Testing: Taste of Home Test Kitchen
Food Photography: Reiman Photo Studio
Cover Photo: James Wieland

Senior Editor, Retail Books: Jennifer Olski
Executive Editor, Books: Heidi Reuter Lloyd
Creative Director: Ardyth Cope
Senior Vice President, Editor in Chief: Catherine Cassidy
President: Barbara Newton
Founder: Roy Reiman

International Standard Book Number (13): 978-0-89821-520-5
International Standard Book Number (10): 0-89821-520-X
Library of Congress Control Number: 2006926771

For other Taste of Home books and products, visit www.tasteofhome.com.
For more Reader's Digest products and information, visit
www.rd.com (in the United States)
www.rd.ca (in Canada)

3 5 7 9 10 8 6 4 2
Printed in China

Pictured on covers:
1. Raspberry Swirls, p. 98
2. Chocolate Peanut Butter Sandwich Cookies, p. 156
3. Cream Cheese Bells, p. 114
4. Mocha Mousse Brownies, p. 171
5. Almond Kiss Cookies, p. 125
6. Chocolate Topped Peanut Butter Spritz, p. 281
7. Cranberry Chip Cookies, p. 55
8. Special Chocolate Treats, p. 133
9. Mocha Crackle Cookies, p. 24
10. Crisp Lemon Cookies, p. 23
11. Apricot Bars, p. 205
12. Chocolate Snowballs, p. 34
13. Meringue Coconut Brownies, p. 179
14. Frosted Spice Cookies, p. 144

Table of Contents

Cookies 101

Before You Begin

Read the entire recipe before you begin and check to see that you have all the ingredients for the recipe. Also make sure you understand the cooking techniques.

Preheat the oven for 10 to 15 minutes before baking. Use an oven thermometer to verify the accuracy of your oven. If the set oven temperature and the oven thermometer do not agree, adjust the oven temperature accordingly.

Mixing It Up

Prepare the ingredients before you start mixing. Let the butter soften, toast the coconut, chop the nuts, etc. Measure the ingredients correctly, using the proper technique and measuring utensils. Prepare recipe according to directions.

Avoid overmixing the dough. If it's handled too much, the cookies will be tough. For even baking, make cookies the same size and thickness.

Use heavy-gauge dull aluminum baking sheets with one or two short sides for cookies. For brownies and bars, use dull aluminum baking pans or glass. It's best to use the size of pan called for in the recipe.

When a recipe calls for greased baking sheets or pans, grease them with shortening or nonstick cooking spray. For easy removal, line the bottom of the pan with parchment paper and grease the paper.

Unless the recipe states otherwise, place cookie dough 2 to 3 in. apart on a cool baking sheet. For brownies and bars, spread the batter evenly in the pan, otherwise they may bake unevenly.

While Baking

Leave at least 2 in. around the baking sheet or pan and the oven walls for good heat circulation. For best results, bake only one sheet of cookies at a time. If you need to bake two sheets at once, switch the position of the baking sheets halfway through the baking time.

Use a kitchen timer to accurately time the recipe. Unless otherwise directed, let cookies cool for 1 minute on the baking sheet before removing to a wire rack. Cool baked goods on a wire rack to allow air to circulate around the food and cool completely before storing.

Let baking sheets cool before placing the next batch of cookie dough on it. Otherwise, the heat from the baking sheet will soften the dough and cause it to spread.

Storing Cookies & Bars

Cookies tend to switch texture upon storing—soft cookies get hard and crisp cookies get soft. Here are some tips to keep these morsels at optimum freshness.

- Allow cookies and bars to cool completely before storing. Cut crisp bar cookies while slightly warm. Allow icing on cookies to completely dry before storing.

- Store soft and crisp cookies in separate airtight containers. If stored together, the moisture from the soft cookies will soften the crisp cookies and they will lose their crunch.

- Flavors can also blend during storage, so don't store strong-flavored cookies with delicate-flavored cookies.

- Arrange cookies in a container with waxed paper between each layer.

- Store cookies in a cool, dry place. Cookies, frosted with a cream cheese frosting, should be covered and stored in the refrigerator.

- If your crisp cookies became soft during storage, crisp them up by heating in a 300° oven for 5 minutes.

- Cover a pan of uncut brownies and bars with foil—or put the pan in a large resealable plastic bag. If made with perishable ingredients, like the cream cheese, store covered in the refrigerator. Once the bars are cut, store them in an airtight container.

- For longer storage, freeze for up to 3 months.

- Wrap unfrosted cookies in plastic wrap, stack in an airtight container, seal and freeze.

- Freeze a pan of uncut bars in an airtight container or resealable plastic bag. Or, wrap individual bars in plastic wrap and stack in an airtight container.

- Thaw wrapped cookies and bars at room temperature before frosting and serving.

Shipping Cookies

Here are some pointers to ensure that cookies arrive at their destination as delicious and attractive as when you baked them.

First, select cookies that are sturdy and will travel well such as bars and brownies, drop, slice and bake, and sandwich cookies. Cutouts and other thin cookies might break or crumble during shipping. Cookies requiring refrigeration are a poor choice for shipping because they'll spoil.

Bake and completely cool cookies just before packing and shipping, so they arrive as fresh as possible.

To help the cookies stay fresh and intact, wrap them in bundles of two (for drop cookies, place their

bottoms together) with plastic wrap (photo 1). Wrap bars individually. Pack the crisp and soft cookies in separate tins and pack strong-flavored cookies such as gingersnaps, separate from mild-flavored cookies.

Line a tin or box with crumbled waxed paper to cushion the cookies. Snugly pack the cookies to within 1 in. of the top. Use crumpled waxed

paper or bubbly wrap to fill in any gaps between cookies and side of container and to cover tops of cookies (photo 2). Close box or tin.

Wrap cookie container in a cardboard box that is slightly larger and cushion with bubble wrap, crumpled paper or shipping peanuts. Seal box and label "Fragile and Perishable."

Problem-Solving Pointers for Cookies & Bars

Cookies spread too much.
- Place cookies on a cool baking sheet.
- Replace part of the butter in the recipe with shortening.
- If using margarine, check label and make sure it contains 80% vegetable oil.

Cookies don't spread enough.
- Use all butter instead of shortening or margarine.
- Add 1 to 2 tablespoons of liquid such as milk or water.
- Let dough stand at room temperature before baking.

Cookies are tough.
- The dough was overhandled or overmixed; use a light touch when mixing.
- Too much flour was worked into the dough.
- Add 1 or 2 tablespoons more of shortening or butter or sugar.

Cookies are too brown.
- Check oven temperature with an oven thermometer.

- Use heavy-gauged, dull aluminum baking sheets. Dark baking sheets will cause the cookies to be overly brown.

Cookies are too pale.
- Check oven temperature with an oven thermometer.
- Use heavy-gauged, dull aluminum baking sheets. Insulated baking sheets cause cookies to be pale in color.
- Use butter, not shortening or margarine.
- Substitute 1 to 2 tablespoons corn syrup for the sugar.

Bars baked unevenly.
- Spread batter evenly in pan.
- Check to make sure oven rack is level.

Bars are overbaked.
- Use pan size called for in recipe, too large a pan will cause batter to be thin and dry.
- Check oven temperature with an oven thermometer.
- Check 5 minutes sooner than the recommended baking time.

Bars are gummy.
- Use pan size called for in recipe, too small a pan will cause batter to be thick and may be gummy or cake-like.

Bars are tough.
- Stir in dry ingredients with a wooden spoon. Overmixing will cause the bars to be tough.

Crust is soggy.
- Crust was not baked long enough before placing filling on top.

Crumb crust is too crumbly.
- Cut in a little more butter so that the crust will stick together.

Brownies crumble when they are cut.
- Cool completely before cutting. Use a sawing motion when cutting. Warm blade of knife in hot water, then dry and make a cut. Clean and rewarm knife after each cut.

Food Equivalents

Item	Equivalent
Butter *or* Margarine	1 pound = 2 cups; 4 sticks 1 stick = 8 tablespoons
Chocolate Chips	6 ounces = 1 cup
Cocoa, baking	1 pound = 4 cups
Coconut, flaked	14 ounces = 5-1/2 cups
Cream Cheese	8 ounces = 16 tablespoons
Flour: all-purpose cake whole wheat	 1 pound = about 3-1/2 cups 1 pound = about 4-1/2 cups 1 pound = about 3-3/4 cups
Frozen Whipped Topping	8 ounces = 3-1/2 cups
Graham Crackers	16 crackers = 1 cup crumbs
Honey	1 pound = 1-1/3 cups
Lemons	1 medium = 3 tablespoons juice; 2 teaspoons grated peel
Limes	1 medium = 2 tablespoons juice; 1-1/2 teaspoons grated peel
Marshmallows: large miniature	 1 cup = 7 to 9 marshmallows 1 cup = about 100 marshmallows
Nuts: almonds ground hazelnuts pecans walnuts	 1 pound = 3 cups halves, 4 cups slivered 3-3/4 ounces = 1 cup 1 pound = 3-1/2 cups whole 1 pound = 4-1/2 cups chopped 1 pound = 3-3/4 cups chopped
Oats: old-fashioned quick-cooking	 1 pound = 5 cups 1 pound = 5-1/2 cups
Oranges	1 medium = 1/3 to 1/2 cup juice; 4 teaspoons grated peel
Raisins	15 ounces = 2-1/2 cups
Shortening	1 pound = 2 cups
Sugar: brown sugar confectioners' sugar granulated	 1 pound = 2-1/4 cups 1 pound = 4 cups 1 pound = 2-1/4 to 2-1/2 cups

Emergency Ingredients Substitutions

Ingredient	Amount	Substitution
Apple Pie Spice	1 teaspoon	1/2 teaspoon ground cinnamon + 1/4 teaspoon ground nutmeg, 1/8 teaspoon ground allspice and dash ground cloves *or* cardamom
Baking Powder	1 teaspoon	1/2 teaspoon cream of tartar + 1/4 teaspoon baking soda
Buttermilk	1 cup	1 tablespoon lemon juice *or* white vinegar + enough milk to measure 1 cup. Stir and let stand for 5 minutes before using. *Or* 1 cup plain yogurt.
Chocolate, semisweet	1 square (1 ounce)	3 tablespoons semisweet chocolate chips *or* 1 square (1 ounce) unsweetened chocolate + 1 tablespoon sugar
Chocolate, unsweetened	1 square (1 ounce)	3 tablespoons baking cocoa + 1 tablespoon shortening *or* vegetable oil
Corn Syrup, dark	1 cup	3/4 cup light corn syrup + 1/4 cup molasses
Corn Syrup, light	1 cup	1 cup sugar + 1/4 cup water
Cream, half-and-half	1 cup	1 tablespoon melted butter + enough whole milk to measure 1 cup
Egg	1 whole	2 egg whites *or* 2 egg yolks *or* 1/4 cup egg substitute
Flour, cake	1 cup	1 cup minus 2 tablespoons (7/8 cup) all-purpose flour
Flour, self-rising	1 cup	Place 1-1/2 teaspoons baking powder and 1/2 teaspoon salt in a measuring cup. Add all-purpose flour to measure 1 cup.
Honey	1 cup	1-1/4 cups sugar + 1/4 cup water
Lemon Juice	1 teaspoon	1 teaspoon cider vinegar
Lemon Peel	1 teaspoon	1/2 teaspoon lemon extract
Milk, whole	1 cup	1/2 cup evaporated milk + 1/2 cup water. *Or* 1 cup water + 1/3 cup nonfat dry milk powder
Molasses	1 cup	1 cup honey
Pumpkin Pie Spice	1 teaspoon	1/2 teaspoon ground cinnamon + 1/4 teaspoon ground ginger, 1/4 teaspoon ground allspice and 1/8 teaspoon ground nutmeg *or* cloves
Sour Cream	1 cup	1 cup plain yogurt
Sugar	1 cup	1 cup packed brown sugar *or* 2 cups sifted confectioners' sugar

Coconut Washboards, p. 15

8 *The Ultimate Cookie Collection*

Pecan Sandies Cookies, p. 10

Icebox Cookies, p. 19

Cookie Jar Gingersnaps, p. 11

Cookie Jar Favorites

Keep the cookie jar filled with plenty of family-pleasing treats. Choose from melt-in-your-mouth sugar cookies, old-time oatmeal cookies, spicy molasses chews and more.

Pecan Sandies Cookies

(Pictured on page 9)
Debbie Carlson, San Diego, California

Whenever Mother made these cookies, there never seemed to be enough! Even now when I make them, they disappear quickly. These buttery treats are great with a cold glass of milk or a steaming mug of hot chocolate.

2 cups butter, softened
1 cup confectioners' sugar
2 tablespoons water
4 teaspoons vanilla extract
4 cups all-purpose flour
2 cups chopped pecans
Additional confectioners' sugar

1. In a mixing bowl, cream butter and sugar. Add water and vanilla; mix well. Gradually add flour; fold in pecans.

2. Roll dough into 1-in. balls. Place on ungreased baking sheets and flatten with fingers. Bake at 300° for 20-25 minutes. Remove to wire racks to cool. When cool, dust with additional confectioners' sugar.

Yield: about 5 dozen.

Scottish Shortbread

Rose Mabee
Selkirk, Manitoba

My mother, who is of Scottish heritage, passed this recipe, as with most of my favorite recipes, on to me. When I entered Scottish Shortbread at our local fair, it won a ribbon.

1 pound butter, softened
1 cup packed brown sugar
4 to 4-1/2 cups all-purpose flour

1. In a mixing bowl, cream the butter and brown sugar. Add 3-3/4 cups flour; mix well.

2. Sprinkle a board with some of the remaining flour. Knead for 5 minutes, adding enough remaining flour to make a soft, nonsticky dough. Roll to 1/2-in. thickness. Cut into 3-in. x 1-in. strips.

3. Place 1 in. apart on ungreased baking sheets. Prick with fork. Bake at 325° for 20-25 minutes or until cookies are lightly browned. Remove to wire racks to cool.

Yield: about 4 dozen.

Cherry Snowballs

Evy Adams
West Seneca, New York

A juicy maraschino cherry is the pleasant surprise tucked inside these cookies. My mother clipped this recipe out of the newspaper many years ago.

- 1 cup butter, softened
- 1/2 cup confectioners' sugar
- 1 tablespoon water
- 1 teaspoon vanilla extract
- 2 cups all-purpose flour
- 1 cup quick-cooking oats
- 1/2 teaspoon salt
- 36 maraschino cherries, well drained

COATING:
- 2 cups confectioners' sugar
- 1/4 to 1/3 cup milk
- 2 cups flaked coconut, finely chopped

1. In a mixing bowl, cream butter, sugar, water and vanilla. Combine the flour, oats and salt; gradually add to the creamed mixture. Shape a tablespoonful of dough around each cherry, forming a ball.

2. Place 2 in. apart on ungreased baking sheets. Bake at 350° for 18-20 minutes or until bottoms are browned. Remove to wire racks to cool.

3. Combine confectioners' sugar and enough milk to achieve smooth dipping consistency. Dip cookies in sugar mixture, then roll in coconut.

Yield: 3 dozen.

Cookie Jar Gingersnaps

(Pictured on page 9)
Deb Handy, Pomona, Kansas

My grandma kept two cookie jars in her pantry. One of the jars, which I now have, always had these crisp and chewy gingersnap cookies in it.

- 3/4 cup shortening
- 1 cup sugar
- 1 egg
- 1/4 cup molasses
- 2 cups all-purpose flour
- 2 teaspoons baking soda
- 1-1/2 teaspoons ground ginger
- 1 teaspoon ground cinnamon
- 1/2 teaspoon salt
- Additional sugar

1. In a large mixing bowl, cream the shortening and sugar. Beat in the egg and molasses. Combine flour, baking soda, ginger, cinnamon and salt; gradually add to creamed mixture.

2. Roll teaspoonfuls of dough into balls. Dip one side of each ball into sugar; place with sugar side up on a greased baking sheet. Bake at 350° for 12-15 minutes or until lightly browned and crinkly. Remove to wire racks to cool.

Yield: 3-4 dozen.

Pecan Meltaways

Alberta McKay
Bartlesville, Oklahoma

These sugared nut-filled balls are a tradition of ours at Christmastime, but they are great anytime of year. And, they melt in your mouth!

1 cup butter, softened
1/2 cup confectioners' sugar
1 teaspoon vanilla extract
2-1/4 cups all-purpose flour
1/4 teaspoon salt
3/4 cup chopped pecans
Additional confectioners' sugar

1. In a mixing bowl, cream the butter, sugar and vanilla. Combine the flour and salt; add to creamed mixture. Stir in pecans. Cover and chill until easy to handle.

2. Roll into 1-inch balls and place 1 in. apart on ungreased baking sheets. Bake at 350° for 10-12 minutes. Roll in confectioners' sugar while still warm. Cool; roll in sugar again.

Yield: about 4 dozen.

Toffee Almond Sandies

Vicki Crowley, Monticello, Iowa

I knew after sampling these cookies from a friend that I had to add the recipe to my bulging files! The cookie is filled with sliced almonds and toffee bits for a crunchy treat.

1 cup butter, softened
1 cup vegetable oil
1 cup sugar
1 cup confectioners' sugar
2 eggs
1 teaspoon almond extract
4-1/2 cups all-purpose flour
1 teaspoon baking soda
1 teaspoon cream of tartar
1 teaspoon salt
2 cups sliced almonds
1 package English toffee bits (10 ounces) *or* almond brickle chips (7-1/2 ounces)

1. In a mixing bowl, cream butter, oil and sugars. Add eggs, one at a time, beating well after each addition. Beat in extract. Combine flour, baking soda, cream of tartar and salt; gradually add to the creamed mixture. Stir in almonds and toffee bits.

2. Drop by teaspoonfuls 2 in. apart onto ungreased baking sheets. Bake at 350° for 10-12 minutes or until golden brown. Remove to wire racks to cool completely.

Yield: 9 dozen.

Raspberry Nut Pinwheels

(Pictured on cover)
Pat Habiger, Spearville, Kansas

I won first prize in a recipe contest with these yummy swirl cookies a number of years ago. The taste of raspberries and walnuts really comes through in each bite, and they're so much fun to make!

1/2 cup butter, softened
1 cup sugar
1 egg
1 teaspoon vanilla extract
2 cups all-purpose flour
1 teaspoon baking powder
1/4 cup seedless raspberry jam
3/4 cup finely chopped walnuts

1. In a large mixing bowl, cream butter and sugar until light and fluffy. Beat in egg and vanilla. Combine the flour and baking powder; gradually add to creamed mixture and mix well.

2. Roll out dough between waxed paper into a 12-in. square. Remove top pieces of waxed paper. Spread dough with jam and sprinkle with nuts. Roll up tightly jelly-roll style, starting with a long side; wrap in plastic wrap. Refrigerate for 2 hours or until firm.

3. Unwrap dough and cut into 1/4-in. slices. Place 2 in. apart on ungreased baking sheets. Bake at 375° for 9-12 minutes or until edges are lightly browned. Remove to wire racks to cool.

Yield: about 3-1/2 dozen.

Double Chocolate Sprinkle Cookies

Barb Meinholz
South Milwaukee, Wisconsin

Chock-full of chocolate chips and sprinkles, these chewy cookies never last long around our house. They're simply outstanding.

2 cups butter, softened
2 cups sugar
2 cups packed brown sugar
4 eggs
2 teaspoons vanilla extract
5 cups old-fashioned oats
4 cups all-purpose flour
2 teaspoons baking soda
2 teaspoons baking powder
1 teaspoon salt
4 cups (24 ounces) semisweet chocolate chips
3 cups chopped walnuts
2 cups chocolate sprinkles

1. In a large mixing bowl, cream the butter and sugars. Add eggs, one at a time, beating well after each addition. Beat in vanilla.

2. Place the oats in a blender or food processor; cover and process until finely ground. Combine oats, flour, baking soda, baking powder and salt; gradually add to creamed mixture. Transfer to a larger bowl if necessary. Stir in chocolate chips, walnuts and sprinkles.

3. Roll into 1-1/2-in. balls. Place 2 in. apart on ungreased baking sheets. Flatten with a glass. Bake at 350° for 12-14 minutes or until golden brown. Remove to wire racks to cool.

Yield: about 9 dozen.

Maple Sugar Cookies

Anna Glaus, Greensburg, Pennsylvania

This recipe is requested by friends and family every time I'm asked to bring cookies for an event. Folks enjoy the subtle maple flavor in this crisp cookie.

- 1 cup butter-flavored shortening
- 1-1/4 cups sugar
- 2 eggs
- 1/4 cup maple syrup
- 1 tablespoon vanilla extract
- 3 cups all-purpose flour
- 3/4 teaspoon baking powder
- 1/2 teaspoon baking soda
- 1/2 teaspoon salt

1. In a mixing bowl, cream shortening and sugar. Add eggs, one at a time, beating well after each addition. Beat in syrup and vanilla. Combine the remaining ingredients; gradually add to the creamed mixture. Cover and refrigerate for 2 hours or until easy to handle.

2. On a lightly floured surface, roll out to 1/8-in. thickness. Cut with floured 2-1/2-in. cookie cutters. Place 1 in. apart on ungreased baking sheets. Bake at 375° for 8-10 minutes or until golden brown. Remove to wire racks to cool.

Yield: 4 dozen.

Crisp Graham Cookies

Lori Daniels
Beverly, West Virginia

I was delighted to find the recipe for these fun cookies. The peanut butter makes them extra special.

- 1/2 cup butter-flavored shortening
- 1/2 cup packed brown sugar
- 1 egg
- 1-1/2 teaspoons vanilla extract
- 1 can (14 ounces) sweetened condensed milk
- 3 tablespoons creamy peanut butter
- 1-1/2 cups all-purpose flour
- 1 cup graham cracker crumbs
- 1 teaspoon baking soda
- 1 teaspoon salt
- 2 cups (1 pound) plain M&M's
- 1/2 cup chopped pecans

1. In a mixing bowl, cream shortening and brown sugar; beat in egg. Add vanilla and milk. Blend in peanut butter. Combine dry ingredients; add to the creamed mixture. Stir in the M&M's and nuts.

2. Drop by teaspoonfuls 1 in. apart on ungreased baking sheets. Bake at 350° for 10-12 minutes or until golden brown. Remove to wire racks to cool completely.

Yield: 7 dozen.

Editor's Note: Reduced-fat or generic brands of peanut butter are not recommended for this recipe.

Championship Cookies

Patricia Miller
North Fork, California

I got this recipe from a friend who baked at a conference center. Snickers candy bar pieces make them irresistible.

2/3 cup shortening
1-1/4 cups packed brown sugar
1 egg
1 teaspoon vanilla extract
1-1/2 cups all-purpose flour
1 teaspoon baking powder
1 teaspoon baking soda
1/2 teaspoon ground cinnamon
1/4 teaspoon salt
2 Snickers candy bars (2.07 ounces *each*), chopped
1/2 cup quick-cooking oats

1. In a mixing bowl, cream shortening and brown sugar. Beat in egg and vanilla. Combine flour, baking powder, baking soda, cinnamon and salt; gradually add to creamed mixture. Stir in chopped candy bars and oats.

2. Drop dough by round tablespoonfuls 2 in. apart onto greased or parchment-lined baking sheets. Bake at 350° for 10-12 minutes or until lightly browned. Remove to wire racks to cool.

Yield: about 5 dozen.

Coconut Washboards

(Pictured on page 8)
Tommie Sue Shaw, McAlester, Oklahoma

My husband loves these cookies. Even my great-grandchildren like to come over to munch on these chewy treats, which resemble an old-fashioned washboard.

1/2 cup butter, softened
1/2 cup shortening
2 cups packed brown sugar
2 eggs
1/4 cup water
1 teaspoon vanilla extract
4 cups all-purpose flour
1-1/2 teaspoons baking powder
1/2 teaspoon baking soda
1/4 teaspoon salt
1 cup flaked coconut

1. In a mixing bowl, cream butter, shortening and sugar for 2 minutes or until fluffy. Add eggs; mix well. Gradually add water and vanilla; mix well. Combine flour, baking powder, baking soda and salt; add to the creamed mixture. Fold in coconut. Cover and refrigerate for 2-4 hours.

2. Roll into 1-in. balls. Place 2 in. apart on greased baking sheets; flatten with fingers into 2-1/2-in. x 1-in. oblong shapes. Press lengthwise with a floured fork. Bake at 400° for 8-10 minutes or until lightly browned. Cool 2 minutes before removing to wire racks.

Yield: 9 dozen.

Forming Coconut Washboard Cookies

With your hands, shape the 1-in. balls of dough into 2-1/2-in. x 1-in. rectangles. Using a floured fork, gently press the tines lengthwise across the cookie dough, giving it a washboard look.

Brownie Mounds

Mary Turner
Blountville, Tennessee

If you crave brownies but not the longer baking time, try these quick chocolaty cookies. I usually make them for the holidays, but they're good anytime of year.

    1/3 cup butter, softened
    3/4 cup sugar
    1/3 cup light corn syrup
      1 egg
      3 squares (1 ounce *each*)
         unsweetened chocolate,
         melted
      1 teaspoon vanilla extract
 1-2/3 cups all-purpose flour
    1/2 teaspoon baking powder
    1/4 teaspoon salt
    1/2 cup chopped walnuts

1. In a large mixing bowl, cream butter and sugar until light and fluffy. Add corn syrup and egg; beat well. Stir in chocolate and vanilla. Combine the flour, baking powder and salt; add to chocolate mixture; beat well. Stir in walnuts.

2. Drop by tablespoonfuls 2 in. apart onto greased baking sheets. Bake at 350° for 10-12 minutes or until edges are firm. Remove to wire racks to cool completely.

Yield: 3 dozen.

Lemon Refrigerator Cookies

Dessa Black, Dallas, Texas

This recipe brings back warm memories of watching my mom bake when I was a girl. To this day, the holidays wouldn't be the same without these cookies. The combination of light lemon flavor and pecans makes a delightful cookie.

    1/2 cup butter, softened
    1/2 cup sugar
    1/2 cup packed brown sugar
      1 egg
      1 teaspoon vanilla extract
      1 teaspoon lemon extract
 1-3/4 cups all-purpose flour
    1/2 teaspoon baking soda
    1/4 teaspoon salt
    1/2 cup finely chopped pecans

1. In a mixing bowl, cream butter and sugars. Beat in the egg and extracts. Combine flour, baking soda and salt; gradually add to the creamed mixture. Stir in pecans. Shape into two 9-in. rolls; wrap each in plastic wrap. Refrigerate for 2 hours or until firm.

2. Unwrap and cut into 1/8-in. slices. Place 2 in. apart on ungreased baking sheets. Bake at 250° for 21-22 minutes or until edges are golden brown. Remove to wire racks to cool.

Yield: about 8 dozen.

Editor's Note: The oven temperature is correct as printed.

Mom's Soft Raisin Cookies

Pearl Cochenour, Williamsport, Ohio

With four sons in service during World War II, my mother sent these favorite cookies as a taste from home to "her boys" in different parts of the world.

2 cups raisins
1 cup water
1 cup shortening
1-3/4 cups sugar
2 eggs, lightly beaten
1 teaspoon vanilla extract
3-1/2 cups all-purpose flour
1 teaspoon baking powder
1 teaspoon baking soda
1 teaspoon salt
1/2 teaspoon ground cinnamon
1/2 teaspoon ground nutmeg
1/2 cup chopped walnuts

1. Combine raisins and water in a small saucepan; bring to a boil. Cook for 3 minutes; remove from the heat and let cool (do not drain).

2. In a mixing bowl, cream shortening; gradually add sugar. Add eggs and vanilla. Combine dry ingredients; gradually add to creamed mixture and blend thoroughly. Stir in nuts and raisins.

3. Drop by teaspoonfuls 2 in. apart on greased baking sheets. Bake at 350° for 12-14 minutes or until set. Remove to wire racks to cool.

Yield: 6 dozen.

Oatmeal Animal Crackers

Bob Dittmar
Trout Run, Pennsylvania

When I was a child, we kids helped Mom cut these crispy crackers into all sorts of shapes. They're not too sweet, but sweet enough that we always wanted more.

2 cups sugar
2 cups old-fashioned oats
1 teaspoon baking soda
1/4 teaspoon salt
1/2 cup shortening
1/2 cup hot water
1 tablespoon vanilla extract
2 to 2-1/2 cups all-purpose flour

1. In a bowl, combine the sugar, oats, baking soda and salt. Cut in the shortening until crumbly. Add water and vanilla; stir until blended. Add enough flour to form a stiff dough.

2. On a lightly floured surface, roll dough to 1/8-in. thickness. Cut into rectangles or use floured cookie cutters. Using a floured spatula, transfer to greased baking sheets, placing 2 in. apart. Bake at 350° for 8-10 minutes or until lightly browned. Remove to wire racks to cool.

Yield: about 4 dozen.

Chocolate Jubilees

LaVera Fenton
Colorado Springs, Colorado

Rich and fudgy, these cookies make many appearances in care packages I send out. I combined several recipes and added maraschino cherries to come up with this winning recipe.

- 1 cup butter, softened
- 1 cup shortening
- 2 cups packed brown sugar
- 1 cup sugar
- 4 eggs
- 2 to 3 teaspoons almond extract
- 4 cups all-purpose flour
- 1 cup quick-cooking oats
- 1 cup baking cocoa
- 2 teaspoons *each* baking soda and salt
- 1 jar (16 ounces) maraschino cherries, drained and chopped
- 3 cups (18 ounces) semisweet chocolate chips
- 1 cup sliced almonds, optional

1. In a mixing bowl, cream butter, shortening and sugars. Add eggs, one at a time, beating well after each addition. Beat in extract. Combine flour, oats, cocoa, baking soda and salt; gradually add to the creamed mixture. Transfer to a larger bowl if necessary. Stir in cherries, chocolate chips and almonds if desired.

2. Roll into 1-1/2-in. balls. Place 3 in. apart on ungreased baking sheets. Bake at 375° for 12-14 minutes or until the edges are firm. Remove to wire racks to cool.

Yield: about 5-1/2 dozen.

Vanilla Wafer Cookies

Edith MacBeath
Gaines, Pennsylvania

Vanilla Wafer Cookies are chewy and irresistible and they're a wonderful way to round out a meal when you're on a budget.

- 1/2 cup butter, softened
- 1 cup sugar
- 1 egg
- 1 tablespoon vanilla extract
- 1-1/3 cups all-purpose flour
- 3/4 teaspoon baking powder
- 1/4 teaspoon salt

1. In a mixing bowl, cream butter and sugar. Beat in egg and vanilla. Combine dry ingredients; add to creamed mixture and mix well.

2. Drop by teaspoonfuls 2 in. apart onto ungreased baking sheets. Bake at 350° for 12-15 minutes or until edges are golden brown. Remove to a wire rack to cool.

Yield: about 3-1/2 dozen.

Icebox Cookies

Chris Paulsen
Glendale, Arizona

This recipe from my grandmother was my grandfather's favorite. I keep the dough in the freezer because I love to make a fresh batch when company drops in.

1/2 cup butter, softened
  1 cup packed brown sugar
  1 egg, beaten
1/2 teaspoon vanilla extract
  2 cups all-purpose flour
1/2 teaspoon baking soda
1/2 teaspoon cream of tartar
1/2 teaspoon salt
  1 cup chopped walnuts, optional

1. In a mixing bowl, cream the butter and brown sugar. Add egg and vanilla; beat well. Combine dry ingredients; add to creamed mixture. Stir in nuts if desired. On a lightly floured surface shape dough into two 10-in. rolls; wrap each in plastic wrap. Freeze for at least 12 hours.

2. Unwrap and cut into 3/8-in. slices. Place 2 in. apart on greased baking sheets. Bake at 350° for 6-8 minutes. Remove to wire racks to cool.

Yield: about 7 dozen.

Orange Drop Cookies

Grace Nevils, Steubenville, Ohio

This recipe comes from a nursing home where I worked, so it makes a lot. Everyone loved the cookie's delicate citrus flavor.

  1 cup butter, softened
  2 cups sugar
  3 eggs
1/3 cup orange juice
  1 tablespoon grated orange peel
  4 cups all-purpose flour
  2 teaspoons baking powder
  1 teaspoon baking soda

1. In a mixing bowl, cream butter and sugar. Beat in eggs, orange juice and peel. Combine the flour, baking powder and baking soda; gradually add to creamed mixture and mix well.

2. Drop by teaspoonfuls 2 in. apart onto greased baking sheets. Bake at 350° for 12-14 minutes or until edges begin to brown. Remove to wire racks to cool completely.

Yield: about 8 dozen.

Family–Favorite Oatmeal Cookies

Virginia Bodner
Sandusky, Ohio

My mother got this recipe in about 1910 when she was a housekeeper and cook for the local physician. The doctor's wife was an excellent cook and taught my mother of lot of her cooking techniques. The cookies soon became a favorite in our home and now are a favorite with my children's families.

- 2 cups packed brown sugar
- 1 cup shortening
- 3 eggs
- 3 cups all-purpose flour
- 1 teaspoon salt
- 1 teaspoon baking powder
- 1 teaspoon baking soda
- 1 teaspoon ground cinnamon
- 1 cup buttermilk
- 2 cups rolled oats
- 1 cup raisins
- 1 cup chopped walnuts

1. In a large mixing bowl, cream sugar and shortening. Add eggs, one at a time, mixing well after each addition. Combine flour, salt, baking powder, soda and cinnamon; add alternately with milk to the creamed mixture. Stir in oats, raisins and nuts.

2. Drop dough by heaping tablespoonfuls onto greased baking sheets. Bake at 350° for about 12 minutes or until lightly browned. Remove to wire racks to cool.

Yield: about 5 dozen.

Butterfinger Cookies

Carol Kitchens, Ridgeland, Mississippi

I prefer chunky peanut butter in this cookie. The candy bars add a touch of chocolate and a sweet crunch. These great cookies don't last long—make a double batch!

- 1/2 cup butter, softened
- 3/4 cup sugar
- 2/3 cup packed brown sugar
- 2 egg whites
- 1-1/4 cups chunky peanut butter
- 1-1/2 teaspoons vanilla extract
- 1 cup all-purpose flour
- 1/2 teaspoon baking soda
- 1/4 teaspoon salt
- 5 Butterfinger candy bars (2.1 ounces *each*), chopped

1. In a mixing bowl, cream butter and sugars. Add egg whites; beat well. Blend in peanut butter and vanilla. Combine flour, baking soda and salt; add to creamed mixture and mix well. Stir in candy bars.

2. Roll into 1-1/2-in. balls and place on greased baking sheets. Bake at 350° for 10-12 minutes or until golden brown. Remove to wire racks to cool.

Yield: 4 dozen.

Editor's Note: Reduced-fat or generic brands of peanut butter are not recommended for this recipe.

Peppermint Wafers

Barrie Citrowske, Canby, Minnesota

I enjoy nibbling on these cookies with a cup of tea or coffee for a midday treat. For even more mint flavor, use mint chocolate chips instead of semisweet.

>   1 cup butter, softened
>   3/4 cup sugar
>   1 egg
>   1/4 teaspoon peppermint extract
>   2-1/4 cups all-purpose flour
>   1/2 teaspoon salt
>   1 cup (6 ounces) semisweet chocolate chips
>   4 teaspoons shortening

1. In a mixing bowl, cream butter and sugar. Beat in egg extract. Combine flour and salt; gradually add to the creamed mixture. Shape into two 8-in. rolls; wrap each in plastic wrap. Refrigerate for 3 hours or until firm.

2. Unwrap and cut into 1/4-in. slices. Place 1 in. apart on ungreased baking sheets. Bake at 350° for 9-10 minutes or until the edges begin to brown. Remove to wire racks to cool.

3. In a microwave or heavy saucepan, melt chocolate and shortening; stir until smooth. Spread or drizzle over cookies.

Yield: about 6 dozen.

Editor's Note: To make mint chocolate chips, place 1 cup (6 ounces) semisweet chocolate chips and 1/8 teaspoon peppermint extract in a plastic bag; seal and toss to coat. Allow chips to stand for 1-2 days.

Coconut Macaroons

Nancy Tafoya
Ft. Collins, Colorado

I keep the ingredients for these easy-to-make cookies in my pantry. That way I can make a fresh batch in just minutes.

>   2-1/2 cups flaked coconut
>   1/3 cup all-purpose flour
>   1/8 teaspoon salt
>   2/3 cup sweetened condensed milk
>   1 teaspoon vanilla extract
>   9 red *or* green candied cherries, halved

1. In a bowl, combine the coconut, flour and salt. Add milk and vanilla; mix well (batter will be stiff).

2. Drop by tablespoonfuls 1 in. apart onto a greased baking sheet. Top each with a candied cherry half. Bake at 350° for 15-20 minutes or until golden brown. Remove to wire racks to cool.

Yield: 1-1/2 dozen.

Malted Milk Cookies

Audrey Metzger, Larchwood, Iowa

My daughter substituted crushed malted milk balls in our favorite chocolate chip cookie recipe to create these crisp treats. They're so yummy, especially fresh from the oven.

    1 cup butter, softened
  3/4 cup packed brown sugar
  1/3 cup sugar
    1 egg
    2 teaspoons vanilla extract
2-1/4 cups all-purpose flour
    2 tablespoons instant chocolate drink mix
    1 teaspoon baking soda
  1/2 teaspoon salt
    2 cups malted milk balls, crushed

1. In a mixing bowl, cream the butter and sugars. Beat in egg and vanilla. Combine the flour, drink mix, baking soda and salt; gradually add to creamed mixture. Stir in malted milk balls.

2. Roll into 1-1/2-in. balls. Place 2 in. apart on greased baking sheets. Bake at 375° for 10-12 minutes or until set. Cool for 1 minute before removing from pans to wire racks.

Yield: about 3 dozen.

Golden Raisin Cookies

Isabel Podeszwa
Lakewood, New Jersey

Since my children are grown, I make these light butter cookies for the neighborhood kids.

    1 cup butter, softened
1-1/2 cups sugar
    1 tablespoon lemon juice
    2 eggs
3-1/2 cups all-purpose flour
1-1/2 teaspoons cream of tartar
1-1/2 teaspoons baking soda
    1 package (15 ounces) golden raisins (2-1/2 cups)

1. In a mixing bowl, cream butter and sugar. Add lemon juice and eggs. Combine dry ingredients; gradually add to creamed mixture. Stir in raisins.

2. Roll into 1-in. balls. Place on greased baking sheets; flatten with a floured fork. Bake at 400° for 8-10 minutes or until lightly browned.

Yield: about 6 dozen.

Crisp Lemon Sugar Cookies

Dollie Ainley
Doniphan, Missouri

I've had this recipe for 40 years. These cookies are my husband's favorite, so I bake them almost every week. One of my daughter's friends still remembers having these special treats when she stopped in on her way home from school.

1/2 cup butter, softened
1/2 cup butter-flavored shortening
1 cup sugar
1 egg
1 tablespoon milk
2 teaspoons lemon extract
1 teaspoon vanilla extract
2-1/2 cups all-purpose flour
3/4 teaspoon salt
1/2 teaspoon baking soda
Additional sugar

1. In a mixing bowl, cream butter, shortening and sugar. Beat in egg, milk and extracts. Combine the flour, salt and baking soda; gradually add to creamed mixture.

2. Roll into 1-in. balls or drop by rounded teaspoonfuls 2 in. apart onto ungreased baking sheets. Flatten with a glass dipped in sugar. Bake at 400° for 9-11 minutes or until edges are lightly browned. Immediately remove to wire racks to cool.

Yield: about 6-1/2 dozen.

Tried 'n' True Peanut Butter Cookies

Emma Lee Granger, La Pine, Oregon

When I want to offer friends and family a tried-and-true cookie, this is the recipe I turn to. Use either creamy or crunchy peanut butter with delicious results.

4 cups butter-flavored shortening
4 cups peanut butter
3 cups sugar
3 cups packed brown sugar
8 eggs
4 teaspoons vanilla extract
2 teaspoons water
9 cups all-purpose flour
4 teaspoons baking soda
4 teaspoons salt

1. In a large mixing bowl, cream shortening, peanut butter and sugars. Add eggs, one at a time, beating well after each addition. Beat in vanilla and water. Combine flour, baking soda and salt; gradually add to the creamed mixture.

2. Drop by heaping tablespoons 2 in. apart onto ungreased baking sheets. Flatten with a fork. Bake at 350° for 12-15 minutes or until golden brown. Remove to wire racks to cool.

Yield: about 8 dozen.

Editor's Note: This recipe can be halved to fit into a mixing bowl. Reduced-fat or generic brands of peanut butter are not recommended for this recipe.

Mocha Crackle Cookies

Louise Beatty
Amherst, New York

These cake-like cookies are better than brownies. They have crackly tops and a subtle coffee flavor.

- 1/2 cup butter
- 5 squares (1 ounce *each*) unsweetened chocolate
- 1 tablespoon instant coffee granules
- 4 eggs
- 1/8 teaspoon salt
- 1 cup sugar
- 1 cup packed brown sugar
- 2 cups plus 3 tablespoons all-purpose flour
- 2 teaspoons baking powder
- 1/3 cup confectioners' sugar

1. In a microwave or saucepan, heat butter, chocolate and coffee until chocolate is melted; cool slightly. In a mixing bowl, combine eggs and salt. Add sugar and brown sugar. Stir in chocolate mixture; mix well. Combine flour and baking powder; gradually add to egg mixture to form a soft dough. Cover and refrigerate for 2 hours or until easy to handle.

2. Roll dough into 3/4-in. balls. Roll in confectioners' sugar; place 2 in. apart on greased baking sheets. Bake at 350° for 12 minutes or until set. Remove to wire racks to cool.

Yield: about 5 dozen.

Soft Ginger Puffs

Marion Lowery, Medford, Oregon

- 1/2 cup butter, softened
- 3/4 cup sugar
- 3 eggs
- 1 cup molasses
- 1 cup (8 ounces) sour cream
- 3-1/2 cups all-purpose flour
- 2 teaspoons ground ginger
- 1 teaspoon baking soda
- 1/2 teaspoon *each* ground allspice, cinnamon and nutmeg
- 1-1/2 cups raisins
- 1-1/2 cups chopped walnuts

These spice cookies loaded with raisins and walnuts really do appeal to all generations—I found the recipe in a 1901 South Dakota cookbook! Sour cream adds a wonderful, unusual flair.

1. In a mixing bowl, cream the butter and sugar. Add eggs, one at a time, beating well after each addition. Beat in the molasses and sour cream. Combine the flour, ginger, baking soda, allspice, cinnamon and nutmeg; gradually add to the creamed mixture. Stir in the raisins and walnuts.

2. Drop by tablespoonfuls 1 in. apart onto greased baking sheets. Bake at 375° for 10-12 minutes or until the edges begin to brown. Remove to wire racks to cool.

Yield: 8 dozen.

Cookie Jar Nut Cookies

Mrs. Terry Robbins
Hendersonville, North Carolina

I started collecting cookie recipes when I was a teenager. These chewy spice cookies were some of the first I ever made, and they're still a favorite today. They can be found in my cookie jar whenever someone stops by.

1 cup butter, softened
2 cups packed brown sugar
2 eggs
1/4 cup milk
1 teaspoon vanilla extract
3 cups all-purpose flour
1 teaspoon baking soda
1 teaspoon salt
1 teaspoon ground nutmeg
1 cup chopped walnuts

1. In a mixing bowl, cream butter and brown sugar. Add eggs, one at a time, beating well after each addition. Beat in milk and vanilla. Combine flour, baking soda, salt and nutmeg; gradually add to the creamed mixture. Stir in walnuts.

2. Drop by rounded teaspoonfuls 2 in. apart onto ungreased baking sheets. Flatten with a glass dipped in sugar. Bake at 350° for 10-12 minutes or until lightly browned. Remove to wire racks to cool.

Yield: 9 dozen.

White Chocolate Oatmeal Cookies

Edith Pluhar
Cohagen, Montana

My sons and grandsons manage our ranch and they always seem to have one hand in the cookie jar; especially when I bake these crunchy morsels!

1 cup butter, softened
1/2 cup sugar
1/2 cup packed brown sugar
1 egg
3 teaspoons vanilla extract
1 teaspoon coconut extract
6 squares (1 ounce *each*) white baking chocolate, melted
1-1/4 cups all-purpose flour
1 teaspoon salt
1 teaspoon baking soda
1-1/2 cups quick-cooking oats
1 cup flaked coconut, toasted
Additional sugar

1. In a mixing bowl, cream the butter and sugars. Add the egg and extracts; mix well. Stir in the melted chocolate. Combine the flour, salt and baking soda; gradually add to creamed mixture. Stir in the oats and the coconut.

2. Drop by tablespoonfuls 3 in. apart onto ungreased baking sheets. Flatten with a glass dipped in sugar. Bake at 350° for 9-11 minutes or until golden brown. Cool for 1 minute before removing to wire racks.

Yield: about 5 dozen.

Sour Cream Chocolate Cookies, p. 42

Chocolate Malted Cookies, p. 30

Five-Chip Cookies, p. 33

Monster Cookies, p. 28

Chock-Full Of Chips

If you're crazy about chips, here's a collection of delicious recipes showcasing semisweet, milk, peanut butter, butterscotch and vanilla chips. You'll discover new variations on classic chocolate chip cookies, as well as chips in delicate meringue cookies or hearty biscotti.

Monster Cookies

(Pictured on page 27)
Patricia Schroedl, Jefferson, Wisconsin

This recipe combines several of my favorites flavors—peanut butter, butterscotch and chocolate—in one monster cookie. Before baking, press a few extra M&M's on top for added color. They won't last long, so you may want to make a double batch.

    1 cup peanut butter
  1/2 cup butter, softened
1-1/4 cups packed brown sugar
    1 cup sugar
    3 eggs
    2 teaspoons baking soda
    1 teaspoon vanilla extract
    4 cups quick-cooking oats
    1 cup M&M's
    1 cup butterscotch chips
    1 cup salted peanuts
    2 cups all-purpose flour

1. In a large mixing bowl, cream peanut butter, butter and sugars. Add eggs, one at a time, beating well after each addition. Add baking soda and vanilla. Add oats, M&M's, butterscotch chips and peanuts; let stand for 10 minutes. Stir in flour (the dough will be crumbly).

2. Shape 1/4 cupfuls into balls. Place on greased baking sheets, about nine cookies on each sheet. Gently flatten cookies. Bake at 325° for 15-18 minutes or until edges are lightly browned. Remove to wire racks to cool.

Yield: about 2-1/2 dozen.

Editor's Note: Reduced-fat or generic brands of peanut butter are not recommended for this recipe.

Snow-Topped Chocolate Mint Cookies

Arlene Hurst
Ephrata, Pennsylvania

Our local newspaper had a cookie contest a while back. This was one of the recipes featured, and it caught my eye because I love mint flavor. My family likes these cookies as much as I do.

    1 package (10 ounces) mint
      semisweet chocolate
      chips, *divided*
    6 tablespoons butter,
      softened
    1 cup sugar
    2 eggs
1-1/2 teaspoons vanilla extract
1-1/2 cups all-purpose flour
1-1/2 teaspoons baking powder
  1/4 teaspoon salt
Confectioners' sugar

1. In a microwave, melt 1 cup chocolate chips; set aside to cool. In a mixing bowl, cream butter and sugar. Add eggs, one at a time, beating well after each addition. Beat in the melted chocolate chips and vanilla. Combine flour, baking powder and salt; gradually add to the creamed mixture. Stir in the remaining chocolate chips. Cover and refrigerate for 2 hours or until easy to handle.

2. Roll into 1-in. balls, then roll in confectioners' sugar. Place 2 in. apart on ungreased baking sheets. Bake at 350° for 10-12 minutes or until edges are set and centers are almost set. Cool for 10 minutes before removing to wire racks.

Yield: 4 dozen.

Chocolate Chip Butter Cookies

Janis Gruca
Mokena, Illinois

At the downtown Chicago law firm where I work, we often bring in goodies for special occasions. When co-workers hear I've baked these melt-in-your-mouth cookies, they make a special trip to my floor to sample them. Best of all, these crisp, buttery treats can be made in no time.

1 cup butter
1/2 teaspoon vanilla extract
2 cups all-purpose flour
1 cup confectioners' sugar
1 cup miniature semisweet chocolate chips

1. In a microwave or heavy saucepan, melt butter; stir in vanilla. Cool completely. In a large bowl, combine flour and sugar; stir in butter mixture and chocolate chips (mixture will be crumbly).

2. Roll dough into 1-in. balls. Place 2 in. apart on ungreased baking sheets; flatten slightly. Bake at 375° for 12 minutes or until edges begin to brown. Remove to wire racks to cool.

Yield: about 4 dozen.

Big Chocolate Cookies

Marie Macy, Fort Collins, Colorado

The combination of different kinds of chocolate makes these cookies irresistible. Friends and family are delighted to have a "big" cookie to enjoy.

6 tablespoons butter
6 squares (1 ounce *each*) semisweet chocolate
2 squares (1 ounce *each*) unsweetened chocolate
2 eggs
3/4 cup sugar
2 teaspoons instant coffee granules
1 tablespoon boiling water
2 teaspoons vanilla extract
1/4 cup all-purpose flour
1/2 teaspoon salt
1/4 teaspoon baking powder
1 cup (6 ounces) semisweet chocolate chips
1 cup coarsely chopped walnuts
1 cup coarsely chopped pecans

1. In a microwave or heavy saucepan, melt butter and the chocolate squares; cool. In a mixing bowl, beat eggs until foamy; gradually add sugar. Dissolve the coffee granules in water. Add the coffee, vanilla and cooled chocolate mixture to egg mixture. Combine the flour, salt and baking powder; gradually add to the egg mixture. Stir in chocolate chips and nuts.

2. Drop by 1/3 cupfuls 4 in. apart onto ungreased baking sheets. Bake at 350° for 15-17 minutes or until firm. Cool for 4 minutes before removing to wire racks.

Yield: 1 dozen.

Editor's Note: 1/4 cup flour is the correct amount.

Cookie Sticks

Kathy Zielicke
Fond du Lac, Wisconsin

If you have a craving for cookies and you want them now, these yummy strips take just a few minutes to make from start to finish. Nothing could be quicker!

- 1/2 cup vegetable oil
- 1/2 cup sugar
- 1/2 cup packed brown sugar
- 1 egg
- 1 teaspoon vanilla extract
- 1-1/2 cups all-purpose flour
- 1/2 teaspoon baking soda
- 1/2 teaspoon salt
- 1 cup (6 ounces) semisweet chocolate chips
- 1/2 cup chopped walnuts, optional

1. In a mixing bowl, combine the oil, sugars, egg and vanilla. Combine the flour, baking soda and salt; gradually add to sugar mixture. Divide dough in half.

2. On a greased baking sheet, shape each portion into a 15-in. x 3-in. rectangle about 3 in. apart. Sprinkle chocolate chips and nuts if desired over dough; press lightly.

3. Bake at 375° for 6-7 minutes. (Bake for 8-9 minutes for crispier cookies.) Cool for 5 minutes. Cut with a serrated knife into 1-in. strips; remove to wire racks to cool.

Yield: about 3 dozen.

Chocolate Malted Cookies

(Pictured on page 27)
Teri Rasey-Bolf, Cadillac, Michigan

These cookies are the next best thing to a good old-fashioned malted milk shake. With malted milk powder, chocolate syrup plus chocolate chips and chunks, these are the best cookies I've ever tasted.

- 1 cup butter-flavored shortening
- 1-1/4 cups packed brown sugar
- 1/2 cup malted milk powder
- 2 tablespoons chocolate syrup
- 1 tablespoon vanilla extract
- 1 egg
- 2 cups all-purpose flour
- 1 teaspoon baking soda
- 1/2 teaspoon salt
- 1-1/2 cups semisweet chocolate chunks
- 1 cup milk chocolate chips

1. In a large mixing bowl, beat the shortening, brown sugar, malted milk powder, chocolate syrup and vanilla for 2 minutes. Add egg. Combine the flour, baking soda and salt; gradually add to creamed mixture, mixing well after each addition. Stir in chocolate chunks and chips.

2. Roll into 2-in. balls; place 3 in. apart on ungreased baking sheets. Bake at 375° for 12-14 minutes or until golden brown. Cool for 2 minutes before removing to a wire rack.

Yield: about 1-1/2 dozen.

Welcome-to-the-Neighborhood Cookies

Susan Bice, Edwards Air Force Base, California

I always share a batch of these cookies with new neighbors. It's a real welcoming treat to adults and children alike. They're easy to make but taste like I really fussed.

1 cup butter, softened
1/2 cup sugar
1/2 cup packed brown sugar
1 egg
2-1/4 cups all-purpose flour
2 to 3 teaspoons grated orange peel
1 teaspoon ground cinnamon
3/4 teaspoon baking soda
1/2 teaspoon salt
Dash *each* ground nutmeg and cloves
1 package (10 to 12 ounces) vanilla *or* white chips

1. In a mixing bowl, cream butter and sugars; beat in egg. Combine flour, orange peel, cinnamon, baking soda, salt, nutmeg and cloves; add to creamed mixture. Stir in chips.

2. Drop by rounded tablespoonfuls onto ungreased baking sheets. Bake at 350° for 12-14 minutes or until lightly browned. Remove to wire racks to cool.

Yield: about 3-1/2 dozen.

Goblin Chewies

Bernice Morris
Marshfield, Missouri

These light, crispy cookies are packed with fun ingredients perfect for Halloween.

1 cup shortening
1 cup packed brown sugar
1 cup sugar
2 eggs
1 teaspoon vanilla extract
2 cups all-purpose flour
1 teaspoon baking soda
1/2 teaspoon baking powder
1/2 teaspoon salt
1-1/2 cups old-fashioned oats
1 cup crisp rice cereal
1 cup diced candy orange slices
1 cup (6 ounces) semisweet chocolate chips *or* raisins
Additional raisins *or* chocolate chips and candy orange slices

1. In a mixing bowl, cream shortening and sugars. Add eggs and vanilla; mix well. Combine the flour, baking soda, baking powder and salt; add to creamed mixture. Stir in oats, cereal, orange slices and chips or raisins.

2. Drop dough by tablespoonfuls 2 in. apart onto greased baking sheets. Flatten slightly with a fork. Decorate with raisin or chocolate chip eyes and orange slice mouths. Bake at 350° for 10-14 minutes. Remove to wire racks to cool.

Yield: about 6 dozen.

Editor's Note: Orange slices cut easier if microwaved for 5 seconds on high and cut with a sharp knife or kitchen scissors.

Macadamia Nut Cookies

These rich cookies—full of Hawaiian macadamia nuts and chocolate chips—make a delectable ending to any meal.

Mary Gaylord, Balsam Lake, Wisconsin

1 cup butter, softened
3/4 cup sugar
3/4 cup packed brown sugar
2 eggs
1 teaspoon vanilla extract
2-1/4 cups all-purpose flour
1 teaspoon baking soda
1 teaspoon salt
2 jars (3-1/2 ounces *each*) macadamia nuts, chopped
2 cups (12 ounces) semisweet chocolate chips
1 cup vanilla *or* white chips

1. In a mixing bowl, cream butter and sugars. Add eggs and vanilla; beat on medium speed for 2 minutes. Combine flour, baking soda and salt; add to creamed mixture and beat for 2 minutes. Stir in nuts and chips. Cover and refrigerate several hours or overnight.

2. Drop by tablespoonfuls 2 in. apart onto ungreased baking sheets. Bake at 375° for 10-12 minutes or until golden brown. Cool on pans for 1 minute before removing to wire racks.

Yield: about 6 dozen.

White Chocolate-Cranberry Biscotti

The original version of this recipe was handed down from my great-aunt. Through the years, my mother and I have tried different flavor combinations...this is a favorite for all.

Brenda Keith, Talent, Oregon

1/2 cup butter, softened
1 cup sugar
4 eggs
1 teaspoon vanilla extract
3 cups all-purpose flour
1 tablespoon baking powder
3/4 cup dried cranberries
3/4 cup vanilla *or* white chips

1. In a mixing bowl, cream butter and sugar. Add the eggs, one at a time, beating well after each addition. Beat in vanilla. Combine the flour and baking powder; gradually add to creamed mixture. Stir in cranberries and vanilla chips. Divide dough into three portions.

2. On ungreased baking sheets, shape each portion into a 10-in. x 2-in. rectangle. Bake at 350° for 20-25 minutes or until lightly browned. Cool for 5 minutes.

3. Transfer to a cutting board; cut diagonally with a serrated knife into 1-in. slices. Place cut side down on ungreased baking sheets. Bake for 15-20 minutes or until golden brown. Remove to wire racks to cool. Store in an airtight container.

Yield: 2-1/2 dozen.

Cutting Biscotti

After the rectangular biscotti dough is baked, it needs to be cut into slices, which will be baked longer. With a serrated knife, cut the cookie diagonally into 1/2- or 3/4-in.-thick slices. Place the sliced cookies cut side down on a baking sheet and bake as directed.

Five-Chip Cookies

Sharon Hedstrom
Minnetonka, Minnesota

With peanut butter, oats and five kinds of chips, these cookies make a hearty snack that appeals to kids of all ages. I sometimes double the recipe to share with friends and neighbors.

1 cup butter, softened
1 cup peanut butter
1 cup sugar
2/3 cup packed brown sugar
2 eggs
1 teaspoon vanilla extract
2 cups all-purpose flour
1 cup old-fashioned oats
2 teaspoons baking soda
1/2 teaspoon salt
2/3 cup *each* milk chocolate chips, semisweet chocolate chips, peanut butter chips, vanilla *or* white chips and butterscotch chips

1. In a large mixing bowl, cream butter, peanut butter and sugars. Add eggs, one at a time, beating well after each addition. Beat in vanilla. Combine flour, oats, baking soda and salt; gradually add to the creamed mixture. Stir in chips.

2. Drop by rounded tablespoonfuls 2 in. apart onto ungreased baking sheets. Bake at 350° for 10-12 minutes or until lightly browned. Cool for 1 minute before removing to wire racks.

Yield: 4-1/2 dozen.

Editor's Note: Reduced-fat or generic brands of peanut butter are not recommended for this recipe.

Pecan Surprises

Jean Ohnigian
Havertown, Pennsylvania

After I bought too many nuts for a different recipe, I decided to put the leftovers to use in a batch of cookies. Coconut and apricots add a little "surprise" to every bite.

1 cup butter, softened
3/4 cup sugar
3/4 cup packed brown sugar
2 eggs
1 teaspoon vanilla extract
2 cups all-purpose flour
3/4 cup ground pecans
1 teaspoon baking soda
1 teaspoon salt
2 cups (12 ounces) semisweet chocolate chips
2/3 cup flaked coconut
2/3 cup finely chopped dried apricots

1. In a mixing bowl, cream butter and sugars. Add the eggs, one at a time, beating well after each addition. Beat in vanilla. Combine flour, pecans, baking soda and salt; gradually add to the creamed mixture. Stir in remaining ingredients.

2. Drop by tablespoonfuls 2 in. apart onto ungreased baking sheets. Bake at 375° for 10-12 minutes or until lightly browned. Cool for 1-2 minutes before removing to wire racks.

Yield: 6 dozen.

Chocolate Snowballs

Dee Derezinski
Waukesha, Wisconsin

This is my favorite Christmas cookie recipe. The cookies remind me of the snowballs I'd packed as a child during winters here in Wisconsin.

- 3/4 cup butter, softened
- 1/2 cup sugar
- 1 egg
- 2 teaspoons vanilla extract
- 2 cups all-purpose flour
- 1/2 teaspoon salt
- 1 cup chopped nuts
- 1 cup (6 ounces) chocolate chips
- Confectioners' sugar

1. In a large mixing bowl, cream butter and sugar. Add egg and vanilla; mix well. Combine flour and salt; stir into creamed mixture. Fold in nuts and chips.

2. Roll into 1-in. balls. Place on ungreased baking sheets. Bake at 350° for 15-20 minutes. Remove to wire racks. Cool cookies slightly before rolling in confectioners' sugar.

Yield: about 4 dozen.

Vanilla Chip Maple Cookies

Debra Hogenson, Brewster, Minnesota

These cookies have a distinct maple flavor and stay moist and soft, although they're never in my cookie jar for long!

- 1 cup shortening
- 1/2 cup butter, softened
- 2 cups packed brown sugar
- 2 eggs
- 1 teaspoon vanilla extract
- 1 teaspoon maple flavoring
- 3 cups all-purpose flour
- 2 teaspoons baking soda
- 2 cups vanilla *or* white chips
- 1/2 cup chopped pecans

FROSTING:
- 1/4 cup butter, softened
- 4 cups confectioners' sugar
- 1 teaspoon maple flavoring
- 4 to 6 tablespoons milk
- 3-1/2 cups pecan halves

1. In a mixing bowl, cream the shortening, butter and brown sugar. Add eggs, one at a time, beating well after each addition. Beat in vanilla and maple flavoring. Combine the flour and baking soda; gradually add to creamed mixture. Stir in vanilla chips and pecans.

2. Drop by rounded tablespoonfuls 2 in. apart onto ungreased baking sheets. Bake at 350° for 8-10 minutes or until golden brown. Cool for 2 minutes before removing to wire racks.

3. In a mixing bowl, cream butter and confectioners' sugar. Beat in maple flavoring and enough milk to achieve spreading consistency. Frost cooled cookies. Top each with a pecan half.

Yield: about 7 dozen.

Cherry Chocolate Nut Cookies

Sybil Brown, Highland, California

Each Christmas, I make about 600 cookies to share with family and friends. The holidays wouldn't be the same without several batches of these colorful goodies. The pecans, maraschino cherries and semisweet chips make a great flavor combination.

- 1/2 cup butter, softened
- 1/2 cup sugar
- 1/2 cup packed brown sugar
- 1 egg
- 1/4 cup milk
- 1 teaspoon vanilla extract
- 2 cups all-purpose flour
- 1 teaspoon baking powder
- 1/2 teaspoon salt
- 1/4 teaspoon baking soda
- 1 cup (6 ounces) semisweet chocolate chips
- 3/4 cup chopped maraschino cherries
- 3/4 cup chopped pecans

1. In a mixing bowl, cream butter and sugars. Beat in egg, milk and vanilla. Combine flour, baking powder, salt and baking soda; gradually add to the creamed mixture. Stir in the remaining ingredients.

2. Drop by tablespoonfuls 2 in. apart onto greased baking sheets. Bake at 375° for 10-12 minutes or until golden brown. Remove to wire racks.

Yield: 5 dozen.

Double Chocolate Chip Cookies

Diane Hixon
Niceville, Florida

The cocoa in the batter gives these treats a double dose of chocolate. They disappear fast from my cookie jar.

- 1 cup butter, softened
- 1 cup sugar
- 1/2 cup packed dark brown sugar
- 1 teaspoon vanilla extract
- 1 egg
- 1/3 cup baking cocoa
- 2 tablespoons milk
- 1-3/4 cups all-purpose flour
- 1/4 teaspoon baking powder
- 1 cup chopped walnuts
- 1 cup (6 ounces) semisweet chocolate chips

1. In a large mixing bowl, cream the butter, sugars and vanilla. Beat in egg. Add cocoa and milk. Combine flour and baking powder; fold into creamed mixture with walnuts and chocolate chips.

2. Roll teaspoonfuls of dough into balls; place 2 in. apart on ungreased baking sheets. Bake at 350° for 10-12 minutes. Cool for 5 minutes before removing to wire racks.

Yield: 3-4 dozen.

Special Oatmeal Chip Cookies

Carol Poskie, Pittsburgh, Pennsylvania

My son dubbed these "the cookie" after just one taste, and they've become my signature cookie since then. I haven't shared my "secret" recipe until now. Now you can bake up a batch and make these your "secret" recipe, too.

    1 cup butter, softened
    1 cup peanut butter
    1 cup sugar
    1 cup packed brown sugar
    2 eggs
    1 teaspoon vanilla extract
    3 cups old-fashioned oats
    1 cup all-purpose flour
    2 teaspoons ground
      cinnamon
    1 teaspoon baking soda
  1/4 teaspoon ground nutmeg
1-1/2 cups semisweet chocolate
      chips

DRIZZLE:
    1 cup white chocolate candy
      coating, melted
    1 cup dark chocolate candy
      coating, melted

1. In a mixing bowl, cream butter, peanut butter and sugars. Add eggs, one at a time, beating well after each addition. Beat in vanilla. Combine oats, flour, cinnamon, baking soda and nutmeg; gradually add to the creamed mixture. Stir in chocolate chips.

2. Roll into 1-in. balls. Place 2 in. apart on greased baking sheets; flatten to 1/2-in. thickness. Bake at 350° for 10-12 minutes or until golden brown. Remove to wire racks to cool.

3. Drizzle with white coating in one direction, then with dark coating in the opposite direction to form a crisscross pattern.

Yield: about 5-1/2 dozen.

Editor's Note: Reduced-fat or generic brands of peanut butter are not recommended for this recipe.

Cookie Pizza

Debbie Johnson
New Bloomfield, Missouri

I contribute this quick-and-easy treat to every bake sale our two daughters are involved in. Everyone seems to love the great-tasting combination of yummy chocolate and marshmallows on a homemade peanut butter cookie crust.

  1/2 cup butter, softened
  1/2 cup peanut butter
  1/2 cup sugar
  1/2 cup packed brown sugar
    1 egg
  1/2 teaspoon vanilla extract
1-1/2 cups all-purpose flour
    2 cups miniature
      marshmallows
    1 cup (6 ounces) semisweet
      chocolate chips

1. In a mixing bowl, cream butter, peanut butter and sugars. Beat in egg and vanilla. Stir in flour until blended.

2. Spread dough onto a greased 12-in. pizza pan. Bake at 375° for 12 minutes. Sprinkle with marshmallows and chocolate chips. Bake 5-6 minutes longer or until lightly browned.

Yield: 10-12 servings.

Editor's Note: Reduced-fat or generic brands of peanut butter are not recommended for this recipe.

Pistachio Thumbprints

Liz Probelski
Port Washington, Wisconsin

These mild pistachio-flavored cookies disappear in a wink.

- 1 cup butter, softened
- 1/3 cup confectioners' sugar
- 1 egg
- 1 teaspoon vanilla extract
- 3/4 teaspoon almond extract
- 2 cups all-purpose flour
- 1 package (3.4 ounces) instant pistachio pudding mix
- 1/2 cup miniature chocolate chips
- 2 cups finely chopped pecans

FILLING:
- 2 tablespoons butter, softened
- 2 cups confectioners' sugar
- 1 teaspoon vanilla extract
- 2 to 3 tablespoons milk

GLAZE:
- 1/2 cup semisweet chocolate chips
- 2 teaspoons shortening

1. In a mixing bowl, cream butter and sugar until smooth. Add egg and extracts; mix well. Combine flour and pudding mix; add to the creamed mixture. Stir in chocolate chips.

2. Roll into 1-in. balls; roll in nuts. Place 2 in. apart on greased baking sheets; make a thumbprint in center of cookie. Bake at 350° for 10-12 minutes. Remove to a wire rack to cool.

3. For filling, cream butter, sugar, vanilla and milk. Spoon into center of cooled cookies.

4. For glaze, if desired, melt chocolate chips with shortening; drizzle over cookies. Let stand until set.

Yield: about 7 dozen.

Chewy Peanut Butter Crisps

Lucy Garrett, Cedartown, Georgia

- 1 cup peanut butter
- 1 cup sugar
- 1/2 cup evaporated milk
- 4 teaspoons cornstarch
- 1/2 cup semisweet chocolate chips

This flourless cookies successfully combines a chewy inside and crisp outside. Plus, chocolate and peanut butter is a classic combination that's hard to beat. It uses only five ingredients and take just minutes to mix up.

1. In a mixing bowl, combine peanut butter and sugar. Stir in milk and cornstarch until smooth. Add chocolate chips.

2. Drop by heaping teaspoonfuls 2 in. apart onto ungreased baking sheets. Bake at 350° for 12-15 minutes or until golden brown. Remove to wire racks to cool.

Yield: 3-1/2 dozen.

Editor's Note: This recipe does not use flour. Reduced-fat or generic brands of peanut butter are not recommended for this recipe.

Crinkle-Top Chocolate Cookies

Maria Groff
Ephrata, Pennsylvania

When I baked these moist fudgy cookies for the first time, my three children loved them! But I like them because they're lower in fat and easy to mix and bake.

2 cups (12 ounces) semisweet chocolate chips, *divided*

2 tablespoons butter, softened

1 cup sugar

2 egg whites

1-1/2 teaspoons vanilla extract

1-1/2 cups all-purpose flour

1-1/2 teaspoons baking powder

1/4 teaspoon salt

1/4 cup water

1/2 cup confectioners' sugar

1. In a microwave, melt 1 cup chocolate chips. Stir until smooth; set aside. In a small mixing bowl, beat butter and sugar until crumbly, about 2 minutes. Add egg whites and vanilla; beat well. Stir in melted chocolate. Combine the flour, baking powder and salt; gradually add to butter mixture alternately with water. Stir in remaining chocolate chips. Cover and refrigerate for 2 hours or until easy to handle.

2. Shape dough into 1-in. balls. Roll in confectioners' sugar. Place 2 in. apart on baking sheets coated with nonstick cooking spray. Bake at 350° for 10-12 minutes or until set. Remove to wire racks to cool.

Yield: 3-1/2 dozen.

Toffee Cranberry Crisps

Ann Quaerna, Lake Geneva, Wisconsin

I've had more friends request this recipe than any other cookie recipe I have. The combination of cranberries, chocolate chips and toffee bits is wonderful.

1 cup butter, softened

3/4 cup sugar

3/4 cup packed brown sugar

1 egg

1 teaspoon vanilla extract

1-1/2 cups all-purpose flour

1-1/2 cups quick-cooking oats

1 teaspoon baking soda

1/4 teaspoon salt

1 cup dried cranberries

1 cup miniature semisweet chocolate chips

1 cup English toffee bits *or* almond brickle chips

1. In a mixing bowl, cream butter and sugars. Beat in egg and vanilla. Combine flour, oats, baking soda and salt; gradually add to creamed mixture. Stir in cranberries, chocolate chips and toffee bits.

2. Shape into three 12-in. rolls; wrap each in plastic wrap. Refrigerate for 2 hours or until firm. Unwrap and cut into 1/2-in. slices. Place 2 in. apart on ungreased baking sheets. Bake at 350° for 8-10 minutes or until golden brown. Remove to wire racks to cool.

Yield: 5-1/2 dozen.

Crispy Scotchies

Joanne Kramer, Manchester, Iowa

I first tasted these cookies as a newlywed in 1959. Over the years, I've made a few modifications, and now they turn out perfectly every time. They're a hit with all my family.

- 6 tablespoons butter, softened
- 6 tablespoons butter-flavored shortening
- 1 cup sugar
- 1 cup packed brown sugar
- 2 eggs
- 1 teaspoon vanilla extract
- 4 cups crisp rice cereal, *divided*
- 1-1/2 cups all-purpose flour
- 1 teaspoon baking soda
- 1/2 teaspoon baking powder
- 1 cup butterscotch chips

TOPPING:
- 1/2 cup sugar
- 1/2 cup packed brown sugar

1. In a mixing bowl, cream butter, shortening and sugars. Add eggs, one at a time, beating well after each addition. Beat in vanilla. Crush 2 cups of cereal; add flour, baking soda and baking powder. Gradually add to the creamed mixture. Stir in butterscotch chips and remaining cereal. Combine topping ingredients in a small bowl.

2. Roll dough into 1-1/4-in. balls, then roll in topping. Place 2 in. apart on ungreased baking sheets; flatten slightly with glass. Bake at 350° for 10-12 minutes or until golden brown. Cool for 1 minute before removing to wire racks.

Yield: about 5-1/2 dozen.

Peanut Butter Maple Cookies

Lois Bowman
Swanton, Maryland

I bake these crispy yet chewy peanut butter cookies often. My grandchildren, can't wait to dig into the cookie jar.

- 1 cup butter, softened
- 1/2 cup peanut butter
- 1 cup sugar
- 1 cup packed brown sugar
- 2 eggs
- 1 tablespoon maple syrup
- 2 teaspoons vanilla extract
- 2 cups all-purpose flour
- 3/4 cup quick-cooking oats
- 1-1/2 teaspoons baking powder
- 1 teaspoon baking soda
- 1 teaspoon salt
- 1 package (10 ounces) peanut butter chips

1. In a mixing bowl, cream the butter, peanut butter and sugars. Add the eggs, one at a time, beating well after each addition. Beat in syrup and vanilla. Combine the flour, oats, baking powder, baking soda and salt; add to the creamed mixture and mix well. Stir in peanut butter chips.

2. Drop by heaping tablespoonfuls 2 in. apart onto ungreased baking sheets. Bake at 325° for 15-18 minutes or until golden brown. Cool for 1 minute before removing to wire racks.

Yield: about 5 dozen.

Editor's Note: Reduced-fat or generic brands of peanut butter are not recommended for this recipe.

Chocolate Raspberry Cookies

Sherri Crotwell, Shasta Lake, California

I moved away from a dear friend some years ago. Knowing she loved raspberries, I created this recipe—a blend of chocolate and raspberry. Now I send her these cookies to help her remember the fun times we had together.

1 cup butter, softened
3/4 cup sugar
3/4 cup packed brown sugar
2 eggs
3/4 cup semisweet chocolate chips, melted and cooled
1/2 cup raspberries, pureed
3 cups all-purpose flour
3/4 teaspoon baking soda
3/4 teaspoon salt
1 cup vanilla *or* white chips

1. In a mixing bowl, cream butter and sugars. Add eggs, one at a time, beating well after each addition. Beat in melted chocolate and raspberries. Combine the flour, baking soda and salt; gradually add to the creamed mixture. Stir in vanilla chips.

2. Drop by teaspoonfuls 2 in. apart onto ungreased baking sheets. Bake at 375° for 10-12 minutes or until edges begin to brown. Remove to wire racks to cool.

Yield: 6 dozen.

Coconut Chocolate Chip Cookies

Laura Bankard
Manchester, Maryland

Here is a delicious twist on traditional chocolate chip cookies. They're great for coconut lovers, who will be delighted with the texture of the coconut and the added flavor of the coconut extract. My whole family agrees this recipe is a winner.

1/2 cup butter, softened
3/4 cup sugar
1 egg
1/2 teaspoon coconut extract
1 cup plus 2 tablespoons all-purpose flour
1/2 teaspoon baking soda
1/2 teaspoon salt
1 cup (6 ounces) semisweet chocolate chips
1/2 cup flaked coconut

1. In a mixing bowl, cream butter and sugar. Beat in egg and coconut extract; mix well. Combine the flour, baking soda and salt; add to the creamed mixture. Stir in chocolate chips and coconut.

2. Drop by rounded tablespoonfuls 2 in. apart onto ungreased baking sheets. Bake at 375° for 11-13 minutes or until golden brown. Remove to wire racks to cool.

Yield: about 1-1/4 dozen.

Double Chocolate Crisps

Marilyn Spangler
Oak Creek, Wisconsin

I received this recipe from my sister-in-law more than 35 years ago. Chock-full of chocolate, these crispy cookies have a tantalizing aroma while baking.

- 1 cup butter, softened
- 2 cups sugar
- 2 eggs
- 4 squares (1 ounce *each*) unsweetened chocolate, melted and cooled
- 2 teaspoons vanilla extract
- 2-1/4 cups all-purpose flour
- 1 teaspoon baking soda
- 1 teaspoon salt
- 1/4 teaspoon ground cinnamon
- 1 cup (6 ounces) semisweet chocolate chips
- 1 cup chopped pecans

1. In a large mixing bowl, cream butter and sugar. Add eggs, one at a time, beating well after each addition. Beat in chocolate and vanilla. Combine the flour, baking soda, salt and cinnamon; gradually add to the creamed mixture. Stir in chocolate chips and pecans.

2. Drop by tablespoonfuls 2 in. apart onto ungreased baking sheets. Bake at 375° for 10-12 minutes or until tops are cracked. Remove to wire racks to cool.

Yield: 4 dozen.

Crisp 'n' Chewy Cookies

Kristen Snyder, Sugar Land, Texas

Knowing I'm a cookie lover, my mother-in-law sent me this recipe years ago. Many folks have told me these are the best. I think the Butterfinger candy bars make them so special.

- 1-1/4 cups butter-flavored shortening
- 3/4 cup sugar
- 3/4 cup packed brown sugar
- 1 egg
- 3 tablespoons maple syrup
- 1 teaspoon vanilla extract
- 3 cups quick-cooking oats
- 1-3/4 cups all-purpose flour
- 1 teaspoon baking soda
- 1 teaspoon salt
- 3/4 cup semisweet chocolate chips
- 2 Butterfinger candy bars (2.1 ounces *each*), chopped

1. In a mixing bowl, cream shortening and sugars. Beat in egg, syrup and vanilla. Combine oats, flour, baking soda and salt; gradually add to the creamed mixture. Stir in chocolate chips and candy bars.

2. Roll into 1-in. balls. Place 2 in. apart on ungreased baking sheets. Bake at 375° for 7-9 minutes or until golden brown. Remove to wire racks to cool completely.

Yield: 7 dozen.

Chocolate Chip Icebox Cookies

Betty Holzinger
West Olive, Michigan

Putting chocolate chips in these refrigerator cookies make them deliciously different. This treat is always welcome at my house.

    3 tablespoons butter, softened
    2 tablespoons shortening
1/4 cup sugar
1/4 cup packed brown sugar
    1 egg yolk
1/2 teaspoon vanilla extract
2/3 cup all-purpose flour
1/4 teaspoon baking soda
1/4 teaspoon salt
1/4 cup miniature semisweet chocolate chips
1/4 cup finely chopped pecans

1. In a small mixing bowl, cream the butter, shortening and sugars. Beat in egg yolk and vanilla; mix well. Combine the flour, baking soda and salt; gradually add to creamed mixture and mix well. Stir in chips and pecans. Shape into a 9-in. roll; wrap in plastic wrap. Refrigerate overnight.

2. Unwrap and cut into 1/4-in. slices. Place 2 in. apart on ungreased baking sheets. Bake at 375° for 8-10 minutes or until edges are golden brown. Cool for 2 minutes before removing to wire racks.

Yield: 20 cookies.

Sour Cream Chocolate Cookies

(Pictured on page 26)
Tina Sawchuk, Ardmore, Alberta

1/2 cup butter, softened
3/4 cup sugar
1/2 cup packed brown sugar
    1 egg
1/2 cup sour cream
    1 teaspoon vanilla extract
1-3/4 cups all-purpose flour
1/2 cup baking cocoa
    1 teaspoon baking powder
1/2 teaspoon baking soda
1/4 teaspoon salt
    1 cup (6 ounces) semisweet chocolate chips
1/2 cup vanilla *or* white chips

My husband and I live on a mixed farm with our young daughter and son. Among my favorite hobbies are baking and gardening. These soft chocolaty cookies can be easily altered to make several different varieties—I've added everything from mints to macadamia nuts to them.

1. In a mixing bowl, cream butter and sugars. Beat in egg, sour cream and vanilla. Combine dry ingredients; gradually add to the creamed mixture. Stir in chips.

2. Drop by rounded tablespoonfuls 2 in. apart onto greased baking sheets. Bake at 350° for 12-15 minutes or until set. Cool for 2 minutes before removing to wire racks.

Yield: about 3 dozen.

Orange Dreams

Susan Warren
North Manchester, Indiana

A fellow teacher shared this recipe with me. We have several great cooks on our teaching staff, and each of us takes turns bringing special treats to the lounge. These moist, chewy cookies with a pleasant orange flavor are a favorite around here.

1 cup butter, softened
1/2 cup sugar
1/2 cup packed brown sugar
1 egg
1 tablespoon grated orange peel
2-1/4 cups all-purpose flour
3/4 teaspoon baking soda
1/2 teaspoon salt
1-1/2 cups vanilla *or* white chips

1. In a mixing bowl, cream butter and sugars. Beat in egg and orange peel. Combine flour, baking soda and salt; gradually add to the creamed mixture. Stir in vanilla chips.

2. Drop by rounded tablespoonfuls 2 in. apart onto ungreased baking sheets. Bake at 350° for 10-12 minutes or until golden brown. Remove to wire racks to cool.

Yield: 4-1/2 dozen.

Minty Meringue Drops

Karen Wissing
Vashon, Washington

These pretty mint green drops are dotted with chocolate chips. My kids don't consider it the Christmas season until I make them.

2 egg whites
1/4 teaspoon cream of tartar
3/4 cup sugar
1/8 teaspoon vanilla extract
2 to 6 drops green food coloring, optional
1 package (10 ounces) mint chocolate chips

1. Lightly grease baking sheets or line with parchment paper; set aside. In a mixing bowl, beat egg whites until foamy. Add cream of tartar, beating until soft peaks form. Gradually beat in sugar, 1 tablespoon at a time, until stiff peaks form. Beat in vanilla and food coloring if desired. Fold in the chocolate chips.

2. Drop by rounded tablespoonfuls 2 in. apart onto prepared baking sheets. Bake at 250° for 30-35 minutes or until dry to the touch. Remove to wire racks to cool. Store in an airtight container.

Yield: About 2-1/2 dozen.

Editor's Note: If mint chocolate chips are not available, place 2 cups (12 ounces) semisweet chocolate chips and 1/4 teaspoon peppermint extract in a plastic bag; seal and toss to coat. Allow chips to stand for 24-48 hours.

Cocoa Surprise Cookies

Debra Himes, Cedar Rapids, Iowa

These rich cookies are truly a chocolate lover's delight. Miniature marshmallows are the delectable surprise in every bite. Plus, you get a double dose of chocolate.

    1 cup butter, softened
    1 cup sugar
    1 cup packed brown sugar
    2 eggs
    2 teaspoons vanilla extract
    3 cups all-purpose flour
  2/3 cup baking cocoa
  1/2 teaspoon baking soda
    2 cups (12 ounces)
      semisweet chocolate chips
    2 cups miniature
      marshmallows, frozen

1. In a mixing bowl, cream butter and sugars. Add the eggs, one at a time, beating well after each addition. Beat in vanilla. Combine flour, cocoa and baking soda; gradually add to the creamed mixture. Stir in chocolate chips.

2. Roll into 1-1/2-in. balls. Press two to three frozen marshmallows into each; reshape balls. Place 2 in. apart on ungreased baking sheets. Bake at 400° for 8-10 minutes or until set. Cool for 5 minutes before removing to wire racks.

Yield: 5 dozen.

Chips Galore Cookies

Shauna Stephens
San Diego, California

This recipe will make a cookie lover's dream come true! Chock-full of pecans, walnuts and three types of chips, these crisp treats will be a hit with your family.

      1 cup butter, softened
    3/4 cup sugar
    3/4 cup packed brown sugar
      2 eggs
      1 tablespoon almond
        extract
  2-1/4 cups all-purpose flour
      1 teaspoon baking soda
    1/2 teaspoon salt
  1-1/2 cups *each* semisweet
        chocolate chips, milk
        chocolate chips and vanilla
        or white chips
  1-1/2 cups chopped pecans
  1-1/2 cups chopped walnuts

1. In a mixing bowl, cream butter and sugars. Add eggs, one at a time, beating well after each addition. Beat in almond extract. Combine the flour, baking soda and salt; gradually add to creamed mixture. Combine chips and nuts; stir into dough. Cover and refrigerate for 1 hour or until easy to handle.

2. Drop by tablespoonfuls 2 in. apart onto greased baking sheets. Bake at 325° for 18-20 minutes or until golden brown. Remove to wire racks to cool completely.

Yield: 9 dozen.

Butterscotch Raisin Cookies

Victoria Zmarzley-Hahn
Northhampton, Pennsylvania

These chewy oatmeal cookies are full of butterscotch chips and raisins. Every so often I add a half cup of chopped pecans to a batch for something different.

1 cup butter, softened
3/4 cup packed brown sugar
1/4 cup sugar
2 eggs
3 cups quick-cooking oats
1-1/2 cups all-purpose flour
1 package (3.4 ounces) instant butterscotch pudding mix
1 teaspoon baking soda
1 cup raisins
1/2 cup butterscotch chips

1. In a large mixing bowl, cream butter and sugars. Add eggs; beat well. Combine the oats, flour, dry pudding mix and baking soda; gradually add to the creamed mixture. Stir in the raisins and butterscotch chips (dough will be stiff).

2. Drop by tablespoonfuls 2 in. apart onto ungreased baking sheets. Bake at 375° for 9-11 minutes or until lightly browned. Remove to wire racks to cool.

Yield: 3-1/2 dozen.

Raspberry Meringues

Iola Egle, McCook, Nebraska

As rosy pink as Santa's cheeks, these merry meringue cookies are drizzled with dark chocolate and are almost too pretty to eat. Pecans add a nice crunch to these chewy treats.

3 egg whites
3 tablespoons plus 1 teaspoon raspberry gelatin powder
3/4 cup sugar
1 teaspoon white vinegar
1/8 teaspoon salt
2 cups (12 ounces) semisweet chocolate chips
1/2 cup finely chopped pecans

TOPPING:
1/4 cup semisweet chocolate chips
1 teaspoon shortening

1. Place egg whites in a small mixing bowl; let stand at room temperature for 30 minutes. Beat the egg whites until soft peaks form. Gradually add gelatin, beating until combined. Gradually add sugar, 1 tablespoon at a time, beating until stiff peaks form. Beat in vinegar and salt. Fold in chocolate chips and nuts.

2. Drop by rounded teaspoonfuls onto parchment-lined baking sheets. Bake at 250° for 20-25 minutes or until firm to the touch. Turn oven off; leave the cookies in the oven with door ajar for about 1-1/2 hours or until cool. In a microwave or heavy saucepan, melt the chocolate chips and shortening; stir until smooth. Drizzle over cookies.

Yield: 7-1/2 dozen.

Coffee Chip Cookies

Maurane Ramsey
Fort Wayne, Indiana

My daughter loves the subtle coffee flavor in these soft cookies. The recipe makes plenty so you can share them with friends.

- 1 cup shortening
- 2 cups packed brown sugar
- 2 eggs
- 1 cup boiling water
- 2 tablespoons instant coffee granules
- 4 cups all-purpose flour
- 2 teaspoons baking powder
- 1 teaspoon baking soda
- 4 cups (24 ounces) semisweet chocolate chips

1. In a mixing bowl, cream shortening and brown sugar. Add eggs, one at a time, beating well after each addition. Combine water and coffee; set aside. Combine the flour, baking powder and baking soda; add to creamed mixture alternately with coffee. Stir in the chocolate chips. Refrigerate for 1 hour.

2. Drop dough by rounded tablespoonfuls 2 in. apart onto greased baking sheets. Bake at 350° for 10-12 minutes or until golden around the edges. Remove to wire racks to cool.

Yield: 3-1/2 dozen.

Chocolate Chip Crispies

Stephanie DiGiovanni, Wakefield, Massachusetts

In this recipe from a cousin, potato chips add crunch while oats make them chewy. It's a fun twist to traditional chocolate chip cookies.

- 1 cup butter, softened
- 1 cup vegetable oil
- 1 cup sugar
- 1 cup packed brown sugar
- 1 egg
- 1 teaspoon vanilla extract
- 3-1/2 cups all-purpose flour
- 1 cup quick-cooking oats
- 1 teaspoon baking soda
- 1 teaspoon cream of tartar
- 1/2 teaspoon salt
- 1 tablespoon milk
- 1 teaspoon white vinegar
- 2 cups (12 ounces) semisweet chocolate chips
- 1 cup crushed potato chips

1. In a large mixing bowl, beat butter, oil and sugars. Beat in egg and vanilla. Combine the flour, oats, baking soda, cream of tartar and salt; gradually add to the sugar mixture. Combine milk and vinegar; add to sugar mixture. Stir in chocolate chips and potato chips.

2. Drop by tablespoonfuls 2 in. apart onto ungreased baking sheets. Bake at 350° for 12-15 minutes or until golden brown. Remove to wire racks to cool.

Yield: about 8 dozen.

Peanut Butter Cup Cookies

Faith Jensen, Meridian, Idaho

With the classic combination of chocolate and peanut butter, it's no surprise these are my family's favorite cookies. They're easy to make.

1 cup butter, softened
2/3 cup peanut butter
1 cup sugar
1 cup packed brown sugar
2 eggs
2 teaspoons vanilla extract
2-1/4 cups all-purpose flour
1 teaspoon baking soda
1/2 teaspoon salt
2 cups (12 ounces) semisweet chocolate chips
2 cups chopped peanut butter cups (about six 1.6-ounce packages)

1. In a large mixing bowl, cream butter, peanut butter and sugars. Add eggs, one at a time, beating well after each addition. Beat in vanilla. Combine flour, baking soda and salt; gradually add to the creamed mixture. Stir in the chocolate chips and peanut butter cups.

2. Drop by rounded tablespoonfuls 2 in. apart onto ungreased baking sheets. Bake at 350° for 10-12 minutes or until edges are lightly browned. Cool for 2 minutes before removing to wire racks.

Yield: 7-1/2 dozen.

Editor's Note: Reduced-fat or generic brands of peanut butter are not recommended for this recipe.

White Chocolate Chip Hazelnut Cookies

Denise DeJong
Pittsburgh, Pennsylvania

This is a cookie you will want to make again and again. I like to take it to church get-togethers and family reunions. It's very delicious...crispy on the outside and chewy on the inside.

1-1/4 cups whole hazelnuts, toasted, *divided*
9 tablespoons butter, softened, *divided*
1/2 cup sugar
1/2 cup packed brown sugar
1 egg
1 teaspoon vanilla extract
1-1/2 cups all-purpose flour
1/2 teaspoon baking soda
1/2 teaspoon salt
1 cup white *or* vanilla chips

1. Coarsely chop 1/2 cup hazelnuts; set aside. Melt 2 tablespoons butter. In a food processor, combine melted butter and remaining hazelnuts. Cover and process until the mixture forms a crumbly paste; set aside.

2. In a mixing bowl, cream the remaining butter. Beat in the sugars. Add egg and vanilla; beat until light and fluffy. Beat in ground hazelnut mixture until blended. Combine the flour, baking soda and salt; add to batter and mix just until combined. Stir in chips and chopped hazelnuts.

3. Drop by rounded tablespoonfuls 2 in. apart onto greased baking sheets. Bake at 350° for 10-12 minutes or until lightly browned. Remove to wire racks to cool.

Yield: 3 dozen.

Apricot Almond Blondies

Amy Forkner, Cheyenne, Wyoming

My mom shared this recipe with me after sampling these cookies at a bed-and-breakfast. I sometimes substitute cranberries and pecans for the apricots and almonds.

3/4 cup butter, softened
1 cup packed brown sugar
1 egg
1 teaspoon vanilla extract
1-2/3 cups all-purpose flour
1/2 teaspoon baking soda
1/4 teaspoon salt
1 package (10 to 12 ounces) vanilla *or* white chips
3/4 cup chopped almonds
3/4 cup chopped dried apricots

1. In a mixing bowl, cream butter and brown sugar. Beat in egg and vanilla. Combine flour, baking soda and salt; gradually add to the creamed mixture. Stir in vanilla chips, almonds and apricots.

2. Drop by heaping tablespoonfuls 2 in. apart onto ungreased baking sheets. Bake at 350° for 7-9 minutes or until lightly browned. Remove to wire racks to cool.

Yield: 6 dozen.

Double Chocolate Biscotti

Taste of Home Test Kitchen
Greendale, Wisconsin

Not fond of biscotti? Try this moister version that's especially good with a hot cup of coffee. It has a chocolaty taste and sweet drizzle on top.

2 eggs
1 teaspoon vanilla extract
1/4 teaspoon almond extract
1/2 cup sugar
1 cup all-purpose flour
1/2 cup finely chopped pecans
1/4 cup baking cocoa
1/4 teaspoon salt
1/2 cup miniature semisweet chocolate chips

ICING:
1-1/2 teaspoons miniature semisweet chocolate chips
3 teaspoons fat-free milk
1/2 cup confectioners' sugar
1/8 teaspoon vanilla extract

1. In a mixing bowl, beat the eggs and extracts. Beat in sugar. Combine the flour, pecans, cocoa and salt; gradually add to egg mixture. Stir in chocolate chips.

2. On a baking sheet coated with nonstick cooking spray, shape dough into a 14-in. x 3-in. rectangle. Bake at 350° for 20-25 minutes or until lightly browned. Cool for 5 minutes.

3. Transfer to a cutting board; cut with a serrated knife into 1-in. slices. Place cut side down on baking sheets coated with nonstick cooking spray. Bake for 15-20 minutes or until firm. Remove to wire racks to cool.

4. For icing, melt chocolate chips. Stir in milk, confectioners' sugar and vanilla. Drizzle over cookies; let stand until set.

Yield: about 1 dozen.

Triple Chocolate Caramel Cookies

Colleen Jennings
Freeburg, Illinois

I love caramel, chocolate and pecans together. I created this cookie recipe.

1-1/2 cups butter, softened
1 cup sugar
1 egg
1 teaspoon vanilla extract
3 cups all-purpose flour
1/2 cup baking cocoa
1 package (12 ounces) miniature semisweet chocolate chips
1 cup chopped pecans, toasted
1 bottle (12-1/2 ounces) caramel ice cream topping
4 to 6 ounces dark chocolate candy coating, melted

1. In a mixing bowl, cream butter and sugar. Beat in egg and vanilla. Combine flour and cocoa; gradually add to the creamed mixture. Stir in chocolate chips and pecans.

2. Roll into 1-in. balls. Place 2 in. apart on ungreased baking sheets. Using the end of a wooden spoon handle, make a 3/8- to 1/2-in.-deep indentation in the center of each ball. Smooth any cracks. Fill each indentation half full with caramel topping.

3. Bake at 350° for 15-18 minutes or until caramel is very bubbly and the cookies are set. Cool for 5 minutes before removing to wire racks. Drizzle cooled cookies with candy coating.

Yield: 6 dozen.

Chunky Mocha Cookies

Janet Sparks, Shirley, Indiana

My Home Economics Club has a cookie exchange every Christmas. These cookies flavored with a hint of coffee are always a big hit.

1 cup butter-flavored shortening
3/4 cup sugar
1/2 cup packed brown sugar
2 eggs
2 tablespoons milk
1 tablespoon instant coffee granules
1 teaspoon vanilla extract
2-1/3 cups all-purpose flour
2 tablespoons baking cocoa
1 teaspoon baking soda
1/2 teaspoon salt
1 cup chopped pecans
1 cup (6 ounces) semisweet chocolate chips
3/4 cup raisins
3/4 cup flaked coconut

1. In a mixing bowl, cream shortening and sugars. Beat in eggs, milk, coffee granules and vanilla. Combine the flour, cocoa, baking soda and salt; add to the creamed mixture and mix well. Stir in pecans, chips, raisins and coconut.

2. Drop by rounded tablespoonfuls 2 in. apart onto ungreased baking sheets. Bake at 375° for 10-12 minutes. Remove to wire racks to cool.

Yield: about 6 dozen.

Frosted Pineapple Cookies, p. 52

Marbled Chocolate Peanut Cookies, p. 59

Oatmeal Crispies, p. 60

Cranberry Chip Cookies, p. 55

Easy Drop Cookies

Drop cookies are some of the simplest to make—just mix, drop and bake. Best of all, these effortless cookies can be baked up in a variety flavors.

Tips for Making Drop Cookies

If your mixer begins to strain because the cookie dough is too thick, use a wooden spoon to stir in the last of the flour or ingredients such as nuts, chips or dried fruit.

For even baking, it's important that you make cookies the same size. Use a teaspoon or tablespoon from your flatware set or a small ice cream scoop (see Using an Ice Cream Scoop to Make Drop Cookies on page 59).

Drop cookies generally melt and spread during baking. But sometimes a recipe may instruct you to flatten the cookies with the bottom of a glass dipped in sugar or with a fork making a crisscross pattern.

Frosted Pineapple Cookies

(Pictured on page 50)
Mary DeVoe, Bradenton, Florida

These are the best pineapple cookies—sweet and moist with real tropical flavor. Because they are unique and look so pretty, these cookies are a hit whenever I serve them. People can't seem to eat just one!

    1 can (8 ounces) crushed pineapple
  1/2 cup shortening
    1 cup packed brown sugar
    1 egg
    1 teaspoon vanilla extract
    2 cups all-purpose flour
1-1/2 teaspoons baking powder
  1/4 teaspoon baking soda
  1/4 teaspoon salt
1-1/2 cups confectioners' sugar

1. Drain pineapple, reserving 3 tablespoons juice. Set pineapple aside; set juice aside for frosting. In a mixing bowl, cream shortening and sugar. Add egg; mix well. Add pineapple and vanilla; mix well. Combine flour, baking powder, baking soda and salt; stir into the creamed mixture.

2. Drop by tablespoonfuls 2 in. apart onto greased baking sheets. Bake at 325° for 17-20 minutes or until golden. Immediately remove to wire racks to cool.

3. For frosting, in a small bowl, combine confectioners' sugar with enough of reserved pineapple juice to achieve a smooth spreading consistency. Frost cooled cookies.

Yield: 3 dozen.

Sesame Seed Cookies

Joan Humphreys, Ellicott City, Maryland

These golden cookies are light inside, chewy outside and really showcase the light nutty flavor of sesame.

  1/2 cup shortening
  1/2 cup butter, softened
    2 cups sugar
    5 eggs
    1 teaspoon vanilla extract
3-1/2 cups all-purpose flour
    5 teaspoons baking powder
  1/2 teaspoon salt
    3 tablespoons milk
    5 tablespoons sesame seeds, toasted

1. In a large mixing bowl, cream the shortening, butter and sugar. Add eggs, one at a time, beating well after each addition. Beat in vanilla. Combine the flour, baking powder and salt; gradually add to creamed mixture.

2. Drop by tablespoonfuls 3 in. apart onto greased baking sheets. Brush with milk; sprinkle with sesame seeds. Bake at 400° for 8-10 minutes or until golden brown. Remove to wire racks to cool.

Yield: about 5-1/2 dozen.

Ginger Drop Cookies

Bethel Walters
Willow River, Minnesota

My mother shared the recipe for these soft spice cookies.

1 cup shortening
1 cup packed brown sugar
1 cup molasses
2 eggs
4 cups all-purpose flour
2 teaspoons baking soda
2 teaspoons ground cinnamon
2 teaspoons ground ginger
1 teaspoon salt
1/2 cup water

1. In a mixing bowl, cream shortening and brown sugar. Add molasses and eggs; mix well. Combine the dry ingredients; add to the creamed mixture alternately with water. Cover and refrigerate for at least 8 hours.

2. Drop dough by tablespoonfuls 2 in. apart onto greased baking sheets. Bake at 350° for 10-12 minutes or until lightly browned. Remove to wire racks to cool.

Yield: about 5-1/2 dozen.

Lemon Zucchini Drops

Barbara Franklin, Tucson, Arizona

When we lived on the East Coast, a nearby fruit and vegetable stand had a bakery featuring these soft cake-like cookies. We missed every bite when we moved away, so I developed this recipe.

1/2 cup butter, softened
1 cup sugar
1 egg
1 cup finely shredded zucchini
1 teaspoon grated lemon peel
2 cups all-purpose flour
1 teaspoon baking soda
1 teaspoon baking powder
1 teaspoon ground cinnamon
1/2 teaspoon salt
1/2 cup raisins
1/2 cup chopped walnuts

LEMON GLAZE:
2 cups confectioners' sugar
2 to 3 tablespoons lemon juice

1. In a mixing bowl, cream butter and sugar. Beat in egg, zucchini and lemon peel. Combine flour, baking soda, baking powder, cinnamon and salt; gradually add to the creamed mixture. Stir in raisins and walnuts.

2. Drop by tablespoonfuls 3 in. apart onto lightly greased baking sheets. Bake at 375° for 8-10 minutes or until lightly browned. Remove to wire racks to cool.

3. For glaze, combine sugar and enough lemon juice to achieve a thin spreading consistency. Spread or drizzle over cooled cookies.

Yield: 3-1/2 dozen.

Frosted Cashew Cookies

Sheila Wyum
Rutland, North Dakota

My sister's sister-in-law discovered this recipe. We enjoy these cookies at Christmas, but they're rich and elegant enough for a special coffee and can be tucked in a lunch box, too.

1/2 cup butter
1 cup packed brown sugar
1 egg
1/3 cup sour cream
1/2 teaspoon vanilla extract
2 cups all-purpose flour
3/4 teaspoon *each* baking powder, baking soda and salt
1-3/4 cups salted cashew halves

BROWNED BUTTER FROSTING:
1/2 cup butter
3 tablespoons half-and-half cream
1/4 teaspoon vanilla extract
2 cups confectioners' sugar
Additional cashew halves, optional

1. In a mixing bowl, cream the butter and brown sugar. Beat in egg, sour cream and vanilla; mix well. Combine dry ingredients; add to creamed mixture and mix well. Fold in the cashews.

2. Drop by rounded teaspoonfuls 2 in. apart onto greased baking sheets. Bake at 375° for 8-10 minutes or until lightly browned. Remove to wire racks to cool.

3. For the frosting, lightly brown butter in a small saucepan. Remove from the heat; add cream and vanilla. Beat in confectioners' sugar until smooth and thick. Frost cookies. Top each with a cashew half if desired.

Yield: about 3 dozen.

Cherry Almond Chews

Alma Chaney, Trenton, Ohio

I make these attractive cherry coconut cookies every Christmas. During that busy time of year, I appreciate the fact that they freeze well, so I can make them ahead.

1 cup shortening
1 cup sugar
1 cup packed brown sugar
2 eggs
3/4 teaspoon almond extract
2-1/2 cups all-purpose flour
1 teaspoon baking soda
1 teaspoon salt
2-1/2 cups flaked coconut
3/4 cup chopped almonds *or* pecans, optional
1 jar (16 ounces) maraschino cherries, drained and halved

1. In a mixing bowl, cream shortening and sugars. Add eggs, one at a time, beating well after each addition. Beat in extract. Combine flour, baking soda and salt; gradually add to the creamed mixture. Stir in coconut and nuts if desired.

2. Drop by rounded teaspoonfuls 2 in. apart onto lightly greased baking sheets. Place a cherry half in the center of each. Bake at 350° for 12-14 minutes or until lightly browned. Remove to wire racks to cool.

Yield: about 7 dozen.

Cranberry Chip Cookies

(Pictured on page 51 and cover)
Jo Ann McCarthy, Canton, Massachusetts

I received these delightful cookies for Christmas a few years ago. I was watching my diet, but I couldn't stay away from them! The tart cranberries blend beautifully with the sweet chocolate and vanilla chips.

- 1/2 cup butter, softened
- 1/2 cup shortening
- 3/4 sugar
- 3/4 cup packed brown sugar
- 2 eggs
- 1 teaspoon vanilla extract
- 2-1/4 cups all-purpose flour
- 1 teaspoon baking soda
- 1/2 teaspoon salt
- 1 cup semisweet chocolate chips
- 1 cup vanilla *or* white chips
- 1 cup dried cranberries
- 1 cup chopped pecans

1. In a mixing bowl, cream butter, shortening and sugars. Add eggs, one at a time, beating well after each addition. Beat in vanilla. Combine flour, baking soda and salt; gradually add to the creamed mixture. Stir in the chips, cranberries and pecans.

2. Drop by tablespoonfuls 2 in. apart onto ungreased baking sheets. Bake at 375° for 9-11 minutes or until golden brown. Cool for 2 minutes before removing to wire racks.

Yield: 9 dozen.

No-Bake Fudgy Oat Cookies

Elizabeth Hunter
Prosperity, South Carolina

I got this recipe from my mother-in-law back in 1949 and my grown daughter asked me to share it with her so she could make them for Christmas.

- 2-1/4 cups quick-cooking oats
- 1 cup flaked coconut
- 1/2 cup milk
- 1/4 cup butter
- 2 cups sugar
- 1/2 cup baking cocoa
- 1 teaspoon vanilla extract

1. In a large bowl, combine oats and coconut; set aside. In a saucepan, combine milk and butter. Stir in sugar and cocoa; mix well. Bring to a boil. Add oat mixture; cook for 1 minute, stirring constantly. Remove from the heat; stir in vanilla.

2. Drop by rounded tablespoonfuls 1 in. apart onto waxed paper. Let stand until set.

Yield: about 3 dozen.

Date Drops

These cake-like cookies are flavorful and firm enough to pack in brown-bag lunches or take on picnics.

Doris Barb, El Dorado, Kansas

1/2 cup butter, softened
3/4 cup packed brown sugar
2 eggs
1/4 cup milk
1/2 teaspoon vanilla extract
1-1/2 cups all-purpose flour
1 teaspoon baking powder
1/4 teaspoon salt
1 cup quick-cooking oats
1 cup chopped dates
1/2 cup chopped walnuts

1. In a mixing bowl, cream the butter and brown sugar. Beat in eggs, milk and vanilla. Combine flour, baking powder and salt; gradually add to creamed mixture and mix well. Stir in oats, dates and nuts.

2. Drop by rounded teaspoonfuls 1 in. apart onto greased baking sheets. Bake at 350° for 12-15 minutes or until edges are lightly browned and tops are firm to the touch. Remove to wire racks to cool.

Yield: about 6 dozen.

Peanut Butter Jumbos

Deborah Huffer
Staunton, Virginia

Oats, peanut butter and chocolate make these soft, chewy cookies hearty. My whole family agrees this recipe is a real winner.

1-1/2 cups peanut butter
1/2 cup butter, softened
1 cup sugar
1 cup packed brown sugar
3 eggs
1 teaspoon vanilla extract
4-1/2 cups quick-cooking oats
2 teaspoons baking soda
1 cup miniature semisweet chocolate chips
1 cup miniature M&M's

1. In a large mixing bowl, cream peanut butter, butter and sugars. Add eggs, one at a time, beating well after each addition. Beat in vanilla. Combine oats and baking soda; gradually add to creamed mixture. Stir in chips and M&M's.

2. Drop by heaping tablespoonfuls 2 in. apart onto ungreased baking sheets. Bake at 350° for 12-14 minutes or until edges are browned. Remove to wire racks.

Yield: 9 dozen.

Editor's Note: This recipe does not use flour. Reduced-fat or generic brands of peanut butter are not recommended.

Golden Raisin Oatmeal Cookies

Marion Lowery
Medford, Oregon

Here's a slightly different twist on a traditional favorite. These crisp, chewy oatmeal cookies feature golden raisins and have a mild orange tang. They're a staple in my picnic basket!

- 3/4 cup butter, softened
- 1 cup packed brown sugar
- 1/2 cup sugar
- 1 egg
- 2 tablespoons water
- 1 teaspoon vanilla extract
- 3 cups quick-cooking oats
- 2/3 cup all-purpose flour
- 2 tablespoons grated orange peel
- 1 teaspoon ground cinnamon
- 1/2 teaspoon baking soda
- 2/3 cup golden raisins

1. In a large mixing bowl, cream butter and sugars until light and fluffy. Beat in egg, water and vanilla. Combine oats, flour, orange peel, cinnamon and baking soda; gradually add to creamed mixture. Stir in the raisins (dough will be stiff).

2. Drop by level tablespoonfuls 2 in. apart onto ungreased baking sheets. Bake at 350° for 12-15 minutes or until the edges are lightly browned. Remove to wire racks to cool.

Yield: 4 dozen.

Pecan Grahams

June Russell
Green Cove Springs, Florida

Years ago, I was eager to enter a recipe contest I'd read about. I went to my pantry and threw together these nutty cookies. Although they didn't win, they've been a hit with my family and friends ever since!

- 1/2 cup shortening
- 1/2 cup sugar
- 1/2 cup packed brown sugar
- 1 egg
- 1 cup all-purpose flour
- 1/2 teaspoon baking powder
- 1/2 teaspoon baking soda
- 1/4 teaspoon salt
- 1 cup graham cracker crumbs
- 1 cup ground pecans
- 54 to 60 pecan halves

1. In a mixing bowl, cream shortening and sugars. Add egg and mix well. Combine flour, baking powder, baking soda and salt; add to the creamed mixture. Stir in cracker crumbs and ground pecans; mix well.

2. Drop by rounded teaspoonfuls 2 in. apart onto ungreased baking sheets. Place a pecan half in the center of each cookie; press down lightly. Bake at 350° for 9-11 minutes or until lightly browned. Cool for 2 minutes before removing to wire racks.

Yield: about 4-1/2 dozen.

Rhubarb-Filled Cookies

Pauline Bondy
Grand Forks, North Dakota

I won a blue ribbon at our local fair for these tender cookies. They're so pretty with the filling peeking through the dough. When not just any cookie will do, try making these and watch the smiles appear.

    1 cup butter, softened
    1 cup sugar
    1 cup packed brown sugar
    4 eggs
4-1/2 cups all-purpose flour
    1 teaspoon baking soda
    1 teaspoon salt

FILLING:
3-1/2 cups chopped fresh *or* frozen rhubarb, thawed
1-1/2 cups sugar
    6 tablespoons water, *divided*
  1/4 cup cornstarch
    1 teaspoon vanilla extract

1. In a mixing bowl, cream the butter and sugars. Add the eggs, one at a time, beating well after each addition. Combine the flour, baking soda and salt; gradually add to creamed mixture and mix well (dough will be sticky).

2. For filling, combine rhubarb, sugar and 2 tablespoons water in a large saucepan. Bring to a boil. Reduce heat; simmer, uncovered, for 10 minutes or until thickened, stirring frequently. Combine cornstarch and remaining water until smooth; stir into rhubarb mixture. Bring to a boil; cook and stir for 2 minutes or until thickened. Remove from the heat; stir in vanilla.

3. Drop dough by tablespoonfuls 2 in. apart onto ungreased baking sheets. Using the end of a wooden spoon handle, make an indentation in the center of each cookie; fill with a rounded teaspoon of filling. Top with 1/2 teaspoon of dough, allowing some filling to show. Bake at 375° for 8-10 minutes or until lightly browned. Remove to wire racks to cool.

Yield: about 4-1/2 dozen.

Coconut Caramel Oat Cookies

When I was a little girl, my grandmother and I used to whip up this no-bake snack to munch on while playing rummy.

Tammy Schroeder, Aitkin, Minnesota

  1/2 cup butter
  1/2 cup milk
    1 cup sugar
    1 teaspoon vanilla extract
  1/2 teaspoon salt
   25 caramels
    3 cups quick-cooking oats
    1 cup flaked coconut

1. In a heavy saucepan, bring butter and milk to a boil; add sugar, vanilla and salt. Cook for 1 minute. Add caramels and stir until melted, about 4 minutes. Stir in oats and coconut.

2. Drop by heaping tablespoonfuls onto waxed paper. Let stand at room temperature until set.

Yield: 4-1/2 dozen.

Marbled Chocolate Peanut Cookies

(Pictured on page 51)
Shirley De Lange, Byron Center, Michigan

This recipe came about when I was making peanut butter and chocolate cookies. I had small portion each dough left and made them into one cookie.

PEANUT BUTTER DOUGH:
- 1 cup butter, softened
- 1 cup peanut butter
- 1-1/4 cups sugar
- 1-1/4 cups packed brown sugar
- 3 eggs
- 2 teaspoons vanilla extract
- 2-1/2 cups all-purpose flour
- 1/2 teaspoon *each* baking soda and salt
- 1 cup chopped peanuts

CHOCOLATE DOUGH:
- 1 cup butter, softened
- 1 cup packed brown sugar
- 3/4 cup sugar
- 3 eggs
- 2 teaspoons vanilla extract
- 2-1/2 cups all-purpose flour
- 1/2 cup baking cocoa
- 1/2 teaspoon *each* baking soda and salt
- 2 cups (12 ounces) semisweet chocolate chips

1. In a mixing bowl, cream butter, peanut butter and sugars. Add eggs, one at a time, beating well after each addition. Beat in vanilla. Combine flour, baking soda and salt; gradually add to the creamed mixture. Stir in peanuts; set aside.

2. For chocolate dough, cream butter and sugars in another mixing bowl. Add eggs, one at a time, beating well after each addition. Beat in vanilla. Combine flour, cocoa, baking soda and salt; gradually add to the creamed mixture. Stir in chocolate chips. Gently fold in peanut butter dough until slightly marbled.

3. Drop by heaping tablespoonfuls 3 in. apart onto greased baking sheets. Bake at 350° for 14-16 minutes or until lightly browned and firm. Remove to wire racks to cool.

Yield: 9-1/2 dozen.

Editor's Note: Reduced-fat or generic brands of peanut butter are not recommended for this recipe.

Using an Ice Cream Scoop to Make Drop Cookies

An ice cream scoop is the perfect utensil for making uniformly sized drop cookies. (A 1 tablespoon-size ice cream scoop will result in a standard-size 2-in. cookie.) Just scoop the dough, even off the top with a flat-edge metal spatula and release onto a baking sheet.

Oatmeal Crispies

(Pictured on page 51)
Karen Henson, St. Louis, Missouri

My husband, who normally isn't fond of oatmeal, thinks these old-fashioned cookies are great. With a hint of nutmeg, their aroma is wonderful as they bake...and they taste even better!

1 cup shortening
1 cup sugar
1 cup packed brown sugar
2 eggs
1 teaspoon vanilla extract
3 cups quick-cooking oats
1-1/2 cups all-purpose flour
1 teaspoon salt
1 teaspoon baking soda
1/4 teaspoon ground nutmeg
1/4 teaspoon ground cinnamon

1. In a mixing bowl, cream shortening and sugars. Add eggs, one at a time, beating well after each addition. Beat in vanilla. Combine the remaining ingredients; gradually add to creamed mixture.

2. Drop by tablespoonfuls 2 in. apart onto ungreased baking sheets. Flatten with a fork. Bake at 350° for 10-12 minutes or until lightly browned. Remove to wire racks to cool.

Yield: 5-1/2 dozen.

Apple Butter Cookies

Dorothy Hawkins
Springhill, Florida

My mother used to bake these mouth-watering cookies for an after-school treat. These cookies stay moist and fresh for a long time, or the dough can be stored in the refrigerator for several days so you can bake as you need them.

1/4 cup butter, softened
1 cup packed brown sugar
1 egg
1/2 cup quick-cooking oats
1/2 cup apple butter
1 cup all-purpose flour
1/2 teaspoon baking soda
1/2 teaspoon baking powder
1/2 teaspoon salt
2 tablespoons milk
1/2 cup chopped nuts
1/2 cup raisins

1. In a small mixing bowl, cream butter and sugar. Beat in egg, oats and apple butter. Combine dry ingredients; gradually add to creamed mixture along with the milk; beat until blended. Stir in nuts and raisins. Cover and refrigerate until easy to handle.

2. Drop by teaspoonfuls 2 in. apart onto lightly greased baking sheets. Bake at 350° for 15 minutes or until set. Remove to wire racks.

Yield: about 2-1/2 dozen.

Frosted Ginger Cookies

Jeanne Matteson
South Dayton, New York

My husband and I just built a new house in a small rural community in western New York. The aroma of these soft delicious cookies in our oven has made our new house smell like home.

1-1/2 cups butter
1 cup sugar
1 cup packed brown sugar
2 eggs
1/2 cup molasses
2 teaspoons vanilla extract
4-1/2 cups all-purpose flour
1 tablespoon ground ginger
2 teaspoons *each* baking soda and ground cinnamon
1/2 teaspoon *each* salt and ground cloves

FROSTING:
1/3 cup packed brown sugar
1/4 cup milk
2 tablespoons butter
2 cups confectioners' sugar
1/2 teaspoon vanilla extract
Dash salt

1. In a mixing bowl, cream butter and sugars. Add the eggs, one at a time, beating well after each addition. Stir in molasses and vanilla; mix well. Combine dry ingredients; gradually add to creamed mixture.

2. Drop by tablespoonfuls 2 in. apart onto ungreased baking sheets. Bake at 325° for 12-15 minutes or until cookies spring back when touched lightly (do not overbake). Remove to wire racks.

3. For frosting, in a medium saucepan, bring brown sugar, milk and butter to a boil; boil for 1 minute, stirring constantly. Remove from the heat (mixture will look curdled at first). Cool for 3 minutes before adding confectioners' sugar, vanilla and salt; mix well. Frost cookies.

Yield: about 6 dozen.

Pecan Puffs

Leslie Link-Terry, Greendale, Wisconsin

I just had to share my mom's recipe for these drop cookies. The light-as-a-cloud taste is simply heavenly.

3 egg whites
Dash salt
1 cup packed brown sugar
1/2 teaspoon vanilla extract
1 cup chopped pecans

1. In a small mixing bowl, beat egg whites and salt on medium speed until soft peaks form. Gradually add sugar, 2 tablespoons at a time, beating on high until stiff peaks form, about 5-8 minutes. Fold in the vanilla and pecans.

2. Drop by well-rounded teaspoonfuls onto greased baking sheets. Bake at 200° for 50-55 minutes or until firm to the touch. Remove to wire racks. Store in airtight container.

Yield: 3 dozen.

Chewy Ginger Drop Cookies

Lois Furcron
Coudersport, Pennsylvania

This recipe originated with my grandmother. My mom also made these cookies. I too baked them for my family, then my daughters made them and now their daughters are making them—a true legacy I'm happy to share.

1/2 cup shortening
1/2 cup sugar
2 cups all-purpose flour
1/2 teaspoon baking soda
1/2 teaspoon ground ginger
1/4 teaspoon salt
1/2 cup molasses
1/4 cup water
Additional sugar

1. In a mixing bowl, cream shortening and sugar. Combine flour, baking soda, ginger and salt. Combine molasses and water. Add dry ingredients to the creamed mixture alternately with molasses mixture.

2. Drop by rounded teaspoonfuls 2 in. apart onto greased baking sheets. Sprinkle with sugar. Bake at 350° for 13-15 minutes or until edges are set. Remove to wire racks to cool.

Yield: about 2-1/2 dozen.

Root Beer Cookies

Violette Bawden
West Valley City, Utah

Since it's too difficult to take along root beer floats on a picnic, pack these cookies instead! I've found the flavor is even better the next day. The hard part is convincing my family to wait that long before sampling them.

1 cup butter, softened
2 cups packed brown sugar
2 eggs
1 cup buttermilk
3/4 teaspoon root beer concentrate *or* extract
4 cups all-purpose flour
1 teaspoon baking soda
1 teaspoon salt
1-1/2 cups chopped pecans

FROSTING:
3-1/2 cups confectioners' sugar
3/4 cup butter, softened
3 tablespoons water
1-1/4 teaspoons root beer concentrate *or* extract

1. In a large mixing bowl, cream butter and brown sugar. Add eggs, one at a time, beating well after each addition. Beat in buttermilk and root beer concentrate. Combine the flour, baking soda and salt; gradually add to creamed mixture. Stir in pecans.

2. Drop by tablespoonfuls 3 in. apart onto ungreased baking sheets. Bake at 375° for 10-12 minutes or until lightly browned. Remove to wire racks to cool.

3. In a mixing bowl, combine frosting ingredients; beat until smooth. Frost cooled cookies.

Yield: about 6 dozen.

Crisp Peppermint Patties

Deborah Kay Collins, Mansfield, Ohio

Mint lovers will delight in every bite of these original crisp cookies. They not only taste wonderful, but they're attractive.

- 1 cup butter-flavored shortening
- 1/2 cup sugar
- 1/2 cup packed brown sugar
- 2 eggs
- 1 package (13 ounces) chocolate-covered peppermint patties, melted
- 1 teaspoon vanilla extract
- 2-1/3 cups all-purpose flour
- 1 teaspoon baking soda
- 1/2 teaspoon salt

1. In a mixing bowl, cream shortening and sugars. Add eggs, one at a time, beating well after each addition. Beat in melted peppermint patties and vanilla. Combine flour, baking soda and salt; gradually add to the creamed mixture. Cover and refrigerate for 30 minutes or until easy to handle.

2. Drop by rounded teaspoonfuls 2 in. apart onto ungreased baking sheets. Bake at 375° for 8-10 minutes or until the surface cracks. Cool for 1-2 minutes before removing to wire racks.

Yield: 5 dozen.

Molasses Raisin Cookies

Denise and George Hymel
Gramercy, Louisiana

These old-fashioned, mildly sweet cookies are dotted with walnuts and raisins. We like them soft right from the oven. Later, they crisp up and are perfect for dunking.

- 3/4 cup shortening
- 1 cup packed brown sugar
- 1/4 cup molasses
- 2 eggs
- 2-1/4 cups all-purpose flour
- 1 teaspoon baking soda
- 1 teaspoon ground ginger
- 1 teaspoon ground cinnamon
- 1/2 teaspoon ground cloves
- 1/2 teaspoon salt
- 1/2 cup raisins
- 1/2 cup chopped walnuts

1. In a large mixing bowl, cream shortening and brown sugar. Beat in molasses. Add eggs, one at a time, beating well after each addition. Combine the flour, baking soda, spices and salt; gradually add to creamed mixture. Stir in raisins and nuts.

2. Drop by rounded tablespoonfuls 2 in. apart onto greased baking sheets. Bake at 375° for 8-10 minutes or until edges are lightly browned. Remove to wire racks to cool.

Yield: about 3-1/2 dozen.

Frosted Raisin Creams

Kay Strain, Norwalk, Iowa

These old-fashioned raisin cookies bring back fond memories of Mom whipping up a batch in her kitchen. The down-home aroma as they bake is a wonderful way to welcome family home.

1 cup raisins
1-1/4 cups boiling water
1 cup butter, softened
1-1/2 cups sugar
2 eggs
3 cups all-purpose flour
2 tablespoons ground cinnamon
1 teaspoon baking soda
1/4 teaspoon salt
1/2 cup chopped walnuts

FROSTING:
1/2 cup packed brown sugar
1/2 hot milk
4-1/2 cups confectioners' sugar

1. Place raisins in a bowl. Add boiling water; let stand for 5 minutes. Drain, reserving 1 cup liquid; set the raisins and liquid aside.

2. In a mixing bowl, cream butter and sugar. Add the eggs, one at a time, beating well after each addition. Combine flour, cinnamon, baking soda and salt; add to the creamed mixture alternately with reserved liquid. Stir in walnuts and raisins.

3. Drop by teaspoonfuls 2 in. apart onto ungreased baking sheets. Bake at 350° for 12-15 minutes or until lightly browned. Cool for 1 minute before removing to wire racks.

4. For frosting, whisk brown sugar and milk until sugar is dissolved. Add confectioners' sugar; mix well. Frost cooled cookies.

Yield: about 9 dozen.

Peanut Butter Oatmeal Cookies

Rollin Barkeim
Trempealeau, Wisconsin

These cookies are soft and chewy with the old-fashioned goodness of oatmeal and peanut butter. I take them to work and on camping trips since they travel very well.

3 egg whites
1 cup packed brown sugar
1 cup reduced-fat peanut butter
1/2 cup unsweetened applesauce
1/4 cup honey
2 teaspoons vanilla extract
3 cups quick-cooking oats
1 cup all-purpose flour
1 cup nonfat dry milk powder
2 teaspoons baking soda

1. In a mixing bowl, beat egg whites and brown sugar. Beat in peanut butter, applesauce, honey and vanilla. Combine the oats, flour, milk powder and baking soda; gradually add to peanut butter mixture, beating until combined.

2. Drop by tablespoonfuls 2 in. apart onto baking sheets coated with nonstick cooking spray. Bake at 350° for 8-10 minutes or until golden brown. Remove to wire racks to cool.

Yield: 5 dozen.

Drop Sugar Cookies

Shirley Brazel
Coos Bay, Oregon

I've been making these cookies for more than 25 years. The cookies have a crisp edge, soft center and subtle lemon flavor. Choose colored sugar to tailor them to any occasion.

2 eggs
3/4 cup sugar
2/3 cup vegetable oil
2 teaspoons vanilla extract
1 teaspoon grated lemon peel
2 cups all-purpose flour
2 teaspoons baking powder
1/2 teaspoon salt
Additional sugar *or* colored sugar

1. In a mixing bowl, beat eggs, sugar, oil, vanilla and lemon peel until blended. Combine the flour, baking powder and salt; gradually beat into egg mixture.

2. Drop by rounded teaspoonfuls 2 in. apart onto greased baking sheets. Flatten with a glass dipped in sugar. Bake at 350° for 8-10 minutes or until edges are lightly browned. Cool for 1-2 minutes before removing to wire racks.

Yield: about 3-1/2 dozen.

Rosemary Honey Cookies

Audrey Thibodeau, Mesa, Arizona

You'll be delighted with this unusual cookie's wonderful flavor. Rosemary combined with cinnamon and nutmeg make this cookie unique from other spice cookies.

1/2 cup shortening
1/4 cup butter, softened
3/4 cup sugar
1 egg
1/4 cup honey
1 tablespoon lemon juice
2 cups all-purpose flour
2 teaspoons dried rosemary, crushed
1 teaspoon baking soda
1/2 teaspoon salt
1/2 teaspoon ground cinnamon
1/4 teaspoon ground nutmeg

1. In a mixing bowl, cream shortening, butter and sugar. Beat in egg, honey and lemon juice. Combine dry ingredients; add to creamed mixture.

2. Drop by teaspoonfuls 2 in. apart onto greased baking sheets. Bake at 325° for 12-14 minutes or until lightly browned. Remove to wire racks to cool.

Yield: about 4 dozen.

Apricot Coconut Cookies

Sara Kennedy
Manassas, Virginia

These fancy, chewy cookies are made without eggs. Our son's allergy got me searching for treats he can enjoy and we love them, too.

1-1/4 cups all-purpose flour
1/4 cup sugar
1-1/2 teaspoons baking powder
1/2 cup butter
1 package (3 ounces) cream cheese
1/2 cup flaked coconut
1/2 cup apricot preserves

GLAZE:
1/2 cup confectioners' sugar
2 tablespoons apricot preserves
1-1/2 teaspoons butter, softened
1-1/2 teaspoons milk

1. In a large bowl, combine flour, sugar and baking powder. Cut in butter and cream cheese until mixture resembles coarse crumbs. Add coconut and preserves; mix well.

2. Drop by rounded teaspoonfuls 2 in. apart onto greased baking sheet. Bake at 350° for 10-12 minutes or until golden brown. Remove to wire racks to cool.

3. Combine glaze ingredients in a small bowl; mix well. Spoon over cooled cookies.

Yield: about 3 dozen.

Double Chocolate Cookies

Chantal Cornwall
Prince Rupert, British Columbia

When I make these yummy treats with my young grandson, Ben, I use an extra-big mixing bowl to prevent the flour and other ingredients from flying all over. He seems to enjoy making the cookies almost as much as eating them!

1-1/4 cups butter, softened
2 cups sugar
2 eggs
2 teaspoons vanilla extract
2 cups all-purpose flour
3/4 cup baking cocoa
1 teaspoon baking soda
1/2 teaspoon salt
2 cups (12 ounces) semisweet chocolate chips

1. In a mixing bowl, cream butter and sugar until smooth. Beat in eggs and vanilla. Combine the flour, cocoa, baking soda and salt; gradually add to creamed mixture and mix well. Stir in chocolate chips.

2. Drop by rounded teaspoonfuls 2 in. apart onto greased baking sheets. Bake at 350° for 8-10 minutes or until set. Cool for 2 minutes; remove to wire racks to cool completely.

Yield: about 9 dozen.

Butter Meltaways

Sue Call, Beech Grove, Indiana

Add variety to this recipe by substituting lemon flavoring for the vanilla plus a teaspoon of lemon peel.

- 1/2 cup butter, softened
- 1/2 cup vegetable oil
- 1/2 cup sugar
- 1/2 cup confectioners' sugar
- 1 egg
- 1/2 teaspoon vanilla extract
- 2-1/4 cups all-purpose flour
- 1/2 teaspoon baking soda
- 1/2 teaspoon cream of tartar
- Additional sugar

1. In a mixing bowl, cream butter, oil and sugars. Add egg and vanilla. Combine flour, baking soda and cream of tartar; gradually add to the creamed mixture. Chill for several hours or overnight.

2. Drop by rounded teaspoonfuls 2 in. apart onto ungreased baking sheets. Flatten with a fork dipped in flour; sprinkle with sugar. Bake at 350° for 13-15 minutes or until lightly browned. Remove to wire racks to cool completely.

Yield: about 4 dozen.

Frosted Orange Cookies

Tammie Young
Mattoon, Illinois

I remember my dad making a big batch of these citrus cookies when I was growing up. They're very moist and have a old-fashioned taste.

- 2 medium navel oranges
- 1/2 cup butter-flavored shortening
- 1 cup sugar
- 1/2 cup milk
- 2 cups all-purpose flour
- 1 teaspoon baking powder
- 1/2 teaspoon baking soda
- 1/2 teaspoon salt
- 2-1/2 cups confectioners' sugar
- 1 tablespoon butter, melted

1. With a sharp paring knife, score each orange into quarters; remove peel. Use knife to remove white pith from the peel and the fruit; discard. Quarter oranges and place in a blender. Add peel; cover and process until smooth (mixture should measure 3/4 cup).

2. In a mixing bowl, cream the shortening and sugar. Beat in the milk and 6 tablespoons orange mixture. Combine the flour, baking powder, baking soda and salt; add to creamed mixture until blended.

3. Drop by rounded teaspoonfuls 2 in. apart onto greased baking sheets. Bake at 350° for 10-13 minutes or until set and edges are lightly browned. Remove to wire racks to cool.

4. For frosting, in a small mixing bowl, combine confectioners' sugar, butter and enough of the remaining orange mixture to achieve spreading consistency. Frost cookies.

Yield: about 4 dozen.

Crisp Sunflower Cookies

Karen Ann Bland, Gove, Kansas

This is the "Sunflower State," and these crisp cookies feature sunflower seeds. It takes just minutes to mix up a batch of these tasty cookies.

- 3/4 cup shortening
- 1 cup sugar
- 1 cup packed brown sugar
- 2 eggs
- 1 teaspoon vanilla extract
- 2 cups all-purpose flour
- 1 teaspoon baking soda
- 1/2 teaspoon baking powder
- 1/2 teaspoon salt
- 2 cups quick-cooking oats
- 1 cup flaked coconut
- 1 cup salted sunflower seeds

1. In a mixing bowl, cream shortening and sugars until light and fluffy. Add eggs and vanilla; mix well. Combine flour, baking soda, baking powder and salt; add to creamed mixture and mix well. Stir in the oats, coconut and sunflower seeds.

2. Drop by teaspoonfuls 2 in. apart onto greased baking sheets. Bake at 350° for 12-15 minutes or until golden brown. Remove to wire racks to cool.

Yield: 5 dozen.

Chewy Maple Cookies

Reba Legrand
Jericho, Vermont

My husband, Bob, and I have a small sugaring operation with Bob's father. I love to put some of our syrup to use in these golden cookies.

- 1/2 cup shortening
- 1 cup packed brown sugar
- 1 egg
- 1/2 cup pure maple syrup
- 1/2 teaspoon vanilla extract *or* maple flavoring
- 1-1/2 cups all-purpose flour
- 2 teaspoons baking powder
- 1/2 teaspoon salt
- 1 cup flaked coconut

1. In a mixing bowl, cream shortening and brown sugar until fluffy. Beat in the egg, syrup and vanilla until well mixed. Combine flour, baking powder and salt; add to the creamed mixture. Stir in coconut.

2. Drop by tablespoonfuls 2 in. apart onto greased baking sheets. Bake at 375° for 12-15 minutes or until lightly browned. Remove to wire racks to cool completely.

Yield: 3 dozen.

Sugar 'n' Spice Cookies

Dottie LaPierre
Woburn, Massachusetts

These sweet and tart cookies are a special treat.

3/4 cup shortening
1 cup sugar
1 egg
1/4 cup molasses
2 cups all-purpose flour
1 teaspoon baking soda
1-1/2 teaspoons ground ginger
1 teaspoon ground cinnamon
3/4 teaspoon ground cloves
1/2 teaspoon salt

LEMON FROSTING:
3 tablespoons butter, softened
2 cups confectioners' sugar
1 teaspoon grated lemon peel
3 to 4 tablespoons lemon juice

1. In a mixing bowl, cream shortening and sugar. Add egg; mix well. Beat in molasses. Combine dry ingredients; add to creamed mixture and mix well.

2. Drop by rounded teaspoonfuls 2 in. apart onto greased baking sheets. Bake at 350° for 8-10 minutes. Remove to wire racks to cool.

3. For frosting, cream the butter, sugar and lemon peel in a mixing bowl. Gradually add enough of the lemon juice to achieve a spreading consistency. Frost cookies.

Yield: about 4-1/2 dozen.

Apricot-Nut Drop Cookies

Patricia Crawford, Garland, Texas

Most everyone who comes to our home asks for my "famous" apricot cookies. They are really good, and I try not to eat them all myself!
If you like apricots, I recommend you make two batches for starters.

3/4 cup butter-flavored shortening
1-1/4 cups packed brown sugar
1 egg
2 tablespoons milk
1 teaspoon vanilla extract
1-3/4 cups all-purpose flour
1 teaspoon baking powder
3/4 teaspoon baking soda
1/2 teaspoon salt
1 cup chopped dried apricots
1 cup chopped pecans

1. In a mixing bowl, cream shortening and brown sugar. Beat in egg, milk and vanilla. Combine dry ingredients; gradually add to creamed mixture. Stir in apricots and pecans.

2. Drop by rounded tablespoonfuls 3 in. apart onto ungreased baking sheets. Bake at 375° for 10-13 minutes or until light golden brown. Cool for 2 minutes before removing to wire racks.

Yield: 4-1/2 dozen.

Sour Cream Drops

Tracy Betzler
Reston, Virginia

My mother is an excellent baker, and this is her recipe. Whether Mom makes these cookies or I do, they always disappear quickly. Friends rave about them and often ask me to bring them to get-togethers.

1/4 cup shortening
3/4 cup sugar
1 egg
1/2 cup sour cream
1/2 teaspoon vanilla extract
1-1/3 cups all-purpose flour
1/4 teaspoon baking soda
1/4 teaspoon baking powder
1/4 teaspoon salt

BURNT SUGAR FROSTING:
2 tablespoons butter
1/2 cup confectioners' sugar
1/4 teaspoon vanilla extract
3 to 4 teaspoons hot water

1. In a mixing bowl, cream shortening, sugar and egg. Add sour cream and vanilla. Combine dry ingredients; add to the creamed mixture. Chill for at least 1 hour.

2. Drop by tablespoonfuls 2 in. apart onto greased baking sheets. Bake at 425° for 7-8 minutes or until lightly browned. Remove to wire racks to cool completely.

3. For frosting, melt the butter in a small saucepan until golden brown. Stir in vanilla and enough water to achieve a spreading consistency. Frost cooled cookies.

Yield: about 2-1/2 dozen.

Nutty Butter Munchies

Zenola Frazier, Tallulah, Louisiana

I developed this delicious recipe for a crisp cookie as a way to satisfy my sweet tooth. Peanuts and pecans are abundant here in Louisiana, so I bake with them often.

1 cup butter, softened
1/2 cup chunky peanut butter
1 cup sugar
1 cup packed brown sugar
3 eggs
1 teaspoon vanilla extract
1/2 teaspoon almond extract
3 cups all-purpose flour
1/2 teaspoon baking soda
1/2 teaspoon salt
1-1/2 cups chopped pecans
1/2 cup salted peanuts

1. In a mixing bowl, cream butter, peanut butter and sugars. Add eggs, one at a time, beating well after each addition. Beat in extracts. Combine flour, baking soda and salt; gradually add to the creamed mixture. Stir in pecans and peanuts.

2. Drop dough by tablespoonfuls 2 in. apart onto greased baking sheets. Flatten with a glass dipped in sugar. Bake at 350° for 10-12 minutes or until the edges are lightly browned. Remove to wire racks to cool.

Yield: 8-1/2 dozen.

Editor's Note: Reduced-fat or generic brands of peanut butter are not recommended for this recipe.

Iced Orange Cookies

Lori DiPietro, New Port Richey, Florida

I usually make these bite-size cookies at Christmastime, when oranges in Florida are plentiful. Every time I sniff their wonderful aroma, I remember my grandmother, who shared the recipe.

1/2 cup shortening
1 cup sugar
2 eggs
1/2 cup orange juice
1 tablespoon grated orange peel
2-1/2 cups all-purpose flour
1-1/2 teaspoons baking powder
1/2 teaspoon salt

ICING:
2 cups confectioners' sugar
1/4 cup orange juice
2 tablespoons butter, melted

1. In a mixing bowl, cream shortening and sugar. Add eggs, one at a time, beating well after each addition. Beat in orange juice and peel. Combine flour, baking powder and salt; gradually add to the creamed mixture.

2. Drop by heaping teaspoonfuls 2 in. apart onto ungreased baking sheets. Bake at 350° for 10-12 minutes or until edges begin to brown. Remove to wire racks to cool.

3. In a small bowl, combine icing ingredients until smooth; drizzle over cooled cookies.

Yield: about 5-1/2 dozen.

Maple Raisin Oatmeal Cookies

Karen Nienaber
Erskine, Minnesota

My five children love maple and brown sugar oatmeal, so I decided to add those ingredients to my oatmeal cookies. The first time I made them, they vanished in just a few days!

1 cup butter, softened
1 cup packed brown sugar
1/2 cup sugar
2 eggs
1 teaspoon maple flavoring
1-1/2 cups all-purpose flour
1 teaspoon baking soda
1 teaspoon ground cinnamon
1/2 teaspoon salt
3 cups quick-cooking oats
1 cup raisins

1. In a mixing bowl, cream the butter and sugars. Add eggs, one at a time, beating well after each addition. Beat in maple flavoring. Combine the flour, baking soda, cinnamon and salt; gradually add to the creamed mixture. Stir in oats and raisins.

2. Drop by rounded teaspoonfuls 2 in. apart onto ungreased baking sheets. Bake at 350° for 10-12 minutes or until golden brown. Remove to wire racks to cool.

Yield: 6 dozen.

Toasted Coconut Cookies

Cindy Colley, Othello, Washington

These cookies have coconut, walnuts and oats to make them a satisfying snack no matter what time of day. They're a hit with everyone who tries them.

1/2 cup butter, softened
1/2 cup shortening
3/4 cup sugar
3/4 cup packed brown sugar
2 eggs
2 teaspoons vanilla extract
2 cups all-purpose flour
1 teaspoon baking powder
1 teaspoon baking soda
3/4 teaspoon salt
1-1/2 cups quick-cooking oats
1-1/2 cups flaked coconut, toasted
3/4 cup chopped walnuts, toasted

1. In a mixing bowl, cream butter, shortening and sugars until fluffy. Add eggs and vanilla; beat well. Combine flour, baking powder, baking soda and salt; gradually add to creamed mixture. Fold in oats, coconut and nuts.

2. Drop by tablespoonfuls onto greased baking sheets. Bake at 375° for 10-11 minutes or until golden brown. Cool 2-3 minutes before removing to wire racks.

Yield: about 5 dozen.

Fudgy No-Bake Cookies

Beth Brown
Naples, Florida

This recipe can be changed to suit your sweet tooth. Try adding almond or mint extract. They make a fun garnish for ice cream, too.

1 cup sugar
2 tablespoons baking cocoa
1/4 cup butter
1/4 cup milk
1 cup quick-cooking oats
1/4 cup flaked coconut
2 tablespoons peanut butter
1/2 teaspoon vanilla extract

1. In a saucepan, combine sugar and cocoa; add butter and milk. Cook and stir over medium heat until mixture comes to a boil; boil for 1 minute. Remove from the heat; stir in oats, coconut, peanut butter and vanilla.

2. Let stand until the mixture mounds when dropped by tablespoonfuls onto waxed paper. Cool.

Yield: 1 dozen.

Editor's Note: Reduced-fat or generic brands of peanut butter are not recommended for this recipe.

Cranberry Oat Yummies

Carol Birkemeier
Nashville, Indiana

I like to think these oatmeal treats are better for you than the standard chocolate chip cookies. Our three sons just can't get enough of them. And they have no idea I've made the cookies healthier.

1/2 cup butter, melted
1/2 cup sugar
1 cup packed brown sugar
1 egg
1/4 cup egg substitute
2 tablespoons corn syrup
1-1/2 teaspoons vanilla extract
3 cups quick-cooking oats
1 cup all-purpose flour
1 teaspoon baking soda
1 teaspoon ground cinnamon
1/2 teaspoon baking powder
1/2 teaspoon salt
1/8 teaspoon ground nutmeg
1 cup dried cranberries

1. In a mixing bowl, beat butter and sugars. Add egg, egg substitute, corn syrup and vanilla; mix well. Combine the oats, flour, baking soda, cinnamon, baking powder, salt and nutmeg; gradually add to egg mixture. Stir in cranberries.

2. Drop by heaping tablespoonfuls 2 in. apart onto ungreased baking sheets. Bake at 375° for 8-10 minutes or until golden brown. Cool for 2 minutes before removing to wire racks.

Yield: 3 dozen.

Banana Spice Cookies

Peggy Burdick, Burlington, Michigan

My grandkids love these tasty drop cookies. The banana makes them soft and moist. The cinnamon and cloves complement the banana flavor.

1/2 cup shortening
1 cup packed brown sugar
2 eggs
1 cup mashed ripe bananas (2 to 3 medium)
2 cups all-purpose flour
2 teaspoons baking powder
1/2 teaspoon ground cinnamon
1/4 teaspoon baking soda
1/4 teaspoon salt
1/4 teaspoon ground cloves
1/2 cup chopped walnuts
1/2 cup raisins

1. In a mixing bowl, cream shortening and brown sugar. Add eggs and bananas; mix well. Combine dry ingredients; add to creamed mixture and mix well. Stir in nuts and raisins. Cover and refrigerate for 2-4 hours (dough will be very soft).

2. Drop by rounded teaspoonfuls 2 in. apart onto greased baking sheets. Bake at 350° for 8-10 minutes or until lightly browned. Remove to wire racks to cool.

Yield: 3 dozen.

Frosted Brown Sugar Cookies

Loretta Patterson
Mentor, Ohio

These old-fashioned, cake-like cookies are sweet and buttery. They pair equally well with a glass of cold milk or a cup of hot coffee.

- 1/2 cup butter, softened
- 1 cup packed brown sugar
- 1 egg
- 1/2 cup sour cream
- 1-3/4 cups all-purpose flour
- 1/2 teaspoon baking soda
- 1/4 teaspoon salt

BROWN SUGAR FROSTING:
- 1/4 cup butter
- 1/2 cup packed brown sugar
- 2 tablespoons milk
- 1 cup confectioners' sugar

1. In a small mixing bowl, cream butter and brown sugar. Beat in egg and sour cream. Combine the flour, baking soda and salt; gradually add to creamed mixture and mix well.

2. Drop by tablespoonfuls 2 in. apart onto greased baking sheets. Bake at 375° for 9-11 minutes or until golden brown. Remove to wire racks to cool completely.

3. For frosting, in a small saucepan, melt butter over low heat; add brown sugar. Cook and stir for 2 minutes. Gradually add the milk. Bring to a boil, stirring constantly. Remove from the heat. Stir in confectioners' sugar. Cool for 20-30 minutes. Frost cooled cookies.

Yield: about 2 dozen.

Cherry Date Cookies

Charlotte Moore, Parkersburg, West Virginia

You can fix these chewy old-fashioned drop cookies with just five ingredients. I received this recipe from a friend more than 40 years ago and have made these cookies every Christmas since.

- 2-1/4 cups graham cracker crumbs (about 27 squares)
- 1 can (14 ounces) sweetened condensed milk
- 2 cups chopped dates
- 2 cups chopped walnuts
- 27 red *or* green maraschino cherries, halved

1. In a bowl, combine cracker crumbs and milk; let stand for 10 minutes. Stir in dates and walnuts (mixture will be very thick).

2. Drop by tablespoonfuls 2 in. apart onto greased baking sheets. Top each with a cherry half. Bake at 350° for 10-15 minutes or until set and edges are lightly browned. Cool for 1 minute before removing to wire racks to cool completely.

Yield: 4-1/2 dozen.

Butter Wafers

Evelyn Starr, Raymond, Washington

These crisp drop cookies are great for folks who don't like their treats too sweet and who don't want to fuss with rolling out the dough. Just beat together four ingredients and you are on your way to a delicious treat.

1 cup butter, softened
1/3 cup confectioners' sugar
1 cup all-purpose flour
2/3 cup cornstarch
Colored sugar, optional

1. In a mixing bowl, cream butter and confectioners' sugar. Combine flour and cornstarch; add to creamed mixture and mix well.

2. Drop by rounded tablespoonfuls 3 in. apart onto ungreased baking sheets (cookies will spread). Sprinkle with colored sugar if desired. Bake at 325° for 12-15 minutes or until edges are lightly browned and tops are set. Cool for 2 minutes before carefully removing to wire racks.

Yield: about 2-1/2 dozen.

Cute Pig Cookies

Becky Baldwin
Annville, Pennsylvania

I created this recipe for a party my friend had for National Pig Day, which is March 1st. They were not only a big hit at the party, but also at my son's school parties.

1 cup butter, softened
1-1/2 cups sugar
2 eggs
1 cup (8 ounces) sour cream
1 teaspoon vanilla extract
3 cups all-purpose flour
1 teaspoon baking powder
1/2 teaspoon salt

FROSTING/DECORATING:
1/2 cup butter
4 cups confectioners' sugar
2 teaspoons vanilla extract
6 tablespoons milk
3 to 4 drops red food coloring
Pink sugar wafer cookies
36 large marshmallows, halved
Reese's candy bar sprinkles

1. Cream butter and sugar. Add eggs, sour cream and vanilla; mix well. Combine dry ingredients; add to creamed mixture and mix well.

2. Drop by tablespoonfuls 2 in. apart onto ungreased baking sheets. Bake at 375° for 10-12 minutes or until edges are lightly browned. Remove to wire racks to cool completely.

3. Melt butter. Add the sugar, vanilla, milk and food coloring; mix until smooth. Frost the cookies. Cut the sugar wafers into triangles; place two pieces on each cookie for ears. With a toothpick, poke two holes in each marshmallow half for nostrils; press light brown candy bar sprinkles into holes. Place nose on cookies. Add dark brown candy bar sprinkles for eyes.

Yield: 6 dozen.

Crispy Cereal Meringues

Beverly Albrecht, Beatrice, Nebraska

Topped with creamy chocolate ribbons, these meringues are rich-tasting but feather-light. You'll think you're biting into a decadent dessert that's off-limits, but it's not.

4 egg whites
1/4 teaspoon cream of tartar
1/4 teaspoon salt
1 cup sugar
2 cups chocolate-flavored crisp rice cereal
1/4 cup semisweet chocolate chips
1/2 teaspoon vegetable shortening

1. In a mixing bowl, beat egg whites, cream of tartar and salt until soft peaks form. Gradually add sugar, 1 tablespoon at a time, until stiff peaks form, about 6 minutes. Fold in cereal.

2. Drop by rounded teaspoonfuls 1 in. apart onto baking sheets coated with nonstick cooking spray. Bake at 300° for 35-40 minutes or until firm to the touch. Remove to wire racks to cool.

3. In a microwave or heavy saucepan, melt the chocolate chips with the shortening. Transfer to a small resealable plastic bag; cut a small hole in the corner of bag. Drizzle melted chocolate over meringues. Place on waxed paper to set.

Yield: about 5 dozen.

Apple Spice Drops

Blanche Whytsell
Arnoldsburg, Wyoming

It's a snap to stir up these soft frosted cookies. With their big apple flavor and abundance of nuts, you'll have a hard time eating just one.

1/2 cup butter, softened
2/3 cup sugar
2/3 cup packed brown sugar
1 egg
1/4 cup apple juice
2 cups all-purpose flour
1 teaspoon ground cinnamon
1/2 teaspoon baking soda
1/2 teaspoon ground nutmeg
1 cup finely chopped peeled tart apple
1 cup chopped walnuts

FROSTING:
1/4 cup butter, softened
3 cups confectioners' sugar
1 teaspoon vanilla extract
3 to 4 tablespoons apple juice

1. In a mixing bowl, cream butter and sugars. Beat in egg and apple juice. Combine the dry ingredients; gradually add to the creamed mixture. Fold in apple and walnuts.

2. Drop by teaspoonfuls 2 in. apart onto greased baking sheets. Bake at 375° for 12-14 minutes or until golden brown. Remove to wire racks to cool completely.

3. For frosting, cream butter, sugar, vanilla and enough apple juice to achieve spreading consistency. Frost cooled cookies.

Yield: about 3-1/2 dozen.

Prune-Pecan Cookies

Lucille Dent
Galesburg, Michigan

The prunes in this recipe are finely chopped so no one will need to know they appear in these crisp, lightly sweet cookies.

> 1 egg
> 7 pitted dried prunes *or* plums
> 1/2 cup sugar
> 1 cup all-purpose flour
> 1/2 teaspoon baking soda
> Dash salt
> 24 pecan halves

1. In a blender, puree egg and prunes until finely chopped. Pour into a mixing bowl. Add sugar. Combine the flour, baking soda and salt; add to prune mixture and mix well.

2. Drop by rounded teaspoonfuls onto greased baking sheets. Top each cookie with a pecan half. Bake at 350° for 13-15 minutes or until golden brown. Remove to wire racks to cool.

Yield: 2 dozen.

Hint O' Mint Cookies

Janet Hartmann, Gibbon, Minnesota

After I experimented in the kitchen mixing and matching ingredients to come up with a new and different cookie recipe, my husband proclaimed these the winner!

> 1/2 cup milk
> 1/2 teaspoon white vinegar
> 1/2 cup butter, softened
> 1 cup sugar
> 1 egg
> 1/2 teaspoon vanilla extract
> 1/4 teaspoon peppermint extract
> 2 cups all-purpose flour
> 1/2 teaspoon baking soda
> 1/4 teaspoon cream of tartar

FROSTING:
> 3 tablespoons butter, softened
> 2 cups confectioners' sugar
> 1/3 cup baking cocoa
> 1/8 teaspoon salt
> 1 teaspoon vanilla extract
> 2 to 4 tablespoons milk

1. In a small bowl, combine milk and vinegar; set aside. In a mixing bowl, cream butter and sugar. Beat in egg and extracts. Combine flour, baking soda and cream of tartar; add to the creamed mixture alternately with milk mixture.

2. Drop by heaping teaspoonfuls 2 in. apart onto ungreased baking sheets. Flatten with a glass dipped in sugar. Bake at 350° for 6 to 8 minutes or until set. Remove to wire racks to cool.

3. In a small mixing bowl, cream the butter, sugar, cocoa and salt. Beat in the vanilla and enough milk to achieve spreading consistency. Frost cooled cookies.

Yield: 4 dozen.

Cheery Cherry Cookies

Judy Clark
Elkhart, Indiana

With a tall glass of ice-cold milk, a couple of cherry cookies really hit the spot for dessert or as a snack. The coconut and bits of cherries provide a fun look and texture.

    1 cup packed brown sugar
  3/4 cup butter, softened
    1 egg
    2 tablespoons milk
    1 teaspoon vanilla extract
    2 cups all-purpose flour
  1/2 teaspoon salt
  1/2 teaspoon baking soda
  1/2 cup maraschino cherries,
        well drained and chopped
  1/2 cup chopped pecans
  1/2 cup flaked coconut

1. In a large mixing bowl, cream brown sugar, butter, egg, milk and vanilla. Combine flour, salt and baking soda; gradually add to creamed mixture. Fold in cherries, pecans and coconut.

2. Drop by teaspoonfuls onto ungreased baking sheets. Bake at 375° for 10-12 minutes or until golden brown. Remove to wire racks to cool.

Yield: 4 dozen.

Marmalade Chews

Shirleene Wilkins, Lake Placid, Florida

  1/4 cup shortening
  1/2 cup sugar
    1 egg
1-1/2 cups all-purpose flour
  1/4 teaspoon baking soda
  1/4 teaspoon salt
  1/2 cup orange marmalade
  1/2 cup chopped pecans,
        optional

FROSTING:
    2 cups confectioners' sugar
    2 tablespoons butter,
        melted
    1 teaspoon grated orange
        peel
    2 to 3 tablespoons orange
        juice

I live in the heart of citrus country and think this cookie really captures that area's flavor. Orange marmalade, juice and peel give the cookie and frosting a delightful tropical taste.

1. In a mixing bowl, cream shortening and sugar. Beat in egg. Combine flour, baking soda and salt; gradually add to the creamed mixture. Stir in marmalade and pecans if desired.

2. Drop by heaping teaspoonfuls 2 in. apart onto greased baking sheets. Bake at 350° for 10-15 minutes or until golden brown. Remove to wire racks to cool.

3. In a small mixing bowl, combine the sugar, butter and orange peel. Add enough orange juice to achieve spreading consistency. Frost the cooled cookies.

Yield: about 4-1/2 dozen.

Almond Sandies

Joyce Pierce, Caledonia, Michigan

Buttery, rich and delicious, Almond Sandies are my husband's favorite cookie. These are very popular wherever I take them and they always disappear quickly.

1 cup butter, softened
1 cup sugar
1 teaspoon almond extract
1-3/4 cups all-purpose flour
1/2 teaspoon baking soda
1/4 teaspoon baking powder
1/4 teaspoon salt
1/2 cup slivered almonds

1. In a mixing bowl, cream butter and sugar. Add extract; mix well. Combine flour, baking soda, baking powder and salt; gradually add to creamed mixture. Fold in almonds.

2. Drop by rounded teaspoonfuls onto ungreased baking sheets. Bake at 300° for 22-24 minutes or until lightly browned. Cool 1-2 minutes before removing to a wire rack.

Yield: about 4 dozen.

Frosted Cranberry Drop Cookies

Shirley Kidd
New London, Minnesota

I started making these treats after tasting a batch my friend whipped up. I immediately requested the recipe and have been baking them by the dozens ever since. The icing is an ideal complement to the tart berries in the cookies.

1/2 cup butter, softened
1 cup sugar
3/4 cup packed brown sugar
1/4 cup milk
1 egg
2 tablespoons orange juice
3 cups all-purpose flour
1 teaspoon baking powder
1/2 teaspoon salt
1/4 teaspoon baking soda
2-1/2 cups chopped fresh *or* frozen cranberries
1 cup chopped walnuts

FROSTING:
1/3 cup butter
2 cups confectioners' sugar
1-1/2 teaspoons vanilla extract
2 to 4 tablespoons hot water

1. In a mixing bowl, cream butter and sugars. Add milk, egg and orange juice; mix well. Combine the flour, baking powder, salt and baking soda; add to the creamed mixture and mix well. Stir in cranberries and nuts.

2. Drop by tablespoonfuls 2 in. apart onto greased baking sheets. Bake at 350° for 12-15 minutes or until golden brown. Remove to wire racks to cool completely.

3. For frosting, heat the butter in a saucepan over low heat until golden brown, about 5 minutes. Cool for 2 minutes; transfer to a small mixing bowl. Add sugar and vanilla. Beat in water, 1 tablespoon at a time, until frosting reaches desired consistency. Frost the cookies.

Yield: about 5 dozen.

Chewy Chocolate Chip Cookies

Iona Hamilton, Rocky Ford, Colorado

Everyone who has tried these cookies says they're the best they've ever eaten. I'm sure the addition of the pudding mix makes all the difference. Try instant chocolate pudding mix for a nice change.

1 cup butter, softened
3/4 cup packed brown sugar
1/4 cup sugar
1 package (3.4 ounces) instant vanilla pudding mix
2 eggs
1 teaspoon vanilla extract
2-1/4 cups all-purpose flour
1 teaspoon baking soda
2 cups (12 ounces) semisweet chocolate chips
1 cup finely chopped walnuts

1. In a mixing bowl, cream butter, sugars and pudding mix. Add eggs, one at a time, beating well after each addition. Beat in vanilla. Combine flour and baking soda; gradually add to creamed mixture. Stir in chocolate chips and walnuts (dough will be stiff).

2. Drop by rounded teaspoonfuls 2 in. apart onto ungreased baking sheets. Bake at 350° for 8-10 minutes or until lightly browned. Remove to wire racks to cool.

Yield: 9-1/2 dozen.

Editor's Note: One 3.9-ounce package of instant chocolate pudding mix may be substituted for the vanilla pudding mix.

Mom's Buttermilk Cookies

Jane Darling
Simi Valley, California

The recipe for these comforting "cookie pillows" originated with my mother. The tender treats are jazzed up with thick frosting and a sprinkling of chopped walnuts.

1/2 cup butter, softened
1 cup sugar
1 egg
1 teaspoon vanilla extract
2-1/2 cups all-purpose flour
1/2 teaspoon baking soda
1/2 teaspoon salt
1/2 cup buttermilk

FROSTING:
3 tablespoons butter, softened
3-1/2 cups confectioners' sugar
1/4 cup milk
1 teaspoon vanilla extract
1/2 cup finely chopped walnuts, optional

1. In a mixing bowl, cream butter and sugar until light and fluffy. Beat in egg and vanilla. Combine flour, baking soda and salt; add to the creamed mixture alternately with buttermilk and mix well.

2. Drop by rounded tablespoonfuls 2 in. apart onto greased baking sheets. Bake at 375° for 10-12 minutes or until edges are lightly browned. Remove to wire racks to cool.

3. For frosting, combine butter, sugar, milk and vanilla in a mixing bowl; beat until smooth. Frost cookies; sprinkle with walnuts if desired.

Yield: 3 dozen.

Macaroons

Penny Ann Habeck
Shawano, Wisconsin

These cookies are my husband's favorites, so I always have to make a few batches if I make them to give away. I also like that it makes a small enough batch for the two of us to nibble on.

1-1/3 cups flaked coconut
1/3 cup sugar
2 tablespoons all-purpose flour
1/8 teaspoon salt
2 egg whites
1/2 teaspoon vanilla extract

1. In a small bowl, combine the coconut, sugar, flour and salt. Stir in egg whites and vanilla; mix well.

2. Drop by rounded teaspoonfuls onto greased baking sheets. Bake at 325° for 18-20 minutes or until golden brown. Remove to wire racks to cool.

Yield: about 1-1/2 dozen.

Ambrosia Bites

Arlene Steinwart
Grand Island, Nebraska

These chewy oatmeal cookies are packed with the refreshing flavors of orange and lemon, plus dates, raisins and coconut. When our children, grandchildren and great-grandchildren ask me to make "Grandma's Cookies," these are the ones they're referring to.

1 cup butter, softened
1 cup sugar
1 cup packed brown sugar
2 eggs
1 tablespoon grated orange peel
1 tablespoon grated lemon peel
1 teaspoon vanilla extract
2 cups all-purpose flour
1-1/2 cups quick-cooking oats
1-1/2 teaspoons baking soda
1 teaspoon baking powder
1 teaspoon salt
1 cup chopped walnuts
1 cup raisins
1 cup chopped dates
1 cup flaked coconut

1. In a mixing bowl, cream butter and sugars. Add the eggs, one at a time, beating well after each addition. Beat in peels and vanilla. Combine flour, oats, baking soda, baking powder and salt; gradually add to the creamed mixture. Stir in remaining ingredients.

2. Drop by heaping tablespoonfuls 3 in. apart onto ungreased baking sheets. Bake at 375° for 8-10 minutes or until golden brown. Remove to wire racks to cool.

Yield: 6 dozen.

Chocolate Waffle Cookies

Pat Oviatt
Zimmerman, Minnesota

I've had this recipe for years. It's economical to make, yet results in a delicious cookie.

- 1/4 cup butter, softened
- 6 tablespoons sugar
- 1 egg
- 1/2 teaspoon vanilla extract
- 1 square (1 ounce) unsweetened chocolate, melted
- 1/2 cup all-purpose flour
- Confectioners' sugar

1. In a mixing bowl, cream butter and sugar; beat in egg and vanilla until light and fluffy. Blend in chocolate. Add flour; mix well.

2. Drop dough by rounded teaspoonfuls 1 in. apart onto a preheated waffle iron. Bake for 1 minute. Remove to wire racks to cool. Dust with confectioners' sugar.

Yield: about 1-1/2 dozen.

Soft Sugar Cookies

Coleen Walter, Bancroft, Michigan

These soft cookies have been a hit in my family for four generations. I often stir up a big batch, and I sometimes add food coloring to the frosting to coordinate with the current holiday.

- 1 cup butter, softened
- 3/4 cup sugar
- 2 eggs
- 1 teaspoon vanilla extract
- 1/2 teaspoon almond extract
- 2 cups all-purpose flour
- 1 teaspoon cream of tartar
- 1/2 teaspoon baking soda
- 1/4 teaspoon salt
- 1/4 teaspoon ground nutmeg

FROSTING:
- 1/4 cup butter, softened
- 3 cups confectioners' sugar
- 1 teaspoon almond extract
- 2 to 4 tablespoons hot water
- Food coloring, optional

1. In a large mixing bowl, cream butter and sugar until light and fluffy. Beat in the eggs, vanilla and almond extract. Combine the flour, cream of tartar, baking soda, salt and nutmeg; gradually add to creamed mixture.

2. Drop by rounded teaspoonfuls 2 in. apart onto ungreased baking sheets. Bake at 350° for 8-10 minutes or until light brown. Remove to wire racks to cool.

3. For frosting, in a large mixing bowl, combine the butter, confectioners' sugar, almond extract and enough water to achieve desired consistency. Tint with food coloring if desired. Frost the cookies.

Yield: about 6 dozen.

Blueberry Oat Cookies

Elaine Gelina, Ladson, South Carolina

It's fun to make these cookies at the height of blueberry season when folks are looking for tasty ways to serve that juicy fruit. A hint of cinnamon adds a special touch.

- 1/2 cup butter, softened
- 1 cup packed brown sugar
- 1 egg
- 1 teaspoon vanilla extract
- 1-1/2 cups quick-cooking oats
- 1 cup all-purpose flour
- 1 to 2 teaspoons ground cinnamon
- 1/2 teaspoon salt
- 1/2 teaspoon baking soda
- 1/4 teaspoon baking powder
- 1 cup fresh *or* frozen blueberries

1. In a mixing bowl, cream butter and brown sugar. Beat in egg and vanilla. Combine oats, flour, cinnamon, salt, baking soda and baking powder; gradually add to the creamed mixture. Stir in the blueberries.

2. Drop by heaping tablespoonfuls 2 in. apart onto lightly greased baking sheets. Bake at 350° for 12-14 minutes or until golden brown. Remove to wire racks to cool.

Yield: 3 dozen.

Soft Lemonade Cookies

Margo Neuhauser
Bakersfield, California

I remember my mother making these cookies. They're perfect for warm days. They're so lovely and moist, you won't be able to stop eating them.

- 1 cup butter, softened
- 1 cup sugar
- 2 eggs
- 3 cups all-purpose flour
- 1 teaspoon baking soda
- 1 can (6 ounces) frozen lemonade concentrate, thawed, *divided*

Additional sugar

1. In a mixing bowl, cream butter and sugar; add eggs. Combine flour and baking soda; add to the creamed mixture alternately with 1/3 cup of lemonade concentrate. Mix well.

2. Drop dough by rounded teaspoonfuls onto ungreased baking sheets. Bake at 400° for 8 minutes or until set. Remove to wire racks. Brush with remaining lemonade concentrate; sprinkle with additional sugar. Cool.

Yield: 6 dozen.

Apple-Oat Breakfast Treats

Dolores Kastello, Waukesha, Wisconsin

Our three grandsons gobble up these soft, chewy oatmeal cookies at breakfast with some yogurt and a glass of juice. If you don't have pie filling handy, use jam to make the cookie's fruity topping.

3/4 cup butter, softened
3/4 cup packed brown sugar
2 eggs
1 teaspoon vanilla extract
2-1/2 cups old-fashioned oats
3/4 cup all-purpose flour
1/2 cup nonfat dry milk powder
1 teaspoon salt
1/2 teaspoon baking powder
1/2 teaspoon ground cinnamon
1 to 1-1/4 cups apple pie filling

1. In a mixing bowl, cream butter and brown sugar. Add the eggs and vanilla. Combine flour, milk powder, salt, baking powder and cinnamon; add to the creamed mixture and mix well.

2. Drop by 1/4 cupfuls 6 in. apart onto ungreased baking sheets. Flatten into 3-in. circles. Make a slight indentation in the center of each; top with a rounded tablespoonful of pie filling.

3. Bake at 350° for 16-20 minutes or until edges are lightly browned. Cool for 5 minutes before removing to wire racks.

Yield: 10 servings.

Giant Cherry Oatmeal Cookies

Irene McDade
Cumberland, Rhode Island

These colossal cookies taste best when golden around the edges and moist and chewy in the center.

1/2 cup shortening
1/2 cup butter, softened
3/4 cup packed brown sugar
1/2 cup sugar
2 eggs
1 teaspoon vanilla extract
2-1/2 cups old-fashioned oats
1-1/3 cups all-purpose flour
2 teaspoons apple pie spice
1/2 teaspoon baking powder
1/4 teaspoon baking soda
1/4 teaspoon salt
1-1/2 cups dried cherries, chopped
1/2 to 1 teaspoon grated orange peel

1. In a large mixing bowl, cream shortening, butter and sugars. Beat in the eggs and vanilla. Combine the oats, flour, apple pie spice, baking powder, baking soda and salt; gradually add to the creamed mixture. Stir in cherries and orange peel.

2. Drop by 1/3 cupfuls onto an ungreased baking sheet. Press to form a 4-in. circle. Bake at 375° for 9-12 minutes or until golden brown. Let stand for 1 minute before removing to wire racks.

Yield: 1 dozen.

Cranberry Crisps

Sandy Furches
Lake City, Florida

I developed this recipe after sampling a similar cookie while traveling in North Carolina. These pretty cookies keep well in the freezer, so I always have some on hand for midday munching.

- 1 cup butter-flavored shortening
- 1 cup sugar
- 1 cup packed brown sugar
- 2 eggs
- 2 teaspoons vanilla extract
- 2-1/2 cups old-fashioned oats
- 2 cups all-purpose flour
- 1 teaspoon baking soda
- 1 teaspoon ground cinnamon
- 1/2 teaspoon salt
- 1/2 teaspoon baking powder
- 1-1/3 cups dried cranberries
- 1 cup coarsely chopped walnuts

1. In a mixing bowl, cream shortening and sugars. Add eggs, one at a time, beating well after each addition. Beat in vanilla. Combine oats, flour, baking soda, cinnamon, salt and baking powder; gradually add to the creamed mixture. Stir in the cranberries and walnuts.

2. Drop by tablespoonfuls 2 in. apart onto lightly greased baking sheets. Bake at 350° for 12-14 minutes or until lightly browned. Remove to wire racks to cool.

Yield: 5 dozen.

Golden Harvest Cookies

Florence Pope, Denver, Colorado

Folks may be skeptical when you tell them the ingredients in these cookies. But what a tantalizing treat for the taste buds! These unique cookies are just slightly sweet.

- 2/3 cup butter, softened
- 1/3 cup packed brown sugar
- 1 egg
- 1 teaspoon vanilla extract
- 3/4 cup self-rising flour
- 1 teaspoon ground cinnamon
- 1/8 teaspoon ground cloves
- 1-1/2 cups quick-cooking oats
- 1 cup shredded carrots
- 1 cup (4 ounces) shredded cheddar cheese
- 1 cup chopped pecans
- 1/2 cup raisins

1. In a mixing bowl, cream butter and brown sugar. Beat in egg and vanilla. Combine flour, cinnamon and cloves; gradually add to the creamed mixture. Stir in remaining ingredients.

2. Drop by heaping tablespoonfuls 2 in. apart onto ungreased baking sheets. Bake at 375° for 12-14 minutes or until golden brown. Remove to wire racks to cool. Store in the refrigerator.

Yield: 3-1/2 dozen.

Editor's Note: As a substitute for self-rising flour, place 1 teaspoon baking powder and 1/4 teaspoon salt in a measuring cup. Add all-purpose flour to measure 3/4 cup.

Double Peanut Butter Cookies, p. 88

Chocolate Coconut Neapolitans, p.89

Peppermint Cookies, p.97

Watermelon Slice Cookies, p.91

Timeless
Slice & Bake

If you need to manage your kitchen tasks but still want to make cookies, mix these treats up ahead of time! Just wrap the logs of dough, then stash them in the refrigerator up to a week before cutting into slices and baking.

Tips for Slice & Bake Cookies

To make refrigerator cookie dough easier to slice, use nuts and fruits that are finely chopped. If the nuts and fruit are too large, the cookie dough may break apart when sliced.

Wrap the dough tightly to prevent it from drying out in the refrigerator. Refrigerate dough until firm. Generally, the dough can be refrigerated up to 1 week or frozen up to 6 months. To keep the shape round, place each roll of dough inside a tall glass and place the glass on its side in the refrigerator. The rounded glass will prevent the bottom of the roll from flattening out.

Use a thin sharp knife to slice through the dough. Cut one roll at a time and keep additional rolls refrigerated until ready to use. After each slice, rotate the roll to avoid having one side that's flat.

Double Peanut Butter Cookies

(Pictured on page 86)
Jeannette Mack, Rushville, New York

The extra taste of peanut butter in the middle of the cookie is a delicious surprise the first time you bite into one. It's a nice, soft cookie and fun to make with little helpers. Kids love to put that extra dab of peanut butter in the middle and snitch some at the same time.

1-1/2 cups all-purpose flour
1/2 cup sugar
1/2 teaspoon baking soda
1/4 teaspoon salt
1/2 cup shortening
1/2 cup creamy peanut butter
1/4 cup light corn syrup
1 tablespoon milk
Additional peanut butter

1. In a large bowl, combine the flour, sugar, baking soda and salt. Cut in the shortening and peanut butter until mixture resembles coarse crumbs. Stir in the corn syrup and milk; mix well. Shape into a 10-in. roll; wrap in plastic wrap. Refrigerate for at least 3 hours.

2. Unwrap and cut into 1/4-in. slices. Place half of the slices 2 in. apart on ungreased baking sheets. Top each with 1/2 teaspoon of peanut butter. Cover with remaining slices; seal edges with a fork. Bake at 350° for 12-14 minutes or until lightly browned. Cool for 2 minutes before removing to wire racks.

Yield: 20 cookies.

Editor's Note: Reduced-fat or generic brands of peanut butter are not recommended for this recipe.

Strawberry-Nut Pinwheel Cookies

Ruth Gillmore, Alden, New York

All the "cookie monsters" I know love these treats. They make a great after-school snack. I enjoy the cookies because they're easy to roll up, cut and bake. The strawberry-walnut filling is very tasty!

1/2 cup butter, softened
1 cup sugar
1 egg
1 teaspoon vanilla extract
2 cups all-purpose flour
1 teaspoon baking powder
1/2 cup strawberry jam
1 cup chopped walnut

1. In a mixing bowl, cream butter and sugar. Add egg and vanilla; mix well. Combine flour and baking powder; gradually add to creamed mixture. On a lightly floured surface, roll dough into a 14-in. x 10-in. rectangle. Spread jam to within 1/2 in. of edges. Sprinkle nuts over jam. Roll up jelly-roll style, starting with a long side; wrap in plastic wrap. Refrigerate for at least 3 hours or overnight.

2. Unwrap and cut into 1/4-in. slices. Place 1 in. apart on greased baking sheets. Bake at 375° for 10-12 minutes or until lightly browned. Remove to wire racks to cool.

Yield: 4 dozen.

Chewy Almond Cookies

Betty Speth
Vincennes, Indiana

These old-fashioned cookies are requested by my grandchildren. The unbaked cookie dough can be frozen (well wrapped) for up to 1 year. When ready to bake, let stand at room temperature for 15-30 minutes. Then just slice and bake.

  3 tablespoons butter, softened
  1 cup packed brown sugar
  1 egg
  1/4 teaspoon vanilla extract
  1/4 teaspoon almond extract
1-1/2 cups all-purpose flour
  1/4 teaspoon baking soda
  1/4 teaspoon ground cinnamon
  1/2 cup sliced almonds

1. In a mixing bowl, beat butter and brown sugar until crumbly. Add egg and extracts; mix well. Combine flour, baking soda and cinnamon; gradually add to the creamed mixture and mix well. Shape into two 6-in. rolls; wrap each in plastic wrap. Refrigerate overnight.

2. Unwrap; cut into 1/4-in. slices. Place 2 in. apart on greased baking sheets. Sprinkle with almonds. Bake at 350° for 7-10 minutes or until lightly browned. Cool for 2-3 minutes before removing to wire racks.

Yield: 4-1/2 dozen.

Chocolate Coconut Neapolitans

(Pictured on page 87)
Lena Marie Brownell, Rockland, Massachusetts

These yummy striped cookies with a chocolaty twist are easy and fun to make, but they do need some time in the freezer. The red layer has an almond flavor, the middle layer has bits of coconut and the brown layer is flavored with chocolate syrup.

  1 cup butter, softened
1-1/2 cups sugar
  1 egg
  1 teaspoon vanilla extract
2-1/2 cups all-purpose flour
1-1/2 teaspoons baking powder
  1/2 teaspoon salt
  1 teaspoon almond extract
  4 drops red food coloring
  1/2 cup flaked coconut, finely chopped
4-1/2 teaspoons chocolate syrup
  1/2 cup semisweet chocolate chips
1-1/2 teaspoons shortening

1. Line a 9-in. x 5-in. x 3-in. loaf pan with waxed paper; set aside. In a mixing bowl, cream butter and sugar. Beat in egg and vanilla. Combine the flour, baking powder and salt; gradually add to creamed mixture and mix well.

2. Divide dough into thirds. Add almond extract and red food coloring to one portion; spread evenly into prepared pan. Add coconut to second portion; spread evenly over first layer. Add chocolate syrup to third portion; spread over second layer. Cover with foil; freeze for 4 hours or overnight.

3. Unwrap loaf and cut in half lengthwise. Cut each portion widthwise into 1/4-in. slices. Place 2 in. apart on ungreased baking sheets. Bake at 350° for 12-14 minutes or until edges are lightly browned. Remove to wire racks to cool.

4. In a microwave or saucepan, melt chocolate chips and shortening, stirring until smooth. Dip one end of each cookie into chocolate. Place on wire racks until set.

Yield: 5-1/2 dozen.

Cherry-Pecan Icebox Cookies

Betye Dalton
Tupelo, Oklahoma

During the holiday season, I keep a roll of dough for these crisp cookies in the freezer. It's nice to offer unexpected company a home-baked treat.

1 cup butter, softened
1-1/4 cups sugar
1 egg
2-1/2 cups all-purpose flour
1-1/2 teaspoons baking soda
1/8 teaspoon salt
1 cup chopped pecans
3/4 cup red *and/or* green candied cherries

1. In a large mixing bowl, cream butter and sugar. Add egg; mix well. Combine the flour, baking soda and salt; add to creamed mixture and mix well. Stir in pecans and candied cherries. Shape into four 8-in. rolls; wrap each in plastic wrap. Refrigerate for at least 4 hours or until firm.

2. Unwrap and cut into 1/8- to 1/4-in. slices. Place 2 in. apart on ungreased baking sheets. Bake at 350° for 7-8 minutes or until lightly browned and edges are set. Cool for 1-2 minutes before removing to wire racks.

Yield: 13 dozen.

Editor's Note: Dough may be frozen for up to 6 months. Remove from the freezer 1-1/2 hours before baking. Unwrap and cut into 1/8- to 1/4-in. slices. Place 2 in. apart on ungreased baking sheets. Bake at 350° for 8-9 minutes or until lightly browned and edges are set. Cool for 1-2 minutes before removing to wire racks.

Peanut Butter Pinwheels

Kandy Dick, Junction, Texas

Chocolate is swirled through these tasty peanut butter cookies. So you get two delicious tastes in one bite—chocolate and peanut butter.

1/2 cup shortening
1/2 cup creamy peanut butter
1 cup sugar
1 egg
2 tablespoons milk
1-1/4 cups all-purpose flour
1/2 teaspoon baking soda
1/2 teaspoon salt
1 cup (6 ounces) semisweet chocolate chips

1. In a mixing bowl, cream shortening, peanut butter and sugar. Beat in egg and milk. Combine the flour, baking soda and salt; gradually add to creamed mixture. Roll out between waxed paper into a 12-in. x 10-in. rectangle. Melt chocolate chips; cool slightly. Spread over dough to within 1/2 in. of edges. Roll up tightly jelly-roll style, starting with a long side; wrap in plastic wrap. Refrigerate for 20-30 minutes or until easy to handle.

2. Unwrap and cut into 1/2-in. slices. Place 1 in. apart on greased baking sheets. Bake at 375° for 10-12 minutes or until edges are lightly browned. Remove to wire racks to cool.

Yield: about 4 dozen.

Editor's Note: Reduced-fat or generic brands of peanut butter are not recommended for this recipe.

Watermelon Slice Cookies

(Pictured on page 87)
Sue Ann Benham, Valparaiso, Indiana

When I made these rich butter cookies for a neighborhood event, one neighbor thought they were so attractive that she kept one in her freezer for the longest time so she could show it to friends and relatives.

   3/4 cup butter, softened
   3/4 cup sugar
     1 egg
   1/2 teaspoon almond extract
     2 cups all-purpose flour
   1/4 teaspoon baking powder
   1/8 teaspoon salt
Red and green gel food coloring
   1/3 cup raisins
     1 teaspoon sesame seeds

1. In a mixing bowl, cream butter and sugar. Beat in egg and extract. Combine flour, baking powder and salt; gradually add to creamed mixture. Set aside 1 cup of dough. Tint remaining dough red and shape into a 3-1/2-in.-long log. Wrap in plastic wrap. Tint 1/3 cup of the reserved dough green; wrap in plastic wrap. Wrap remaining plain dough in a plastic bag. Refrigerate for 2 hours or until firm.

2. On a lightly floured surface, roll plain dough into an 8-1/2-in. x 3-1/2-in. rectangle. Place red dough log on the end of a short side of the rectangle; roll up. Roll green dough into a 10-in. x 3-1/2-in. rectangle. Place red and white log on the end of a short side on green dough; roll up. Wrap in plastic wrap; refrigerate overnight.

3. Unwrap and cut into 3/16-in. slices (just less than 1/4 in.). Place 2 in. apart on ungreased baking sheets. Cut raisins into small pieces. Lightly press raisin bits and sesame seeds into red dough to resemble watermelon seeds. Bake at 350° for 9-11 minutes or until firm. Immediately cut the cookies in half. Remove to wire racks to cool.

Yield: about 3 dozen.

Rolled Oat Cookies

Kathi Peters
Chilliwack, British Columbia

I like to keep some of this dough in the freezer at all times since it's so handy to slice, bake and serve at a moment's notice. These wholesome cookies are super with a cup of coffee—in fact, we occasionally grab a few for breakfast when we're in a hurry.

     1 cup butter, softened
     1 cup packed brown sugar
   1/4 cup water
     1 teaspoon vanilla extract
     3 cups quick-cooking oats
 1-1/4 cups all-purpose flour
     1 teaspoon salt
   1/4 teaspoon baking soda

1. In a mixing bowl, cream butter and sugar. Add water and vanilla; mix well. Combine dry ingredients; add to creamed mixture and mix well. Chill for 30 minutes. Shape into two 1-1/2-in.-diameter rolls; wrap each in plastic wrap. Refrigerate for 2 hours or until firm.

2. Unwrap and cut into 1/2-in. slices. Place 2 in. apart on greased baking sheets. Bake at 375° for 12 minutes or until lightly browned. Remove to wire racks to cool.

Yield: 3-1/2 dozen.

Honey Spice Cookies

Joan Gerber, Bluffton, Indiana

With four children, I bake a lot of cookies. These nicely seasoned sweets are a favorite of my family. When I bake them up they go fast—it's a good thing the recipe makes a lot.

2 cups honey
2 cups sugar
3 eggs
7-1/2 cups all-purpose flour
3 teaspoons baking soda
3 teaspoons ground cinnamon
1 teaspoon salt
1 teaspoon ground allspice
1 teaspoon ground cloves
2 cups confectioners' sugar
3 tablespoon fat-free milk

1. In a mixing bowl, beat honey and sugar. Add the eggs, one at a time, beating well after each addition. Combine flour, baking soda, cinnamon, salt, allspice and cloves; gradually add to honey mixture. Shape dough into five 10-in. rolls; wrap each in plastic wrap. Refrigerate for 2 hours or until firm.

2. Unwrap and cut into 1/4-in. slices. Place 2 in. apart on baking sheets coated with nonstick cooking spray. Combine confectioners' sugar and milk; lightly brush over cookies. Bake at 350° for 8-10 minutes or until lightly browned. Remove to wire racks to cool.

Yield: 12-1/2 dozen.

Hazelnut Shortbread

Karen Morrell
Canby, Oregon

We have several acres of hazelnut trees here in the Willamette Valley, where the climate is perfect for this crop. Harvesttime is a big family event with everyone pitching in to help. I try to incorporate this wonderful flavorful nut into our recipes, and this cookie is always a hit.

1 cup butter, softened
1/2 cup sugar
2 tablespoons maple syrup *or* honey
2 teaspoons vanilla extract
2 cups all-purpose flour
1-1/4 cups finely chopped hazelnuts
1/2 cup semisweet chocolate chips

1. In a mixing bowl, cream butter and sugar. Add syrup and vanilla. Add flour and mix just until combined; fold in the nuts. Shape into two 1-1/2-in.-diameter rolls; wrap each in plastic wrap. Refrigerate for 2 hours or until firm.

2. Unwrap and cut into 1/4-in. slices. Place 2 in. apart on ungreased baking sheets. Bake at 325° for 14-16 minutes or until edges begin to brown. Remove to wire racks to cool. Melt chocolate chips; drizzle over cookies. Let stand until chocolate is set.

Yield: 6 dozen.

Brown Sugar Icebox Cookies

Eilene Bogar
Minier, Illinois

My daughters and I have been "fairly" successful competitors at county fairs and bake-offs for years. This is one of those tasty winning recipes.

1/2 cup butter, softened
1 cup packed brown sugar
1 egg
1 teaspoon vanilla extract
1-3/4 cups all-purpose flour
1/2 teaspoon baking soda
1/4 teaspoon salt
2/3 cup chopped pecans *or* flaked coconut

1. In a large mixing bowl, cream the butter and sugar. Add the egg and vanilla; mix well. Combine the flour, baking soda and salt; gradually add to cream mixture. Fold in pecans or coconut (dough will be sticky). Shape into two rolls; wrap each in plastic wrap. Refrigerate for 4 hours or overnight.

2. Unwrap and cut into 1/4-in. slices. Place 2 in. apart on ungreased baking sheets. Bake at 375° for 7 to 10 minutes or until set. Remove to wire racks to cool.

Yield: about 3-1/2 dozen.

Caramel Swirls

Jan Smith, Star, Texas

In my opinion, cookies are the best dessert to make and to eat! With a crisp outside and chewy caramel filling, these are likely one of my favorites. I'm sure your family will like them, too!

1 cup butter, softened
4 ounces cream cheese, softened
1 cup packed brown sugar
1 egg yolk
1 teaspoon maple flavoring
2-3/4 cups all-purpose flour

FILLING:
30 caramels
2 packages (3 ounces *each*) cream cheese, softened

1. In a mixing bowl, cream the butter, cream cheese and brown sugar. Add egg yolk and maple flavoring; mix well. Gradually add flour. Cover and refrigerate for 2 hours or until easy to handle.

2. Meanwhile, in a microwave or saucepan, melt caramels, stirring until smooth. Stir in cream cheese until blended; set aside. Divide dough in half. Roll each portion between waxed paper to 1/4-in. thickness. Spread caramel mixture over dough to within 1/2 in. of edges. Roll up tightly jelly-roll style, starting with a long side. Wrap each roll in plastic wrap. Refrigerate for 4 hours or until firm.

3. Unwrap and cut into 1/4-in. slices. Place 1 in. apart on greased baking sheets. Bake at 350° for 12-14 minutes or until golden brown. Remove to wire racks to cool.

Yield: 6-1/2 dozen.

Peppermint Candy Cookies

Gloria McKenzie
Panama City, Florida

These buttery mint treats practically melt in your mouth. Plus, bright food coloring gives them a lively look for wintertime parties.

1-1/4 cups butter, softened
 3/4 cup confectioners' sugar
2-1/2 cups all-purpose flour
 1/2 teaspoon salt
 1/2 teaspoon peppermint extract
Green and red paste *or* gel food coloring

1. In a mixing bowl, cream butter and sugar. Add the flour, salt and extract; mix well. Divide dough into fourths. Tint one portion green and one red; leave the remaining portions plain.

2. Divide each portion into thirds; shape each into a 6-in. log. Flatten into triangular logs, bending the top of one point slightly (to give finished cookies a pinwheel effect). Assemble one large roll by alternating three green and three plain logs. Wrap in plastic wrap. Repeat with red and remaining plain dough. Refrigerate for 4 hours or until firm.

3. Unwrap and cut into 1/4-in. slices. Place 2 in. apart on ungreased baking sheets. Bake at 375° for 8-10 minutes or until edges are golden brown. Cool for 1 minute before removing to wire racks. Cut 6-in.-square pieces of cellophane or plastic wrap to wrap each cookie; twist ends securely or tie with a ribbon.

Yield: about 4 dozen.

Shaping Peppermint Candy Cookies

1. Shape each piece into a 6-in. log. Flatten into triangular logs, bending the top of one point slightly.

2. Assemble one large roll by alternating three green and three plain logs. Repeat with red dough and remaining plain dough.

Mom's Coconut Cookies

Shirley Secrest, Mattoon, Illinois

Mom worked hard to keep us fed during the Depression, and there was never a day we went hungry. These cookies could always be found in the cookie jar. They are still a favorite today.

1/2 cup butter, softened
1 cup sugar
1/4 cup packed brown sugar
1 egg
1-1/2 teaspoons vanilla extract
2 cups all-purpose flour
1-1/2 teaspoons baking powder
1/8 teaspoon salt
1 cup flaked coconut

1. In a mixing bowl, cream butter and sugar. Beat in egg and vanilla. Combine the flour, baking powder and salt; gradually add to the creamed mixture. Stir in coconut. Shape into two 3-1/2-in. rolls; wrap each in plastic wrap. Refrigerate for 2 hours or until firm.

2. Unwrap and cut into 1/8-in. slices. Place 2 in. apart on ungreased baking sheets. Bake at 425° for 5-7 minutes or until lightly browned. Remove to wire racks to cool.

Yield: 4-1/2 dozen.

Chocolate Pinwheels

Patricia Kile
Greentown, Pennsylvania

My husband's grandfather was always intrigued with how the swirls got in these cookies!

1/2 cup butter, softened
1 cup sugar
1/4 cup packed brown sugar
1 egg
1-1/2 teaspoons vanilla extract
2 cups all-purpose flour
1 teaspoon baking powder
Dash salt

FILLING:
2 cups (12 ounces) semisweet chocolate chips
2 tablespoons butter
1/4 teaspoon vanilla extract
Dash salt

1. In a mixing bowl, cream butter and sugars. Add egg and vanilla; beat until light and fluffy. Combine dry ingredients; beat into creamed mixture. Divide dough in half; place each half between two sheets of waxed paper. Roll into 12-in. x 10-in. rectangles. Chill until almost firm, about 30 minutes.

2. In a saucepan over low heat, melt chips and butter. Add vanilla and salt; mix well. Spread over dough. Carefully and tightly roll up jelly-roll style, starting with a long side. Wrap each in plastic warp. Refrigerate for 2 hours or until firm.

3. Cut rolls into 1/8-in. slices with a sharp thin knife; place on greased or parchment-lined baking sheets. Bake at 350° for 7-10 minutes or until lightly browned. Remove to wire racks to cool.

Yield: 9 dozen.

Lemon Pecan Slices

These attractive morsels are my daughter's favorite. The lemon glaze pairs well with the delicate nut-topped cookie.

Melissa Branning, Fontana, Wisconsin

- 1 cup butter, softened
- 3/4 cup packed brown sugar
- 1/2 cup sugar
- 2 eggs
- 1-1/2 teaspoons vanilla extract
- 1 tablespoon grated lemon peel
- 3 cups all-purpose flour
- 1-1/2 teaspoons baking powder
- 3/4 teaspoon salt

TOPPING:
- 3/4 cup finely chopped pecans
- 1/4 cup sugar

LEMON GLAZE:
- 1-1/4 cups confectioners' sugar
- 5 teaspoons lemon juice
- 1 drop yellow food coloring, optional

1. In a large mixing bowl, cream the butter and sugars. Separate one egg; refrigerate egg white. Add the egg yolk, second egg, vanilla and lemon peel to creamed mixture; mix well. Combine the flour, baking powder and salt; gradually beat into creamed mixture. Shape into three 7-in. rolls; wrap each in plastic wrap. Refrigerate for 2 hours or until firm.

2. Unwrap logs. Lightly beat reserved egg white. Combine pecans and sugar. Brush each log with egg white, then roll in pecan mixture; press firmly into dough.

3. Cut into 1/4-in. slices. Place 2 in. apart on ungreased baking sheets. Bake at 400° for 6-7 minutes or until very lightly browned. Remove to wire racks to cool. Combine glaze ingredients; drizzle over cookies.

Yield: about 7 dozen.

Pastelitos De Boda

Terri Lins
San Diego, California

In Mexico, these rich cookies are called "Little Wedding Cakes" and are usually served with hot chocolate. Since moving here close to Mexico from the Midwest, I've enjoyed trying authentic recipes—they're a sharp departure from the Iowa favorites I grew up with! I love introducing these to relatives and friends!

- 3/4 cup butter, softened
- 1/2 cup confectioners' sugar
- 2 teaspoons vanilla extract
- 2 cups sifted all-purpose flour
- 1/4 teaspoon salt
- 1 cup finely chopped walnuts
- 1/4 cup heavy whipping cream

Additional confectioners' sugar

1. In a large mixing bowl, cream butter and sugar; add vanilla. Combine the flour, salt and nuts; gradually add to creamed mixture. Add cream; knead lightly. Shape into a 2-1/2-in.-diameter roll. Wrap in plastic wrap. Refrigerate for several hours or overnight.

2. Unwrap and cut into 1/4-in. slices. Place 2 in. apart on ungreased baking sheets. Bake at 375° for 15 minutes or until delicately browned around edges. Remove to wire racks. While warm, roll in additional confectioners' sugar.

Yield: about 3 dozen.

Peppermint Cookies

Mrs. Robert Nelson
Des Moines, Iowa

The crushed peppermint candy adds a fun twist to these icebox sugar cookies.

- 1 cup shortening
- 1/2 cup sugar
- 1/2 cup packed brown sugar
- 2 eggs
- 1-1/2 teaspoons vanilla extract
- 2-3/4 cups all-purpose flour
- 1 teaspoon salt
- 1/2 teaspoon baking soda
- 1/2 cup crushed peppermint candies

1. In a mixing bowl, cream shortening and sugars. Add eggs, one at a time, beating well after each addition. Beat in vanilla. Combine dry ingredients; gradually add to the creamed mixture. Stir in crushed candies. Shape into a 15-in. roll; wrap in plastic wrap. Refrigerate for 4 hours or until firm.

2. Unwrap and cut into 1/8-in. slices. Place 2 in. apart on ungreased baking sheets. Bake at 375° for 6-8 minutes or until edges begin to brown. Remove to wire racks to cool.

Yield: about 6 dozen.

Cream Cheese-Filled Cookies

My aunt baked these cookies as part of my wedding day dinner. Everyone was impressed with their eye-catching appeal and rich flavor. They were a memorable treat on that wonderful day.

Ruth Glick, New Holland, Pennsylvania

- 1/3 cup butter, softened
- 1/3 cup shortening
- 3/4 cup sugar
- 1 egg
- 1 teaspoon vanilla extract
- 1-3/4 cups all-purpose flour
- 1 teaspoon baking powder
- 1/2 teaspoon salt

FILLING:
- 2 packages (3 ounces *each*) cream cheese, softened
- 1-1/2 cups confectioners' sugar
- 2 tablespoons all-purpose flour
- 1 teaspoon vanilla extract
- 1 drop yellow food coloring, optional

TOPPING:
- 3/4 cup semisweet chocolate chips
- 3 tablespoons butter

1. In a large mixing bowl, cream butter, shortening and sugar. Beat in egg and vanilla. Combine flour, baking powder and salt; gradually add to the creamed mixture. Shape into two 12-in. rolls; wrap each in plastic wrap. Refrigerate for 4 hours or overnight.

2. Unwrap and cut into 1-in. slices. Place 1 in. apart on greased baking sheet. Bake at 375° for 10-12 minutes or until lightly browned. Immediately make an indentation in the center of each cookie using the end of a wooden spoon handle. Remove to wire racks to cool.

3. Combine filling ingredients in a mixing bowl; mix well. Place 2 teaspoonfuls in the center of each cookie. Let stand until set. In a microwave or saucepan, melt chocolate chips and butter; stir until smooth. Drizzle over cookies. Store in the refrigerator.

Yield: about 2-1/2 dozen.

Cappuccino Flats

Jacqueline Cline
Drummond, Wisconsin

These coffee-flavored cookies are so delicious most people can't believe they're made in my own kitchen instead of a gourmet bakery!

- 1/2 cup butter, softened
- 1/2 cup shortening
- 1/2 cup sugar
- 1/2 cup packed brown sugar
- 1 tablespoon instant coffee granules
- 1 teaspoon warm water
- 1 egg
- 2 squares (1 ounce *each*) unsweetened chocolate, melted and cooled
- 2 cups all-purpose flour
- 1 teaspoon ground cinnamon
- 1/4 teaspoon salt
- 1-1/2 cups semisweet chocolate chips
- 3 tablespoons shortening

1. In a mixing bowl, cream butter, shortening and sugars. Dissolve coffee in water; add to creamed mixture with egg and melted chocolate. Mix well. Combine flour, cinnamon and salt; gradually add to creamed mixture (dough will be sticky). Shape into two 6-1/2-in. rolls; wrap in plastic wrap. Refrigerate for 4 hours or until firm.

2. Unwrap and cut into 1/4-in. slices. Place 2 in. apart on ungreased baking sheets. Bake at 350° for 10-12 minutes or until firm. Remove to wire racks to cool.

3. In a microwave or small heavy saucepan, melt chocolate chips and shortening, stirring until smooth. Dip each cookie halfway; shake off excess. Place on waxed paper to set.

Yield: 4-1/2 dozen.

Raspberry Swirls

Marcia Hostetter, Canton, New York

My mother-in-law shared the recipe for these old-fashioned cookies. Swirls of raspberry jam give them a yummy yuletide twist.

- 1 cup butter, softened
- 2 cups sugar
- 2 eggs
- 1 teaspoon vanilla extract
- 1/2 teaspoon lemon extract
- 3-3/4 cups all-purpose flour
- 2 teaspoons baking powder
- 1 teaspoon salt
- 1 jar (12 ounces) seedless raspberry jam
- 1 cup flaked coconut
- 1/2 cup chopped pecans

1. In a mixing bowl, cream butter and sugar. Add the eggs and extracts; mix well. Combine flour, baking powder and salt; add to creamed mixture and mix well. Cover and chill for at least 2 hours.

2. Divide dough in half. On a lightly floured surface, roll each half into a 12-in. x 9-in. rectangle. Combine jam, coconut and pecans; spread over rectangles. Carefully roll up rectangle jelly-roll style, starting with a long side; wrap in plastic wrap. Refrigerate overnight or freeze for 2-3 hours.

3. Unwrap and cut into 1/4-in. slices; place 1-1/2 in. apart on parchment-lined baking sheets. Bake at 375° for 10-12 minutes or until lightly browned. Remove to wire racks to cool completely.

Yield: 8 dozen.

Icebox Sugar Cookies

Louise Worsham, Kalamazoo, Michigan

I've been making light, buttery and easily portable Icebox Sugar Cookies since I was a girl. They are always well received when I serve them.

1 cup butter, softened
2 cups sugar
2 eggs
1 teaspoon vanilla extract
3-1/2 cups all-purpose flour
1 teaspoon baking soda
1/2 teaspoon salt

1. In a mixing bowl, cream butter and sugar. Beat in eggs and vanilla. Combine flour, baking soda and salt; gradually add to creamed mixture. On a lightly floured surface, shape dough into three 10-in. long rolls. Wrap each roll in plastic wrap. Refrigerate for 1 hour or until firm.

2. Unwrap and cut into 3/8-in. slices; place on greased baking sheets. Sprinkle with sugar. Bake at 375° for 8-10 minutes or until lightly browned. Remove to wire racks to cool.

Yield: about 8 dozen.

Owl Cookies

Liz Clemons
Sumter, South Carolina

These are fun to serve at grade school parties or at Halloween.

1 cup packed brown sugar
3/4 cup butter, softened
1 egg
1 teaspoon vanilla extract
2-1/2 cups all-purpose flour
2 teaspoons baking powder
1/4 teaspoon salt
1 square (1 ounce) unsweetened chocolate, melted
1/4 teaspoon baking soda
Orange and yellow M&M's
Whole cashews

1. In a mixing bowl, cream brown sugar and butter. Add egg and vanilla; mix well. Combine flour, baking powder and salt; add to creamed mixture.

2. Remove two-thirds of the dough; roll into an 8-in. square on waxed paper and set aside. Combine chocolate and baking soda until thoroughly blended; beat into remaining dough. Shape into an 8-in. long roll; place on edge of white dough. Wrap white dough around roll and pinch seam together. Wrap in plastic wrap. Refrigerate for at least 2 hours.

3. Unwrap and cut into 1/4-in. slices. To form owl's face, place two slices side by side on a lightly greased baking sheet. Pinch dough at the top of the circles to form ears. Place M&M's in the center of each circle for eyes. Place a cashew in the center of the face for the beak.

4. Bake at 350° for 9-11 minutes or until edges are lightly browned. Cool for 2 minutes before removing to a wire rack.

Yield: about 1-1/2 dozen.

Pecan Rounds

Clara Avilla, San Martin, California

I developed these recipes when a friend shared her pecan crop with me. These cookies are always on my family's "must make" list.

1 cup butter, softened
1-1/2 cups confectioners' sugar, *divided*
1 teaspoon vanilla extract
2-1/4 cups all-purpose flour
3/4 cup finely ground pecans, toasted
1/2 teaspoon salt
1 tablespoon ground cinnamon

1. In a mixing bowl, cream the butter and 1/2 cup sugar. Beat in vanilla. Combine flour, pecans and salt; gradually add to the creamed mixture. Shape into two 8-in. rolls; wrap each in plastic wrap. Refrigerate for 2 hours or until firm.

2. Unwrap and cut into 1/4-in. slices. Place 1-1/2 in. apart on ungreased baking sheets. Bake at 375° for 8-10 minutes or until edges are lightly browned. Remove to wire racks. Meanwhile, combine cinnamon and remaining sugar. Roll warm cookies in cinnamon-sugar. Cool completely on wire racks.

Yield: 6-1/2 dozen.

Ginger Thins

Eleanor Senske
Rock Island, Illinois

I like to serve these spiced treats with a dollop of lemon sherbet.

6 tablespoons butter, softened
1/2 cup plus 2 tablespoons sugar, *divided*
2 tablespoons molasses
1 tablespoon cold strong brewed coffee
1-1/4 cups all-purpose flour
3/4 teaspoon ground ginger
1/2 teaspoon baking soda
1/2 teaspoon ground cinnamon
1/4 teaspoon ground cloves
1/8 teaspoon salt

1. In a mixing bowl, cream butter and 1/2 cup sugar; set remaining sugar aside. Add molasses and coffee to creamed mixture; mix well. Combine the remaining ingredients; add to creamed mixture. Mix well (dough will be soft). Cover and freeze for 15 minutes. Shape into a 7-in. roll; flatten to 1-in. thickness. Wrap in plastic wrap. Freeze for 8 hours or overnight.

2. Unwrap and cut into 1/8-in. slices; place 2 in. apart on parchment paper-lined baking sheets. Sprinkle with reserved sugar. Bake at 350° for 8-10 minutes or until firm. Remove to wire racks to cool.

Yield: 3-1/2 dozen.

Double Butterscotch Cookies

Beverly Duncan
Big Prairie, Ohio

I've made this old-fashioned recipe for years. It can also be made with miniature chocolate chips or coconut in place of the toffee bits. This recipe makes seven dozen cookies, so it is good for bake sales and potlucks.

- 1/2 cup butter, softened
- 1/2 cup shortening
- 4 cups packed brown sugar
- 4 eggs
- 1 tablespoon vanilla extract
- 6 cups all-purpose flour
- 3 teaspoons baking soda
- 3 teaspoons cream of tartar
- 1 teaspoon salt
- 1 package English toffee bits (10 ounces) *or* almond brickle chips (7-1/2 ounces)
- 1 cup finely chopped pecans

1. In a large mixing bowl, cream the butter, shortening and brown sugar until light and fluffy. Add the eggs, one at a time, beating well after each addition. Beat in vanilla. Combine flour, baking soda, cream of tartar and salt; gradually add to the creamed mixture and mix well. Stir in toffee bits and pecans. Shape into three 14-in. rolls; wrap each roll in plastic wrap. Refrigerate for 4 hours or until firm.

2. Unwrap and cut into 1/2-in. slices. Place 2 in. apart on greased baking sheets. Bake at 375° for 9-11 minutes or until lightly browned. Cool for 1-2 minutes before removing from pans to wire racks.

Yield: about 7 dozen.

Chocolate Peppermint Pinwheels

Ellen Johnson, Hampton, Virginia

My cookie-loving family is never satisfied with just one batch of these minty pinwheels, so I automatically double the recipe each time I bake them. Even then the cookie tin is quickly emptied.

- 1/2 cup shortening
- 3/4 cup sugar
- 1 egg
- 1 tablespoon milk
- 1 teaspoon peppermint extract
- 1-1/4 cups all-purpose flour
- 1/4 teaspoon salt
- 1/4 teaspoon baking powder
- 1 square (1 ounce) unsweetened chocolate, melted

1. In a mixing bowl, cream shortening and sugar. Add egg, milk and extract; mix well. Combine the flour, salt and baking powder; gradually add to creamed mixture. Divide dough in half. Add the chocolate to one portion; mix well. Roll each portion between waxed paper into a rectangle about 1/2 in. thick. Remove top sheet of waxed paper; place plain dough over chocolate dough. Roll up jelly-roll style, starting with a long side. Wrap in each plastic warp. Refrigerate for 2 hours or until firm.

2. Unwrap and cut into 1/4-in. slices. Place 2 in. apart on greased baking sheets. Bake at 375° for 8-10 minutes or until lightly browned. Remove to wire racks to cool.

Yield: about 3 dozen.

Two-Tone Butter Cookies

Kathy Kittell
Lenexa, Kansas

During the hectic holiday season, you'll appreciate the ease of these irresistible butter cookies. It's wonderful to pull the two-tone dough from the freezer and bake a festive batch in no time.

- **1 cup butter, softened**
- **1 cup confectioners' sugar**
- **1 teaspoon vanilla extract**
- **2 cups all-purpose flour**
- **Red and green liquid *or* paste food coloring**
- **Red colored sugar, optional**

1. In a mixing bowl, cream butter and confectioners' sugar. Beat in vanilla. Add flour and mix well. Divide dough in half; with food coloring, tint half the dough red and half green. Shape each portion into an 8-in. log; wrap each in plastic wrap. Refrigerate for at least 1 hour.

2. Unwrap and cut each log in half lengthwise. Press red and green halves together. Tightly wrap each roll in plastic wrap; freeze for up to 6 months.

3. To prepare cookies: Let dough stand at room temperature for 15 minutes. Cut into 1/4-in. slices; place 2 in. apart on ungreased baking sheets. Sprinkle with colored sugar if desired. Bake at 350° for 12-14 minutes or until set. Cool on wire racks.

Yield: about 5 dozen.

Aunt Ione's Icebox Cookies

Jenny Hill, Meridianville, Alabama

Whenever we went to visit my Aunt Ione in southern Georgia, her icebox cookies were our favorite treat. I enjoy them now, which brings back memories of my aunt.

- **6 cups all-purpose flour**
- **1-1/2 teaspoons baking powder**
- **1 teaspoon baking soda**
- **1 teaspoon ground nutmeg**
- **1 teaspoon ground cinnamon**
- **2 cups butter, softened**
- **1 cup sugar**
- **1 cup packed brown sugar**
- **3 eggs**
- **1 teaspoon vanilla extract**
- **1 teaspoon lemon extract**
- **2 cups chopped nuts**

1. Sift together first five ingredients; set aside. In a mixing bowl, cream butter and sugars. Add eggs, vanilla and lemon extracts; beat well. Add dry ingredients; mix well. Stir in nuts. Divide dough into four pieces. Shape into four 11-in. rolls; wrap each in plastic wrap. Refrigerate overnight.

2. Unwrap and cut into 3/8-in. slices. Place 2 in. apart on greased baking sheets. Bake at 350° for about 10 minutes or until set. Remove to wire racks to cool completely.

Yield: about 17 dozen.

Orange Pecan Cookies

Eleanor Henry, Derry, New Hampshire

This cookie is pure heaven with a glass of milk. It has a subtle orange flavor and just a sprinkling of crunchy pecans throughout.

1 cup butter, softened
1/2 cup sugar
1/2 cup packed brown sugar
1 egg
2 tablespoons orange juice
1 tablespoon grated orange peel
2-1/2 cups all-purpose flour
1/2 teaspoon baking soda
1/2 teaspoon salt
1/2 cup chopped pecans

1. In a mixing bowl, cream butter and sugars. Beat in egg, orange juice and peel. Combine flour, baking soda and salt; gradually add to creamed mixture. Stir in pecans. Shape dough into two 11-1/2-in. rolls; wrap each in plastic wrap. Refrigerate for 4 hours or overnight.

2. Unwrap and cut into 1/4-in. slices. Place 2 in. apart on lightly greased baking sheet. Bake at 400° for 7-8 minutes or until golden brown. Remove to wire racks to cool.

Yield: about 6 dozen.

Date Swirls Cookies

Donna Grace
Clancy, Montana

My granddaughter nicknamed my mother "Cookie Grandma" because she made wonderful cookies. Mom made these crisp and chewy cookies every Christmas.

FILLING:

2 cups chopped dates
1 cup water
1 cup sugar
1 cup chopped nuts
2 teaspoons lemon juice

DOUGH:

1 cup butter, softened
1 cup packed brown sugar
1 cup sugar
3 eggs
1 teaspoon lemon extract
4 cups all-purpose flour
1 teaspoon salt
3/4 teaspoon baking soda

1. In a saucepan, combine filling ingredients. Cook over medium-low heat, stirring constantly, until mixture becomes stiff, about 15-20 minutes. Chill.

2. For dough, in a mixing bowl, cream butter and sugars. Add eggs, one at a time, beating well after each addition. Add extract. Combine the flour, salt and baking soda; gradually add to creamed mixture and mix well. Cover and refrigerate for at least 1 hour.

3. On a lightly floured surface, roll out half of the dough to a 12-in. x 9-in. rectangle, about 1/4 in. thick. Spread with half of the filling. Roll up jelly-roll style, starting with the long side. Repeat with remaining dough and filling. Wrap with plastic wrap; refrigerate overnight.

4. Unwrap and cut rolls into 1/4-in. slices. Place 2 in. apart on greased baking sheets. Bake at 375° for 8-10 minutes or until lightly browned. Remove to wire racks to cool.

Yield: 4 dozen.

Sesame Coconut Cookies

Roberta Myers, Elwood, Indiana

Even folks who normally pass on coconut treats can't resist these crisp butter cookies. They make a nice accompaniment to a hot cup of coffee or tea.

- 2 cups butter, softened
- 1-1/2 cups sugar
- 1 teaspoon vanilla extract
- 3 cups all-purpose flour
- 1/2 teaspoon salt
- 2 cups flaked coconut
- 1 cup sesame seeds
- 1/2 cup finely chopped almonds

1. In a mixing bowl, cream butter and sugar. Beat in vanilla. Combine flour and salt; gradually add to creamed mixture. Stir in the coconut, sesame seeds and almonds. Shape into three 10-in. rolls; wrap each in plastic wrap. Refrigerate for 1-2 hours or until firm

2. Unwrap dough and cut into 1/4-in. slices. Place 1 in. apart on ungreased baking sheets. Bake at 300° for 25-30 minutes or until lightly browned. Cool for 2 minutes before removing to wire racks.

Yield: 10 dozen.

Fruit 'n' Nut Cookies

Jennie Loftus
Gasport, New York

Once after making a fruitcake, I had some fruit and nuts left over. I mixed them into a basic cookie dough along with pineapple and coconut.

- 3/4 cup butter, softened
- 3/4 cup shortening
- 1-1/4 cups packed brown sugar
- 2 eggs
- 1 teaspoon vanilla extract
- 4 cups all-purpose flour
- 2 teaspoons baking powder
- 1/2 teaspoon salt
- 1 can (8 ounces) crushed pineapple, drained
- 1/2 cup chopped dates
- 1/2 cup chopped red maraschino cherries
- 1/2 cup chopped green maraschino cherries
- 1/2 cup flaked coconut
- 1/2 cup chopped pecans *or* walnuts

1. In a large mixing bowl, cream the butter, shortening and brown sugar. Add eggs, one at a time, beating well after each addition. Beat in vanilla. Combine flour, baking powder and salt; gradually add to the creamed mixture. Stir in remaining ingredients. Shape into three 10-in. rolls; wrap each in plastic wrap. Refrigerate for 2 hours or until firm.

2. Unwrap and cut into 1/4-in. slices. Place 2 in. apart on ungreased baking sheets. Bake at 375° for 8-10 minutes or until golden brown. Remove to wire racks to cool.

Yield: 7 dozen.

Cute Kitty Cookies

Kay Curtis
Guthrie, Oklahoma

An oatmeal refrigerator cookie recipe proved "purrfect" for cat cookies. Half of the dough is chocolate, which frames the playful faces. It was a game of cat and mouse to see what dessert plate would be emptied first!

1/2 cup butter, softened
1/4 cup shortening
  1 cup sugar
  2 eggs
  1 teaspoon vanilla extract
2-1/4 cups all-purpose flour
3/4 teaspoon baking powder
1/2 teaspoon salt
  1 cup quick-cooking oats
  2 squares (1 ounce *each*) unsweetened chocolate, melted and cooled

Semisweet chocolate chips

Red-hot candies

Black shoestring licorice, cut into 1-1/2-inch pieces

1. In a mixing bowl, cream butter, shortening and sugar. Add eggs, one at a time, beating well after each addition. Beat in vanilla. Combine flour, baking powder and salt; gradually add to the creamed mixture. Stir in oats.

2. Divide dough in half. Add melted chocolate to one portion. Roll plain dough into an 8-in. log. Roll chocolate dough between waxed paper into an 8-in. square. Place log at one end of square; roll up. Wrap in plastic wrap; refrigerate for at least 3 hours.

3. Unwrap and cut into 1/2-in. slices. Place slices on ungreased baking sheets. To form ears, pinch two triangles on the top of each cookie. Bake at 350° for 8-10 minutes or until lightly browned. Immediately place two chocolate chips for eyes, a red-hot for the nose and six pieces of licorice on each for whiskers. Remove to wire racks to cool.

Yield: 3 dozen.

Making Cute Kitty Cookies

Cute Kitty Cookies have a solid center of vanilla dough encased in a chocolate dough. To make these two-toned cookies, shape the vanilla dough into an 8-in. roll. Roll out the chocolate dough into an 8-in. square between two sheets of waxed paper. Remove the top sheet of waxed paper and place the vanilla roll at one edge of the square. Trim if necessary. Roll up jelly-roll style, peeling waxed paper away while rolling. Seal seam. Wrap the roll in plastic wrap and refrigerate.

Peanut Butter Baskets, p. 111

Festive Shortbread Logs, p. 110

Meringue Bunnies, p. 109

Almond Kiss Cookies, p. 125

Shaped Sensations

Dig into cookie making by forming dough into balls, logs, crescents and cups and other fanciful, fun shapes. These treats may take a bit longer to make but the yummy results will be worth it.

Tips for Shaped Cookies

For easier handling, refrigerate the dough until it is chilled. If there is a high butter content in the dough, the heat from your hands can soften the butter in the dough, making it harder to shape. Dust hands lightly with flour to prevent dough from sticking while shaping it.

Peanut Butter Delights

Jennifer Moran
Elizabethtown, Kentucky

With their chocolate-dipped bottoms, peanut butter thumbprint filling and pretty chocolate drizzle on top, these cookies are fancy and fun! The recipe is from my mother.

1/2 cup shortening
1/2 cup butter, softened
1/2 cup creamy peanut butter
1-1/2 cups sugar, *divided*
1 cup packed brown sugar
2 eggs
3 cups all-purpose flour
3/4 teaspoon baking soda
1/2 teaspoon salt

FILLING:
1/2 cup creamy peanut butter
4 ounces cream cheese, softened
1/4 cup sugar
1 egg yolk
1/2 teaspoon vanilla extract
2-1/2 cups milk chocolate chips

TOPPING:
1 tablespoon butter
1-1/2 cups confectioners' sugar
6 tablespoons baking cocoa
3 tablespoons water
1/4 teaspoon vanilla extract

1. In a large mixing bowl, cream the shortening, butter, peanut butter, 1 cup sugar and brown sugar. Add eggs, one at a time, beating well after each addition. Combine the flour, baking soda and salt; gradually add to creamed mixture.

2. Roll into 1-1/2-in. balls; roll in remaining sugar. Place 2 in. apart on ungreased baking sheets. Using the end of a wooden spoon handle, make an indentation in the center of each ball.

3. In a small mixing bowl, beat peanut butter and cream cheese until smooth. Beat in the sugar, egg yolk and vanilla. Spoon about 3/4 teaspoon of filling into each indentation. Bake at 350° for 12-15 minutes or until firm to the touch. Remove to wire racks to cool.

4. Melt the chocolate chips; stir until smooth. Dip bottoms of cookies in chocolate; shake off excess. Place chocolate side up on waxed paper-lined baking sheets. Refrigerate until set.

5. For topping, melt butter in a saucepan. Whisk in confectioners' sugar and cocoa. Gradually add water, whisking until smooth. Stir in vanilla. Drizzle over tops of cookies. Chill until chocolate is set. Store in an airtight container in the refrigerator.

Yield: about 5 dozen.

Editor's Note: Reduced-fat or generic brands of peanut butter are not recommended for this recipe.

Braided Sweetheart Cookies

Rhonda Berstad
Melfort, Saskatchewan

Everyone had a "hay day" when our daughter, Naomi, married. Naomi's grandmother, who made these tender cookies for 48 years, fixed them in the shape of hearts for the wedding. Make the cookies ahead and freeze until serving.

1 cup butter, softened
1-1/2 cups confectioners' sugar
1 egg
1/2 teaspoon vanilla extract
2-1/2 cups all-purpose flour
1/2 teaspoon baking powder
1/2 teaspoon salt
6 to 8 drops red food coloring

1. In a mixing bowl, cream butter and sugar. Beat in egg and vanilla. Combine the flour, baking powder and salt; gradually add to creamed mixture.

2. Divide dough in half; tint one portion pink, leaving the remaining portion white. Wrap each portion in plastic wrap; refrigerate for 4 hours or overnight.

3. For each cookie, shape a 1-in. ball of each color into an 8-in. rope. Place a pink and white rope side-by-side; press together gently and twist. Place 2 in. apart on ungreased baking sheets; shape into a heart and pinch ends to seal. Bake at 350° for 8-11 minutes or until edges are lightly browned. Remove to wire racks to cool.

Yield: 2 dozen.

Meringue Bunnies

(Pictured on page 107)
Taste of Home Test Kitchen
Greendale, Wisconsin

These cute cookies created by our home economists are a great addition to your table when entertaining at Easter. Enlist the kids to help shape the bunnies.

2 egg whites
1/8 teaspoon cream of tartar
1/2 cup sugar
1/4 cup pink candy coating disks
36 heart-shaped red decorating sprinkles

1. In a mixing bowl, beat the egg whites and cream of tartar on medium speed until soft peaks form. Gradually add sugar, 1 tablespoon at a time, beating on high until stiff peaks form.

2. Transfer to a pastry or plastic bag; cut a small hole in a corner of the bag. On parchment-lined baking sheets, pipe the meringue into 4-3/4-in. bunny shapes. Bake at 225° for 1-1/2 hours or until firm. Remove to wire racks to cool.

3. In a microwave or heavy saucepan, melt candy coating, stirring until smooth. Place in a pastry or plastic bag. Pipe ears, whiskers and mouths on bunnies. Attach hearts for eyes and nose with melted candy coating.

Yield: 1 dozen.

Almond-Tipped Shortbread Fingers

Cindy Sifford
Mt. Zion, Illinois

My husband enjoys these cookies so much that he usually can't wait until they're set to start eating them. If you'd like, try dipping them into melted semisweet chocolate and chopped pecans.

1 cup butter, softened
3/4 cup packed brown sugar
2 teaspoons vanilla extract
2 cups all-purpose flour
6 squares (1 ounce *each*) white baking chocolate
1-1/4 cups chopped almonds

1. In a large mixing bowl, cream butter and brown sugar. Beat in vanilla. Gradually add flour. Shape 1/2 cupfuls of dough into 1/2-in.-thick logs. Cut logs into 2-in. pieces.

2. Place 2 in. apart on ungreased baking sheets. Bake at 325° for 15-17 minutes or until lightly browned. Remove to wire racks to cool.

3. In a microwave-safe bowl, melt white chocolate, stir until smooth. Dip one end of each cookie into chocolate, then into almonds. Place on waxed paper until set.

Yield: 4 dozen.

Dipping Cookies in Chocolate

Melt the chocolate chips, baking chocolate or candy coating according to recipe directions. If necessary, transfer chocolate to a narrow container.

Dip cookie partway into chocolate and scrape bottom of the cookie across the edge of the container to remove excess chocolate. Place on a baking sheet lined with waxed paper and allow to set at room temperature.

Toward the end of the process, when the chocolate is running low, it might be necessary to spoon the chocolate over the cookies. If chocolate cools too much to coat the cookies properly, rewarm before finishing dipping.

Peanut Butter Baskets

(Pictured on page 106)
Darlene Brenden, Salem, Oregon

- 30 green gumdrops
- 3/4 cup creamy peanut butter
- 1/2 cup shortening
- 3/4 cup sugar, *divided*
- 1/2 cup packed brown sugar
- 1 egg
- 2 tablespoons milk
- 1 teaspoon vanilla extract
- 1-1/3 cups all-purpose flour
- 1/2 teaspoon baking soda
- 1/2 teaspoon salt
- 30 miniature peanut butter cups, halved
- 60 cake decorator candy flowers

Rich, buttery cookies become more delightful when topped with peanut butter cups and candy. These are cute for spring, but I've used appropriately colored decorations to match occasions at any time of the year.

1. Flatten the gumdrops; cut into small leaf shapes and set aside. In a mixing bowl, cream peanut butter, shortening, 1/2 cup sugar and brown sugar. Add the egg, milk and vanilla; mix well. Combine the flour, baking soda and salt; add to the creamed mixture and mix well.

2. Shape into 1-in. balls. Roll in remaining sugar; place 2 in. apart on ungreased baking sheets. Bake at 350° for 10-12 minutes or until lightly browned.

3. Remove from the oven and immediately lightly press one peanut butter cup cut side down into each cookie to form a basket. Press a candy flower onto cookie so it appears as if a flower is coming out of the basket; press gumdrop leaves next to flowers. Remove to wire racks to cool.

Yield: about 5 dozen.

Editor's Note: Reduced-fat or generic brands of peanut butter are not recommended for this recipe.

Cardamom Cookies

Mary L. Steiner
West Bend, Wisconsin

These melt-in-your-mouth morsels are sure to be a hit at your house. Cardamom, almond extract and walnuts enhance the flavor of these delicate cookies.

- 2 cups butter, softened
- 2-1/2 cups confectioners' sugar, *divided*
- 1-1/2 teaspoons almond extract
- 3-3/4 cups all-purpose flour
- 1 cup finely chopped walnuts
- 1 teaspoon ground cardamom
- 1/8 teaspoon salt

1. In a mixing bowl, cream butter and 1-1/2 cups confectioners' sugar until smooth. Beat in extract. Combine the flour, walnuts, cardamom and salt; gradually add to the creamed mixture.

2. Roll into 1-in. balls. Place 2 in. apart on ungreased baking sheets. Bake at 350° for 15-17 minutes or until edges are golden. Roll warm cookies in remaining confectioners' sugar. Remove to wire racks to cool.

Yield: 6 dozen.

Strawberry Cream Cookies

Glenna Aberle, Sabetha, Kansas

This cream cheese cookie looks lovely on a tea tray. The sweet jam complements the buttery cookie. You can use raspberry, cherry or blueberry jam instead of strawberry.

1 cup butter, softened
1 cup sugar
1 package (3 ounces) cream cheese, softened
1 tablespoon vanilla extract
1 egg yolk
2-1/2 cups all-purpose flour
Strawberry jam, room temperature

1. In a mixing bowl, cream butter, sugar and cream cheese. Add vanilla and egg yolk; mix well. Add flour and blend. Cover and refrigerate.

2. Roll into 1-in. balls. Place 2 in. apart on ungreased baking sheets. Using the end of a wooden spoon handle, make an indentation in the center of each ball. Fill with 1/4 teaspoon jam. Bake at 350° for 10-12 minutes or until set. Remove to wire racks to cool.

Yield: 5 dozen.

Farm Mouse Cookies

Kay Curtis
Guthrie, Oklahoma

Eeeek! The whimsical mice I made evoked shrieks of delight from the kids at our party. Peanut-half "ears" and the licorice "tails" transformed these peanut butter cookies into country critters.

1 cup creamy peanut butter
1/2 cup butter, softened
1/2 cup sugar
1/2 cup packed brown sugar
1 egg
1 teaspoon vanilla extract
1-1/2 cups all-purpose flour
1/2 teaspoon baking soda
Peanut halves
Black shoestring licorice, cut into 2-1/2-inch pieces

1. In a mixing bowl, cream peanut butter, butter and sugars. Beat in egg and vanilla. Combine flour and baking soda; gradually add to creamed mixture. Cover and chill dough for 1 hour or overnight.

2. Roll into 1-in. balls. Dash one end, forming a teardrop shape. Place 2 in. apart on ungreased baking sheets; press to flatten. For ears, press two peanuts into each cookie near the pointed end. Using a toothpick, make a 1/2-in.-deep hole for the tail in the end opposite the ears. Bake at 350° for 8-10 minutes or until golden. While cookies are warm, insert licorice for tails. Cool on wire racks.

Yield: 4 dozen.

Editor's Note: Reduced-fat or generic brands of peanut butter are not recommended for this recipe.

Walnut Horn Cookies

Sharon Allen
Allentown, Pennsylvania

At our house, it wouldn't be Christmas without these delicious Pennsylvania Dutch cookies that are known locally as "kiffels."

1 pound butter, softened

2 packages (one 8 ounces, one 3 ounces) cream cheese, softened

4 egg yolks

4-1/4 cups all-purpose flour

FILLING:

4 cups ground walnuts (about 1 pound)

5-3/4 cups confectioners' sugar, *divided*

4 egg whites

1/2 teaspoon vanilla extract

1/2 teaspoon almond extract

1. In a mixing bowl, combine butter, cream cheese, egg yolks and flour; beat until smooth.

2. Roll into 1-in. balls; place in a container with waxed paper separating each layer. Cover and refrigerate overnight.

3. For filling, combine walnuts and 3-3/4 cups sugar (the mixture will be dry). In a small mixing bowl, beat egg whites until soft peaks form; fold into nut mixture. Add extracts and a few drops of water if necessary until filling reaches a spreading consistency. Place remaining sugar in a bowl; roll cream cheese balls in sugar until completely covered. Place a few balls at a time between two sheets of waxed paper. Roll balls into 2-1/2-in. circles. Gently spread about 2 teaspoons of filling over each. Roll up.

4. Place seam side down 2 in. apart on ungreased baking sheets. Curve the ends slightly. Bake at 350° for 20 minutes or until lightly browned. Remove to wire racks to cool.

Yield: about 8 dozen.

Nutty Orange Spritz Strips

Jeannie Mayfield, Santa Rosa, California

At the annual office cookie exchange my co-workers raved about these cookies. The unique recipe now holds a treasured place in our family cookbook.

3/4 cup butter, softened

1 cup sugar

1 egg

4 teaspoons grated orange peel

2-3/4 cups all-purpose flour

1 teaspoon baking powder

1/4 teaspoon salt

2 tablespoons orange juice

1 cup (6 ounces) semisweet chocolate chips

1 tablespoon shortening

1 cup ground walnuts

1. In a mixing bowl, cream butter and sugar. Beat in egg and orange peel. Combine flour, baking powder and salt; add to the creamed mixture alternately with orange juice.

2. Using a cookie press fitted with a bar disk, press dough into long strips on ungreased baking sheets. Cut each strip into 3-in. pieces (there is no need to separate the pieces). Bake at 350° for 12-14 minutes or until edges are golden. Cut into pieces again if necessary. Remove to wire racks to cool completely.

3. In a microwave or heavy saucepan, melt the chocolate and shortening, stirring until smooth. Dip each end of cookies in chocolate mixture, then in walnuts. Place on waxed paper; let stand until set.

Yield: about 4-1/2 dozen.

Cream Cheese Bells

Charlene Grimminger
Paris, Ohio

Since I was raised on a dairy farm, the ingredients in this recipe suit me fine! These delicious cookies freeze well, although most of them get gobbled up before I have a chance to get them in the freezer.

7 tablespoons butter, softened
1 package (8 ounces) cream cheese, softened
2 egg yolks
2-1/2 cups all-purpose flour

FILLING:
2-1/2 cups ground pecans *or* walnuts
1/2 cup sugar
1/4 cup butter, melted
1 egg white
Confectioners' sugar

1. In a mixing bowl, cream butter and cream cheese. Beat in egg yolks. Gradually add the flour. Cover and refrigerate overnight. Remove from refrigerator about 1 hour before rolling.

2. For filling, combine the nuts, sugar, butter and egg white; set aside. Divide dough into fourths. On a floured surface, roll out each portion to 1/8-in. thickness. Cut with a 2-3/4-in. round cookie cutter. Place 1 in. apart on ungreased baking sheets. Place 1 teaspoon filling in center of each circle. Shape into a bell by folding edges of dough to meet over filling. Moisten edges with water and pinch edges together.

3. Bake at 350° for 12-15 minutes or until lightly browned. Remove to wire racks. Sprinkle cooled cookies with confectioners' sugar.

Yield: about 4 dozen.

Apricot Pecan Tassies

Paula Magnus, Republic, Washington

The apricot filling makes these adorable little tarts extra special. They never last long when I fix them for the holidays. For variety use your favorite dried fruit for the apricots.

1/2 cup plus 1 tablespoon butter, softened, *divided*
6 tablespoons cream cheese, softened
1 cup all-purpose flour
3/4 cup packed brown sugar
1 egg, lightly beaten
1/2 teaspoon vanilla extract
1/4 teaspoon salt
2/3 cup diced dried apricots
1/3 cup chopped pecans

1. In a mixing bowl, cream 1/2 cup butter and cream cheese. Gradually add the flour, beating until mixture forms a ball. Cover and refrigerate for 15 minutes.

2. Meanwhile, in a bowl, combine brown sugar, egg, vanilla, salt and remaining butter. Stir in apricots and pecans; set aside. Roll dough into 1-in. balls. Press onto the bottom and up the sides of greased miniature muffin cups. Spoon 1 teaspoon apricot mixture into each cup. Bake at 325° for 25 minutes or until golden brown. Cool in pans on wire racks.

Yield: 2 dozen.

Chocolate Macadamia Meltaways

Barbara Sepcich, Galt, California

I came up with this recipe by accident one day when I wanted to make some cookies. I decided to use some ingredients already in my cupboard, and these were the delicious result.

1/2 cup butter, softened
1/4 cup confectioners' sugar
1/2 teaspoon vanilla extract
1-1/4 cups all-purpose flour
1 jar (3-1/2 ounces) macadamia nuts, finely chopped

FILLING:
1 cup (6 ounces) semisweet chocolate chips
1/2 cup coarsely chopped macadamia nuts
Additional confectioners' sugar

1. In a mixing bowl, cream butter and sugar. Beat in vanilla. Gradually add flour. Stir in nuts (dough will be stiff); set aside.

2. For filling, melt chocolate chips; stir until smooth. Stir in the nuts; cool slightly. Drop by 1/2 teaspoonfuls onto a waxed paper-lined baking sheet; cover and refrigerate for 30 minutes.

3. Shape teaspoonfuls of dough around each piece of chocolate-nut mixture so it is completely covered. Place 2 in. apart on ungreased baking sheets. Bake at 375° for 12-14 minutes or until lightly browned. Roll warm cookies in confectioners' sugar; cool on wire racks.

Yield: 2-1/2 dozen.

Frosted Snowmen

Leah Gallington
Corona, California

These cookies were created when I made an error and used regular sugar for the confectioners' sugar called for in the original recipe. I didn't notice the error until I tasted one and thought it was even better than the original recipe!

1-1/2 cups butter, softened
2-1/4 cups sugar
1 egg
3 teaspoons vanilla extract
3-3/4 cups all-purpose flour
1/2 teaspoon baking powder
1 can (16 ounces) vanilla frosting
72 pretzel sticks
Red and blue decorating icing

1. In a mixing bowl, cream butter and sugar. Gradually beat in egg and vanilla. Combine flour and baking powder; add to creamed mixture. Roll dough into 1-in., 5/8-in. and 1/4-in. balls.

2. For each snowman, place one of each size ball 1/4 in. apart on ungreased baking sheets; place snowmen 2 in. apart. Break pretzel sticks in half; press into sides of middle ball.

3. Bake at 375° for 10-12 minutes or until bottoms are lightly browned. Cool 1 minute before removing to wire racks.

4. Frost cooled cookies. Decorate with blue icing for eyes, mouth and buttons, and red for nose and scarf.

Yield: 6 dozen.

Festive Shortbread Logs

(Pictured on page 107)
Michele Fenner, Girard, Pennsylvania

I first made these rich and tender cookies as a teenager and now make them for my husband and our two sons. I enjoy seeing the smiles on their faces when I serve these cookies.

1 cup butter, softened
1/2 cup confectioners' sugar
1 teaspoon vanilla extract
2 cups all-purpose flour
1-1/2 cups semisweet chocolate chips
4 teaspoons shortening
3/4 cup ground walnuts

1. In a mixing bowl, cream butter and confectioners' sugar. Add vanilla. Gradually add flour; mix well.

2. With lightly floured hands, shape tablespoonfuls into 2-in. logs. Place 2 in. apart on ungreased baking sheets. Bake at 350° for 9-11 minutes or until edges and bottom are lightly browned. Cool for 2-3 minutes before removing to wire racks.

3. In a microwave or heavy saucepan, melt chips and shortening, stirring until smooth. Drizzle chocolate over half of the cookies. Dip one end of remaining cookies into chocolate, then sprinkle with walnuts.

Yield: 4 dozen.

Beary Cute Cookies

Susan Schuller
Brainerd, Minnesota

These cheery cookie cubs, served at my teddy bear picnic, will delight "kids" of all ages! I like to make fun foods but don't care to spend a whole lot of time fussing. So the idea of using candy for the bears' features was right up my alley.

3/4 cup shortening
1/2 cup sugar
1/2 cup packed brown sugar
1 egg
1 teaspoon vanilla extract
2 cups all-purpose flour
1 teaspoon salt
1/2 teaspoon baking soda
Additional sugar
30 miniature milk chocolate kisses
60 miniature M&M baking bits

1. In a mixing bowl, cream shortening and sugars. Beat in egg and vanilla; mix well. Combine the flour, salt and baking soda; gradually add to creamed mixture and mix well (dough will be crumbly).

2. Set aside about 1/2 cup of dough for ears. Shape remaining dough into 1-in. balls; roll in additional sugar. Place 3 in. apart on ungreased baking sheets. Flatten to about 1/2-in. thickness. Roll the reserved dough into 1/2-in. balls; roll in the sugar. Place two smaller balls about 1 in. apart touching each flattened ball (do not flatten smaller balls).

3. Bake at 375° for 10-12 minutes or until set and edges are lightly browned. Remove from oven; immediately press one kiss and two baking bits into each cookie for nose and eyes. Cool for 5 minutes before removing to wire racks.

Yield: 2-1/2 dozen.

Lo-Cal Molasses Cookies

Kim Marie Van Rheenen
Mendota, Illinois

Whenever we want a super snack, I bake up a batch of these lighter, yummy molasses cookies. Underneath the pretty crackled tops are soft, chewy centers.

 1/2 cup vegetable oil
 1/4 cup molasses
 1/4 cup plus 2 tablespoons sugar, *divided*
 1 egg
 2 cups all-purpose flour
 2 teaspoons baking soda
 1 teaspoon ground cinnamon
 1/2 teaspoon ground ginger
 1/4 teaspoon ground cloves

1. In a mixing bowl, beat oil, molasses, 1/4 cup sugar and egg. Combine flour, baking soda, cinnamon, ginger and cloves; add to molasses mixture and mix well. Cover and refrigerate for at least 2 hours.

2. Shape into 1-in. balls; roll in remaining sugar. Place 2 in. apart on ungreased baking sheets. Bake at 375° for 10-12 minutes or until cookies are set and surface cracks. Remove to wire racks to cool.

Yield: 5 dozen.

Mexican Wedding Cakes

Sarita Johnston, San Antonio, Texas

As part of a Mexican tradition, I tucked these tender cookies into small gift boxes for the guests at my sister's wedding. Most folks ate them up before they got home!

 2 cups butter, softened
 1 cup confectioners' sugar
 4 cups all-purpose flour
 1 teaspoon vanilla extract
 1 cup finely chopped pecans
Additional confectioners' sugar

1. In a mixing bowl, cream butter and sugar. Gradually add flour; mix well. Beat in vanilla. Stir in pecans.

2. Shape tablespoonfuls into 2-in. crescents. Place 2 in. apart on ungreased baking sheets. Bake at 350° for 12-15 minutes or until lightly browned. Roll warm cookies in confectioners' sugar; cool on wire racks.

Yield: about 6 dozen.

Making Crescent-Shaped Cookies

Shape rounded teaspoonfuls of dough into 2 to 2-1/2-in. logs, then bend slightly to form the crescent shape.

Peanut Cookies

Kristen Proulx
Canton, New York

I made these cookies as part of a circus theme for my son's birthday party. To shape the Peanut Cookies, just flatten each dough log with a fork, then pinch in the center before baking.

     1 cup butter, softened
     1 cup creamy peanut butter
     1 cup sugar
     1 cup packed brown sugar
     2 eggs
     1 teaspoon vanilla extract
2-1/2 cups all-purpose flour
     1 teaspoon baking powder
     1 teaspoon baking soda
Additional sugar

1. In a large mixing bowl, cream butter, peanut butter and sugars. Add eggs, one at a time, beating well after each addition. Beat in vanilla. Combine the flour, baking powder and baking soda; gradually add to creamed mixture. Refrigerate for 1 hour.

2. Roll dough into 1-in. balls; roll in sugar. Shape into logs. Place 2 in. apart on ungreased baking sheets. Flatten with a fork. Pinch center to form peanut shape. Bake at 375° for 7-10 minutes or until golden brown. Cool for 2 minutes before removing to wire racks.

Yield: about 5-1/2 dozen.

Editor's Note: Reduced-fat or generic brands of peanut butter are not recommended for this recipe.

Caramel Pecan Treasures

Glenda MacEachern, Crown Point, Indiana

Fancy-looking cookies like these may take an extra step or two to make, but family and friends will be impressed! No one can resist these caramel-topped shortbread cookies.

     1 cup butter, softened
   3/4 cup packed brown sugar
     1 teaspoon vanilla extract
1-3/4 cups all-purpose flour
   1/2 teaspoon baking powder
    30 caramels, halved and
        flattened
     2 cups (12 ounces)
        semisweet chocolate chips
     1 tablespoon shortening
   1/2 cup finely chopped pecans

1. In a mixing bowl, cream butter and brown sugar. Beat in vanilla. Combine the flour and baking powder; gradually add to the creamed mixture.

2. Roll into 1-in. balls. Place 2 in. apart on baking sheets; flatten slightly. Bake at 325° for 12-15 minutes or until golden brown. Remove to wire racks to cool completely.

3. Place one caramel on each cooled cookie. In a microwave or heavy saucepan, melt the chocolate chips and shortening, stirring until smooth. Spread over cookies. Sprinkle with pecans. Let stand until set.

Yield: 5 dozen.

Apricot Sesame Cookies

Jeanne Allen, Webster, New York

This recipe is a favorite of mine to make for special events. The cookies freeze beautifully, so you can conveniently make them ahead of time.

1 cup butter, softened
1/2 cup sugar
1 teaspoon almond extract
2 cups all-purpose flour
1/2 teaspoon salt
7 tablespoons sesame seeds
6 tablespoons apricot jam

1. In a mixing bowl, cream butter and sugar. Beat in extract. Combine the flour and salt; gradually add to the creamed mixture.

2. Roll into 1-in. balls, then roll in sesame seeds. Place 2 in. apart on ungreased baking sheets. Using the end of a wooden spoon handle, make an indentation in the center of each ball. Fill with jam. Bake at 400° for 10-12 minutes or until lightly browned. Remove to wire racks to cool completely.

Yield: 4 dozen.

Chocolate Thumbprints Cookies

Laura Bryant German
W. Warren, Massachusetts

A group of friends had a weekly "movie night" during winters in Martha's Vineyard, and we'd take turns making a chocolate treat to share. These terrific cookies were an instant success.

1/2 cup butter, softened
2/3 cup sugar
1 egg, *separated*
2 tablespoons milk
1 teaspoon vanilla extract
1 cup all-purpose flour
1/3 cup baking cocoa
1/4 teaspoon salt
1 cup finely chopped walnuts

FILLING:
1/2 cup confectioners' sugar
1 tablespoon butter, softened
2 teaspoons milk
1/4 teaspoon vanilla extract
26 milk chocolate kisses, unwrapped

1. In a mixing bowl, beat butter, sugar, egg yolk, milk and vanilla until light and fluffy. Combine flour, cocoa and salt; gradually add to creamed mixture. Cover and chill for 1 hour or until firm enough to roll into balls.

2. Meanwhile, in a small bowl, lightly beat egg white. Roll dough into 1-in. balls; dip in egg white, then roll in nuts. Place 2 in. apart on greased baking sheets. Make an indentation with thumb in center of each cookie. Bake at 350° for 10-12 minutes or until center is set.

3. Combine the first four filling ingredients in small bowl until smooth. Spoon 1/4 teaspoon into each warm cookie; gently press a chocolate kiss in the center. Carefully remove from baking sheet to wire racks to cool completely.

Yield: 2 dozen.

Pistachio Orange Drops

Susan Zarzycki, Saratoga, California

These shaped sugar cookies are topped with melted chocolate and chopped pistachios. They're a pretty treat for special occasions or just everyday dessert.

1 cup butter, softened
1 cup confectioners' sugar
1 teaspoon grated orange peel
2 cups all-purpose flour
1 cup finely chopped pistachios
1 cup (6 ounces) semisweet chocolate chips
2 tablespoons shortening

1. In a mixing bowl, cream the butter, sugar and orange peel. Gradually add flour. Set aside 3 tablespoons pistachios for topping; stir remaining pistachios into dough.

2. Roll into 1-in. balls. Place 1-1/2 in. apart on ungreased baking sheets. Bake at 375° for 8-10 minutes or until lightly browned. Remove to wire racks to cool.

3. In a saucepan over low heat, melt chocolate chips and shortening; stir until smooth. Dip tops of cooled cookies in chocolate, then in reserved pistachios.

Yield: about 4-1/2 dozen.

Apricot Cheese Crescents

Ruth Gilhousen
Knoxdale, Pennsylvania

Traditionally, I bake these for Christmas. A cross between sweet breads and cookies, they're also something that I have been asked to make for weddings.

2 cups all-purpose flour
1/2 teaspoon salt
1 cup cold butter
1 cup (8 ounces) small-curd cottage cheese

FILLING:
1 package (6 ounces) dried apricots
1/2 cup water
1/2 cup sugar

TOPPING:
3/4 cup finely chopped almonds
1/2 cup sugar
1 egg white, lightly beaten

1. In a large bowl, combine flour and salt; cut in butter until crumbly. Add cottage cheese; mix well. Shape into 1-in. balls. Cover and refrigerate several hours or overnight.

2. For the filling, combine apricots and water in a saucepan. Cover and simmer for 20 minutes. Cool for 10 minutes. Pour into a blender; cover and process on high speed until smooth. Transfer to a bowl; stir in sugar. Cover and refrigerate.

3. For topping, combine almonds and sugar; set aside. On a floured surface, roll the balls into 2-1/2-in. circles. Spoon about 1 teaspoon of filling onto each. Fold dough over filling and pinch edges to seal. Place on greased baking sheets. Brush tops with egg white; sprinkle with almond mixture. Bake at 375° for 12-15 minutes or until lightly browned. Remove to wire racks to cool.

Yield: 4-1/2 dozen.

Tassies

Joy Corie
Ruston, Louisiana

Any cookie tray will be perked up with the addition of these pretty tarts. If you don't have miniature tart pans, use miniature muffin pans instead.

PASTRY:

- 1 package (3 ounces) cream cheese, softened
- 1/2 cup butter
- 1 cup all-purpose flour

FILLING:

- 3/4 cup packed brown sugar
- 1 tablespoon butter, softened
- 1 egg
- 1 teaspoon vanilla extract

Dash salt

- 2/3 cup finely chopped pecans, *divided*

Maraschino cherries, halved, optional

1. For pastry, blend cream cheese and butter until smooth; stir in flour. Cover and refrigerate for about 1 hour.

2. Roll into twenty-four 1 in. balls. Place in ungreased miniature muffin tins or small cookie tarts; press the dough against bottom and sides to form shell. Set aside.

3. In a bowl, beat brown sugar, butter and egg until combined. Add vanilla, salt and half the pecans; spoon into pastry. Top with remaining pecans. Bake at 375° for 20 minutes, or until filling is set and pastry is light golden brown. Cool and remove from pans. Top each with a maraschino half if desired.

Yield: 24 tarts.

Crispy Oat Cookies

Stephanie Malszycki, Ft. Myers, Florida

These tasty oat cookies have added crunch from the crisp rice cereal and walnuts. Send them for a classroom party or share them with friends.

- 1 cup butter, softened
- 1 cup vegetable oil
- 1-1/3 cups sugar, *divided*
- 1 egg
- 1 teaspoon vanilla extract
- 3-1/2 cups all-purpose flour
- 1 teaspoon baking soda
- 1 teaspoon cream of tartar
- 1 teaspoon salt
- 1 cup crisp rice cereal
- 1 cup quick-cooking oats
- 1 cup flaked coconut
- 1 cup chopped walnuts

1. In a mixing bowl, beat the butter, oil and 1 cup sugar. Beat in egg and vanilla. Combine flour, baking soda, cream of tartar and salt; gradually add to the butter mixture. Stir in the cereal, oats, coconut and nuts.

2. Roll into 1-in. balls; roll in some of the remaining sugar. Place 2 in. apart on ungreased baking sheets. Flatten with a glass dipped in remaining sugar. Bake at 350° for 10-12 minutes or until lightly browned. Remove to wire racks to cool.

Yield: 8 dozen.

Pecan Cheddar Crisps

Ozela Haynes
Emerson, Arkansas

Serve up these crispy snacks for a super party appetizer or just keep a batch on hand to nibble on anytime.

- 1/2 cup butter, softened
- 1/2 cup finely shredded cheddar cheese
- 1 cup all-purpose flour
- 1/4 teaspoon paprika
- 1/4 teaspoon salt
- 1/2 cup pecan halves

1. In a mixing bowl, cream the butter and cheese. Combine flour, paprika and salt; add to creamed mixture.

2. Shape dough into 1-in. balls. Place 2 in. apart on ungreased baking sheets. Top each with a pecan; press down to flatten. Bake at 350° for 15-20 minutes or until golden brown. Remove to wire rack to cool.

Yield: about 2 dozen.

Chocolate-Covered Cherry Cookies

Barbara Hart, Hickory, North Carolina

My five brothers and I lost our mother when we were young, so we started cooking at an early age. Being successful in the kitchen is easy with tried-and-true recipes like this one.

- 1/2 cup butter, softened
- 1 cup sugar
- 1 egg
- 1-1/2 teaspoons vanilla extract
- 1-1/2 cups all-purpose flour
- 1/2 cup baking cocoa
- 1/2 teaspoon salt, *divided*
- 1/4 teaspoon baking powder
- 1/4 teaspoon baking soda
- 1 jar (10 ounces) maraschino cherries
- 1 cup (6 ounces) semisweet chocolate chips
- 1/2 cup sweetened condensed milk

1. In a mixing bowl, cream the butter and sugar. Add egg and vanilla; mix well. Combine the flour, cocoa, 1/4 teaspoon salt, baking powder and baking soda; gradually add to the creamed mixture.

2. Drain cherries, reserving 1-1/2 teaspoons juice. Pat cherries dry. Shape 1 tablespoon of dough around each cherry. Place 2 in. apart on ungreased baking sheets. Bake at 350° for 8-10 minutes or until set. Remove to wire racks to cool.

3. For frosting, in a saucepan, heat chocolate chips and milk until chips are melted; stir until smooth. Remove from the heat. Add reserved cherry juice and remaining salt. Frost cookies.

Yield: about 2-1/2 dozen.

Chocolate-Filled Poppy Seed Cookies

While it's been around for years, this recipe remains a favorite to this day. A co-worker prepared these at a cookie exchange a while back...they were the biggest hit of the party.

Karen Mead, Granville, New York

1 cup butter, softened
1/2 cup sugar
2 egg yolks
1 teaspoon vanilla extract
2 cups all-purpose flour
3 tablespoons poppy seeds
1/4 teaspoon salt
1 cup (6 ounces) semisweet chocolate chips, melted

1. In a mixing bowl, cream butter and sugar. Beat in egg yolks and vanilla. Combine flour, poppy seeds and salt; gradually add to the creamed mixture.

2. Roll into 1-in. balls. Place 2 in. apart on ungreased baking sheets. Using the end of a wooden spoon handle, make an indentation in the center of each. Bake at 375° for 10-12 minutes or until lightly browned. Immediately make an indentation in the center again. Remove to wire racks to cool slightly; fill with melted chocolate.

Yield: 6-1/2 dozen.

Thumbprint Cookies

Taste of Home Test Kitchen
Greendale, Wisconsin

Looking for a lighter alternative to traditional Christmas cookies? Try these pretty jam-filled thumbprints. The melt-in-your-mouth treats have a buttery taste and get a nice crunch from chopped pecans.

6 tablespoons butter, softened
1/2 cup sugar
1 egg
2 tablespoons canola oil
1 teaspoon vanilla extract
1/4 teaspoon butter flavoring *or* almond extract
1-1/2 cups all-purpose flour
1/4 cup cornstarch
1 teaspoon baking powder
1/4 teaspoon salt
1 egg white
1/3 cup chopped pecans
7-1/2 teaspoons assorted jams

1. In a mixing bowl, cream butter and sugar. Beat in egg. Beat in oil, vanilla and butter flavoring. Combine the flour, cornstarch, baking powder and salt; stir into creamed mixture.

2. Roll into 1-in. balls. In a small bowl, lightly beat egg white. Dip each ball halfway into egg white, then into pecans. Place nut side up 2 in. apart on baking sheets coated with nonstick cooking spray. Using the end of a wooden spoon handle, make an indentation in the center of each. Bake at 350° for 8-10 minutes or until the edges are lightly browned. Remove to wire racks. Fill each cookie with 1/4 teaspoon jam; cool.

Yield: 2-1/2 dozen.

Chocolate Puddles

Kathie Griffin, Antelope, California

The variations on this original recipe are almost endless. For a great twist, use peanut butter chips and peanuts for the vanilla chips and mixed nuts.

> 1 cup butter, softened
> 1 cup sugar
> 1 cup packed brown sugar
> 2 eggs
> 2 teaspoons vanilla extract
> 3 cups all-purpose flour
> 3/4 cup baking cocoa
> 1 teaspoon baking soda

FILLING:
> 1 cup vanilla *or* white chips
> 1/2 cup plus 2 tablespoons sweetened condensed milk
> 3/4 cup coarsely chopped mixed nuts

1. In a mixing bowl, cream butter and sugars. Add the eggs, one at a time, beating well after each addition. Beat in vanilla. Combine flour, cocoa and baking soda; gradually add to creamed mixture. Cover and refrigerate for 2 hours or until dough is stiff.

2. Meanwhile, for filling, heat chips and milk in a heavy saucepan over low heat until chips are melted, stirring constantly. Stir in nuts. Cover and refrigerate for 1 hour or until easy to handle.

3. Roll cookie dough into 1-1/4-in. balls. Place the balls 2 in. apart on lightly greased baking sheets. Using the end of a wooden spoon handle, make an indentation in the center; smooth any cracks. Roll filling into 1/2-in. balls; gently push one into each cookie. Bake at 375° for 8-10 minutes or until cookies are set. Remove to wire racks to cool.

Yield: about 5 dozen.

Butter Cookies

Ruth Griggs
South Hill, Virginia

These cookies are favorites of my nephews, who love the creamy frosting.

> 1 cup butter, softened
> 3/4 cup sugar
> 1 egg
> 1/2 teaspoon vanilla extract
> 2-1/2 cups all-purpose flour
> 1 teaspoon baking powder
> 1/4 teaspoon salt

FROSTING:
> 1/2 cup butter, softened
> 4 cups confectioners' sugar
> 1 teaspoon vanilla extract
> 3 to 4 tablespoons milk
> Red food coloring, optional

1. In a mixing bowl, cream butter and sugar. Add egg and vanilla; mix well. Combine the flour, baking powder and salt; add to creamed mixture and mix well.

2. Place the dough in a cookie press fitted with a heart plate; press dough 2 in. apart on ungreased baking sheets. Bake at 375° for 6-8 minutes or until set (do not brown). Remove to wire racks to cool.

3. Beat butter, sugar and vanilla until smooth. Blend in enough milk until desired spreading consistency is reached. Add food coloring to a portion or all of the frosting if desired. Frost cookies.

Yield: about 6-1/2 dozen.

Almond Kiss Cookies

Kathy Aldrich
Webster, New York

These cookies are unbelievable! They're easy to make, look elegant and are absolutely delicious with almond, raspberry and chocolate flavors.

1/2 cup butter, softened
1/2 cup sugar
1/2 cup packed brown sugar
1 egg
1 teaspoon almond extract
2 cups all-purpose flour
1 teaspoon baking soda
1/4 teaspoon salt
Additional sugar
40 milk chocolate kisses with almonds

GLAZE:
1 cup confectioners' sugar
1 tablespoon milk
4 teaspoons raspberry jam
1/4 teaspoon almond extract

1. In a mixing bowl, cream butter and sugars. Beat in egg and extract. Combine the flour, baking soda and salt; gradually add to creamed mixture. Cover and chill for 1 hour or until easy to handle.

2. Roll dough into 1-in. balls, then roll in additional sugar. Place 2 in. apart on ungreased baking sheets. Bake at 325° for 13-15 minutes or until golden brown. Immediately press a chocolate kiss into the center of each cookie. Remove to wire racks to cool. Combine glaze ingredients; drizzle over cooled cookies.

Yield: 40 cookies.

Chocolate Mint Crisps

Karen Ann Bland, Gove, Kansas

If you like chocolate and mint, you can't help but love these yummy, crispy cookies with their creamy icing. We always make them for the holidays and guests can never eat just one!

1-1/2 cups packed brown sugar
3/4 cup butter, cubed
2 tablespoons plus 1-1/2 teaspoons water
2 cups (12 ounces) semisweet chocolate chips
2 eggs
2-1/2 cups all-purpose flour
1-1/4 teaspoons baking soda
1/2 teaspoon salt
3 packages (4.67 ounces *each*) mint Andes candies

1. In a heavy saucepan, cook and stir the brown sugar, butter and water over low heat until butter is melted and mixture is smooth. Remove from the heat; stir in chocolate chips until melted. Transfer to a mixing bowl. Let stand for 10 minutes.

2. With mixer on high speed, add eggs one at a time, beating well after each addition. Combine the flour, baking soda and salt; add to chocolate mixture, beating on low until blended. Cover and refrigerate for 8 hours or overnight.

3. Roll dough into 1-in. balls. Place the balls 3 in. apart on lightly greased baking sheets. Bake at 350° for 11-13 minutes or until edges are set and the tops are puffed and cracked (cookies will become crisp after cooling). Immediately top each cookie with a mint. Let stand for 1-2 minutes; spread over cookie. Remove to wire racks; let stand until chocolate is set and cookies are cooled.

Yield: 6-1/2 dozen.

Frosted Cocoa Cookies

Diane Moran, Rhame, North Dakota

Almond flavor in the chocolate frosting accents these soft cookies nicely. My husband and two sons gobble them up quickly! They also make a nice take-along to potlucks.

1 cup shortening
2 cups sugar
4 eggs
2 teaspoons vanilla extract
3-1/2 cups all-purpose flour
1 cup baking cocoa
2 teaspoons baking soda
1 teaspoon salt

FROSTING:
3 cups confectioners' sugar
1/3 cup baking cocoa
1/3 cup butter, softened
1/4 teaspoon almond extract
3 to 4 tablespoons milk

1. In a large mixing bowl, cream shortening and sugar. Add eggs, one at a time, beating well after each addition. Beat in vanilla. Combine the flour, cocoa, baking soda and salt; gradually add to creamed mixture.

2. Roll into 1-1/2-in. balls. Place 2 in. apart on ungreased baking sheets. Bake at 350° for 13-16 minutes or until set. Remove to wire racks to cool.

3. For frosting, in a mixing bowl, combine the confectioners' sugar, cocoa, butter and extract. Add enough milk to achieve spreading consistency. Frost cooled cookies.

Yield: 3-1/2 dozen.

Honey-Peanut Butter Cookies

Lucile H. Proctor, Panguitch, Utah

When my husband wants a treat, he requests these chewy cookies. The honey adds sweetness and a subtle flavor to the peanut butter cookies.

1/2 cup shortening
1 cup creamy peanut butter
1 cup honey
2 eggs, lightly beaten
3 cups all-purpose flour
1 cup sugar
1-1/2 teaspoons baking soda
1 teaspoon baking powder
1/2 teaspoon salt

1. In a mixing bowl, mix shortening, peanut butter and honey. Add eggs; mix well. Combine flour, sugar, baking soda, baking powder and salt; add to peanut butter mixture and mix well.

2. Roll into 1- to 1-1/2-in. balls. Place 2 in. apart on ungreased baking sheets. Flatten with a fork dipped in flour. Bake at 350° for 8-10 minutes or until set. Remove to wire racks to cool.

Yield: 5 dozen.

Editor's Note: Reduced-fat or generic brands of peanut butter are not recommended for this recipe.

Shaping Peanut Butter Cookies

Peanut butter cookie dough is generally a stiff dough and needs to be flattened before baking. Using a floured fork, press the balls of dough until 3/8 in. thick. Press again in the opposite direction to make a crisscross pattern.

Favorite Molasses Cookies

Marjorie Jenkins, Lees Summit, Missouri

Clove and ginger spiced these chewy molasses cookies. One bite and you'll know why they are "my favorite."

3/4 cup butter, softened
1 cup sugar
1/4 cup molasses
1 egg
2 cups all-purpose flour
2 teaspoons baking powder
1/2 teaspoon baking soda
1 teaspoon ground cinnamon
1/2 teaspoon ground cloves
1/2 teaspoon ground ginger

1. In a mixing bowl, cream butter and sugar. Beat in molasses and egg. Combine dry ingredients; gradually add to creamed mixture. Cover and refrigerate for 1 hour or until firm.

2. Roll into 1-in. balls. Place 2 in. apart on greased baking sheets. Press flat with a glass dipped in sugar. Bake at 375° for 8-10 minutes or until lightly browned. Remove to wire racks to cool.

Yield: 6 dozen.

Cinnamon Crackle Cookies

Vicki Lair
Apple Valley, Minnesota

This recipe is the compilation of many years of baking. I make these cookies for a holiday bazaar and year-round for our family.

1/2 cup butter, softened
1/2 cup shortening
1 cup sugar
1/2 cup packed brown sugar
1 egg
1 teaspoon vanilla extract
1/2 teaspoon almond extract
2-1/2 cups all-purpose flour
1 tablespoon ground cinnamon
2 teaspoons baking soda
2 teaspoons cream of tartar
2 teaspoons ground nutmeg
2 teaspoons grated orange peel
1 teaspoon grated lemon peel
1/2 teaspoon salt
Additional sugar

1. In a mixing bowl, cream butter, shortening and sugars. Add egg and extracts; mix well. Combine the next eight ingredients; gradually add to the creamed mixture.

2. Roll into 1-in. balls; roll in sugar. Place 2 in. apart on ungreased baking sheets. Bake at 350° for 10-15 minutes or until lightly browned. Remove to wire racks to cool.

Yield: about 6 dozen.

Cinnamon Almond Crescents

Jennifer Branum, O'Fallen, Illinois

I set out these cookies as we open our gifts on Christmas Eve. Before long, the plate is empty and I'm being asked to refill it! The cinnamon-sugar coating adds a special touch to these cookies.

1 cup butter, softened
1/3 cup sugar
1/2 teaspoon vanilla extract
1-2/3 cups all-purpose flour
1/2 cup finely ground blanched almonds

TOPPING:
1/2 cup sugar
1/2 teaspoon ground cinnamon

1. In a mixing bowl, cream butter and sugar. Beat in vanilla. Combine flour and almonds; gradually add to creamed mixture.

2. Roll into 1-in. balls; shape into crescents. Place 2 in. apart on lightly greased baking sheets. Bake at 350° for 10-12 minutes or until set (do not brown). Combine sugar and cinnamon in a small bowl. Roll the warm cookies in cinnamon-sugar; cool on wire racks.

Yield: about 3-1/2 dozen.

Chocolate Pecan Thumbprints

Jim Ries
Milwaukee, Wisconsin

Every Christmas for over 30 years, I have rolled, cut, shaped and baked batches of cookies for family and friends. These melt-in-your-mouth morsels with a dollop of chocolate in the center are among my favorites.

1/2 cup plus 1 tablespoon butter, softened, *divided*
1/4 cup packed brown sugar
1 egg yolk
1 teaspoon vanilla extract
1 cup all-purpose flour
1 egg white, lightly beaten
3/4 cup finely chopped pecans
3/4 cup semisweet chocolate chips

1. In a mixing bowl, cream 1/2 cup butter and brown sugar. Beat in egg yolk and vanilla. Gradually add flour; mix well. Cover and refrigerate for 2 hours or until easy to handle.

2. Roll dough into 1-in. balls. Dip in egg white, then coat with pecans. Place 2 in. apart on greased baking sheets. Using the end of a wooden spoon handle, make a 1/2-in. indentation in the center of each ball. Bake at 325° for 10 minutes. Press again into indentations with the spoon handle. Bake 10-15 minutes longer or until pecans are golden brown. Remove to wire racks to cool.

3. In a microwave or heavy saucepan, melt the chocolate chips and remaining butter, stirring until smooth. Spoon into cooled cookies.

Yield: about 1-1/2 dozen.

Chocolate Cappuccino Cookies

Eleanor Senske
Rock Island, Illinois

A touch of coffee gives these cookies a mocha flavor. The corn syrup makes them chewy.

- 1 tablespoon instant coffee granules
- 1 tablespoon hot water
- 1 egg white
- 3/4 cup plus 1 tablespoon sugar, *divided*
- 1/4 cup canola oil
- 2 tablespoons corn syrup
- 2 teaspoons corn syrup
- 2 teaspoons vanilla extract
- 1-1/4 cups all-purpose flour
- 1/2 cup baking cocoa
- 1/4 teaspoon salt

1. In a small bowl, dissolve coffee granules in hot water. In a mixing bowl, combine the egg white, 3/4 cup sugar, oil, corn syrup, vanilla and coffee; beat until well blended. Combine the flour, cocoa and salt; gradually add to coffee mixture.

2. Roll into 1-in. balls. Place the balls 2 in. apart on ungreased baking sheets. Flatten to 1/4-in. thickness with a glass dipped in the remaining sugar. Bake at 350° for 5-7 minutes or until center is set. Remove to wire racks to cool. Store in an airtight container.

Yield: 3-1/2 dozen.

Butterscotch Snickerdoodles

Nancy Radenbaugh, White Lake, Michigan

This recipe is a combination of the traditional Snickerdoodle recipe and my mother's best spritz recipe. Everyone raves about this combination.

- 1 cup butter, softened
- 1/3 cup vegetable oil
- 1-1/4 cups sugar
- 1/3 cup confectioners' sugar
- 2 eggs
- 3 tablespoons plain yogurt
- 1-1/2 teaspoons almond extract
- 1/8 teaspoon lemon extract
- 3-1/2 cups all-purpose flour
- 1 cup whole wheat flour
- 1 teaspoon cream of tartar
- 1 teaspoon baking soda
- 1/2 teaspoon salt
- 1 cup butterscotch chips
- 1/2 cup chopped almonds
- Additional sugar

1. In a mixing bowl, beat the butter, oil and sugars. Add eggs, one at a time, beating well after each addition. Add yogurt and extracts. Combine the flours, cream of tartar, baking soda and salt; gradually add to the butter mixture. Stir in butterscotch chips and almonds.

2. Roll into 1-in. balls, then in sugar. Place 2 in. apart on ungreased baking sheets. Flatten with a fork dipped in sugar. Bake at 350° for 12-15 minutes or until lightly browned. Remove to wire racks to cool.

Yield: 8 dozen.

Chocolate Caramel Cookies

Melissa Vannoy
Childress, Texas

This is my favorite recipe for bake sales and bazaars. Each delightfully sweet chocolate cookie has a fun caramel surprise in the middle, thanks to Rolo candy. Dipped in pecans before baking, they look so nice that they sell in a hurry.

   1 **cup butter, softened**
   1 **cup plus 1 tablespoon sugar,** *divided*
   1 **cup packed brown sugar**
   2 **eggs**
   2 **teaspoons vanilla extract**
2-1/2 **cups all-purpose flour**
 3/4 **cup baking cocoa**
   1 **teaspoon baking soda**
   1 **cup chopped pecans,** *divided*
   1 **package (13 ounces) Rolo candies**

1. In a mixing bowl, cream butter, 1 cup sugar and brown sugar. Add eggs and vanilla; mix well. Combine flour, cocoa and baking soda; add to the creamed mixture and beat just until combined. Stir in 1/2 cup pecans.

2. Shape dough by tablespoonfuls around each candy. In a small bowl, combine remaining pecans and sugar; dip each cookie halfway. Place with nut side up on ungreased baking sheets.

3. Bake at 375° for 7-10 minutes or until top is slightly cracked. Cool for 3 minutes before removing to wire racks.

Yield: about 5 dozen.

Cream Filberts

Deanna Richter
Elmore, Minnesota

These cookies remind me of "mothball candy" I used to buy with dimes Grandma gave me. The fillbert, which is another name for hazelnut, is a nice crunchy surprise in the middle of the cookie.

   1 **cup shortening**
 3/4 **cup sugar**
   1 **egg**
   1 **teaspoon vanilla extract**
2-1/2 **cups all-purpose flour**
 1/2 **teaspoon baking powder**
 1/8 **teaspoon salt**
 3/4 **cup whole filberts** *or* **hazelnuts**

GLAZE:
   2 **cups confectioners' sugar**
   3 **tablespoons water**
   2 **teaspoons vanilla extract**
Granulated sugar

1. In a mixing bowl, cream shortening and sugar. Add egg and vanilla; mix well. Combine the dry ingredients and add to creamed mixture.

2. Roll heaping teaspoonfuls into balls; press a filbert into each and reshape so dough covers nut. Place on ungreased baking sheets. Bake at 375° for 12-15 minutes or until lightly browned. Remove to wire racks to cool completely.

3. Combine the confectioners' sugar, water and vanilla. Dip entire top of cookies into glaze, then roll in sugar.

Yield: about 5 dozen.

Coffee Bonbons

Leitzel Malzahn
Fox Point, Wisconsin

When I first sampled this unique cookie, I decided it was the best cookie I'd ever tasted! The coffee flavor and chocolate icing make it a delightful treat at buffets and church socials.

1 cup butter, softened
3/4 cup confectioners' sugar
1/2 teaspoon vanilla extract
1 tablespoon instant coffee granules
1-3/4 cups all-purpose flour

CHOCOLATE GLAZE:
1 tablespoon butter
1/2 ounce unsweetened chocolate
1 cup confectioners' sugar
2 tablespoons milk

1. In a mixing bowl, cream butter and sugar until light and fluffy. Add vanilla. Combine coffee and flour; stir into creamed mixture and mix well. Cover and refrigerate until easy to handle.

2. Roll into 3/4-in. balls. Place 2 in. apart on ungreased baking sheets. Bake at 350° for 18-20 minutes or until set. Remove to wire racks.

3. Meanwhile, for glaze, melt butter and chocolate together. Add melted mixture to the sugar along with milk; beat until smooth. Frost the cookies while still warm.

Yield: 5 dozen.

Angel Wings

R. Lane
Tenafly, New Jersey

The shape of these delicate cookies remind me of angel wings. They are a favorite at my house for the holidays.

1 cup cold butter, cubed
1-1/2 cups all-purpose flour
1/2 cup sour cream
10 tablespoons sugar, *divided*
1 tablespoon ground cinnamon, *divided*
Colored sugar, optional

1. In a bowl, cut butter into flour until the mixture resembles coarse crumbs. Stir in the sour cream. Turn onto a lightly floured surface; knead 6-8 times or until mixture holds together. Shape into four balls; flatten slightly. Wrap in plastic wrap; refrigerate for 4 hours or overnight.

2. Unwrap one ball. Sprinkle 2 tablespoons sugar on waxed paper; coat all sides of ball with sugar. Roll into a 12-in. x 5-in. rectangle between two sheets of waxed paper. Remove top sheet of waxed paper. Sprinkle dough with 3/4 teaspoon cinnamon. Lightly mark a line down the center of dough, making two 6-in. x 5-in. rectangles. Starting with a short side, roll up jelly-roll style to center mark; peel waxed paper away while rolling. Repeat with other side. Wrap; freeze for 30 minutes. Repeat three times.

3. Place remaining sugar or place colored sugar if desired on waxed paper. Cut rolls into 1/2-in. slices; dip each side into sugar. Place 2 in. apart on ungreased baking sheets. Bake at 375° for 12 minutes or until golden brown. Turn cookies; bake for 5-8 minutes. Remove to wire racks.

Yield: about 3 dozen.

Peppermint Snowballs

Judith Scholovich, Waukesha, Wisconsin

You'll smile in delight when you taste the surprise peppermint filling in these cookies. Topped with crushed peppermint candy, they make a great treat when served with hot cocoa.

1 cup butter, softened

1/2 cup confectioners' sugar

1 teaspoon vanilla extract

2-1/2 cups all-purpose flour

FILLING:

2 tablespoons cream cheese, softened

1 tablespoon milk

1/2 cup confectioners' sugar

2 tablespoons finely crushed peppermint candy *or* candy canes

1 drop red food coloring

TOPPING:

1/4 cup confectioners' sugar

6 tablespoons finely crushed peppermint candy *or* candy canes

1. In a mixing bowl, cream butter and sugar; add vanilla. Stir in flour; knead until mixed well. Reserve 1/2 cup of dough; shape remaining dough into 1-in. balls.

2. For filling, combine cream cheese and milk in a small bowl. Stir in sugar, candy and food coloring; mix well. Make a deep well in the center of each ball; fill with 1/4 teaspoon filling. Use reserved dough to cover filling. Reshape if necessary into smooth balls.

3. Place 2 in. apart on ungreased baking sheets. Bake at 350° for 12-14 minutes. Combine topping ingredients; roll cookies in mixture while still warm. Cool on wire racks.

Yield: about 4 dozen.

Scandinavian Pecan Cookies

Laurie Knoke
DeKalb, Illinois

We enjoyed these rich, buttery cookies at a bed-and-breakfast in Galena, Illinois, and the hostess was kind enough to share her simple recipe. The pretty nut-topped treats are so special you could give a home-baked batch as a gift.

1 cup butter, softened

3/4 cup packed brown sugar

1 egg, *separated*

2 cups all-purpose flour

1/2 cup finely chopped pecans

1. In a mixing bowl, cream butter, brown sugar and egg yolk. Gradually add flour.

2. Roll into 1-in. balls. In a small bowl, beat egg white. Dip balls in egg white, then roll in pecans. Place 2 in. apart on ungreased baking sheets; flatten slightly. Bake at 375° for 8-12 minutes or until edges are lightly browned. Remove to wire racks to cool.

Yield: 4-5 dozen.

Special Chocolate Treats

Mrs. Walter Max
Wabasha, Minnesota

I serve these lovely cookies to guests. They freeze well so you can keep some in the freezer and you'll always have a tasty treat to offer unexpected company.

3/4 cup butter, softened
3/4 cup packed brown sugar
1-1/2 teaspoons vanilla extract
1/2 teaspoon salt
1-3/4 cups all-purpose flour

FILLING/GLAZE:
1 cup (6 ounces) semisweet chocolate chips
1 tablespoon shortening
2/3 cup finely chopped pecans
1/2 cup sweetened condensed milk
1 teaspoon vanilla extract
1/8 teaspoon salt
1 tablespoon light corn syrup
1 teaspoon water

1. In a mixing bowl, cream butter and sugar until fluffy. Beat in vanilla and salt. Add flour; mix well. Cover and refrigerate.

2. For filling, melt the chocolate chips and shortening in a microwave or heavy saucepan until smooth. Remove from the heat; set aside 1/4 cup for glaze. To remaining chocolate, add pecans, milk, vanilla and salt; blend well. Cover and refrigerate until cool, about 15 minutes.

3. Place a 16-in. x 12-in. piece of foil in a greased baking sheet; lightly sprinkle with flour. Divide dough in half; place one portion on foil. Roll into a 14-in. x 5-in. rectangle. Spread half of the filling lengthwise on half of the dough to within 1/2 in. of edges. Using the foil, fold the dough over filling; seal edges. Repeat with the remaining dough and filling. Bake at 350° for 15-20 minutes or until golden brown. Cool on a wire rack for 10 minutes.

4. For glaze, warm reserved chocolate; stir in corn syrup and water. Spread over cookies. Cool completely. Cut widthwise into 3/4-in. strips.

Yield: about 3-1/2 dozen.

Buttery Almond Cookies

Elaine Anderson, Aliquippa, Pennsylvania

My husband loves these cookies. They have an old-fashioned flavor that goes well with a cup of tea. Plus they're simple to put together.

1 cup butter, softened
1 cup confectioners' sugar, *divided*
2 cups all-purpose flour
1 teaspoon vanilla extract
3/4 cup chopped almonds

1. In a mixing bowl, cream butter and 1/2 cup confectioners' sugar. Add flour and vanilla; mix well. Stir in almonds.

2. Shape into 1-in. balls. Place 2 in. apart on ungreased baking sheets. Bake at 350° for 13-16 minutes or until bottoms are golden brown and cookies are set. Cool for 1-2 minutes before removing to wire racks. Roll in remaining confectioners' sugar.

Yield: about 4 dozen.

Apple Cutout Sugar Cookies, p. 151

Finnish Pinwheels, p. 137

Shortbread Hearts, p. 147

Austrian Nut Cookies, p. 146

Cookie Cutter Delights

These fun-to-make cookies can by stylized to reflect any holiday, season or occasion. Just let your creativity loose as you decorate them. Or, simply frost these cookies or add a sprinkle of colored sugar for a quick finish.

Tips for Making Cutout Cookies

When handling the dough use a light touch; overhandling will cause the cookies to be tough. For easier handling, refrigerate the dough before rolling. This is especially true if the dough was made with butter rather than shortening.

Lightly dust the rolling pin and work surface with flour to prevent sticking. Working too much extra flour into the dough will result in tough cookies.

Roll out a portion of the dough at a time and keep the remaining dough in the refrigerator. Roll out from the center to the edge; keep a uniform thickness and check the thickness with a ruler. If the thickness of the dough is uneven, the cookies will bake unevenly. Thinner cookies will be crisp and may burn, while thicker cookies will be chewy.

To prevent the dough from sticking to the cookie cutter, dip the cutter in flour or spray it with nonstick cooking spray.

After the dough is rolled out, position the shapes from the cookie cutters close together to avoid having too many scraps. Save all the scraps and reroll them just once to prevent tough cookies.

To keep the cutouts intact before and after baking, transfer them to and from the baking sheet with a large metal spatula or pancake turner that supports the entire cutout.

Orange Sugar Rollouts

Margaret Hancock, Camp Verde, Arizona

When my children were young, we would bake and decorate these cookies every Christmas. Now I carry on the tradition with my grandchildren.

- 2/3 cup shortening
- 3/4 cup sugar
- 1/2 to 1 teaspoon grated orange peel
- 1 egg
- 4 teaspoons milk
- 1/2 teaspoon vanilla extract
- 2 cups all-purpose flour
- 1-1/2 teaspoons baking powder
- 1/4 teaspoon salt

FROSTING:
- 1/2 cup butter, softened
- 4 cups confectioners' sugar
- 1 teaspoon vanilla extract
- 1/2 teaspoon grated orange peel
- 2 to 4 tablespoons orange juice

Yellow food coloring, optional

1. In a mixing bowl, cream shortening, sugar and orange peel. Beat in egg, milk and vanilla. Combine flour, baking powder and salt; gradually add to the creamed mixture.

2. On a lightly floured surface, roll dough to 1/4-in. thickness. Cut with floured 2-1/2-in. cookie cutters.

3. Place 1 in. apart on greased baking sheets. Bake at 375° for 6-8 minutes or until lightly browned. Remove to wire racks to cool.

4. In a mixing bowl, combine butter, confectioners' sugar, vanilla, orange peel and enough orange juice to achieve spreading consistency. Add food coloring if desired. Frost cookies.

Yield: about 3-1/2 dozen.

Anise Cutout Cookies

Jerri Moror
Rio Rancho, New Mexico

Mother prepared these soft cookies for holidays and special-occasion meals. My seven siblings and I gobbled them up as fast as she made them. I still can't resist the cinnamon-sugar coating.

2 cups shortening
1 cup sugar
2 eggs
2 teaspoons aniseed
6 cups all-purpose flour
1 tablespoon baking powder
1 teaspoon salt
1/4 cup apple juice
1/2 cup sugar
1 teaspoon ground cinnamon

1. In a mixing bowl, cream shortening and sugar until fluffy; add eggs and aniseed. Combine flour, baking powder and salt; add to the creamed mixture. Add apple juice and mix well.

2. On a floured surface, knead until well blended, about 4-5 minutes. Roll dough to 1/2-in. thickness. Cut into 2-in. shapes.

3. Place 2 in. apart on greased baking sheets. Bake at 375° for 12-16 minutes or until lightly browned. Combine sugar and cinnamon; roll cookies in the mixture while still warm. Cool on wire racks.

Yield: about 5 dozen.

Finnish Pinwheels

(Pictured on page 135)
Ilona Barron, Ontonagon, Michigan

When my sister was hosting an exchange student from Finland, she served these cookies I'd made to her guest. The young lady instantly recognized what they were. So I know they're still being made in our ancestors' country!

FILLING:
1/2 pound pitted dried plums, chopped
1/2 pound pitted dates, chopped
1 cup boiling water
2 tablespoons sugar
1 tablespoon butter

PASTRY:
3 cups all-purpose flour
1 cup sugar
2 teaspoons baking powder
1/2 teaspoon salt
1 cup butter
1 egg, beaten
3 tablespoons cream
1 teaspoon vanilla extract

1. In a saucepan, combine plums, dates, water and sugar. Cook over low heat, stirring constantly, until thickened. Remove from the heat and stir in butter. Cool.

2. Meanwhile, in a mixing bowl, sift together flour, sugar, baking powder and salt. Cut in butter as for a pie pastry. Blend in egg, cream and vanilla. Form into two balls.

3. On a floured surface, roll one portion to 1/8-in. thickness. Cut into 2-in. squares. Place 2 in. apart on ungreased baking sheets. Make 1-in. slits in corners. Place 1/2 teaspoon filling in the center of each square. Bring every other corner up into center to form a pinwheel and press lightly. Repeat with remaining dough and filling. Bake at 325° for 12 minutes or until the points are light golden brown. Remove to wire racks to cool.

Yield: about 7 dozen.

Stained Glass Cutouts

Dixie Terry
Goreville, Illinois

These delicious and festive-looking cookies have a "stained glass" heart in the center.

- 1/2 cup butter, softened
- 3/4 cup sugar
- 2 eggs
- 1 teaspoon vanilla extract
- 2-1/3 cups all-purpose flour
- 1 teaspoon baking powder
- 1/3 cup crushed clear red hard candy
- 1 cup vanilla frosting, optional
- 4 drops red food coloring, optional

1. In a mixing bowl, cream the butter and sugar. Add the eggs, one at a time, beating well after each addition. Beat in vanilla. Combine the flour and baking powder; gradually add to creamed mixture. Cover and refrigerate for 3 hours or until easy to handle.

2. On a lightly floured surface, roll dough to 1/8-in. thickness. Cut with a floured 4-in. heart-shaped cookie cutter. Cut out centers with a floured 1-1/4-in. heart-shaped cookie cutter; set aside to reroll.

3. Place 1 in. apart on lightly greased foil-lined baking sheets. Fill centers with crushed candy. Bake at 375° for 7-9 minutes or until candy is melted and edges of cookies begin to brown. Cool completely on baking sheets.

4. Carefully peel cookies off foil. If desired, combine frosting and food coloring; pipe around edges.

Yield: about 1-1/2 dozen.

Chocolate Oatmeal Stars

Edna Hall, Aitkin, Minnesota

Fans of oatmeal cookies will love this variation that combines oats, chocolate and coconut. These star-shaped cookies "shine" wherever I take them!

- 2/3 cup shortening
- 1 cup sugar
- 1 egg
- 1 teaspoon vanilla extract
- 1/2 teaspoon almond extract
- 1 cup (6 ounces) semisweet chocolate chips, melted
- 1 cup all-purpose flour
- 1 teaspoon salt
- 1/2 teaspoon baking soda
- 1 cup quick-cooking oats
- 1 cup flaked coconut, finely chopped

Colored sugar *or* nonpareils

1. In a mixing bowl, cream shortening and sugar. Beat in egg and extracts. Stir in melted chocolate chips. Combine the flour, salt and baking soda; gradually add to the creamed mixture. Stir in oats and coconut. Cover and refrigerate for 2 hours or until easy to handle.

2. On a lightly floured surface, roll dough to 1/8-in. thickness. Cut with a floured 3-in. star-shaped cookie cutter.

3. Place 1 in. apart on ungreased baking sheets. Sprinkle with colored sugar or nonpareils. Bake at 350° for 7-9 minutes or until firm. Remove to wire racks to cool.

Yield: about 3 dozen.

Chewy Tangerine Cookies

Janyce Barstad, Anchorage, Alaska

This recipe represents my Scandinavian heritage. The blend of spices and hint of tangerine have made these cookies a favorite to serve with a mug of hot coffee.

1/2 cup butter, softened
1/2 cup sugar
1/2 cup dark corn syrup
1 egg
1 tablespoon grated tangerine *or* orange peel
2-1/4 cups all-purpose flour
1/2 teaspoon baking soda
1/2 teaspoon ground cloves
1/2 teaspoon ground nutmeg
1/4 teaspoon salt

1. In a mixing bowl, cream butter and sugar. In a small saucepan, bring corn syrup to a boil; gradually add to the creamed mixture. Beat in egg and tangerine peel. Combine flour, baking soda, cloves, nutmeg and salt; gradually add to the creamed mixture. Cover and refrigerate for 2 hours or until easy to handle.

2. On a lightly floured surface, roll dough to 1/4-in. thickness. Cut with floured 2-1/2-in. cookie cutters.

3. Place 1 in. apart on greased baking sheets. Bake at 375° for 8-10 minutes or until edges are firm. Remove to wire racks to cool.

Yield: about 3 dozen.

Frosted Butter Cutouts

Stephanie McKinnon
West Valley City, Utah

With their soft tender insides, these cookies quickly disappear from the cookie jar. Vanilla pudding mix gives the frosting a velvety texture and fabulous flavor.

1/2 cup butter, softened
1 cup sugar
1 egg
1/2 cup sour cream
1 teaspoon vanilla extract
3-1/2 cups all-purpose flour
1 teaspoon baking soda
1/2 teaspoon salt

FROSTING:
1/4 cup cold milk
3 tablespoons instant vanilla pudding mix
1/4 cup butter, softened
2-1/2 cups confectioners' sugar
1 teaspoon vanilla extract
Food coloring, optional

1. In a mixing bowl, cream butter and sugar. Beat in egg, sour cream and vanilla. Combine flour, baking soda and salt; gradually add to creamed mixture. Cover and refrigerate for 1 hour or until easy to handle.

2. On a work surface sprinkled heavily with confectioners' sugar, roll dough to 1/8-in. thickness. Cut with floured 2-1/2-in. cookie cutters.

3. Place 1 in. apart on greased baking sheets. Bake at 375° for 8-10 minutes or until lightly browned. Immediately remove to wire racks to cool.

4. For frosting, combine milk and pudding mix until smooth; set aside. In a mixing bowl, cream butter. Beat in pudding mixture. Gradually add confectioners' sugar, vanilla and food coloring if desired; beat on high speed until light and fluffy. Frost cookies.

Yield: 5-1/2 dozen.

Lemon Nut Star Cookies

Taste of Home Test Kitchen, Greendale, Wisconsin

Family and friends will say "Hooray!" when they see these star-spangled cookies. Make these treats throughout the year by using different cookie cutters and food coloring.

1 cup butter, softened
2 cups confectioners' sugar
2 eggs
2 tablespoons lemon juice
4 teaspoons half-and-half cream
2 teaspoons grated lemon peel
3-1/4 cups all-purpose flour
1/2 cup ground almonds
1/2 teaspoon baking soda
1/8 teaspoon salt

GLAZE:
2 cups confectioners' sugar
1/4 cup light corn syrup
2 tablespoons lemon juice
Red and blue food coloring

1. In a large mixing bowl, cream butter and confectioners' sugar until light and fluffy. Add eggs, one at a time, beating well after each addition. Beat in the lemon juice, cream and lemon peel. Combine the flour, almonds, baking soda and salt; gradually add to creamed mixture. Cover and refrigerate for 2 hours or until easy to handle.

2. On a lightly floured surface, roll dough to 1/8-in. thickness. Cut with a floured star-shaped cookie cutter.

3. Place 1 in. apart on ungreased baking sheets. Bake at 350° for 8-10 minutes or until lightly browned. Remove to wire racks to cool.

4. For glaze, in a small bowl, combine the confectioners' sugar, corn syrup and lemon juice until smooth. Divide into three bowls. Tint one portion red and one portion blue; leave the third portion plain. Spread over the cookies; let stand overnight for glaze to set.

Yield: about 5-1/2 dozen.

Coffee Shortbread

Dixie Terry
Marion, Illinois

You'll be remembered for these cookies when you serve them for a morning coffee or at a gathering. Melted chips drizzled on top these easy-to-do cookies cookies look fancy, but they're so easy to make.

1 cup butter, softened
1/2 cup packed brown sugar
1/4 cup sugar
2 tablespoons instant coffee granules
2 cups all-purpose flour
1/4 teaspoon salt
1/2 cup semisweet chocolate chips, melted
1/2 cup vanilla *or* white chips, melted

1. In a mixing bowl, cream butter, sugars and coffee granules. Gradually beat in flour and salt.

2. On a lightly floured surface, roll dough to 1/4-in. thickness. Cut with floured 2-in. to 3-in. cookie cutters.

3. Place 2 in. apart on ungreased baking sheets. Bake at 300° for 20-22 minutes or until set. Remove to wire racks to cool. Drizzle with melted chips.

Yield: about 5 dozen.

Feathered Friend Cookies

Taste of Home Test Kitchen
Greendale, Wisconsin

The sky's the limit when you fix a flock of these tempting treats. Let your imagination soar as egg yolk glaze transforms plain sugar cookies into fanciful winged wonders.

1/2 cup butter, softened
1/4 cup shortening
1 cup sugar
2 eggs
2 tablespoons sour cream
1 teaspoon vanilla extract
1/4 teaspoon almond extract
2-3/4 cups all-purpose flour
1-1/2 teaspoons baking powder
1 teaspoon salt

GLAZE:
4 to 6 egg yolks
1 to 1-1/2 teaspoons water
Paste food coloring

1. In a mixing bowl, cream butter, shortening and sugar. Beat in eggs, sour cream and extracts. Combine flour, baking powder and salt; add to the creamed mixture and mix well. Cover and refrigerate for about 1 hour or until easy to handle.

2. On a floured surface, roll dough to 1/4-in. thickness. Cut with a floured 4-in. bird cookie cutter.

3. Place 1 in. apart on ungreased baking sheets. For each color of glaze, beat 1 egg yolk and 1/4 teaspoon water in a custard cup; tint with paste food coloring. Decorate cookies as desired (see tip box below).

4. Bake at 375° for 7-9 minutes or until edges are lightly browned. Cool for 1-2 minutes before removing to wire racks.

Yield: 3-1/2 dozen.

"Painting" with Egg Yolks

In a small bowl combine egg yolk, water and food coloring. With a new small paintbrush, decorate the unbaked cookies, then bake as directed. If the glaze thickens, stir in a few drops of water.

Lemon Leaves

Karen Minthorne
Rancho Cucamonga, California

Sugar, chopped pistachios and lemon peel sprinkled on top of these cookies make them extra special. Feel free to use whatever cookie cutters you have on hand.

1/2 cup butter, softened

1-1/3 cups sugar, *divided*

1 egg

1 tablespoon half-and-half cream

1 teaspoon lemon extract

2-1/4 cups all-purpose flour

3 teaspoons baking powder

1/2 teaspoon salt

2 egg yolks

1 teaspoon water

1/4 cup finely chopped pistachios

1-1/2 teaspoons grated lemon peel

1. In a mixing bowl, cream butter and 1 cup of sugar. Beat in egg, cream and extract. Combine the flour, baking powder and salt; gradually add to the creamed mixture. Cover and refrigerate for 2 hours or until easy to handle.

2. In a small bowl, beat egg yolks and water. In another bowl, combine the pistachios, lemon peel and remaining sugar.

3. On a lightly floured surface, roll dough to 1/8-in. thickness. Cut with a floured 2-1/2-in. leaf-shaped cookie cutter.

4. Place 1 in. apart on ungreased baking sheets. Brush with egg yolk mixture; sprinkle with pistachio mixture. Bake at 350° for 6-8 minutes or until edges are set (do not brown). Remove to wire racks to cool.

Yield: about 4-1/2 dozen.

Easter Sugar Cookies

Julie Brunette, Green Bay, Wisconsin

Cream cheese contributes to the rich taste of these melt-in-your-mouth cookies. They have such nice flavor, you can skip the frosting and sprinkle them with colored sugar for a change.

1 cup butter, softened

1 package (3 ounces) cream cheese, softened

1 cup sugar

1 egg yolk

1/2 teaspoon vanilla extract

1/4 teaspoon almond extract

2-1/4 cups all-purpose flour

1/2 teaspoon salt

1/4 teaspoon baking soda

Tinted frosting *or* colored sugar

1. In a mixing bowl, cream butter, cream cheese and sugar. Beat in egg yolk and extracts. Combine the flour, salt and baking soda; gradually add to creamed mixture. Cover and refrigerate for 3 hours or until easy to handle.

2. On a lightly floured surface, roll out dough to 1/8-in. thickness. Cut with a floured 2-1/2-in. egg- or chick-shaped cookie cutter.

3. Place 1 in. apart on ungreased baking sheets. Bake at 375° for 8-10 minutes or until edges begin to brown. Cool for 2 minutes before removing to wire racks. Decorate as desired.

Yield: 4 dozen.

Chocolate Orange Cookies

Ruth Rumple, Rockford, Ohio

My three sisters like the combination of chocolate and orange as much as I do, so we all really enjoy these beautiful cookies.

1 cup butter, softened
3/4 cup sugar, *divided*
1 egg
1 teaspoon vanilla extract
2-1/2 cups all-purpose flour
1/2 teaspoon salt
1/4 cup finely grated orange peel
1 cup (6 ounces) semisweet chocolate chips, melted

1. In a mixing bowl, cream butter and 1/2 cup sugar. Add egg and vanilla. Gradually add flour and salt; mix well. Cover and refrigerate for 15 minutes.

2. On a floured surface, roll dough to 1/4-in. thickness. Cut with a floured 2-in. cookie cutter or shape into 2-in. x 1-in. rectangles.

3. Place 2 in. apart on ungreased baking sheets. Combine orange peel and remaining sugar; spread over cookies. Bake at 350° for 14-16 minutes or until the edges just begin to brown. Remove to wire racks to cool completely. Decorate cookies with melted chocolate.

Yield: about 3 dozen.

Vanilla Butter Rollouts

Colleen Sickman
Charles City, Iowa

Even cooks who normally shy away from rolled cookies can make these with confidence. The dough is a breeze to work with after just 30 minutes of chilling.

1-1/2 cups butter, softened
1-1/2 cups sugar
2 eggs
3 teaspoons vanilla extract
4 cups all-purpose flour
1 teaspoon baking soda
1 teaspoon cream of tartar
1 teaspoon salt

FROSTING:
6 tablespoons butter, softened
3 cups confectioners' sugar
1/4 cup milk
3 teaspoons vanilla extract
Colored frosting and sugar, optional

1. In a large mixing bowl, cream butter and sugar. Add eggs, one at a time, beating well after each addition. Beat in vanilla. Combine flour, baking soda, cream of tartar and salt; gradually add to the creamed mixture. Cover and refrigerate for 30 minutes or until easy to handle.

2. On a lightly floured surface, roll dough to 1/4-in. thickness. Cut with floured 2-1/2-in. cookie cutters.

3. Place 2 in. apart on ungreased baking sheets. Bake at 350° for 8-10 minutes or until lightly browned. Remove to wire racks to cool.

4. For frosting, combine butter, confectioners' sugar, milk and vanilla in a mixing bowl; beat until smooth. Spread or drizzle over cooled cookies. Decorate with colored frosting and sugar if desired.

Yield: about 7 dozen.

Buttery Walnut Cutouts

Grance Simons, Orange City, Florida

Chopped walnuts add flavor and crunch to a typical butter cookie plus give them a pretty golden color.

1 cup butter, softened
3/4 cup sugar
1 egg
1 teaspoon vanilla extract
2-1/2 cups all-purpose flour
2 teaspoons baking powder
1/2 teaspoon salt
1 cup chopped walnuts

1. In a mixing bowl, cream butter and sugar. Beat in egg and vanilla. Combine flour, baking powder and salt; gradually add to the creamed mixture. Stir in the walnuts. Cover and refrigerate for 1 hour or until easy to handle.

2. On a floured surface, roll dough to 1/8-in. thickness. Cut with floured 2-in. cookie cutters.

3. Place 1 in. apart on ungreased baking sheets. Bake at 375° for 6-8 minutes or until edges are golden brown. Remove to wire racks to cool.

Yield: 4 dozen.

Frosted Spice Cookies

Debbie Hurlbert
Howard, Ohio

My husband's grandmother always had these cookies for him when he visited. Today, he enjoys them more than ever—and so I do.

1 cup butter, softened
1 cup sugar
1 cup molasses
1 egg
1 cup buttermilk
6 cups all-purpose flour
1 tablespoon baking powder
1 teaspoon baking soda
1 teaspoon ground cinnamon
1 teaspoon ground ginger
1/2 teaspoon salt
1 cup chopped walnuts
1 cup golden raisins
1 cup chopped dates

FROSTING:
3-3/4 cups confectioners' sugar
1/3 cup orange juice
2 tablespoons butter, melted

1. In a large mixing bowl, cream butter and sugar. Add molasses, egg and buttermilk; mix well. Combine the flour, baking powder, baking soda, cinnamon, ginger and salt; gradually add to creamed mixture. Stir in walnuts, raisins and dates. Cover and refrigerate for 2 hours until easy to handle.

2. On a floured surface, roll dough to 1/4-in. thickness. Cut with a floured 2-1/2-in.-round cookie cutter.

3. Place 2 in. apart on greased baking sheets. Bake at 350° for 12-15 minutes. Remove to wire racks to cool.

4. For frosting, beat all ingredients in a small bowl until smooth. Frost cookies.

Yield: 5-6 dozen.

Handprint Turkey Cookies

Pat Thompson
Sun Prairie, Wisconsin

Creating these tom treats is just as much fun as gobbling them up! When preparing this delicious cookie recipe years ago, I used to help our children cut out their own hand shapes from the rolled dough. Today they're all grown, but they still remember how much they enjoyed "baking" their hands!

 1/4 **cup shortening**
 1/4 **cup butter, softened**
   1 **cup sugar**
   1 **egg**
   1 **teaspoon vanilla extract**
2-2/3 **cups all-purpose flour**
   1 **teaspoon baking powder**
 1/2 **teaspoon baking soda**
 1/2 **teaspoon salt**
 1/4 **teaspoon ground nutmeg**
 1/2 **cup sour cream**

GLAZE:
   5 **cups confectioners' sugar**
   3 to 4 **tablespoons water**
2-1/4 **teaspoons light corn syrup**
 3/4 **teaspoon vanilla extract**
Red, yellow, orange, green and brown gel food coloring

1. In a mixing bowl, cream shortening, butter and sugar. Beat in the egg and vanilla. Combine the flour, baking powder, baking soda, salt and nutmeg, then add to the creamed mixture alternately with sour cream. Cover and refrigerate for 2 hours or until easy to handle.

2. Use a hand-shaped cookie cutter or trace a child's hand onto a piece of cardboard with pencil and cut out for a pattern.

3. On a well-floured surface, roll out dough to a 1/2-in. thickness. Either use a sharp knife to cut around the cardboard hand pattern in dough or use cookie cutter to cut out hand shapes.

4. Place 2 in. apart on ungreased baking sheets. Bake at 425° for 7-9 minutes or until lightly browned. Remove to wire racks to cool.

5. In a mixing bowl, combine the glaze ingredients and beat until smooth. Set aside 1 teaspoon of white glaze for eyes. Place 1/4 cup of glaze into each of four bowls. Tint one red, one yellow, one orange and one green. Place 1 tablespoon of glaze in another bowl and tint dark brown. Tint the remaining glaze light brown.

6. Frost the palm and thumb of each cookie light brown. Frost each finger a different color, using red, yellow, orange and green. Place remaining yellow glaze in a pastry or plastic bag. Cut a small hole in the corner of bag. Pipe a beak on each thumb.

7. In the same way, use dark brown glaze to pipe a pupil in the center of each eye and to pipe wings in the center of each cookie. Use remaining red glaze to pipe wattles on each thumb. Let dry completely.

Yield: about 3 dozen.

Sour Cream Cutout Cookies

Marlene Jackson
Kingsburg, California

These soft cookies make a comforting evening snack. They have a delicious, delicate flavor and cake-like texture.

1 cup butter, softened
1-1/2 cups sugar
3 eggs
1 cup (8 ounces) sour cream
2 teaspoons vanilla extract
3-1/2 cups all-purpose flour
2 teaspoons baking powder
1 teaspoon baking soda

FROSTING:
1/3 cup butter, softened
2 cups confectioners' sugar
2 to 3 tablespoons milk
1-1/2 teaspoons vanilla extract
1/4 teaspoon salt

1. In a mixing bowl, cream butter and sugar. Beat in eggs. Add sour cream and vanilla; mix well. Combine flour, baking powder and baking soda; add to the creamed mixture and mix well. Cover and refrigerate for at least 2 hours or overnight.

2. On a heavily floured surface, roll dough to 1/4-in. thickness. Cut with a floured 3-in. cutter.

3. Place 2 in. apart on lightly greased baking sheets. Bake at 350° for 10-12 minutes or until cookie springs back when lightly touched. Remove to wire racks to cool. Mix all frosting ingredients until smooth; spread over cooled cookies.

Yield: about 3-1/2 dozen.

Austrian Nut Cookies

(Pictured on page 135)
Marianne Weber, South Beach, Oregon

These are my family's favorite Christmas cookies. If you arrange the slivered almonds in pinwheel fashion, the cookie looks just like a poinsettia.

1 cup all-purpose flour
2/3 cup finely chopped almonds
1/3 cup sugar
1/2 cup cold butter
1/2 cup raspberry jam

FROSTING:
1 square (1 ounce) unsweetened chocolate, melted and cooled
1/3 cup confectioners' sugar
2 tablespoons butter, softened
Slivered almonds

1. In a bowl, combine the flour, chopped almonds and sugar. Cut in butter until mixture resembles coarse crumbs. Form into a ball; cover and chill for 1 hour.

2. On a floured surface, roll dough to 1/8-in. thickness. Cut with a floured 2-in. round cutter.

3. Place 1 in. apart on greased baking sheets. Bake at 375° for 7-10 minutes or until the edges are lightly browned. Remove to wire racks to cool completely.

4. Spread 1/2 teaspoon jam on half of the cookies; top with another cookie. For frosting, combine chocolate, confectioners' sugar and butter. Spread on tops of cookies. Decorate with slivered almonds.

Yield: about 1-1/2 dozen.

Shortbread Hearts

(Pictured on page 135)
Barbara Birk, St. George, Utah

These flaky cookies melt in your mouth. Dipped in chocolate, they look so festive. If you have time, it's nice to write names on the hearts with white icing.

2 cups all-purpose flour
1/2 cup sugar
Dash salt
1 cup cold butter
1 tablespoon cold water
1 teaspoon almond extract
1/2 pound dark chocolate candy coating, melted

1. In a large bowl, combine flour, sugar and salt; cut in butter until mixture resembles coarse crumbs. Stir in water and extract until mixture forms a ball.

2. On a lightly floured surface, roll out dough to 1/4-in. thickness. Cut with a floured 2-1/2-in. cookie cutter. Place 1 in. apart on ungreased baking sheets. Cover and refrigerate for 30 minutes.

3. Bake at 325° for 13-16 minutes or until edges are lightly browned. Cool for 2 minutes before removing to wire racks. Dip one side of cookies in candy coating; place on waxed paper until set.

Yield: about 2 dozen.

Decorated Easter Cookies

Sue Gronholz
Columbus, Wisconsin

The idea to hang Easter egg-shaped cookies from a tree came from hanging gingerbread cookies on a Christmas tree. You can use the tree as a decoration, then at the end of the meal, kids and adults alike can help themselves to dessert.

1 cup butter, softened
1 cup sugar
2 eggs
1/4 cup cold water
1 teaspoon vanilla extract
3-1/4 cups all-purpose flour
1 teaspoon baking soda
1/2 teaspoon salt
GLAZE:
2 cups confectioners' sugar
1/4 cup water
2 tablespoons light corn syrup
Food coloring
Decorator's gel

1. In a mixing bowl, cream butter and sugar. Add eggs, water and vanilla. Combine flour, baking soda and salt; gradually add to creamed mixture. Cover and refrigerate for several hours.

2. On a lightly floured surface, roll dough to 1/4-inch thickness. Cut with a floured egg-shaped cookie cutter (or cutters with other Easter themes such as chicks and rabbits). Make a hole with a plastic straw or toothpick in the top of at least 27 cookies.

3. Place 2 in. apart on greased baking sheets. Bake at 350° for 8-10 minutes or until light golden brown. Remove to wire racks to cool completely.

4. For glaze, combine confectioners' sugar, water and corn syrup until smooth. Depending on how many colors are desired, divide glaze into several small bowls and tint with food coloring. Using a small brush and stirring glaze often, brush glaze on cookies (or leave some plain if desired). Allow glazed cookies to set for at least 1 hour.

5. Add designs with tinted glaze or decorator's gel, referring to photo above for ideas. Allow to set.

Yield: 7-8 dozen (2-1/2-inch cookies).

Cherry-Filled Cookies

Mrs. Delbert Benton, Guthrie Center, Iowa

The luscious cherry filling peeking out of these rounds is just a hint of how scrumptious they are. Using a doughnut cutter to shape each cookie top really speeds up the process.

- 1/2 cup shortening
- 1 cup packed brown sugar
- 1/2 cup sugar
- 2 eggs
- 1/4 cup buttermilk
- 1 teaspoon vanilla extract
- 3-1/2 cups all-purpose flour
- 1/2 teaspoon salt
- 1/2 teaspoon baking soda
- 1 can (21 ounces) cherry pie filling

1. In a mixing bowl, cream shortening and sugars. Add eggs, buttermilk and vanilla; mix well. Combine flour, salt and baking soda; gradually add to creamed mixture and mix well. Cover and refrigerate for 1 hour or until firm.

2. Divide dough in half. On a floured surface, roll each portion to 1/8-in. thickness. Cut with a floured 2-3/4-in. round cutter.

3. Place half of circles 2 in. apart on greased baking sheets; top each with a heaping teaspoon of pie filling. Cut holes in the center of remaining circles with a floured 1-in. round cutter; place over filled circles. Seal edges.

4. Bake at 375° for 10 minutes or until golden brown. Remove to wire racks to cool.

Yield: about 3 dozen.

Surprise Sugar Stars

Joyce Berry
Sandpoint, Idaho

I make dozens of these buttery cutout cookies at holiday time. The basic sugar cookie recipe is my mother's and I came up with the sweet "surprise" inside.

- 1 cup butter, softened
- 1-1/4 cups sugar
- 2 eggs
- 1 teaspoon vanilla extract
- 4 cups all-purpose flour
- 2 teaspoons baking powder
- 2 teaspoons ground nutmeg
- 1 teaspoon baking soda
- 1/2 teaspoon salt
- 2/3 cup buttermilk
- 1 can (21 ounces) cherry pie filling

ICING:
- 2 cups confectioners' sugar
- 2 to 3 tablespoons milk
- 1/2 teaspoon almond extract

Colored sugar, optional

1. In a mixing bowl, cream the butter and sugar. Add the eggs, one at a time, beating well after each addition. Stir in the vanilla. Combine the dry ingredients; add to the creamed mixture alternately with buttermilk. Cover and refrigerate for 2-3 hours or until easy to handle.

2. On a floured surface, roll dough to 1/4-in. thickness. Cut with a floured 2-in star cookie cutter or the cutter of your choice. Place half of the stars on ungreased baking sheets. Spoon 1-1/2 teaspoonfuls of pie filling into the centers of each. Top with remaining stars. Pinch edges to seal; cut a small slit in top of each cookie.

3. Bake at 350° for 12-15 minutes or until lightly browned. Remove to wire racks to cool.

4. For icing, combine confectioners' sugar, milk and extract in a bowl; whisk until smooth. Spread over cooled cookies. Sprinkle with colored sugar if desired.

Yield: 4 dozen.

Smooth Sailing Sugar Cookies

Martha Conaway
Pataskala, Ohio

With a fresh breeze, my longtime-favorite sugar cookie recipe got under way on a new track. I cut out sailboats and frisky fish, frosting them brightly for the nautical gathering. My guests ate their limit!

      1 cup butter, softened
    3/4 cup sugar
      1 egg
      2 tablespoons milk
  1-1/2 teaspoons vanilla extract
      3 cups all-purpose flour
      1 teaspoon baking powder
    1/2 teaspoon salt

FROSTING:
      1 cup confectioners' sugar
    1/2 teaspoon vanilla *or*
          almond extract
    1/4 teaspoon salt
      1 to 2 tablespoons milk
Food coloring, optional

1. In a mixing bowl, cream butter and sugar. Add egg, milk and vanilla. Combine the flour, baking powder and salt; gradually add to the creamed mixture. Cover and refrigerate for 1 hour or until easy to handle.

2. On a lightly floured surface, roll dough to 1/8-in. thickness. Cut with floured cookie cutters of your choice.

3. Place 2 in. apart on greased baking sheets. Bake at 375° for 5-8 minutes or until lightly browned. Remove to wire racks to cool.

4. In a mixing bowl, combine sugar, extract, salt and enough milk to achieve spreading consistency. Add food coloring if desired. Frost cookies; decorate as desired.

Yield: about 4 dozen.

Cottage Cheese Cookies

These delicate, puffy turnover cookies are sparked with raspberry and almond—delightful with afternoon tea.

Linda Hobbs, Albion, New York

      2 cups sifted all-purpose
          flour
      1 cup cold butter
      1 cup plus 2 tablespoons
          small-curd cottage cheese
Raspberry jam

GLAZE:
      1 cup confectioners' sugar
    1/8 teaspoon almond extract
Milk

1. Place flour in a medium mixing bowl; cut in butter until crumbly. Blend in cottage cheese until mixture forms a ball. Cover and chill for 1 hour.

2. On a floured surface, roll dough to 1/8-in. thickness. Cut with a floured 3-in. round cutter. Place a level 1/4 teaspoon of jam in center of each cookie. Moisten edges and fold in half; seal tightly with a fork.

3. Place 2 in. apart on lightly greased baking sheets; prick tops with fork. Bake at 400° for 15 minutes or until lightly browned. Remove to wire racks to cool.

4. For glaze, mix sugar, extract and enough milk to make thin spreading consistency; drizzle on cooled cookies.

Yield: 4 dozen.

Frosted Valentine Cookies

Marcy Cella
L'Anse, Michigan

Sharing delicious sweets has long been the way to show affection. I demonstrate my love every Valentine's Day by making batches of these buttery cookies.

- 2 cups butter, softened
- 1 cup confectioners' sugar
- 4 cups all-purpose flour
- 2 cups quick-cooking oats
- 2 teaspoons vanilla extract
- 1/2 teaspoon almond extract
- 1/2 teaspoon salt
- 1/2 pound semisweet *or* milk chocolate confectionery coating, melted

Confectioners' sugar icing, optional

1. In a mixing bowl, cream butter and sugar. Add flour, oats, extracts and salt; mix well.

2. On a lightly floured surface, roll dough to 1/4-in thickness. Cut with a floured 3-in. heart-shaped cookie cutter.

3. Place 2 in. apart on ungreased baking sheets. Bake at 350° for 12-15 minutes. While cookies are warm, spread melted chocolate on tops. Cool on wire racks. Using a pastry bag, decorate with confectioners' sugar icing if desired.

Yield: 3-1/2-dozen.

Lime Hazelnut Zingers

Karen Morrell, Canby, Oregon

The tangy lime and mellow hazelnut flavors are a unique combination that sets these apart from other cutout cookies. When you serve them, they won't last long!

- 1 cup butter, softened
- 1/2 cup sugar
- 1/4 cup lime juice
- 2 teaspoons grated lime peel
- 1 teaspoon vanilla extract
- 2-1/4 cups all-purpose flour
- 3/4 cup finely chopped hazelnuts

FROSTING:
- 1 package (3 ounces) cream cheese, softened
- 3/4 cup confectioners' sugar
- 2 teaspoons lime juice *or* water
- 1/2 teaspoon vanilla extract
- 1 to 2 drops green food coloring, optional

1. In a mixing bowl, cream butter and sugar. Add lime juice, peel and vanilla. Gradually add flour. Stir in hazelnuts. Cover and refrigerate for 1 hour or until easy to handle.

2. On a lightly floured surface, roll out dough to 1/4-in. thickness. Cut with a floured 2-in. cookie cutter.

3. Place 1 in. apart on ungreased baking sheets. Bake at 350° for 10-12 minutes or until the edges are lightly browned. Remove to wire racks to cool completely.

4. In a small mixing bowl, combine the frosting ingredients; beat until smooth. Transfer to a resealable plastic bag. Cut a small hole in a corner of the bag; drizzle frosting over cookies. Store in an airtight container.

Yield: 4 dozen.

Apple Cutout Sugar Cookies

(Pictured on page 134)
Marlys Benning, Wellsburg, Iowa

Not only are these pretty cookies fun to serve, but they bake up delicate and flaky and taste wonderful. Even the dough is a treat to work with—so easy to roll out and cut.

1-1/2 cups confectioners' sugar
1 cup butter, softened
1 egg
1-1/2 teaspoons vanilla extract
2-1/4 cups all-purpose flour
1 teaspoon baking soda
1 teaspoon cream of tartar
FROSTING:
2 cups confectioners' sugar
1/4 cup light corn syrup
2 tablespoons water
Red and green food coloring

1. In a large mixing bowl, combine the first seven ingredients in order given. Cover and refrigerate dough for 2-3 hours or until easy to handle.

2. On a lightly floured surface, roll dough into 1/4-in. thickness. Cut with a floured apple-shaped cookie cutter.

3. Place 2 in. apart on greased baking sheets. Bake at 375° for 7-8 minutes or until lightly browned. Remove to wire racks to cool.

4. For frosting, combine sugar, corn syrup and water in a small bowl. Transfer three-fourths of the frosting into another bowl; add red food coloring for apples. Add green food coloring to remaining frosting for stems. Frost cookies. Allow to sit overnight for frosting to set.

Yield: 4 dozen.

Spiced Cherry Bells

Peggy Graving
Butte, Montana

I always bake up a batch of these cookies for the dessert buffet I host on Christmas Eve.

1 cup butter, softened
1-1/4 cups packed brown sugar
1/4 cup dark corn syrup
1 egg
1 tablespoon heavy whipping cream
3-1/4 cups all-purpose flour
1 teaspoon ground ginger
1/2 teaspoon instant coffee granules
1/2 teaspoon baking soda
1/2 teaspoon salt
FILLING:
1/3 cup packed brown sugar
3 tablespoons maraschino cherry juice
1 tablespoon butter, softened
1-1/2 cups finely chopped pecans
14 maraschino cherries, quartered

1. In a mixing bowl, cream butter and brown sugar. Beat in corn syrup, egg and cream. Combine dry ingredients; gradually add to the creamed mixture and mix well. Cover and refrigerate for 2-4 hours or overnight.

2. On a lightly floured surface, roll dough to 1/8-in. thickness. Cut with a floured 2-1/2-in.-round cookie cutter.

3. Place 2 in. apart on ungreased baking sheets. In a bowl, combine the first three filling ingredients; mix well. Stir in pecans. Place 1/2 teaspoon of filling in the center of each cookie. Shape into a bell by folding edges of dough to meet over filling; pinch edges together. Place a piece of cherry at open end of each bell for clapper.

4. Bake at 350° for 12-15 minutes or until golden brown. Immediately remove to wire racks to cool.

Yield: about 4-1/2 dozen.

Lemon Cutouts

Bonnie Lytle
Coal Township, Pennsylvania

My grandmother passed away when I was 5 years old, so I treasure this recipe of hers. Grated lemon peel adds a refreshing flavor that makes these cookies stand out from other butter cookies.

1	cup butter, softened
1-1/4	cups sugar
2	eggs
2	teaspoons vanilla extract
3-1/2	cups all-purpose flour
2	teaspoons baking powder
1/2	teaspoon grated lemon peel

Yellow colored sugar, optional

1. In a mixing bowl, cream the butter and sugar. Add the eggs, one at a time, beating well after each addition. Beat in vanilla. Combine the flour, baking powder and lemon peel; gradually add to the creamed mixture. Cover and refrigerate for 1 hour or until easy to handle.

2. On a lightly floured surface, roll dough to 1/8-in. thickness. Cut with floured 2-1/2-in. cookie cutters.

3. Place 1 in. apart on ungreased baking sheets. Sprinkle with colored sugar if desired. Bake at 350° for 8-10 minutes or until golden brown. Remove to wire racks to cool.

Yield: about 6 dozen.

Shamrock Cookies

Edna Hoffman
Hebron, Indiana

A handy cookie cutter shapes these sensation sweets. With a hint of mint flavor, they're especially yummy.

1	cup shortening
1	cup confectioners' sugar
1	egg
1	teaspoon peppermint extract
2-1/2	cups all-purpose flour
1	teaspoon salt

Green paste food coloring
Green colored sugar, optional

1. In a mixing bowl, cream the shortening and confectioners' sugar. Beat in the egg and extract. Add flour and salt; mix well. Tint with food coloring; mix well. Cover and refrigerate for 1 hour or until easy to handle.

2. On a lightly floured surface, roll dough to 1/4-in. thickness. Cut with a floured 2-in. shamrock cookie cutter.

3. Place 1 in. apart on ungreased baking sheets. Sprinkle with colored sugar if desired. Bake at 375° for 10-12 minutes or until edges are lightly browned. Cool for 1 minute before removing to wire racks.

Yield: 3 dozen.

Old-Fashioned Raisin Cookies

Darlene Markel
Stayton, Oregon

My mother has been making these morsels for over 40 years, much to the delight of our family. The fruit-filled sugar cookies will please any sweet tooth. They disappear quickly!

- 1/2 cup sugar
- 1-1/2 teaspoons cornstarch
- 1/4 teaspoon ground cinnamon
- 1 cup chopped dates
- 1/2 cup raisins
- 1/2 cup water

DOUGH:
- 1 cup butter, softened
- 2 cups sugar
- 3 eggs
- 1 teaspoon vanilla extract
- 4 cups all-purpose flour
- 1/2 teaspoon salt

1. In a saucepan, combine the first six ingredients. Cook and stir over medium heat until thickened and bubbly. Cool.

2. In a mixing bowl, cream the butter and sugar. Add the eggs, one at a time, beating well after each addition. Beat in vanilla. Combine flour and salt; gradually add to the creamed mixture. Cover and refrigerate for 2-3 hours or until easy to handle.

3. On a lightly floured surface, roll half of the dough to 1/8-in. thickness. Cut with a floured 2-in. round cookie cutter. Place 1 in. apart on ungreased baking sheets. Place 1 teaspoon of raisin filling in the center of each cookie. Roll out remaining dough. Cut with a 2-in.-round cookie cutter. With a 1-in. round cookie cutter, cut a hole in the center of each; place over filling. With a fork, press edges to seal.

4. Bake at 400° for 10-12 minutes or until edges begin to brown. Remove to wire racks to cool.

Yield: about 4 dozen.

Dipped Coconut Shortbread

Toni Petroskey, Lorain, Ohio

These cookies are great for Sweetest Day. If your heart's desire doesn't like semisweet chocolate, use milk or white chocolate instead.

- 3/4 cup butter, softened
- 1/4 cup sugar
- 2 teaspoons vanilla extract
- 1-3/4 cups all-purpose flour
- 1/2 teaspoon baking powder
- 1 cup flaked coconut
- 1-1/2 cups semisweet chocolate chips
- 1 tablespoon shortening

1. In a mixing bowl, cream butter, sugar and vanilla until light and fluffy. Combine flour and baking powder; gradually add to creamed mixture and mix well. Stir in coconut. Cover and refrigerate for 1 hour or until firm.

2. On a floured surface, roll out the dough to 1/4-in. thickness. Cut with a 2-1/2-in. round cookie cutter. Place 2 in. apart on ungreased baking sheets. Bake at 300° for 20-25 minutes or until edges begin to brown. Remove to wire racks to cool.

3. In a saucepan over low heat, melt chocolate chips and shortening. Remove from the heat; dip cookies halfway into chocolate. Place on waxed paper-lined baking sheets until set.

Yield: about 2 dozen.

Oatmeal Sandwich Cookies, p. 156

Rainbow Cookies, p. 166

Dipped Sandwich Cookies, p. 157

Almond Jelly Cookies, p. 159

Snazzy Sandwich Cookies

What could be better than one cookie? Two cookies with a marvelous filling in between them. Sandwich cookies are delightfully different and are easy to assemble, too.

Oatmeal Sandwich Cookies

(Pictured on page 154)
Jan Woodall, Cadiz, Kentucky

These fun treats put a sweet fluffy filling between two chewy oatmeal cookies. They're perfect for snacking or for packing in lunch boxes.

1-1/2 cups shortening
2-2/3 cups packed brown sugar
    4 eggs
    2 teaspoons vanilla extract
2-1/4 cups all-purpose flour
    2 teaspoons ground cinnamon
1-1/2 teaspoons baking soda
    1 teaspoon salt
  1/2 teaspoon ground nutmeg
    4 cups old-fashioned oats

FILLING:
  3/4 cup shortening
    3 cups confectioners' sugar
    1 jar (7 ounces) marshmallow creme
    1 to 3 tablespoons milk

1. In a mixing bowl, cream shortening and brown sugar. Add eggs, one at a time, beating well after each addition. Beat in the vanilla. Combine the flour, cinnamon, baking soda, salt and nutmeg; add to creamed mixture. Stir in oats.

2. Drop by rounded teaspoonfuls 2 in. apart onto lightly greased baking sheets. Bake at 350° for 10-12 minutes or until golden brown. Remove to wire racks to cool.

3. For filling, in a mixing bowl, cream the first three ingredients. Add enough milk to achieve spreading consistency. Spread filling on the bottom of half of the cookies; top with remaining cookies.

Yield: about 4-1/2 dozen.

Chocolate Peanut Butter Sandwich Cookies

Vickie Rhoads, Eugene, Oregon

Sandwich cookies are always a hit, and homemade ones like these that feature peanut butter and chocolate are guaranteed to please! Whenever we visit out-of-town friends, they ask if we'll bring a batch of these cookies.

    2 cups butter
  1/4 cup shortening
    2 cups baking cocoa
    1 cup chocolate syrup
  1/2 cup peanut butter
    6 eggs
    5 cups sugar
    5 teaspoons vanilla extract
    5 cups all-purpose flour
    3 teaspoons baking soda
    1 teaspoon salt

FILLING:
  1/2 cup butter, softened
    1 cup chunky peanut butter
    1 cup milk
    2 teaspoons vanilla extract
  11 cups confectioners' sugar

1. In a saucepan over low heat, melt butter and shortening. Remove from heat; stir in cocoa, chocolate syrup and peanut butter until smooth. Cool.

2. In a large mixing bowl, beat eggs and sugar until lemon-colored. Beat in the chocolate mixture and vanilla. Combine the flour, baking soda and salt; gradually add to creamed mixture.

3. Drop by teaspoonfuls 2 in. apart onto ungreased baking sheets. Flatten with a glass dipped in sugar. Bake at 350° for 10-12 minutes or until surface cracks. Cool for 2 minutes before removing to wire racks.

4. In a mixing bowl, beat butter and peanut butter. Beat in milk and vanilla. Gradually add confectioners' sugar, beating until blended. Spread on the bottom of half of the cookies; top with remaining cookies.

Yield: 11 dozen.

Editor's Note: Reduced-fat or generic brands of peanut butter are not recommended for this recipe.

Linzer Heart Cookies

Jane Pearcy
Verona, Wisconsin

I bake these tender jam-filled hearts when I need something fancy to serve for Valentine's Day.

1-1/4 cups butter, softened
1 cup sugar
1/2 teaspoon salt
2 eggs
2 cups ground almonds
1 tablespoon baking cocoa
1/4 teaspoon ground cinnamon
1/4 teaspoon ground nutmeg
1/8 teaspoon ground cloves
3 cups all-purpose flour
Raspberry jam
Confectioners' sugar

1. In a mixing bowl, cream the butter, sugar and salt. Add eggs, one at a time, beating well after each addition. Add the almonds, cocoa, cinnamon, nutmeg and cloves; mix well. Add flour; mix well. Cover and refrigerate for 1 hour or until easy to handle.

2. On a lightly floured surface, roll dough to 1/8-in. thickness. Cut with a floured 3-in. heart-shaped cookie cutter. Cut a 1-1/2-in. heart from the center of half the cookies.

3. Place 2 in. apart on ungreased baking sheets. Bake at 350° for 10-12 minutes or until edges are golden brown. Remove to wire racks to cool.

4. Spread 1/2 teaspoon jam over the bottom of the solid cookies; place cutout cookies over jam. Sprinkle with confectioners' sugar.

Yield: 3 dozen.

Dipped Sandwich Cookies

(Pictured on page 155)
Jane Delahoyde, Poughkeepsie, New York

With a lemon filling and chocolate coating, these buttery sandwich cookies are often requested at my house— particularly for special occasions.

1 cup butter, softened
1/2 cup sugar
1 egg yolk
1 teaspoon vanilla extract
2 cups all-purpose flour

LEMON FILLING:
1/2 cup butter, softened
2 cups confectioners' sugar
2 tablespoons lemon juice

DIPPING CHOCOLATE:
4 squares (1 ounce *each*) semisweet chocolate
2 tablespoons butter
1/2 cup finely chopped nuts

1. In a large mixing bowl, cream butter and sugar. Beat in egg yolk and vanilla. Gradually add flour.

2. Shape into 1-in. balls. Place 2 in. apart on ungreased baking sheets. With a glass dipped in sugar, flatten into 2-in. circles. Bake at 350° for 10-12 minutes or until firm. Remove to wire racks to cool.

3. Combine filling ingredients. Spread on the bottom of half of the cookies; top with remaining cookies. Melt chocolate and butter; stir until smooth. Dip each cookie halfway in chocolate, then in nuts. Place on waxed paper until set.

Yield: 2 dozen.

S'more Sandwich Cookies

Abby Metzger
Larchwood, Iowa

Capture the taste of campfire s'mores in your kitchen! Graham cracker crumbs added to chocolate chip cookie dough bring out the flavor of the fireside favorite.

3/4 cup butter, softened
1/2 cup sugar
1/2 cup packed brown sugar
1 egg
2 tablespoons milk
1 teaspoon vanilla extract
1-1/4 cups all-purpose flour
1-1/4 cups graham cracker crumbs (about 20 squares)
1/2 teaspoon baking soda
1/4 teaspoon salt
1/8 teaspoon ground cinnamon
2 cups (12 ounces) semisweet chocolate chips
24 to 28 large marshmallows

1. In a mixing bowl, cream butter and sugars. Beat in egg, milk and vanilla. Combine flour, graham cracker crumbs, baking soda, salt and cinnamon; gradually add to creamed mixture. Stir in chocolate chips.

2. Drop by tablespoonfuls 2 in. apart onto ungreased baking sheets. Bake at 375° for 8-10 minutes or until golden brown. Remove to wire racks to cool completely.

3. Place four cookies bottom side up on a microwave-safe plate; top each with a marshmallow. Microwave, uncovered, on high for 16-20 seconds or until marshmallows begin to puff (do not overcook). Top each with another cookie. Repeat.

Yield: about 2 dozen.

Editor's Note: This recipe was tested with an 850-watt microwave.

Lemon-Cream Sandwich Cookies

A light lemon filling spread between flaky butter cookies makes these a perfect accompaniment to hot tea or coffee. They also make a delicious dessert.

Carol Steiner, Arrowwood, Alberta

3/4 cup butter, softened
1/2 cup confectioners' sugar
2 teaspoons lemon extract
1-1/2 cups all-purpose flour
1/4 cup cornstarch

LEMON FILLING:
1/4 cup butter, softened
1-1/2 cups confectioners' sugar
2 tablespoons lemon juice
2 teaspoons grated lemon peel

1. In a mixing bowl, cream butter and confectioners' sugar. Beat in extract. Combine flour and cornstarch; beat into creamed mixture. Divide into two balls; wrap in plastic wrap and refrigerate for 1 hour.

2. On a lightly floured surface, roll out each portion of dough to 1/8-in. thickness. Cut out with a floured 2-in.-round cookie cutter.

3. Place 2 in. apart on ungreased baking sheets. Bake at 350° for 10-12 minutes or until edges are lightly browned. Remove to wire racks to cool.

4. For filling, in a small mixing bowl, cream butter and confectioners' sugar. Beat in lemon juice and peel. Spread over the bottoms of half of the cookies; top with remaining cookies.

Yield: 2 dozen.

Editor's Note: This recipe does not use eggs.

Almond Jelly Cookies

(Pictured on page 155)
Laraine Hadley, Moretown, Vermont

My mother-in-law used to send these wonderful cookies in her special "care" packages to our family. We could hardly wait to open the box and dig in!

1-1/2 cups butter, softened
    1 cup sugar
1-1/2 cups ground almonds
    1 teaspoon vanilla extract
2-1/2 cups all-purpose flour
   1/2 teaspoon salt
    1 cup jelly *or* jam of your choice

1. In a mixing bowl, cream butter and sugar. Add almonds and vanilla; mix well. Combine flour and salt; gradually add to the creamed mixture. Cover and refrigerate for 2 hours or until easy to handle.

2. On a lightly floured surface, roll out half of dough to 1/8-in. thickness. Cut with a floured 2-in.-round cookie cutter. Repeat with remaining dough, using a 2-in. doughnut cutter so the center is out of each cookie.

3. Place 1 in. apart on ungreased baking sheets. Bake at 350° for 10-12 minutes or until edges are lightly browned. Remove to wire racks to cool. Spread 1/2 teaspoon jelly over the bottom of solid cookies; place cookies with cutout center over jelly.

Yield: 5 dozen.

Strawberry Sandwich Cookies

Barbara Sessoyeff
Redwood Valley, California

These yummy Strawberry Sandwich Cookies are made with a nutty tender cookie.

    1 cup blanched almonds
  3/4 cup butter, softened
    1 cup confectioners' sugar, *divided*
    1 egg
  1/2 teaspoon almond extract
1-1/2 cups all-purpose flour
  1/8 teaspoon salt
    1 tablespoon lemon juice
    3 tablespoons strawberry jam

1. In a food processor or blender, process almonds until ground; set aside. In a mixing bowl, cream butter and 1/2 cup sugar. Beat in egg and extract. Combine flour and salt; gradually add to creamed mixture. Stir in the ground almonds. Divide dough in half; cover and refrigerate for 2 hours or until easy to handle.

2. On a lightly floured surface, roll out each portion of the dough into a 12-in. x 9-in. rectangle. Cut lengthwise into three strips; cut each strip widthwise into six pieces. With a floured 3/4-in.-round cookie cutter, cut out a circle in the center of half of the pieces (discard circles).

3. Place 1 in. apart on ungreased baking sheets. Bake at 375° for 8-10 minutes or until golden brown. Remove to wire racks to cool.

4. For glaze, combine lemon juice and remaining sugar; thinly spread over whole cookies. Top with cutout cookies; fill center with 1/2 teaspoon jam.

Yield: 1-1/2 dozen.

Chocolate Mint Cookies

Christina Burbage, Spartanburg, South Carolina

My dad sandwiches mint patties between two chocolate cookies to create these chewy treats. Best of all, these cookies are easy and fun to make.

1-1/4 cups butter, softened
    2 cups sugar
    2 eggs
    2 teaspoons vanilla extract
    2 cups all-purpose flour
  3/4 cup baking cocoa
    1 teaspoon baking soda
  1/2 teaspoon salt
   32 round thin chocolate-covered mint patties

1. In a mixing bowl, cream the butter and sugar. Add the eggs, one at a time, beating well after each addition. Beat in vanilla. Combine the flour, cocoa, baking soda and salt; gradually add to the creamed mixture, beating until well combined.

2. Drop by tablespoonfuls 2 in. apart onto ungreased baking sheets. Bake at 350° for 8-9 minutes or until puffy and tops are cracked. Invert half of the cookies onto wire racks. Immediately place a mint patty on each, then top with remaining cookies. Press lightly to seal. Cool.

Yield: 32 sandwich cookies.

Fruit-Filled Spritz Cookies

Ingeborg Keith
Newark, Delaware

From the first time I baked these cookies, they've been a delicious lip-smacking success.

1-1/2 cups chopped dates
    1 cup water
  1/2 cup sugar
    2 teaspoons orange juice
    2 teaspoons grated orange peel
    1 cup maraschino cherries, chopped
  1/2 cup flaked coconut
  1/2 cup ground nuts

DOUGH:
    1 cup butter, softened
    1 cup sugar
  1/2 cup packed brown sugar
    3 eggs
  1/2 teaspoon almond extract
  1/2 teaspoon vanilla extract
    4 cups all-purpose flour
  1/2 teaspoon baking soda
  1/2 teaspoon salt
Confectioners' sugar

1. In a saucepan, combine the first five ingredients; bring to a boil, stirring constantly. Reduce heat; cook and stir for 8 minutes or until thickened. Cool completely. Stir in cherries, coconut and nuts; set aside.

2. In a mixing bowl, cream butter and sugars. Beat in eggs and extracts. Combine the flour, baking soda and salt; gradually add to creamed mixture.

3. Using a cookie press fitted with a bar disk, press a 12-in.-long strip of dough onto an ungreased baking sheet. Spread fruit filling over dough. Press another strip over filling. Cut into 1-in. pieces (there is no need to separate the pieces). Repeat with remaining dough and filling.

4. Bake at 375° for 12-15 minutes or until edges are golden. Recut into pieces if necessary. Remove to wire racks to cool. Dust with confectioners' sugar.

Yield: about 7-1/2 dozen.

Old-Fashioned Whoopie Pies

Maria Costello
Monroe, North Carolina

Who can resist soft chocolate sandwich cookies filled with a layer of fluffy white frosting—my family can't!

- 1/2 cup baking cocoa
- 1/2 cup hot water
- 1/2 cup shortening
- 1-1/2 cups sugar
- 2 eggs
- 1 teaspoon vanilla extract
- 2-2/3 cups all-purpose flour
- 1 teaspoon baking powder
- 1 teaspoon baking soda
- 1/4 teaspoon salt
- 1/2 cup buttermilk

FILLING:
- 3 tablespoons all-purpose flour
- Dash salt
- 1 cup milk
- 3/4 cup shortening
- 1-1/2 cups confectioners' sugar
- 2 teaspoons vanilla extract

1. In a small bowl, combine cocoa and water; mix well. Cool for 5 minutes. In a mixing bowl, cream shortening and sugar. Add cocoa mixture, eggs and vanilla; mix well. Combine dry ingredients. Add to creamed mixture alternately with buttermilk; mix well.

2. Drop by rounded tablespoonfuls 2 in. apart onto greased baking sheets. Flatten slightly with a spoon. Bake at 350° for 10-12 minutes or until firm to the touch. Remove to wire racks to cool.

3. In a saucepan, combine flour and salt. Gradually whisk in milk until smooth; cook and stir over medium-high heat until thick, 5-7 minutes. Remove from heat. Cover and refrigerate until completely cool.

4. In a mixing bowl, cream shortening, sugar and vanilla. Add chilled milk mixture; beat for 7 minutes or until fluffy. Spread filling on half of the cookies; top with remaining cookies. Store in the refrigerator.

Yield: 2 dozen.

Lacy Oat Sandwich Wafers

Ruth Lee, Troy, Ontario

These cookies appear on my table for various special occasions. I'm often asked for the recipe, so I'm sure to have a few copies on hand.

- 2/3 cup butter
- 2 cups quick-cooking oats
- 1 cup sugar
- 2/3 cup all-purpose flour
- 1/4 cup milk
- 1/4 cup corn syrup
- 2 cups semisweet chocolate, milk chocolate, vanilla *or* white chips, melted

1. Line a baking sheet with parchment paper or foil; set aside. In a saucepan, melt butter over low heat. Remove from the heat. Stir in the oats, sugar, flour, milk and corn syrup; mix well.

2. Drop by teaspoonfuls 2 in. apart onto the prepared baking sheets. Bake at 375° for 8-10 minutes or until golden brown. Cool completely; peel cookies off paper or foil. Spread melted chocolate on the bottom of half of the cookies; top with remaining cookies.

Yield: about 3-1/2 dozen.

Cherry-Filled Heart Cookies

Audrey Groe
Lake Mills, Iowa

These crisp, flaky cookies are a wonderful way to show you care. The compliments you'll receive makes them worth the effort.

1/2 cup butter, softened
1/2 cup shortening
1 cup sugar
1 egg
1/2 cup milk
1 teaspoon vanilla extract
3-1/2 cups all-purpose flour
2 teaspoons baking powder
1 teaspoon baking soda
1/2 teaspoon salt

FILLING:
1/2 cup sugar
4-1/2 teaspoons cornstarch
1/2 cup orange juice
1/4 cup red maraschino cherry juice
12 red maraschino cherries, chopped
1 tablespoon butter
Additional sugar

1. In a mixing bowl, cream the butter and shortening; gradually add sugar. Add the egg, milk and vanilla. Combine dry ingredients; gradually add to creamed mixture and mix well. Cover and chill for at least 2 hours.

2. Meanwhile, for filling, combine sugar and cornstarch in small saucepan. Add juices, cherries and butter. Bring to a boil; boil and stir for 1 minute. Chill.

3. On a lightly floured surface, roll dough to 1/8-in. thickness. Cut with a floured 2-1/2-in. heart-shaped cookie cutter.

4. Place half of the cookies 2 in. apart on greased baking sheets; spoon 1/2 teaspoon filling in the center of each. Use a 1-1/2-in. heart-shaped cutter to cut small hearts out of the other half of the cookies. (Bake small heart cutouts separately.) Place the remaining hearts over filled cookies; press edges together gently. Fill centers with additional filling if needed. Sprinkle with sugar.

5. Bake at 375° for 8-10 minutes or until lightly browned. Remove to wire racks to cool.

Yield: about 4-1/2 dozen.

Shaping Cookie Dough into Balls

Roll the dough between your palms until it forms a ball. A 1-in. ball requires about 2 teaspoons of dough. If the dough is sticky, you can refrigerate it until it is easy to handle. You can also lightly flour your hands or spray your hands with nonstick cooking spray to prevent the dough from sticking.

Maple Sandwich Cookies

Barbara Scacchi, Limestone, New York

Mom loves maple flavoring, so I created this recipe just for her. Now the whole family loves these tasty cookies.

1 cup butter, softened
3/4 cup packed brown sugar
1 egg yolk
2 cups all-purpose flour
Sugar

FILLING:
1-1/4 cups confectioners' sugar
2 tablespoons milk
2 tablespoons butter, softened
1/2 teaspoon maple flavoring

1. In a mixing bowl, cream butter and brown sugar. Beat in the egg yolk and flour; mix well. Roll into 1-in. balls. Dip the tops in sugar.

2. Place sugar side up 2 in. apart on ungreased baking sheets. Flatten with a fork. Bake at 325° for 10-12 minutes or until golden brown. Remove to wire racks to cool.

3. Combine filling ingredients in a small mixing bowl; beat until smooth. Spread on the bottom of half of the cookies; top with remaining cookies.

Yield: about 3 dozen.

Chocolaty Double Crunchers

Cheryl Johnson
Upper Marlboro, Maryland

I first tried these fun crispy cookies at a family picnic when I was a child. Packed with oats, cornflakes and coconut, they quickly became a "regular" at our house. Years later, I still make them for my own family.

1/2 cup butter, softened
1/2 cup sugar
1/2 cup packed brown sugar
1 egg
1/2 teaspoon vanilla extract
1 cup all-purpose flour
1/2 teaspoon baking soda
1/4 teaspoon salt
1 cup quick-cooking oats
1 cup crushed cornflakes
1/2 cup flaked coconut

FILLING:
2 packages (3 ounces *each*) cream cheese, softened
1-1/2 cups confectioners' sugar
2 cups (12 ounces) semisweet chocolate chips, melted

1. In a mixing bowl, cream butter and sugars. Add egg and vanilla; mix well. Combine flour, baking soda and salt; add to creamed mixture and mix well. Add oats, cornflakes and coconut.

2. Roll into 1-in. balls. Place 2 in. apart on greased baking sheets. Flatten with a glass dipped lightly in flour. Bake at 350° for 8-10 minutes or until lightly browned. Remove to wire racks to cool.

3. For filling, beat cream cheese and sugar until smooth. Add chocolate; mix well. Spread about 1 tablespoon on half of the cookies and top each with another cookie. Store in refrigerator.

Yield: 2 dozen.

Toffee Sandwich Cookies

April McDavid, Centerburg, Ohio

My brother's quest to find a filled toffee cookie inspired me to spend hours in the kitchen coming up with a winning combination.

1 cup butter, softened
1 cup packed brown sugar
1/2 cup sugar
2 eggs
2 teaspoons vanilla extract
2-1/2 cups all-purpose flour
1/2 teaspoon baking soda
1/4 teaspoon salt
1 cup English toffee bits *or* almond brickle chips

FILLING:
2/3 cup butter, softened
4 cups confectioners' sugar
1 teaspoon vanilla extract
3 to 5 tablespoons half-and-half cream *or* milk

1. In a mixing bowl, cream butter and sugars. Add eggs, one at a time, beating well after each addition. Beat in vanilla. Combine flour, baking soda and salt; gradually add to the creamed mixture. Stir in toffee bits (dough will be stiff).

2. Drop by rounded teaspoonfuls 2 in. apart onto ungreased baking sheets. Bake at 350° for 10 minutes or until firm (do not brown). Remove to wire racks to cool.

3. In a mixing bowl, combine butter, sugar, vanilla and enough cream to achieve spreading consistency. Spread on the bottom of half of the cookies; top with remaining cookies.

Yield: 4 dozen.

Caramel Creams

Barbara Yongers
Kingman, Kansas

These cookies are delicious plain, but I like to make them into sandwich cookies with the brown butter filling. In a pinch, you can use a can of frosting.

1 cup butter, softened
2/3 cup packed brown sugar
2 egg yolks
1/2 teaspoon vanilla extract
2-1/2 cups all-purpose flour
1/3 cup finely chopped pecans
1/4 teaspoon salt

FILLING:
2 tablespoons plus 1-1/2 teaspoons butter
1-1/2 cups confectioners' sugar
1/2 teaspoon vanilla extract
2 to 3 tablespoons heavy whipping cream

1. In a mixing bowl, cream butter and brown sugar. Beat in egg yolks and vanilla. Combine flour, pecans and salt; gradually add to the creamed mixture. Shape into two 10-in. rolls; wrap each in plastic wrap. Refrigerate for 1-2 hours.

2. Unwrap and cut into 1/4-in. slices. Place 2 in. apart on ungreased baking sheets. Bake at 350° for 11-13 minutes or until golden brown. Remove to wire racks to cool.

3. For filling, heat butter in a saucepan over medium heat until golden brown. Remove from the heat; add confectioners' sugar, vanilla and enough cream to achieve spreading consistency. Spread on the bottom of half of the cookies; top with remaining cookies.

Yield: about 3 dozen.

Apricot-Filled Cookies

Bonnie Waliezer
Brush Prairie, Washington

This recipe for these rich, buttery cookies originally called for dates. Apricots have long been my favorite fruit, so using them as a substitute seemed natural.

- 1/2 cup shortening
- 1 cup sugar
- 2 eggs
- 1 teaspoon vanilla extract
- 2-1/2 cups all-purpose flour
- 1/2 teaspoon salt
- 1/4 teaspoon baking soda

FILLING:
- 2 cups canned apricots, mashed
- 2/3 cup sugar
- 2/3 cup water
- 1/2 cup finely chopped almonds
- 1 teaspoon lemon juice

1. In a mixing bowl, cream shortening and sugar. Beat in eggs and vanilla. Combine flour, salt and baking soda; gradually add to the creamed mixture. Cover and refrigerate for 1 hour.

2. Meanwhile, in a saucepan, combine filling ingredients. Cook and stir until thickened, about 15 minutes. Cool completely. Divide dough in half.

3. On a lightly floured surface, roll out each portion to 1/8-in. thickness. Cut one portion with a floured 2-1/2-in.-round cookie cutter. Cut second portion with a floured 2-1/2-in. doughnut cutter.

4. Place 1 in. apart on ungreased baking sheets. Bake at 375° for 8-10 minutes or until edges are very lightly browned. Remove to wire racks to cool. Spread bottom of solid cookies with filling; top with cutout cookies.

Yield: about 1-1/2 dozen.

Making Sandwich Cookies

Spread filling over the bottoms of half of the cookies. Place another cookie over the filling, bottom side down.

Rainbow Cookies

Mary Ann Lee
Marco Island, Florida

I always bake my Rainbow Cookies two weeks ahead. That gives them enough time to "mellow," leaving them moist and full of almond flavor!

- 1 can (8 ounces) almond paste
- 1 cup butter, softened
- 1 cup sugar
- 4 eggs, *separated*
- 2 cups all-purpose flour
- 6 to 8 drops red food coloring
- 6 to 8 drops green food coloring
- 1/4 cup seedless red raspberry jam
- 1/4 cup apricot jam
- 1 cup (6 ounces) semisweet chocolate chips

1. Grease the bottoms of three matching 13-in. x 9-in. x 2-in. baking pans. Line the pans with waxed paper; grease the paper.

2. Place almond paste in a large mixing bowl; break up with a fork. Cream with butter, sugar and egg yolks until light, fluffy and smooth. Stir in flour. In another mixing bowl, beat egg whites until soft peaks form. Fold into dough, mixing until thoroughly blended.

3. Divide dough into three portions (about 1-1/3 cups each). Color one portion with red food coloring and one with green; leave the remaining portion uncolored. Spread each portion into the prepared pans. Bake at 350° for 10-12 minutes or until edges are light golden brown.

4. Invert onto wire racks; remove waxed paper. Place another wire rack on top and turn over. Cool completely.

5. Place green layer on a large piece of plastic wrap. Spread evenly with raspberry jam. Top with uncolored layer and spread with apricot jam. Top with pink layer. Bring plastic wrap over layers. Slide onto a baking sheet and set a cutting board or heavy, flat pan on top to compress layers. Refrigerate overnight.

6. The next day, melt chocolate in a microwave or heavy saucepan. Spread over top layer; allow to set. With a sharp knife, trim edges. Cut into 1/2-in. strips across the width; then cut each strip into 4-5 pieces. Store in airtight containers.

Yield: about 8 dozen.

Chocolate Almond Cookies

Kathryn Werner, Peterborough, Ontario

Special occasions around our house have always been celebrated with these chocolate-dipped, jam-filled cookies. They not only look appealing, they taste terrific, too.

1/2 cup butter, softened
6 tablespoons sugar
1-1/2 teaspoons vanilla extract
1 cup all-purpose flour
1 cup finely chopped blanched almonds
1/4 to 1/2 cup raspberry jam *or* jam of your choice
3 squares (1 ounce *each*) semisweet chocolate, melted

1. In a mixing bowl, cream the butter, sugar and vanilla. Combine flour and almonds; gradually add to the creamed mixture. Shape into one 12-in. roll; wrap in plastic wrap. Refrigerate for 4 hours or until firm.

2. Unwrap; cut into 1/4-in. slices. Place 2 in. apart on ungreased baking sheets. Bake at 350° for 8-10 minutes or until lightly browned. Remove to wire racks to cool.

3. Spread 1 teaspoon jam on the bottom of half of the cookies; top with remaining cookies. Dip cookies halfway into melted chocolate; shake off excess. Place on waxed paper-lined baking sheets until set.

Yield: 2 dozen.

Pumpkin Whoopie Pies

Deb Stuber
Carlisle, Pennsylvania

My kids start begging me for these cake-like sandwich cookies as soon as autumn arrives. I haven't met a person yet who doesn't like these fun treats.

1 cup shortening
2 cups packed brown sugar
2 eggs
1 teaspoon vanilla extract
3-1/2 cups all-purpose flour
1-1/2 teaspoons baking powder
1-1/2 teaspoons baking soda
1 teaspoon salt
1 teaspoon ground cinnamon
1 teaspoon ground ginger
1-1/2 cups canned pumpkin

FILLING:
1/4 cup all-purpose flour
Dash salt
3/4 cup milk
1 cup shortening
2 cups confectioners' sugar
2 teaspoons vanilla extract

1. In a mixing bowl, cream shortening and brown sugar. Add eggs, one at a time, beating well after each addition. Beat in vanilla. Combine the flour, baking powder, baking soda, salt, cinnamon and ginger; add to creamed mixture alternately with pumpkin.

2. Drop by rounded tablespoonfuls 2 in. apart onto greased baking sheets; flatten slightly with the back of a spoon. Bake at 400° for 10-11 minutes. Remove to wire racks to cool.

3. For filling, combine the flour and salt in a saucepan. Gradually whisk in milk until smooth; cook and stir over medium heat for 5-7 minutes or until thickened. Cover and refrigerate until completely cooled.

4. In a mixing bowl, cream shortening, confectioners' sugar and vanilla. Add chilled milk mixture; beat for 7 minutes or until fluffy. Spread on the bottom of half of the cookies; top with remaining cookies. Store in the refrigerator.

Yield: about 2 dozen.

Fudgy Walnut Brownies, p. 170

eanut Butter Brownies, p. 172

Apricot Angel Brownies, p. 174

Rich Chocolate Brownies, p. 173

Unbeatable Brownies

Whether you crave moist, fudgy brownies or comforting cake-like brownies...classic chocolate treats or new taste twists...simple frosted bars or elaborately decorated ones, you'll discover the perfect brownie here!

Fudgy Walnut Brownies

(Pictured on page 168)
Diane Truver, Valencia, Pennsylvania

We have lots of great cooks in our clan, so adding to our collection of family recipes is a tradition. I came up with these moist, nut-covered brownies while doing my Christmas baking. Now everyone requests them.

- 3/4 cup butter
- 4 squares (1 ounce *each*) unsweetened chocolate
- 4 eggs
- 2 cups sugar
- 1 teaspoon vanilla extract
- 1 cup all-purpose flour

WALNUT CRUNCH TOPPING:
- 3/4 cup packed brown sugar
- 1/4 cup butter, cubed
- 2 eggs, lightly beaten
- 2 tablespoons all-purpose flour
- 1 teaspoon vanilla extract
- 4 cups chopped walnuts

1. In a microwave or heavy saucepan, melt butter and chocolate; stir until smooth. Cool slightly. In a bowl, beat eggs and sugar; stir in the vanilla and chocolate mixture. Stir in flour until well blended. Pour into a greased 13-in. x 9-in. x 2-in. baking pan; set aside.

2. For topping, in a saucepan, combine brown sugar and butter. Cook and stir over low heat until butter is melted. Stir in the eggs, flour and vanilla until well blended. Stir in nuts. Spread evenly over brownie batter.

3. Bake at 350° for 40-45 minutes or until a toothpick inserted near the center comes out with moist crumbs (do not overbake). Cool in pan on a wire rack. Cut into bars.

Yield: 1-1/2 dozen.

Peppermint Patty Brownies

Clara Bakke
Coon Rapids, Minnesota

I've added my own special ingredient to these sweet and fudgy brownies. A layer of mint patties make a refreshing surprise.

- 1-1/2 cups butter, softened
- 3 cups sugar
- 5 eggs
- 1 tablespoon vanilla extract
- 2 cups all-purpose flour
- 1 cup baking cocoa
- 1 teaspoon baking powder
- 1 teaspoon salt
- 1 package (13 ounces) chocolate-covered peppermint patties

1. In a mixing bowl, cream the butter and sugar. Add the eggs, one at a time, beating well after each addition. Beat in vanilla. Combine dry ingredients; add to creamed mixture and mix well.

2. Spread about two-thirds of the batter in a greased 13-in. x 9-in. x 2-in. baking pan. Arrange peppermint patties over top. Carefully spread remaining batter over patties.

3. Bake at 350° for 35-40 minutes or until edges begin to pull away from sides of pan and a toothpick inserted near the center comes out clean (top will appear uneven). Cool in pan on a wire rack. Cut into bars.

Yield: 2 to 2-1/2 dozen.

Mocha Mousse Brownies

Stacy Waller
Eagan, Minnesota

Coffee-flavored mousse tops a rich fudge brownie for a perfect pairing.

- 2/3 cup semisweet chocolate chips
- 1/2 cup butter
- 1 cup plus 2 tablespoons sugar
- 2 eggs
- 1/4 cup hot water
- 2 tablespoons instant coffee granules
- 1/2 cup all-purpose flour
- 1/2 cup baking cocoa
- 1 teaspoon baking powder

MOCHA MOUSSE:
- 1 package (3 ounces) cream cheese, softened
- 1/4 cup sweetened condensed milk
- 1/2 cup semisweet chocolate chips, melted
- 1 envelope unflavored gelatin
- 1/4 cup cold water
- 2 tablespoons instant coffee granules
- 1 cup heavy whipping cream

1. In a saucepan over low heat, melt the chips and butter; pour into a mixing bowl. Beat in sugar until smooth. Add eggs, one at a time, beating well after each addition. Combine hot water and coffee granules; add to chocolate mixture. Combine the flour, cocoa and baking powder; beat into chocolate mixture.

2. Spread into a greased 13-in. x 9-in. x 2-in. baking pan. Bake at 350° for 15-20 minutes or until a toothpick inserted near the center comes out clean (brownies will be thin). Cool in pan on a wire rack.

3. For mousse, in a small mixing bowl, beat cream cheese until smooth; beat in milk and melted chips. In a saucepan, sprinkle gelatin over cold water; let stand for 1 minute. Cook and stir over low heat until gelatin is dissolved. Remove from the heat; stir in coffee granules until dissolved.

4. In a mixing bowl, beat whipping cream until slightly thickened. Beat in gelatin. Fold into cream cheese mixture. Spread over brownies. Cover and refrigerate for 3 hours or until firm. Cut into squares. Store in the refrigerator.

Yield: 2 dozen.

Blonde Brownie Nut Squares

Edie Farm, Farmington, New Mexico

These moist bars get a small but satisfying crunch from pecans. They are a tasty change of pace from traditional chocolate brownies.

- 1/4 cup butter, melted
- 1 cup packed brown sugar
- 1 egg
- 1 teaspoon vanilla extract
- 3/4 cup all-purpose flour
- 1 teaspoon baking powder
- 1/4 teaspoon salt
- 1/2 cup finely chopped pecans

1. In a mixing bowl, beat the butter, sugar, egg and vanilla. Combine the flour, baking powder and salt; gradually add to sugar mixture and mix well. Fold in nuts.

2. Spread in a greased 8-in. baking dish. Bake at 350° for 15-20 minutes or until a toothpick comes out clean. Cool in pan on a wire rack. Cut into squares.

Yield: 16 squares.

Maple Butterscotch Brownies

Grace Vonhold
Rochester, New York

Generally, I'll make a double recipe of these brownies—they go so fast, no matter where I take them! I've baked them for family dinners and church suppers, and never had any left over. They're very easy plus they keep and freeze well.

1-1/4 cups packed brown sugar
1/2 cup butter, melted
1-1/2 teaspoons maple flavoring
2 eggs
1-1/2 cups all-purpose flour
1 teaspoon baking powder
1 cup chopped walnuts
Confectioners' sugar, optional

1. In a bowl, combine brown sugar, butter and maple flavoring. Beat in the eggs, one at a time. Combine flour and baking powder; add to egg mixture. Stir in walnuts.

2. Pour into a greased 9-in. square baking pan. Bake at 350° for 27-32 minutes or until a toothpick inserted near the center comes out clean. Cool in pan on a wire rack. Dust with confectioners' sugar if desired. Cut into bars.

Yield: 16 brownies.

Peanut Butter Brownies

(Pictured on page 169)
Margaret McNeil, Memphis, Tennessee

The combination of chocolate and peanut butter makes these brownies a real crowd-pleaser. They're so good, they won a ribbon at the fair.

3 eggs
1 cup butter, melted
2 teaspoons vanilla extract
2 cups sugar
1-1/4 cups all-purpose flour
3/4 cup baking cocoa
1/2 teaspoon baking powder
1/4 teaspoon salt
1 cup milk chocolate chips

FILLING:
2 packages (8 ounces *each*) cream cheese, softened
1/2 cup creamy peanut butter
1/4 cup sugar
1 egg
2 tablespoons milk

1. In a large mixing bowl, combine eggs, butter and vanilla. Combine dry ingredients; add to egg mixture and mix well. Stir in chocolate chips. Set aside 1 cup for topping. Spread remaining batter into a greased 13-in. x 9-in. x 2-in. baking pan.

2. In a small mixing bowl, beat cream cheese, peanut butter and sugar until smooth. Add the egg and milk, beating on low just until combined. Carefully spread over batter. Drop reserved batter by tablespoonfuls over filling. Cut through batter with a knife to swirl.

3. Bake at 350° for 35-40 minutes or until a toothpick inserted in the center comes out clean. Cool in pan on a wire rack. Cut into bars. Store in the refrigerator.

Yield: 3 dozen.

Editor's Note: Reduced-fat or generic brands of peanut butter are not recommended for this recipe.

One-Bowl Brownies

Cheryl Smith, Hart, Texas

With just one bowl to clean up after mixing, these no-fuss brownies make many appearances at our dinner table.

1 cup butter, softened
2 cups sugar
4 eggs
1 teaspoon vanilla extract
6 tablespoons baking cocoa
2 cups all-purpose flour
Dash salt
1/2 cup chopped nuts

1. In a mixing bowl, cream butter and sugar. Beat in eggs and vanilla. Combine cocoa, flour and salt; stir into creamed mixture. Add nuts.

2. Pour into a greased 13-in. x 9-in. x 2-in. baking pan. Bake at 375° for 20-25 minutes or until brownies test done. Cool in pan on a wire rack. Cut into bars.

Yield: 2-1/2 dozen.

Rich Chocolate Brownies

Karen Trapp
North Weymouth, Massachusetts

I'm one of those people who need chocolate on a regular basis. I looked high and low for a rich brownie recipe that called for cocoa instead of chocolate squares and this is it. My family loves these brownies—they never last more than a day at our house.

1 cup sugar
2 eggs
1/2 teaspoon vanilla extract
1/2 cup butter, melted
1/2 cup all-purpose flour
1/3 cup baking cocoa
1/4 teaspoon baking powder
1/4 teaspoon salt

FROSTING:
3 tablespoons butter, melted
3 tablespoons baking cocoa
2 tablespoons warm water
1 teaspoon instant coffee granules
1-1/2 cups confectioners' sugar

1. In a mixing bowl, beat sugar, eggs and vanilla. Add butter; mix well. Combine dry ingredients; add to batter and mix well.

2. Pour into a greased 8-in. square baking dish. Bake at 350° for 25-30 minutes or until a toothpick inserted near the center comes out with moist crumbs. Cool in pan on a wire rack.

3. For frosting, combine butter, cocoa, water and coffee; mix well. Gradually stir in sugar until smooth, adding additional warm water if necessary to achieve a spreading consistency. Frost the brownies. Cut into bars.

Yield: 12-16 servings.

Apricot Angel Brownies

(Pictured on page 169)
Tamara Sellman, Barrington, Illinois

To tell the truth, I'm not a "chocoholic." I enjoy fruit desserts and custards more than anything. So my brownies have neither milk nor dark chocolate—but still satisfy every sweet tooth.

4 squares (1 ounce *each*) white baking chocolate
1/3 cup butter
1/2 cup packed brown sugar
2 eggs, beaten
1/4 teaspoon vanilla extract
3/4 cup all-purpose flour
1/2 teaspoon baking powder
1/4 teaspoon salt
1 cup finely chopped dried apricots
1/4 cup sliced almonds
1/4 cup flaked coconut

1. In a saucepan, melt chocolate and butter over low heat, stirring constantly until all of the chocolate is melted. Remove from the heat; stir in brown sugar, eggs and vanilla until blended. Set aside.

2. In a bowl, combine flour, baking powder and salt. Stir in chocolate mixture. Combine the apricots, almonds and coconuts; stir half into the batter.

3. Pour into a greased 9-in. square baking pan. Sprinkle the remaining apricot mixture on top. Bake at 350° for 25-30 minutes or until golden brown. Cool in pan on a wire rack. Cut into bars.

Yield: about 2 dozen.

Really Rocky Road Brownies

Brenda Wood
Egbert, Ontario

This mouth-watering recipe is from a family reunion cookbook that I compiled. My niece, Olivia Fallon, contributed the recipe.

8 squares (1 ounce *each*) unsweetened chocolate
1-1/2 cups butter
6 eggs
3 cups sugar
1 tablespoon vanilla extract
1-1/2 cups all-purpose flour
1 cup chopped walnuts, optional

TOPPING:
2 cups miniature marshmallows
1 square (1 ounce) unsweetened chocolate, melted

1. In a heavy saucepan over medium heat, cook and stir chocolate and butter until melted; cool slightly. In a mixing bowl, beat eggs for 2 minutes. Gradually add sugar; beat until thick, about 3 minutes. Stir in chocolate mixture and vanilla. Fold in flour and nuts if desired.

2. Pour into two greased and floured 9-in. square baking pans. Bake at 350° for 25-30 minutes or until a toothpick inserted in the center comes out with moist crumbs (do not overbake). Sprinkle each pan with 1 cup of marshmallows. Broil until marshmallows are golden brown, about 30-60 seconds. Drizzle with melted chocolate. Cool in pans on wire racks. Cut into bars.

Yield: 4 dozen.

Treasured Brownies

Marianne Wolfe
Westlock, Alberta

This treat is in a book of good-but-easy recipes my sister compiled as a wedding present for me. She refers to them as "money-back guaranteed" brownies.

1 cup butter, melted and cooled

3 eggs

1-1/2 teaspoons vanilla extract

1 cup all-purpose flour

1 cup sugar

1 cup packed brown sugar

3/4 cup baking cocoa

1-1/2 teaspoons baking powder

1 cup chopped nuts

ICING:

1/2 cup butter, softened

1-1/4 cups confectioners' sugar

2/3 cup baking cocoa

2 tablespoons milk

2 tablespoons hot brewed coffee

1 teaspoon vanilla extract

1. In a mixing bowl, combine butter, eggs and vanilla. Combine the dry ingredients; gradually add to butter mixture. Stir in nuts (do not overmix).

2. Spread into a greased 13-in. x 9-in. x 2-in. baking pan. Bake at 350° for 25-30 minutes or until a toothpick inserted near the center comes out clean. Cool in pan on a wire rack.

3. Combine icing ingredients in a mixing bowl; beat until smooth. Spread over cooled brownies. Cut into bars.

Yield: 1-1/2 dozen.

Blonde Brownies

Anne Weiler
Philadelphia, Pennsylvania

My family has enjoyed these bars as a potluck dessert, brown-bag treat and anytime snack many times throughout the years. Butterscotch or peanut butter chips can be used in place of the chocolate chips.

1/4 cup butter-flavored shortening

1-1/2 cups packed brown sugar

2 eggs

1/2 teaspoon vanilla extract

1 cup all-purpose flour

1-1/2 teaspoons baking powder

1/2 teaspoon salt

1 cup chopped walnuts

1/2 cup semisweet chocolate chips

1. In a mixing bowl, cream shortening and brown sugar. Add eggs, one at a time, beating well after each addition. Beat in vanilla. Combine flour, baking powder and salt; gradually add to the creamed mixture. Stir in nuts and chocolate chips.

2. Spread into a greased 11-in. x 7-in. x 2-in. baking pan. Bake at 350° for 25-30 minutes or until a toothpick inserted near the center comes out clean. Cool in pan on wire rack. Cut into bars.

Yield: 2 dozen.

Swiss Chocolate Brownies

Gloria Stange
Claresholm, Alberta

When our two grown children were at home, I baked these brownies often. These days, I make them for big occasions—everyone thinks that they're quite nice. As a bonus, they're a good way to use up leftover sour cream.

      1 cup water
    1/2 cup butter
  1-1/2 squares (1-1/2 ounces)
         unsweetened chocolate
      2 cups all-purpose flour
      2 cups sugar
      1 teaspoon baking soda
    1/2 teaspoon salt
      2 eggs, lightly beaten
    1/2 cup sour cream
    1/2 teaspoon vanilla extract
      1 cup chopped walnuts

ICING:
    1/2 cup butter
  1-1/2 squares (1-1/2 ounces)
         unsweetened chocolate
      3 cups confectioners' sugar,
         divided
      5 tablespoons milk
      1 teaspoon vanilla extract

1. In a saucepan, bring water, butter and chocolate to a boil. Boil for 1 minute. Remove from the heat; cool. In a mixing bowl, combine flour, sugar, baking soda and salt. Add chocolate mixture and mix. Add eggs, sour cream and vanilla; mix. Fold in walnuts.

2. Pour into a greased 15-in. x 10-in. x 1-in. baking pan. Bake at 350° for 20-25 minutes or until brownies test done. Cool for 10 minutes.

3. For icing, melt butter and chocolate. Place in a mixing bowl; mix in 1-1/2 cups confectioners' sugar. Add milk, vanilla and remaining sugar; beat until smooth. Spread over the warm brownies. Cool completely. Cut into bars.

Yield: about 3 dozen.

Cream Cheese Brownies

A friend from church shared this recipe with me. Cream cheese lends itself to a moist and chewy bar that's finger-lickin' good!

Carolyn Reed, North Robinson, Ohio

      2 packages (8 ounces *each*)
         cream cheese, softened
      2 cups sugar, *divided*
      3 tablespoons milk
      1 cup butter, softened
    2/3 cup instant hot cocoa mix
      4 eggs
      2 teaspoons vanilla extract
  1-1/2 cups all-purpose flour
      1 cup chopped nuts

1. In a small mixing bowl, beat cream cheese, 1/2 cup sugar and milk until fluffy; set aside. In a large mixing bowl, cream the butter, hot cocoa mix and remaining sugar. Beat in eggs and vanilla. Stir in flour and nuts.

2. Pour half of the batter into a greased 13-in. x 9-in. x 2-in. baking pan. Spread with the cream cheese mixture. Top with remaining batter. Cut through batter with a knife to swirl the cream cheese.

3. Bake at 350° for 35-40 minutes or until a toothpick inserted near the center comes out clean. Cool in pan on a wire rack. Cut into bars.

Yield: 2-1/2 dozen.

Editor's Note: This recipe was tested with Swiss Miss instant cocoa.

Frosted Fudge Brownies

Sue Soderlund, Elgin, Illinois

A neighbor brought over a pan of these rich brownies along with the recipe when I came home from the hospital with our baby daughter 12 years ago. I've made them ever since.

1 cup plus 3 tablespoons butter
3/4 cup baking cocoa
4 eggs
2 cups sugar
1-1/2 cups all-purpose flour
1 teaspoon baking powder
1 teaspoon salt
1 teaspoon vanilla extract

FROSTING:
6 tablespoons butter, softened
2-2/3 cups confectioners' sugar
1/2 cup baking cocoa
1 teaspoon vanilla extract
1/4 to 1/3 cup milk

1. In a saucepan, melt butter. Remove from the heat. Stir in cocoa; cool. In a mixing bowl, beat eggs and sugar. Combine flour, baking powder and salt; gradually add to egg mixture. Stir in vanilla and the cooled chocolate mixture; mix well.

2. Spread into a greased 13-in. x 9-in. x 2-in. baking pan. Bake at 350° for 25-28 minutes or until a toothpick inserted near the center comes out clean (do not overbake). Cool in pan on a wire rack.

3. For frosting, in a mixing bowl, cream butter, confectioners' sugar, cocoa and vanilla. Add enough milk until the frosting achieves spreading consistency. Spread over brownies. Cut into bars.

Yield: 2 dozen.

Walnut Brownies

Lorraine Silver
Chicopee, Massachusetts

I learned to make these brownies in 1957 in home economics class. They were the first goodies I'd ever baked by myself. Now years later, I still make a batch occasionally. Best of all the recipe calls for basic ingredients found in most every kitchen.

1/4 cup shortening
3 tablespoons baking cocoa
1 egg
1/2 cup sugar
1/4 teaspoon vanilla extract
1/2 cup all-purpose flour
1/4 teaspoon baking powder
1/8 teaspoon salt
1/4 cup chopped walnuts

1. In a small mixing bowl, cream shortening and cocoa; beat in egg, sugar and vanilla. Combine dry ingredients; gradually add to creamed mixture. Beat on low speed until thoroughly combined. Stir in walnuts.

2. Pour into a greased 8-in. x 4-in. x 2-in. loaf pan. Bake at 350° for 15-20 minutes or until a toothpick inserted near the center comes out clean. Cool in pan on a wire rack. Cut into bars.

Yield: 8 brownies.

Fudgy Brownies

Denise Baumert, Dalhart, Texas

No one will ever guess that these soft, chocolaty brownies are made with lighter ingredients like yogurt and egg whites.

1 cup sugar
1/2 cup baking cocoa
6 tablespoons fat-free plain *or* vanilla yogurt
2 egg whites
1 teaspoon vanilla extract
1/2 cup all-purpose flour
1/4 cup chopped walnuts
Confectioners' sugar

1. In a bowl, combine sugar, cocoa and yogurt. Add egg whites and vanilla; mix well. Stir in flour and nuts.

2. Pour into an 8-in. square baking dish coated with nonstick cooking spray. Bake at 350° for 25-28 minutes or until a toothpick inserted near the center comes out clean. Cool in pan. Dust with confectioners' sugar. Cut into bars.

Yield: 16 servings.

Chocolate Peanut Butter Brownies

Patsy Burgin
Lebanon, Indiana

My husband and I have two sons and I sent these brownies to them regularly when they were in college. They told me that they used to hide a few from their roommates just so they could make sure there would be some left!

2 squares (1 ounce *each*) unsweetened chocolate
1/2 cup butter
2 eggs
1 cup sugar
1/2 cup all-purpose flour

FILLING:
1-1/2 cups confectioners' sugar
1/2 cup creamy peanut butter
1/4 cup butter, softened
2 to 3 tablespoons half-and-half cream *or* milk

GLAZE:
1 square (1 ounce) semisweet baking chocolate
1 tablespoon butter

1. In a small saucepan, melt chocolate and butter over low heat; set aside. In a mixing bowl, beat eggs and sugar until light and pale colored. Add flour and melted chocolate; stir well.

2. Pour into a greased 9-in. square baking pan. Bake at 350° for 25 minutes or until the brownies test done. Cool in pan on a wire rack.

3. For filling, beat confectioners' sugar, peanut butter and butter in a mixing bowl. Stir in cream until mixture achieves spreading consistency. Spread over cooled brownies; cover and refrigerate until firm.

4. For glaze; melt chocolate and butter in a saucepan, stirring until smooth. Drizzle over the filling. Chill before cutting. Store in the refrigerator.

Yield: about 5 dozen.

Editor's Note: Reduced-fat or generic brands of peanut butter are not recommended for this recipe.

Meringue Coconut Brownies

Diane Bridge
Clymer, Pennsylvania

Looking for an ooey-gooey brownie that's delicious and different? This sweet recipe combines a short-bread-like crust and a brown sugar meringue with chocolate, coconut and nuts. These never last long!

3/4 cup butter, softened

1-1/2 cups packed brown sugar, *divided*

1/2 cup sugar

3 eggs, *separated*

1 teaspoon vanilla extract

2 cups all-purpose flour

1 teaspoon baking powder

1/4 teaspoon baking soda

1/4 teaspoon salt

2 cups (12 ounces) semisweet chocolate chips

1 cup flaked coconut

3/4 cup chopped walnuts

1. In a large mixing bowl, cream the butter, 1/2 cup brown sugar and sugar. Add egg yolks and vanilla. Beat on medium speed for 2 minutes. Combine the flour, baking powder, baking soda and salt; add to creamed mixture and mix well (batter will be thick). Spread into a greased 13-in. x 9-in. x 2-in. baking pan. Sprinkle with the chocolate chips, coconut and walnuts.

2. In another large mixing bowl, beat egg whites on medium speed until soft peaks form. Gradually beat in remaining brown sugar, 1 tablespoon at a time, beating on high until stiff peaks form. Spread over the top.

3. Bake at 350° for 30-35 minutes or until a toothpick inserted near the center comes out clean. Cool in pan on a wire rack. Cut into bars. Store in the refrigerator.

Yield: 3 to 3-1/2 dozen.

Praline Brownies

Mindy Weiser
Southport, North Carolina

I created these brownies as a tribute to that luscious candy that is so popular in the Deep South.

1/2 cup packed dark brown sugar

3/4 cup butter, *divided*

2 tablespoons evaporated milk

1/2 cup coarsely chopped pecans

2 cups packed light brown sugar

2 eggs

1-1/2 cups all-purpose flour

1 teaspoon vanilla extract

1/2 teaspoon salt

1. In a saucepan, combine the dark brown sugar, 1/4 cup butter and milk. Stir over low heat just until butter is melted. Pour into an ungreased 8-in. square baking pan; sprinkle evenly with pecans.

2. In a mixing bowl, cream light brown sugar and remaining butter; add eggs. Stir in flour, vanilla and salt until moistened. Spread over pecans.

3. Bake at 350° for 40-45 minutes or until brownies test done. Cool for 5 minutes before inverting on to a tray or serving plate. Cool slightly before cutting.

Yield: 16 brownies.

Double Brownies

Rosanne Stevenson
Melfort, Saskatchewan

Living on a farm, I'm quite busy. I do, however, like to bake—and these are favorites of mine.

BOTTOM LAYER:
   1/2 cup butter, softened
1-1/4 cups packed brown sugar
   2 eggs
   2 teaspoons vanilla extract
   1/4 teaspoon salt
1-1/2 cups all-purpose flour
   1/2 cup chopped walnuts

MIDDLE LAYER:
   1/2 cup butter, softened
   1 cup sugar
   2 eggs
   1/8 teaspoon salt
   3/4 cup all-purpose flour
   1/4 cup baking cocoa
   1/2 cup chopped walnuts

CARAMEL ICING:
   6 tablespoons butter
   3/4 cup packed brown sugar
   4 to 6 tablespoons milk
2-1/2 cups confectioners' sugar

1. In a mixing bowl, cream the butter and brown sugar; beat in eggs, vanilla and salt. Stir in flour and nuts. Spread into a greased 13-in. x 9-in. x 2-in. baking pan; set aside.

2. For middle layer, cream butter and sugar; beat in eggs and salt. Stir in flour, cocoa and nuts. Spread over the bottom layer. Bake at 350° for 35-40 minutes or until a toothpick inserted near the center comes out clean. Cool in pan on a wire rack.

3. For icing, melt butter in a saucepan over medium heat. Stir in brown sugar and milk; bring to a boil. Remove from the heat. Cool just until warm; beat in confectioners' sugar until smooth. Spread over brownies. Cut into bars.

Yield: 2 dozen.

Cinnamon Brownies

Christopher Wolf, Belvidere, Illinois

No frosting is needed on top of these chewy, fudge-like brownies. This nice, basic bar packs a delicious burst of cinnamon in every bite.

1-2/3 cups sugar
   3/4 cup butter, melted
   2 tablespoons strong
      brewed coffee
   2 eggs
   2 teaspoons vanilla extract
1-1/3 cups all-purpose flour
   3/4 cup baking cocoa
   1 tablespoon ground
      cinnamon
   1/2 teaspoon baking powder
   1/4 teaspoon salt
   1 cup chopped walnuts
Confectioners' sugar

1. In a mixing bowl, beat the sugar, butter and coffee. Add eggs and vanilla. Combine the flour, cocoa, cinnamon, baking powder and salt; gradually add to the sugar mixture and mix well. Stir in walnuts.

2. Spread into a greased 13-in. x 9-in. x 2-in. baking pan. Bake at 350° for 18-22 minutes or until a toothpick inserted near the center comes out clean. Cool in pan on a wire rack. Dust with confectioners' sugar. Cut into bars.

Yield: 2 dozen.

Cashew Blondies

Kathey Skarie, Vergas, Minnesota

These easy-to-make white chocolate brownies are a hit at potlucks and other gatherings—I always come home with an empty plate and lots of glowing compliments.

2 eggs
2/3 cup sugar
1 teaspoon vanilla extract
8 squares (1 ounce *each*) white baking chocolate, melted and cooled
1/3 cup butter, melted
1-1/2 cups all-purpose flour
1-1/2 teaspoons baking powder
1/4 teaspoon salt
1/2 to 1 cup chopped salted cashews *or* pecans

1. In a mixing bowl, beat eggs, sugar and vanilla on medium speed for 1 minute. Beat in chocolate and butter. Combine the flour, baking powder and salt; gradually add to chocolate mixture. Stir in cashews.

2. Spread into a greased 9-in. square baking pan. Bake at 350° for 25-30 minutes or until a toothpick inserted near the center comes out clean. Cool in pan on a wire rack. Cut into bars.

Yield: 2 dozen.

Peppermint Chocolate Bars

Christine Harrell
Chester, Virginia

I received this treasured recipe from a dear friend years ago. The frosting and topping makes these thin brownies eye-catching.

1/2 cup butter
2 squares (1 ounce *each*) unsweetened chocolate
2 eggs
1 cup sugar
2 teaspoons vanilla extract
1/2 cup all-purpose flour
1/2 teaspoon salt
1/2 cup chopped pecans *or* walnuts

FROSTING:
1/4 cup butter, softened
2 cups confectioners' sugar
1 teaspoon peppermint extract
3 to 4 tablespoons heavy whipping cream

TOPPING:
1 square (1 ounce) semisweet chocolate
1 tablespoon butter

1. In a microwave or heavy saucepan, melt butter and chocolate; stir until smooth. Set aside to cool. In a mixing bowl, beat the eggs, sugar and vanilla. Add the chocolate mixture and mix well. Combine flour and salt; gradually add to chocolate mixture. Stir in nuts.

2. Spread into a greased 13-in. x 9-in. x 2-in. baking pan. Bake at 350° for 16-20 minutes or until a toothpick inserted near the center comes out clean. Cool in pan on a wire rack.

3. In a mixing bowl, cream butter, sugar and extract. Add enough cream until frosting achieves spreading consistency. Frost cooled bars. Melt chocolate and butter; drizzle over frosting. Cut into bars.

Yield: 4 dozen.

Chocolate Macaroon Brownies

Emily Engel, Quill Lake, Saskatchewan

The brownie base makes this recipe different from other macaroon bars. If time is short, substitute a boxed brownie mix for the base.

1-1/2 cups sugar
  2/3 cup vegetable oil
    4 eggs, beaten
    2 teaspoons vanilla extract, *divided*
1-1/3 cups all-purpose flour
  2/3 cup baking cocoa
    1 teaspoon baking powder
  1/2 teaspoon salt
    1 can (14 ounces) sweetened condensed milk
    3 cups flaked coconut

BUTTER FROSTING:
    2 cups confectioners' sugar
  1/2 cup baking cocoa
  1/2 cup butter, softened
    1 teaspoon vanilla extract
    1 to 2 tablespoons milk

1. In a large mixing bowl, combine sugar and oil. Add eggs and 1 teaspoon vanilla; mix well. Combine dry ingredients; add to bowl and mix until smooth.

2. Pour into a greased 13-in. x 9-in. x 2-in. baking pan. In a small bowl, combine condensed milk, coconut and remaining vanilla; spoon over brownie base. Bake at 350° for 30-35 minutes or until a toothpick inserted near the center comes out clean. Cool in pan on a wire rack.

3. For frosting, in a small mixing bowl, combine the sugar, cocoa, butter, vanilla and enough milk to achieve desired spreading consistency. Spread over filling. Cut into bars.

Yield: about 2 dozen.

Candy Bar Brownies

Sharon Evans
Rockwell, Iowa

Two kinds of candy bars baked into these brownies make them an extra-special treat.

  3/4 cup butter, melted
    2 cups sugar
    4 eggs
    2 teaspoons vanilla extract
1-1/2 cups all-purpose flour
  1/3 cup baking cocoa
  1/2 teaspoon baking powder
  1/4 teaspoon salt
    4 Snickers bars (2.07 ounces *each*), cut into 1/4-inch pieces
    3 plain milk chocolate candy bars (1.55 ounces *each*), coarsely chopped

1. In a bowl, combine the butter, sugar, eggs and vanilla. Combine the flour, cocoa, baking powder and salt; set aside 1/4 cup. Add remaining dry ingredients to the egg mixture; mix well. Toss Snickers pieces with reserved flour mixture; stir into batter.

2. Transfer to a greased 13-in. x 9-in. x 2-in. baking pan. Sprinkle with the milk chocolate candy bar pieces. Bake at 350° for 30-35 minutes or until a toothpick inserted near the center comes out clean (do not overbake). Cool in pan on a wire rack. Chill before cutting.

Yield: 3 dozen.

Favorite Frosted Brownies

Barbara Birk
St. George, Utah

I used candy sprinkles to dress up my tried-and-true Favorite Frosted Brownies for Valentine's Day. Everyone always agrees that they are so yummy!

1 cup butter, softened
2 cups sugar
4 eggs
2 teaspoons vanilla extract
1-3/4 cups all-purpose flour
6 tablespoons baking cocoa
1 teaspoon baking powder
1/4 teaspoon salt

FROSTING:
1/2 cup butter, softened
1/4 cup evaporated milk
1 teaspoon vanilla extract
2 tablespoons baking cocoa
3 cups confectioners' sugar
Decorating sprinkles, optional

1. In a large mixing bowl, cream butter and sugar. Add eggs, one at a time, beating well after each addition. Beat in vanilla. Combine the flour, cocoa, baking powder and salt; gradually add to creamed mixture and mix well.

2. Spread into a greased 13-in. x 9-in. x 2-in. baking pan. Bake at 350° for 25-30 minutes or until a toothpick inserted near the center comes out clean. Cool in pan on a wire rack.

3. For frosting, in a mixing bowl, beat the butter, milk and vanilla; add cocoa. Gradually beat in confectioners' sugar until smooth. Spread over cooled brownies. Decorate with sprinkles if desired. Cut into bars.

Yield: 12-15 servings.

Coconut Pecan Blondies

Anna Tokash Henry, Keller, Texas

Here's a classic white chocolate brownie that I've entered in the state fair and frequently made for the men I work with— I'm a landscaper.

1 egg
3/4 cup plus 2 tablespoons packed brown sugar
1/2 cup butter, melted and cooled
1-1/2 teaspoons vanilla extract
3/4 cup plus 2 tablespoons all-purpose flour
1/2 teaspoon baking soda
1/8 teaspoon salt
3/4 cup coarsely chopped pecans, toasted
2/3 cup flaked coconut
4 squares (1 ounce *each*) white baking chocolate, coarsely chopped

1. In a mixing bowl, beat egg and brown sugar for 3 minutes. Add butter and vanilla; mix well. Combine flour, baking soda and salt; gradually add to the brown sugar mixture, beating just until blended. Stir in pecans, coconut and white chocolate.

2. Spread into a greased 8-in. square baking dish. Bake at 325° for 30-40 minutes or until a toothpick inserted near the center comes out with moist crumbs (do not overbake). Cool in pan on a wire rack. Cut into bars.

Yield: 16 brownies.

Granola Blondies

Janet Farley
Snellville, Georgia

A mix of tasty, good-for-you ingredients makes these chewy blond brownies impossible to pass up. The granola adds crunch while dried fruit lends pleasing sweetness. I serve them to just about anybody who walks in our front door.

1 egg
1 egg white
1-1/4 cups packed brown sugar
1/4 cup canola oil
1 cup all-purpose flour
1 teaspoon baking powder
1/2 teaspoon salt
2 cups reduced-fat granola with raisins
1 cup dried cranberries *or* cherries

1. In a mixing bowl, combine the egg, egg white, brown sugar and oil; mix well. Combine the flour, baking powder and salt; stir into sugar mixture just until blended. Stir in granola and cranberries (batter will be thick).

2. Spread into a 9-in. square baking pan coated with nonstick cooking spray. Bake at 350° for 25-30 minutes or until golden and set. Cool in pan on a wire rack. Cut into bars.

Yield: 1 dozen.

Choco-Cloud Brownies

Linda Roecker, Hazelton, North Dakota

True to its name, this mild chocolate brownie is covered by a cloud of fluffy frosting. The recipe has earned lots of raves at our table.

1 cup butter, softened
2 cups sugar
4 eggs
1 milk chocolate candy bar (7 ounces), melted
3 teaspoons vanilla extract
2 cups all-purpose flour
1/2 teaspoon salt
2 cups chopped pecans

FROSTING:
5 tablespoons all-purpose flour
1 cup milk
1 cup butter, softened
1 cup confectioners' sugar
2 teaspoons vanilla extract
Baking cocoa

1. In a mixing bowl, cream butter and sugar. Add the eggs, one at a time, beating well after each. Add chocolate and vanilla; mix well. Gradually add flour and salt. Stir in pecans.

2. Spread into a greased 13-in. x 9-in. x 2-in. baking pan. Bake at 350° for 35-40 minutes or until center is set and edges pull away from pan. Cool in pan on a wire rack.

3. For frosting, combine flour and milk in a small saucepan until smooth. Bring to a boil; cook and stir for 2 minutes or until thickened. Remove from the heat; cool completely. In a mixing bowl, cream butter and confectioners' sugar. Add vanilla; mix well. Gradually add milk mixture; beat for 5 minutes or until fluffy. Frost brownies; dust with cocoa. Cut into bars. Store in the refrigerator.

Yield: about 2-1/2 dozen.

Marbling Batters

To give batters a marbled look, spoon one batter in a random pattern over the other batter. Cut through the batter with a knife. Be careful not to overdo it, or the two batters will blend together and you'll lose the effect.

Cookies 'n' Cream Brownies

Darlene Brenden
Salem, Oregon

You won't want to frost these brownies, since the marbled top is too pretty to cover up. Besides, the tasty cream cheese layer makes them taste like they're already frosted. The crushed cookies add extra chocolate flavor and a fun crunch.

CREAM CHEESE LAYER:
- 1 package (8 ounces) cream cheese, softened
- 1/4 cup sugar
- 1 egg
- 1/2 teaspoon vanilla extract

BROWNIE LAYER:
- 1/2 cup butter, melted
- 1/2 cup sugar
- 1/2 cup packed brown sugar
- 1/2 cup baking cocoa
- 2 eggs
- 1/2 cup all-purpose flour
- 1 teaspoon baking powder
- 1 teaspoon vanilla extract
- 12 cream-filled chocolate sandwich cookies, crushed

1. In a small mixing bowl, beat the cream cheese, sugar, egg and vanilla until smooth; set aside.

2. For brownie layer, combine butter, sugars and cocoa in a large mixing bowl; blend well. Add eggs, one at a time, beating well after each addition. Combine flour and baking powder; stir into the cocoa mixture. Stir in vanilla and cookie crumbs.

3. Pour into a greased 11-in. x 7-in. x 2-in. baking pan. Spoon cream cheese mixture over batter; cut through batter with a knife to swirl. Bake at 350° for 25-30 minutes or until a toothpick inserted near the center comes out with moist crumbs. Cool in pan on a wire rack. Cut into bars.

Yield: 2 dozen.

Blond Toffee Brownies

Mary Williams, Lancaster, California

Whenever my co-worker brought these to company bake sales, they sold in minutes. After getting the recipe from her, I was happy to discover how quickly they could be thrown together.

1/2 cup butter, softened
1 cup sugar
1/2 cup packed brown sugar
2 eggs
1 teaspoon vanilla extract
1-1/2 cups all-purpose flour
2 teaspoons baking powder
1/4 teaspoon salt
1 cup English toffee bits *or* almond brickle bits

1. In a mixing bowl, cream butter and sugars. Add eggs, one at a time, beating well after each addition. Beat in vanilla. Combine the flour, baking powder and salt; gradually add to creamed mixture. Stir in toffee bits.

2. Spread evenly into a greased 13-in. x 9-in. x 2-in. baking pan. Bake at 350° for 35-40 minutes or until a toothpick inserted near the center comes out clean. Cool in pan on a wire rack. Cut into bars.

Yield: 1-1/2 dozen.

Black Forest Brownies

Toni Reeves
Medicine Hat, Alberta

Although I enjoy sweets, other recipes have failed me (I'm a beginning baker!). But not this one! It's easy, and the ingredients are always on hand.

1-1/3 cups all-purpose flour
1 teaspoon baking powder
1/2 teaspoon salt
1 cup butter
1 cup baking cocoa
4 eggs, beaten
2 cups sugar
1-1/2 teaspoons vanilla extract
1 teaspoon almond extract
1 cup maraschino cherries
1/2 cup chopped nuts

ICING:
1/4 cup butter, softened
1 teaspoon vanilla extract
2 cups confectioners' sugar
6 tablespoons baking cocoa
1/4 cup milk
1/4 cup chopped nuts

1. Combine flour, baking powder and salt; set aside. In a large saucepan, melt butter. Remove from the heat and stir in cocoa until smooth. Blend in eggs, sugar and extracts. Stir in flour mixture, cherries and nuts.

2. Pour into a greased 13-in. x 9-in. x 2-in. baking pan. Bake at 350° for 35 minutes or until a toothpick inserted near the center comes out clean.

3. For icing, blend butter, vanilla, sugar, cocoa and milk until smooth; spread over hot brownies. Sprinkle with nuts. Cool in pan on a wire rack. Cut into bars.

Yield: 3 dozen.

Banana Nut Brownies

Christine Mol
Grand Rapids, Michigan

This recipe comes from my Grandma Schlientz. Anytime there are ripe bananas around our house, it's Banana Nut Brownie time! People are always surprised to learn there are bananas in the brownies.

1/2 cup butter, melted and cooled
1 cup sugar
3 tablespoons baking cocoa
2 eggs, lightly beaten
1 tablespoon milk
1 teaspoon vanilla extract
1/2 cup all-purpose flour
1 teaspoon baking powder
1/4 teaspoon salt
1 cup mashed ripe bananas (2-1/2 to 3 medium)
1/2 cup chopped walnuts
Confectioners' sugar, optional

1. In a bowl, combine butter, sugar and cocoa. Stir in eggs, milk and vanilla. Blend in flour, baking powder and salt. Stir in bananas and nuts.

2. Pour into a greased 9-in. square baking pan. Bake at 350° for 40-45 minutes or until the top of brownie springs back when lightly touched. Cool in pan on a wire rack. Just before serving, dust with confectioners' sugar if desired. Cut into bars.

Yield: 16 servings.

Very Chocolate Brownies

Jan Mock, Dillon, Montana

These brownies have chocolate chips and melted chocolate in the batter, making them doubly delicious. It's a crowd-pleasing treat that I count on when I need a special and delicious dessert to share.

2/3 cup butter
1-1/2 cups sugar
1/4 cup water
4 cups (24 ounces) semisweet chocolate chips, *divided*
2 teaspoons vanilla extract
4 eggs
1-1/2 cups all-purpose flour
1/2 teaspoon baking soda
1/2 teaspoon salt

1. In a heavy saucepan, bring butter, sugar and water to a boil, stirring constantly. Remove from the heat. Stir in 2 cups of chocolate chips until melted; cool slightly. Beat in vanilla. Cool to room temperature.

2. In a large mixing bowl, beat eggs. Gradually add chocolate mixture; mix well. Combine flour, baking soda and salt; gradually add to chocolate mixture. Stir in remaining chocolate chips.

3. Spread into a greased 13-in. x 9-in. x 2-in. baking pan. Bake at 325° for 35-40 minutes or until a toothpick inserted near the center comes out clean. Cool in pan on a wire rack. Cut into bars.

Yield: 3 dozen.

Apricot Meringue Bars, p. 191

Cereal Cookie Bars, p. 192

Blueberry Lattice Bars, p. 199

Fudge-Topped Shortbread, p. 193

Delectable Bars

One pan, so many tantalizing varieties! Bar cookies, whether they're patted or poured, layered or filled, frosted or sprinkled are satisfying sweets for so many reasons.

Tips for Making Bars

For a bake shop appearance, remove bars without soft fillings and toppings from pan before cutting. Trim sides and then cut into rectangles, squares or diamonds. The trimming can be crumbled and used as a topping for ice cream or pudding.

For bars with a soft filling, leave in the pan. With a knife, use a gentle sawing motion to cut into bars or squares. Remove the corner piece first. Then the rest will be easier to remove.

For perfectly sized bars or squares, use a ruler and make cut marks with point of a knife. Then lay ruler on top of bars between guide marks and use the edge as a cutting guide.

An 8-in. square dish will yield 16 (2-in.) squares or 64 (1-in.) squares. A 9-in. square pan will yield 54 (1-1/2-in. x 1-in.) bars or 81 (1-in.) squares. A 13-in. x 9-in. x 2-in. pan will yield 78 (1-1/2-in. x 1-in.) bars.

Cherry Coconut Bars

Marguerite Emery
Orland, California

I came across these bars while stationed at a Michigan Air Force base in 1964 and have been making them ever since. My children don't think an event is special unless these bars are part of it.

- 1 cup all-purpose flour
- 3 tablespoons confectioners' sugar
- 1/2 cup cold butter

FILLING:
- 2 eggs
- 1 cup sugar
- 1 teaspoon vanilla extract
- 1/4 cup all-purpose flour
- 1/2 teaspoon baking powder
- 1/4 teaspoon salt
- 3/4 cup chopped walnuts
- 1/2 cup quartered maraschino cherries
- 1/2 cup flaked coconut

1. In a bowl, combine flour and confectioners' sugar; cut in butter until crumbly. Press into a lightly greased 13-in. x 9-in. x 2-in. baking pan. Bake at 350° for 10-12 minutes or until lightly browned. Cool in pan on wire rack.

2. For filling, combine the eggs, sugar and vanilla in a bowl. Combine flour, baking powder and salt; add to the egg mixture. Stir in walnuts, cherries and coconut. Spread over crust. Bake at 350° 20-25 minutes longer or until firm. Cool in pan on a wire rack. Cut into bars.

Yield: 3 dozen.

Best Date Bars

Dorothy DeLeske
Scottsdale, Arizona

These wholesome bar cookies freeze well. Simply cool in the pan, cut into squares. Wrap each bar in plastic wrap, then freeze.

2-1/2 cups pitted dates, cut up
  1/4 cup sugar
1-1/2 cups water
  1/3 cup coarsely chopped walnuts, optional
1-1/4 cups all-purpose flour
    1 teaspoon salt
  1/2 teaspoon baking soda
1-1/2 cups quick-cooking oats
    1 cup packed brown sugar
  1/2 cup butter, softened
    1 tablespoon water

1. In a saucepan, combine dates, sugar and water. Cook, stirring frequently, until very thick. Stir in walnuts; cool. Meanwhile, sift flour, salt and baking soda together in a mixing bowl; add oats and brown sugar. Cut in butter until crumbly. Sprinkle water over mixture; stir lightly.

2. Pat half into a greased 13-in. x 9-in. x 2-in. baking pan. Spread with date mixture; cover with remaining oat mixture and pat lightly. Bake at 350° for 35-40 minutes or until lightly browned. Cool in pan on a wire rack. Cut into bars.

Yield: 40 bars.

Apricot Meringue Bars

(Pictured on page 188)
Krissy Fossmeyer, Huntley, Illinois

    3 cups all-purpose flour
    1 cup sugar, *divided*
    1 cup cold butter
    4 eggs, *separated*
    1 teaspoon vanilla extract
    2 cans (12 ounces *each*) apricot filling
  1/2 cup chopped pecans

I'm expected to bring these wonderful treats to our family picnic each year. Their sweet apricot filling and delicate meringue topping make them everyone's favorite. I wouldn't dream of hosting a get-together without serving these bars.

1. In a large bowl, combine flour and 1/2 cup sugar; cut in butter until crumbly. Add egg yolks and vanilla; mix well. Press into a greased 15-in. x 10-in. x 1-in. baking pan. Bake at 350° for 12-15 minutes or until lightly browned. Spread apricot filling over crust.

2. In a large mixing bowl, beat egg whites until soft peaks form. Gradually add the remaining sugar, 1 tablespoon at a time, beating until stiff peaks form. Spread over apricot layer; sprinkle with pecans.

3. Bake for 25-30 minutes or until lightly browned. Cool in pan on a wire rack. Cut into bars. Store in the refrigerator.

Yield: 32 bars.

Cereal Cookie Bars

(Pictured on page 189)
Connie Craig, Lakewood, Washington

These chewy crowd-pleasers feature all sorts of goodies, including chocolate chips, raisins, coconut and candy-coated baking bits. For a more colorful look, press the baking bits on top of the bars instead of stirring them into the cereal mixture.

    9 cups crisp rice cereal
6-1/2 cups quick-cooking oats
    1 cup cornflakes
    1 cup flaked coconut
    2 packages (one 16 ounces, one 10-1/2 ounces) miniature marshmallows
    1 cup butter, cubed
1/2 cup honey
1/2 cup chocolate chips
1/2 cup raisins
1/2 cup M&M miniature baking bits

1. In a large bowl, combine the cereal, oats, cornflakes and coconut; set aside. In a large saucepan, cook and stir the marshmallows and butter over low heat until melted and smooth. Stir in honey. Pour over cereal mixture; stir until coated. Cool for 5 minutes.

2. Stir in chocolate chips, raisins and baking bits. Press into two greased 15-in. x 10-in. x 1-in. pans. Cool for 30 minutes before cutting.

Yield: 6 dozen.

Lattice Fruit Bars

Betty Keisling
Knoxville, Tennessee

These attractive bars make a beautiful addition to any table. I like the fact that one batch goes a long way.

    3 cups all-purpose flour
    1 cup sugar
    1 teaspoon baking powder
1/2 teaspoon salt
    1 cup cold butter
    2 eggs
    2 teaspoons vanilla extract
3/4 cup apricot preserves
3/4 cup raspberry preserves

1. In a bowl, combine the flour, sugar, baking powder and salt; cut in butter until crumbly. Combine eggs and vanilla; add to crumb mixture until blended. Cover and refrigerate a fourth of the dough for at least 45 minutes.

2. Press remaining dough into an ungreased 15-in. x 10-in. x 1-in. baking pan. Spread 1/4 cup apricot preserves in a 1-3/4-in. strip over one long side of crust. Spread 1/4 cup of raspberry preserves in a 1-3/4-in. strip adjoining the apricot strip. Repeat twice. Roll out reserved dough to 1/8-in. thickness. Cut into 1/2-in. strips; make a lattice top.

3. Bake at 325° for 30-35 minutes or until lightly browned. Cool in pan on wire rack. Cut into bars.

Yield: about 3-1/2 dozen.

Glazed Lebkuchen

Taste of Home Test Kitchen
Greendale, Wisconsin

Honey and spices give great flavor to these cake-like bars topped with a thin sugar glaze.

- 3/4 cup honey
- 1/2 cup sugar
- 1/4 cup packed brown sugar
- 2 eggs
- 2-1/2 cups all-purpose flour
- 1-1/4 teaspoons ground cinnamon
- 1 teaspoon baking soda
- 1/4 teaspoon ground cloves
- 1/8 teaspoon ground allspice
- 3/4 cup chopped slivered almonds
- 1/2 cup finely chopped citron
- 1/2 cup finely chopped candied lemon peel

FROSTING:
- 1 cup confectioners' sugar
- 3 tablespoons hot milk *or* water
- 1/4 teaspoon vanilla extract

Candied cherries and additional citron

1. In a saucepan, bring honey to a boil. Remove from the heat; cool to room temperature. In a mixing bowl, combine honey and sugars; mix well. Add eggs, one at a time, beating well after each addition. Combine the flour, cinnamon, baking soda, cloves and allspice; gradually add to honey mixture. Stir in nuts, citron and lemon peel (mixture will be thick).

2. Press into a greased 15-in. x 10-in. x 1-in. baking pan. Bake at 350° for 20-28 minutes or until top springs back with lightly touched.

3. Meanwhile, combine the confectioners' sugar, milk and vanilla; mix well. Spread over bars while warm. Immediately cut into bars. Decorate with cherries and citron. Cool in pan on a wire rack.

Yield: about 2 dozen.

Fudge-Topped Shortbread

(Pictured on page 189)
Valarie Wheeler, DeWitt, Michigan

This combination of buttery shortbread and sweet chocolate is wonderful. Whenever I make it, there is nothing but crumbs left. Be sure to cut these into small squares because they are very rich.

- 1 cup butter, softened
- 1/2 cup confectioners' sugar
- 1/4 teaspoon salt
- 1-1/4 cups all-purpose flour
- 1 can (14 ounces) sweetened condensed milk
- 2 cups (12 ounces) semisweet chocolate chips
- 1/2 teaspoon almond extract
- 1/3 cup sliced almonds, toasted

1. In a mixing bowl, cream the butter, sugar and salt until fluffy. Gradually beat in flour. Spread into a greased 13-in. x 9-in. x 2-in. baking pan. Bake at 350° for 16-20 minutes or until lightly browned.

2. In a microwave-safe bowl, combine condensed milk and chocolate chips. Microwave, uncovered, on high for 1-2 minutes or until chips are melted; stir until smooth. Stir in extract. Spread over the shortbread. Sprinkle with almonds and press down. Chill until set. Cut into squares.

Yield: 4 dozen.

Blarney Stone Bars

Taste of Home Test Kitchen
Greendale, Wisconsin

A lip-smacking layer of tinted frosting is the crowning touch to these butterscotch bars ladened with crunchy pecans.

- 1/2 cup butter, softened
- 3/4 cup packed brown sugar
- 2 eggs
- 1 tablespoon milk
- 1 teaspoon vanilla extract
- 3/4 cup all-purpose flour
- 3/4 cup quick-cooking oats
- 1/2 teaspoon baking powder
- 1/4 teaspoon salt
- 3/4 cup English toffee bits *or* almond brickle chips
- 1/3 cup chopped pecans
- 4 drops green food coloring
- 3/4 cup vanilla frosting

1. In a mixing bowl, cream butter and sugar. Beat in eggs, milk and vanilla. Combine flour, oats, baking powder and salt; add to the creamed mixture. Fold in the toffee bits and pecans.

2. Spread into a greased 9-in. square baking pan. Bake at 350° for 20-24 minutes or until a toothpick comes out clean. Cool in pan on a wire rack. Add food coloring to frosting; spread over the bars. Cut into diamond shapes.

Yield: about 3-1/2 dozen.

Crunchy Cheesecake Bars

Try this lemon-flavored bar when you're looking for something that's not too sweet.

Shelia Kales, Sceptre, Saskatchewan

- 1 cup all-purpose flour
- 1/3 cup packed brown sugar
- 6 tablespoons cold butter
- 1 package (8 ounces) cream cheese, softened
- 1/4 cup sugar
- 1 egg
- 2 tablespoons milk
- 1/4 teaspoon grated lemon peel
- 2 tablespoons lemon juice
- 1/2 teaspoon vanilla extract
- 3/4 cup chopped nuts

1. In a medium bowl, mix flour and brown sugar. Cut in butter until mixture resembles fine crumbs. Set aside 1/2 cup for topping. Press remaining crumbs into bottom of an ungreased 8-in. square baking dish. Bake at 350° for 15 minutes.

2. Meanwhile, in a mixing bowl, beat cream cheese on medium speed for 30 seconds. Add sugar; beat until fluffy. Add the egg, milk, lemon peel, juice and vanilla; mix well. Spread over baked crust. Combine nuts with reserved crumbs; sprinkle over cream cheese mixture.

3. Bake 20-25 minutes longer or until done. Cool in pan on wire rack. Cut into bars. Store in the refrigerator.

Yield: 2 dozen.

Chocolaty Raisin Oat Bars

Linda Ploeg, Rockford, Michigan

These attractive layered bars have a similar taste to chocolate-covered raisins. "Yum!" is usually how folks describe every bite.

1 can (14 ounces) sweetened condensed milk
2 squares (1 ounce *each*) unsweetened chocolate
2 cups raisins
1 cup butter, softened
1-1/3 cups packed brown sugar
1-1/2 teaspoons vanilla extract
2-1/2 cups quick-cooking oats
2 cups all-purpose flour
3/4 teaspoon salt
1/2 teaspoon baking soda

1. In a microwave-safe bowl, combine milk and chocolate. Microwave on high for 2 minutes or until chocolate is melted; stir until smooth. Stir in raisins; set aside to cool slightly.

2. In a mixing bowl, cream butter and brown sugar. Beat in vanilla. Combine the remaining ingredients; gradually add to creamed mixture (dough will be crumbly). Set aside half for topping.

3. Press remaining crumb mixture into an ungreased 13-in. x 9-in. x 2-in. baking pan. Spread with the chocolate raisin mixture. Sprinkle with reserved crumb mixture; press down lightly. Bake at 375° for 25-30 minutes or until golden brown. Cool in pan on a wire rack. Cut into bars.

Yield: 4 dozen.

Crimson Crumble Bars

Paula Eriksen
Palm Harbor, Florida

Baking is my favorite pastime. These moist cranberry bars have a refreshing sweet-tart taste and a pleasant crumble topping. They're great as a snack or anytime treat.

1 cup sugar
2 teaspoons cornstarch
2 cups fresh *or* frozen cranberries
1 can (8 ounces) unsweetened crushed pineapple, undrained
1 cup all-purpose flour
2/3 cup old-fashioned oats
2/3 cup packed brown sugar
1/4 teaspoon salt
1/2 cup cold butter
1/2 cup chopped pecans

1. In a saucepan, combine the sugar, cornstarch, cranberries and pineapple; bring to a boil, stirring often. Reduce heat; cover and simmer for 10-15 minutes or until the berries pop. Remove from the heat.

2. In a large bowl, combine the flour, oats, brown sugar and salt. Cut in butter until mixture resembles coarse crumbs. Stir in pecans. Set aside 1-1/2 cups for topping.

3. Press remaining crumb mixture onto bottom of a 13-in. x 9-in. x 2-in. baking pan coated with nonstick cooking spray. Bake at 350° for 8-10 minutes or until firm. Cool for 10 minutes.

4. Pour fruit filling over crust. Sprinkle with reserved crumb mixture. Bake 25-30 minutes longer or until golden brown. Cool in pan on a wire rack. Cut into bars.

Yield: 2 dozen.

Springtime Strawberry Bars

Marna Heitz, Farley, Iowa

Warmer weather calls for a lighter dessert like these fruity bars. The recipe makes a big batch, so it's perfect for company.

1 cup butter, softened
1-1/2 cups sugar
2 eggs
1 teaspoon grated lemon peel
3-1/4 cups all-purpose flour
3/4 cup slivered almonds, chopped
1 teaspoon baking powder
1/2 teaspoon salt
1 jar (12 ounces) strawberry preserves

1. In a large mixing bowl, cream the butter and sugar. Add eggs, one at a time, beating well after each addition. Beat in lemon peel. Combine 3 cups flour, almonds, baking powder and salt; gradually add to creamed mixture until mixture resembles coarse crumbs (do not over mix).

2. Set aside 1 cup of dough. Press remaining dough into a greased 15-in. x 10-in. x 1-in. baking pan. Spread preserves to within 1/4 in. of edges. Combine the reserved dough with the remaining flour; sprinkle over preserves. Bake at 350° for 25-30 minutes or until lightly browned. Cool in pan on wire rack. Cut into bars.

Yield: about 3 dozen.

Lemon Bars

Etta Soucy
Mesa, Arizona

This dessert is a delightful recipe from my mother's file. I've been serving it for many years. The bars have a wonderful tangy flavor, and they're always a hit. For variety of color and shape, they're a nice addition to a platter of cookies.

1 cup all-purpose flour
1/2 cup butter, softened
1/4 cup confectioners' sugar

FILLING:
2 eggs
1 cup sugar
2 tablespoons all-purpose flour
1/2 teaspoon baking powder
2 tablespoons lemon juice
1 teaspoon grated lemon peel
Additional confectioners' sugar

1. Combine the first three ingredients; pat into an ungreased 8-in. square baking dish. Bake at 350° for 20 minutes.

2. Meanwhile, beat eggs in a mixing bowl. Add sugar, flour, baking powder, lemon juice and peel; beat until frothy. Pour over the crust. Bake at 350° for 25 minutes longer or until light golden brown. Cool in pan on a wire rack. Dust with confectioners' sugar. Cut into bars.

Yield: 9 servings.

Frosted Raspberry Bars

Esther Horst
Augusta, Wisconsin

While visiting a friend, I tried one of these tempting treats that her daughter made. After one bite, I knew I had to have the recipe. The cake-like bars with a fruity filling and creamy frosting are a sweet solution for any potluck or party.

1 cup butter, softened
1/4 cup sugar
3 cups all-purpose flour
3 teaspoons baking powder
1 teaspoon salt
2 eggs
1/2 cup milk
1 teaspoon vanilla extract
1 can (21 ounces) raspberry pie filling

FROSTING:
1 tablespoon butter, softened
1 tablespoon shortening
1 ounce cream cheese, softened
2 tablespoons marshmallow creme
1/2 cup plus 1 tablespoon confectioners' sugar
1 tablespoon milk

1. In a mixing bowl, cream butter and sugar. Combine the flour, baking powder and salt. Combine eggs, milk and vanilla. Add dry ingredients to the creamed mixture alternately with egg mixture; mix well. Divide dough in half; cover and refrigerate for 2 hours or until firm.

2. Roll out one portion of dough into a 15-in. x 10-in. rectangle; carefully transfer to a greased 15-in. x 10-in. x 1-in. baking pan. Spread with the raspberry filling. Roll out remaining dough to 1/4-in. thickness. Cut into 1/2-in.–wide strips; make a lattice crust over filling. Bake at 350° for 30 minutes or until golden brown. Cool in pan on a wire rack.

3. In a small mixing bowl, beat the butter, shortening, cream cheese and marshmallow cream until smooth. Add the confectioners' sugar and milk; mix well. Drizzle over bars. Refrigerate until set before cutting into bars. Store in the refrigerator.

Yield: about 2 dozen.

Graham Coconut Treats

Renee Schwebach, Dumont, Minnesota

To satisfy a sweet tooth, try these deliciously different bars. A tasty variety of flavors and textures guarantees that the treats never last long.

3 eggs, lightly beaten
1-1/2 cups sugar
1 cup butter
4 cups miniature marshmallows
3 cups graham cracker crumbs (about 48 squares)
3/4 cup flaked coconut
3/4 cup chopped pecans
1-1/2 teaspoons vanilla extract

1. In a heavy saucepan over low heat or double boiler over simmering water, combine the eggs, sugar and butter. Cook and stir until mixture thickness and reaches 160°. Remove from the heat; cool.

2. Add remaining ingredients; mix well. Spoon into a greased 13-in. x 9-in. x 2-in. baking pan. Refrigerate for at least 2 hours. Cut into squares.

Yield: 3 dozen.

Rhubarb Custard Bars

Shari Roach
South Milwaukee, Wisconsin

Once I tried these rich gooey bars, I just had to have the recipe so I could make them for my family and friends. The shortbread-like crust and rhubarb and custard layers inspire people to find rhubarb they can use to fix a batch for themselves.

2 cups all-purpose flour

1/4 cup sugar

1 cup cold butter

FILLING:

2 cups sugar

7 tablespoons all-purpose flour

1 cup heavy whipping cream

3 eggs, beaten

5 cups finely chopped fresh *or* frozen rhubarb, thawed and drained

TOPPING:

2 packages (3 ounces *each*) cream cheese, softened

1/2 cup sugar

1/2 teaspoon vanilla extract

1 cup heavy whipping cream, whipped

1. In a bowl, combine the flour and sugar; cut in butter until the mixture resembles coarse crumbs. Press into a greased 13-in. x 9-in. x 2-in. baking pan. Bake at 350° for 10 minutes.

2. Meanwhile, for filling, combine sugar and flour in a bowl. Whisk in cream and eggs. Stir in the rhubarb. Pour over crust. Bake at 350° for 40-45 minutes or until custard is set. Cool in pan on a wire rack.

3. For topping, beat cream cheese, sugar and vanilla until smooth; fold in whipped cream. Spread over top. Cover and refrigerate. Cut into bars. Store in the refrigerator.

Yield: 3 dozen.

Caramel Pecan Bars

Emma Manning, Crosset, Arkansas

This recipe won first place at a cookie contest held where I work. Everyone agreed that these rich bars really capture the flavor of pecan pie.

1 cup butter

2-1/4 cups packed brown sugar

2 eggs

2 teaspoons vanilla extract

1-1/2 cups all-purpose flour

2 teaspoons baking powder

2 cups chopped pecans

Confectioners' sugar, optional

1. In a saucepan, heat butter and brown sugar over medium heat until sugar is dissolved. In a mixing bowl, combine the eggs, vanilla and butter mixture. Combine flour and baking powder; gradually add to the butter mixture. Stir in pecans.

2. Spread into a greased 13-in. x 9-in. x 2-in. baking pan. Bake at 350° for 20-25 minutes or until a toothpick inserted near the center comes out with moist crumbs and edges are crisp. Cool in pan on a wire rack. Dust with confectioners' sugar if desired. Cut into bars.

Yield: 4 dozen.

Blueberry Lattice Bars

(Pictured on page 189)
Debbie Ayers, Baileyville, Maine

Since our area has an annual blueberry festival, my daughters and I are always looking for great new berry recipes to enter in the cooking contest. These lovely yummy bars won a blue ribbon one year.

1 cup butter, softened
1/2 cup sugar
1 egg
2-3/4 cups all-purpose flour
1/2 teaspoon vanilla extract
1/4 teaspoon salt

FILLING:
3 cups fresh *or* frozen blueberries
1 cup sugar
3 tablespoons cornstarch

1. In a mixing bowl, cream butter and sugar. Add the egg, flour, vanilla and salt; mix well. Cover and refrigerate for 2 hours. Meanwhile, in a saucepan, combine the blueberries, sugar and cornstarch. Bring to a boil; cook and stir for 2 minutes or until thickened.

2. Roll two-thirds of the dough into a 14-in. x 10-in. rectangle. Place in a greased 13-in. x 9-in. x 2-in. baking dish. Top with the filling. Roll out remaining dough to 1/4-in. thickness. Cut into 1/2-in.-wide strips; make a lattice crust over filling.

3. Bake at 375° for 30-35 minutes or until top is golden brown. Cool in pan on a wire rack. Cut into bars. Store in the refrigerator.

Yield: 2 dozen.

Cheerio Treats

Penny Reifenrath
Wynot, Nebraska

Peanut butter, Cherrios and candies put a tooth-tingling spin on marshmallow-cereal bars. Whether I take them to picnics or bake sales, I'm always asked for the recipe.

3 tablespoons butter
1 package (10-1/2 ounces) miniature marshmallows
1/2 cup peanut butter
5 cups Cheerios
1 cup milk chocolate M&M's

1. Place the butter and marshmallows in a large microwave-safe bowl. Microwave, uncovered, on high for 2 minutes or until puffed. Stir in the peanut butter until blended. Add the cereal and M&M's; mix well.

2. Spoon into a greased 13-in. x 9-in. x 2-in. pan; press down gently. Cool slightly before cutting.

Yield: 15 servings.

Editor's Note: Reduced-fat or generic brands of peanut butter are not recommended for this recipe.

Raspberry Almond Bars

A pan of these thick bars makes a pretty presentation at any gathering. The buttery crust has a light almond flavor.

Ann Midkiff, Jackson, Michigan

2 cups butter, softened

2 cups sugar

2 eggs

1 teaspoon almond extract

5 cups all-purpose flour

1 teaspoon baking powder

1 jar (12 ounces) raspberry jam

1. In a mixing bowl, cream the butter and sugar. Add eggs, one at a time, beating well after each addition. Beat in extract. Combine flour and baking powder; gradually add to the creamed mixture.

2. Press into a greased 13-in. x 9-in. x 2-in. baking pan. With a moistened finger, make diagonal indentations every 2 in. in both directions, about 1/3 in. deep. Fill indentations with jam. Bake at 350° for 40 minutes or until lightly browned. Cool in pan on a wire rack. Cut into bars.

Yield: about 3 dozen.

Lime Coconut Bars

Mary Jane Jones
Williamstown, West Virginia

I found this dessert in my mother's recipe collection. I also garnish them with whipped cream and lime.

3/4 cup finely crushed crisp sugar cookies

3 tablespoons cold butter

2-1/4 cups flaked coconut

FILLING:

1/4 cup butter

3/4 cup sugar

1/2 cup lime juice

4-1/2 teaspoons yellow cornmeal

Dash salt

4 egg yolks

1 teaspoon grated lime peel

Confectioners' sugar

1. Place the crushed cookies in a bowl. Cut in butter until mixture resembles coarse crumbs. Stir in coconut; set aside 1 cup for topping. Press the remaining mixture into a greased 8-in. baking dish. Bake at 350° for 13-15 minutes or until golden brown.

2. Meanwhile, for filling, combine the butter, sugar, lime juice, cornmeal and salt in a heavy saucepan. Cook and stir over low heat until sugar is dissolved and cornmeal is softened, about 10 minutes. Remove from the heat.

3. In a small bowl, lightly beat the egg yolks. Stir a small amount of hot lime mixture into the yolks; return all to the pan, stirring constantly. Cook and stir over low heat until a thermometer reads 160° and mixture coats the back of a metal spoon, about 20 minutes. Remove from the heat; stir in lime peel.

4. Pour over the crust; sprinkle with reserved coconut mixture. Bake at 350° for 18-20 minutes or until golden brown. Cool in pan on a wire rack. Dust with confectioners' sugar. Cut into bars.

Yield: 16 bars.

Editor's Note: The cornmeal is used as a thickener in the filling.

Scotch Shortbread Cookies

Marlene Hellickson
Big Bear City, California

This simple three-ingredient recipe makes wonderfully rich, bars. Serve them with fresh berries of the season for a nice, light dessert. You'll get miles of smiles with these at an afternoon tea or at a bridal shower.

4 cups all-purpose flour
1 cup sugar
1 pound cold butter

1. In a large mixing bowl, combine flour and sugar. Cut in butter until mixture resembles fine crumbs. Knead dough until smooth, about 6 to 10 minutes.

2. Pat dough into an ungreased 15-in. x 10-in. x 1-in. baking pan. Pierce with a fork if desired. Bake at 325° for 25 to 30 minutes or until lightly browned. While warm if desired, cut into squares. Cool.

Yield: 4 dozen.

Fruit 'n' Nut Bars

Mrs. John Nagel
Deerbrook, Wisconsin

1-1/4 cups chopped almonds
1 jar (2 ounces) sesame seeds
4 cups quick-cooking oats
1 cup dark seedless raisins
1 cup light corn syrup
2/3 cup vegetable oil
1/2 cup hulled sunflower seeds
1/2 cup toasted wheat germ
1/2 cup nonfat dry milk powder
2 teaspoons ground cinnamon
1 teaspoon vanilla extract
1/2 teaspoon salt

Here's a healthy treat that grandchildren are sure to enjoy. These granola-like bars are filled with flavor and good-for-you ingredients. For convenient snacking, wrap the bars individually in plastic wrap.

1. In a large bowl, combine all ingredients; mix well. Press mixture firmly and evenly into a greased 15-in. x 10-in. x 1-in. baking pan.

2. Bake at 350° for 25 minutes or until golden brown. Cool in pan on wire rack for at least 2 hours. Cut into bars. Store in refrigerator.

Yield: 1-1/2 dozen.

Raspberry Nut Bars

Beth Ask
Ulster, Pennsylvania

Raspberry jam adds sweetness to these pretty bars. I revised the original recipe to reduce fat and calories. The end result is a treat so delicious you'll never know it's good for you.

    1/2 cup margarine
    1/4 cup reduced-fat margarine
    1/3 cup packed brown sugar
    1/4 cup sugar
      1 egg
      1 teaspoon vanilla extract
      2 cups all-purpose flour
      1 teaspoon baking powder
    1/4 teaspoon baking soda
    1/4 teaspoon salt
    3/4 cup chopped pecans,
         divided
    2/3 cup raspberry jam
      2 tablespoons lemon juice

GLAZE:
    1/2 cup confectioners' sugar
      2 teaspoons fat-free milk

1. In a mixing bowl, cream margarines and sugars. Beat in egg and vanilla. Combine flour, baking powder, baking soda and salt; add to creamed mixture and mix well. Stir in 1/2 cup pecans.

2. Spread half of the dough into a 13-in. x 9-in. x 2-in. baking pan coated with nonstick cooking spray. Combine jam and lemon juice; spread over dough. Dollop remaining dough over top. Sprinkle with remaining pecans.

3. Bake at 325° for 30-35 minutes or until lightly browned. Cool in pan on a wire rack. Combine glaze ingredients; drizzle over bars. Let stand until cooled. Cut into bars.

Yield: 3 dozen.

Rhubarb Dream Bars

Marion Tomlinson, Madison, Wisconsin

Dreaming of a different way to use rhubarb? Try these sweet bars. The tender shortbread-like crust is topped with rhubarb, walnuts and coconut for delicious results.

1-1/4 cups all-purpose flour,
       divided
  1/3 cup confectioners' sugar
  1/2 cup cold butter
1-1/4 to 1-1/2 cups sugar
    2 eggs
    2 cups finely chopped
       rhubarb
  1/2 cup chopped walnuts
  1/2 cup flaked coconut

1. In a bowl, combine 1 cup flour and confectioners' sugar. Cut in the butter until crumbly. Pat into a lightly greased 13-in. x 9-in. x 2-in. baking dish. Bake at 350° for 13-15 minutes or until edges are lightly browned.

2. In a bowl, combine the sugar and remaining flour. Add eggs; mix well. Stir in rhubarb, walnuts and coconut; pour over crust. Bake 30-35 minutes longer or until set. Cool in pan on a wire rack. Cut into bars. Store in the refrigerator.

Yield: 2-1/2 to 3 dozen.

Peppermint Crumb Squares

Martha Kerr, Abilene, Texas

Although I have a boxful of recipes, I often opt to make up my own. My granddaughter likes to eat these bars when she visits.

3/4 cup butter, softened
1/2 cup packed brown sugar
2 cups all-purpose flour
1 can (14 ounces) sweetened condensed milk
1 package (10 to 12 ounces) vanilla *or* white chips
2/3 cup crushed peppermint candies

1. In a mixing bowl, cream butter and brown sugar. Add flour; beat until crumbly. Press 2 cups into a greased 13-in. x 9-in. x 2-in. baking pan; set remaining crumb mixture aside. Bake the crust at 350° for 8-10 minutes.

2. Meanwhile, in a microwave or heavy saucepan, heat milk and vanilla chips until chips are melted, stirring until smooth. Pour over hot crust and spread evenly. Combine candy and reserved crumb mixture; sprinkle over top.

3. Bake for 18-22 minutes or until lightly browned. Cool in pan on a wire rack. Cut into squares.

Yield: 4 dozen.

Banana Nut Bars

Susan Huckaby
Smiths, Alabama

My sister gave me this recipe, which is always in demand with family, friends and co-workers. It's amazing how fast these tempting bars vanish when I serve them! The cream cheese frosting is heavenly.

1 cup butter, cubed
1/2 cup water
2 cups all-purpose flour
1-1/2 cups sugar
1/2 cup packed brown sugar
1 teaspoon baking soda
2 eggs
1 cup mashed ripe bananas (about 2 medium)
1/2 cup buttermilk
1 teaspoon vanilla extract
1/2 cup chopped pecans *or* walnuts

FROSTING:
1 package (8 ounces) cream cheese, softened
1/2 cup butter, softened
1 teaspoon vanilla extract
3-1/2 cups confectioners' sugar

1. In a saucepan, bring butter and water to a boil. Remove from the heat; set aside. In a mixing bowl, combine the flour, sugars, baking soda, eggs, bananas, buttermilk and vanilla. Beat until blended. Carefully add butter mixture; mix well. Stir in nuts.

2. Pour into a greased 15-in. x 10-in. x 1-in. baking pan. Bake at 350° for 18-22 minutes or until a toothpick inserted near the center comes out clean. Cool in pan on a wire rack.

3. For frosting, in a mixing bowl, beat cream cheese and butter until light and fluffy. Beat in vanilla. Gradually add confectioners' sugar. Spread over bars. Store in the refrigerator.

Yield: 3 dozen.

Windmill Cookie Bars

Edna Hoffman, Hebron, Indiana

When I went to my grandma's house as a child, she was often baking Dutch windmill cookies. Like her cookies, my bars feature crisp slivered almonds.

- 1 cup butter, softened
- 1 cup sugar
- 1 egg, *separated*
- 2 cups all-purpose flour
- 1 teaspoon ground cinnamon
- 1/4 teaspoon baking soda
- 1 cup slivered almonds

1. In a bowl, cream butter and sugar. Add egg yolk; mix well. Combine the flour, cinnamon and baking soda; gradually add to creamed mixture.

2. Press into a greased 15-in. x 10-in. x 1-in. baking pan. Beat the egg white; brush over dough. Sprinkle with almonds.

3. Bake at 350° for 20-25 minutes or until a toothpick inserted near the center comes out clean. Cool for 5 minutes, before cutting into bars; cool completely.

Yield: 2-1/2 dozen.

Teddy Carrot Bars

Susan Schuller
Brainerd, Minnesota

I made these for a baby shower and pointed out to the mother-to-be and shower guests that these yummy bars include two jars of baby food!

- 1-1/4 cups all-purpose flour
- 1 cup sugar
- 1 teaspoon baking soda
- 1 teaspoon ground cinnamon
- 1/2 teaspoon salt
- 1 jar (6 ounces) carrot baby food
- 1 jar (6 ounces) applesauce baby food
- 2 eggs
- 2 tablespoons vegetable oil

CREAM CHEESE FROSTING:
- 1 package (3 ounces) cream cheese, softened
- 1 teaspoon vanilla extract
- 2 to 2-1/2 cups confectioners' sugar
- 1 to 3 teaspoons milk
- 24 cinnamon-flavored bear-shaped graham crackers

1. In a mixing bowl, combine the flour, sugar, baking soda, cinnamon and salt. Combine the baby foods, eggs and oil; add to dry ingredients just until blended.

2. Pour into a greased 13-in. x 9-in. x 2-in. baking pan. Bake at 350° for 20-25 minutes or until a toothpick inserted near the center comes out clean. Cool in pan on a wire rack. Cut into bars.

3. For frosting, in a mixing bowl, beat the cream cheese and vanilla until smooth. Gradually add confectioners' sugar. Add enough to milk to achieve desired consistency. Place a dollop of frosting on each bar; top with a bear-shaped graham cracker.

Yield: 2 dozen.

Apricot Bars

Jill Moritz
Irvine, California

This recipe is elegant enough to serve for dessert yet casual enough to take to a picnic. For a change of flavor, substitute hazelnuts for the walnuts.

3/4 cup butter, softened
1 cup sugar
1 egg
1/2 teaspoon vanilla extract
2 cups all-purpose flour
1/4 teaspoon baking powder
1-1/3 cups flaked coconut
1/2 cup chopped walnuts
1 jar (12 ounces) apricot preserves

1. In a large mixing bowl, cream the butter and sugar. Add the egg and vanilla; mix well. In separate bowl, combine the flour and baking powder. Gradually add to creamed mixture. Add the coconut and walnuts; mix thoroughly.

2. Press two-thirds of dough into a greased 13-in. x 9-in. x 2-in. baking pan. Spread with preserves; crumble remaining dough over preserves. Bake at 350° for 30-35 minutes or until golden brown. Cool in pan on wire rack. Cut into bars.

Yield: 3 dozen.

Cinnamon Raisin Bars

Nancy Rohr, St. Louis, Missouri

1/2 cup butter, softened
1 cup packed brown sugar
1-1/2 cups all-purpose flour
1-1/2 cups quick-cooking oats
1/2 teaspoon baking soda
1/2 teaspoon salt
2 tablespoons water

RAISIN FILLING:
1/4 cup sugar
1 tablespoon cornstarch
1 cup water
2 cups raisins

ICING:
1 cup confectioners' sugar
1/4 teaspoon ground cinnamon
1 to 2 tablespoons milk

Although these bars keep well, they don't last long with my husband around. As soon as the house fills with their wonderful aroma, he comes running!

1. In a mixing bowl, cream butter and brown sugar. Combine the flour, oats, baking soda and salt; add to creamed mixture with water. Beat until crumbly. Firmly press half into a greased 13-in. x 9-in. x 2-in. baking pan; set the remaining oat mixture aside.

2. In a saucepan, combine the sugar, cornstarch and water until smooth; stir in raisins. Cook and stir over medium heat until thick and bubbly. Cool to room temperature; spread over crust. Top with reserved oat mixture and pat down. Bake at 350° for 30-35 minutes or until golden brown. Cool in pan on a wire rack.

3. In a small bowl, combine the confectioners; sugar and cinnamon; stir in enough milk to reach drizzling consistency. Drizzle over the bars. Cut into bars.

Yield: about 3 dozen.

Pear Custard Bars

Jeannette Nord
San Juan Capistrano, California

When I take this crowd-pleasing treat to a potluck, I come home with an empty pan every time. Cooking and baking come naturally for me— as a farm girl, I helped my mother feed my 10 siblings.

1/2 cup butter, softened
1/3 cup sugar
3/4 cup all-purpose flour
1/4 teaspoon vanilla extract
2/3 cup chopped macadamia nuts

FILLING:
1 package (8 ounces) cream cheese, softened
1/2 cup sugar
1 egg
1/2 teaspoon vanilla extract
1 can (15-1/4 ounces) pear halves, drained

TOPPING:
1/2 teaspoon sugar
1/2 teaspoon ground cinnamon

1. In a mixing bowl, cream butter and sugar. Beat in the flour and vanilla until combined. Stir in the nuts. Press into a greased 8-in. square baking dish. Bake at 350° for 20 minutes or until lightly browned. Cool on a wire rack. Increase temperature to 375°.

2. In a mixing bowl, beat cream cheese until smooth. Add sugar, egg and vanilla; mix until combined. Pour over crust. Cut pears into 1/8-in. slices; arrange in a single layer over filling. Combine sugar and cinnamon; sprinkle over pears.

3. Bake at 375° for 28-30 minutes (center will be soft set and will become firmer upon cooling). Cool in pan on a wire rack for 45 minutes. Cover and refrigerate for at least 2 hours before cutting. Store in the refrigerator.

Yield: 16 bars.

Cranberry Nut Bars

Karen Jarocki, Monte Vista, Colorado

My husband's aunt sent us these bars one Christmas. The fresh cranberry flavor was such a nice change from the usual cookies. I had to have the recipe, and she was gracious enough to provide it.

1/2 cup butter, softened
3/4 cup sugar
3/4 cup packed brown sugar
2 eggs
1 teaspoon vanilla extract
1-1/2 cups all-purpose flour
1 teaspoon baking powder
1/2 teaspoon salt
1 cup chopped fresh *or* frozen cranberries
1/2 cup chopped walnuts

1. In a mixing bowl, cream butter and sugars. Add the eggs, one at a time, beating well after each addition. Beat in vanilla. Combine the flour, baking powder and salt; gradually add to creamed mixture. Stir in cranberries and walnuts.

2. Spread into a greased 13-in. x 9-in. x 2-in. baking pan. Bake at 350° for 20-25 minutes or until golden brown. Cool in pan on a wire rack. Cut into bars.

Yield: 3 dozen.

Ginger-Cream Bars

Carol Nagelkirk, Holland, Michigan

I rediscovered this old-time recipe recently and found it's everyone's favorite. Even 4-year-olds have asked for these frosted bars as nursery school treats.

1 cup butter, softened
1 cup sugar
2 cups all-purpose flour
1 teaspoon salt
2 teaspoons baking soda
1 tablespoon ground cinnamon
1 tablespoon ground cloves
1 tablespoon ground ginger
2 eggs
1/2 cup molasses
1 cup hot coffee

FROSTING:
1/2 cup butter, softened
1 package (3 ounces) cream cheese, softened
2 cups confectioners' sugar
2 teaspoons vanilla extract
Chopped nuts, optional

1. In a medium bowl, cream butter and sugar. Sift together flour, salt, soda and spices; add to creamed mixture. Add eggs, one at a time, beating well after each addition. Beat in molasses. Blend in coffee.

2. Spread in a 15-in. x 10-in. x 1-in. baking pan. Bake at 350° for 20-25 minutes. Cool in pan on a wire rack.

3. For frosting, cream butter and cream cheese; add sugar and vanilla. Spread over bars. Top with nuts if desired. Cut into bars. Store in the refrigerator.

Yield: 5-6 dozen.

Toffee Crunch Grahams

Carol Horne
Perth, Ontario

Only four ingredients make up these toffee bars loaded with crunchy almonds. My sister gave me the recipe years ago, and it's still a family favorite.

12 whole graham crackers (about 5 inches x 2-1/2 inches)
1-1/2 cups butter
1 cup packed brown sugar
2 cups sliced almonds

1. Line a 15-in. x 10-in. x 1-in. baking pan with heavy-duty foil. Place graham crackers in pan. In a saucepan, combine butter and brown sugar; bring to a boil, stirring constantly. Carefully pour over graham crackers. Sprinkle with almonds.

2. Bake at 400° for 6-8 minutes or until bubbly. Cool in pan for 4 minutes. Cut each cracker into four sections; transfer to wire racks to cool completely.

Yield: 4 dozen.

Blueberry Oat Bars

Oats add crunch to the tasty crust and crumbly topping of these fruity bars. I often bake them for church parties. Men especially love them.

Deena Hubler, Jasper, Indiana

1-1/2 cups all-purpose flour
1-1/2 cups quick-cooking oats
1-1/2 cups sugar, *divided*
1/2 teaspoon baking soda
3/4 cup cold butter
2 cups fresh *or* frozen blueberries
2 tablespoons cornstarch
2 tablespoons lemon juice

1. In a bowl, combine flour, oats, 1 cup sugar and baking soda. Cut in butter until mixture resembles coarse crumbs. Reserve 2 cups for topping. Press remaining crumb mixture into a greased 13-in. x 9-in. x 2-in. baking pan; set aside.

2. In a small saucepan, combine the blueberries, cornstarch, lemon juice and remaining sugar. Bring to a boil; cook and stir for 2 minutes or until thickened. Spread evenly over crust. Sprinkle with the reserved crumb mixture.

3. Bake at 375° for 25 minutes or until lightly browned. Cool in pan on a wire rack. Cut into bars. Store in the refrigerator.

Yield: 2-1/2 to 3 dozen.

Apple Walnut Squares

Jennifer Dzubinski
San Antonio, Texas

If you need a homespun snack or bake sale treat that can be assembled in a hurry, try these moist nutty bars. The squares are sweet, flavorful and loaded with chopped apple and nuts.

1/2 cup butter, softened
1 cup sugar
1 egg
1 cup all-purpose flour
1/2 teaspoon baking powder
1/2 teaspoon baking soda
1/2 teaspoon ground cinnamon
1 medium tart apple, peeled and chopped
3/4 cup chopped walnuts

1. In a mixing bowl, cream butter and sugar. Add the egg. Combine the flour, baking powder, baking soda and cinnamon; gradually add to the creamed mixture, beating just until combined. Stir in apple and walnuts.

2. Pour into a greased 8-in. square baking dish. Bake at 350° for 35-40 minutes or until a toothpick inserted near the center comes out clean. Cool on a wire rack.

Yield: 16 servings.

Grandma's Date Bars

Marilyn Reid
Cherry Creek, New York

These nicely textured bars are delicious. It's a good recipe for today's diet awareness, because there's no shortening used. My great-grandmother made these bars, and the recipe has come down through the generations. Now my children are making them.

  1 cup sugar
  1 cup all-purpose flour
  1 teaspoon baking powder
1/2 teaspoon salt
  1 cup chopped dates
  1 cup chopped walnuts
  3 eggs, well beaten
Confectioners' sugar

1. In a bowl, combine the first seven ingredients. Transfer to a greased 8-in. square baking pan. Bake at 350° for 25 minutes or until a toothpick inserted near the center comes out clean.

2. Cool in pan on a wire rack. Dust with confectioners' sugar. Cut into squares.

Yield: 16 servings.

Spiced Pumpkin Bars

Richard Case, Johnstown, Pennsylvania

These bars are moist, with bold pumpkin and spice flavors. When I want to lower the cholesterol, I use egg whites in place of the eggs.

    2 cups all-purpose flour
1-1/2 cups sugar
    1 tablespoon baking powder
    2 teaspoons ground cinnamon
    1 teaspoon baking soda
  1/2 teaspoon salt
  1/2 teaspoon ground ginger
  1/4 teaspoon ground nutmeg
  1/4 teaspoon ground cloves
    4 eggs
1-3/4 cups canned pumpkin
    1 cup unsweetened applesauce
Confectioners' sugar, optional

1. In a bowl, combine the dry ingredients. In another bowl, combine eggs, pumpkin and applesauce; mix well. Stir into the dry ingredients.

2. Spread into a greased 15-in. x 10-in. x 1-in. baking pan. Bake at 350° for 20-25 minutes or until lightly browned. Do not overbake. Cool in pan on a wire rack. Cut into bars. Dust with confectioners' sugar if desired.

Yield: 2-1/2 dozen.

Pineapple Almond Bars

Janice Smith
Cynthiana, Kentucky

Oats and almonds are a crunchy complement to the sweet pineapple filling in these yummy bars.

- 3/4 cup all-purpose flour
- 3/4 cup quick-cooking oats
- 1/3 cup packed brown sugar
- 5 tablespoons cold butter
- 1/2 teaspoon almond extract
- 3 tablespoons sliced almonds
- 1 cup pineapple preserves

1. In a food processor, combine the flour, oats and brown sugar; cover and process until blended. Add butter and extract; cover and pulse until crumbly. Remove 1/2 cup crumb mixture to a bowl; stir in sliced almonds.

2. Press remaining crumb mixture into a 9-in. square baking pan coated with nonstick cooking spray. Spread preserves over crust. Sprinkle with reserved crumb mixture. Bake at 350° for 25-30 minutes or until golden. Cool in pan on a wire rack. Cut into bars.

Yield: 1 dozen.

Coconut Graham Cracker Squares

These bar cookies travel well and feed a lot of people at potlucks and family reunions. Kids, as well as adults, like their rich flavor.

Mrs. Victor Wheeler, Girard, Pennsylvania

- 1 cup butter
- 1 cup sugar
- 1/2 cup milk
- 1 egg, beaten
- 1 cup flaked coconut
- 1 cup chopped walnuts
- 1 cup graham cracker crumbs (about 16 squares)
- 24 whole graham crackers

FROSTING:
- 1/4 cup butter, softened
- 2 cups confectioners' sugar
- 2 tablespoons milk
- 1 teaspoon vanilla extract
- 1/8 teaspoon salt

1. In a heavy saucepan, melt butter. Stir in sugar, milk and egg. Bring to a boil; cook and stir for 10 minutes. Remove from the heat. Stir in coconut, nuts and cracker crumbs.

2. Line a greased 15-in. x 10-in. x 1-in. baking pan with 12 whole crackers. Spread with the coconut mixture. Top with remaining crackers; press down gently. Cover with plastic wrap and refrigerate for 30 minutes.

3. Meanwhile, in a mixing bowl, combine frosting ingredients; beat until smooth. Break each cracker into four portions; spread with frosting.

Yield: 4 dozen.

Toffee Squares

Judith Scholovich
Waukesha, Wisconsin

Here's a traditional holiday bar cookie that is a wonderful timesaver and goes well with cutout cookies. In less than an hour, you can have 4-1/2 dozen cookies that are sure to please everyone!

1 cup butter, softened
1 cup packed brown sugar
1 egg yolk
1 teaspoon vanilla extract
2 cups all-purpose flour
1/4 teaspoon salt
2 packages (4 ounces *each*) German sweet chocolate
1/2 cup chopped nuts

1. In a mixing bowl, cream butter and sugar. Add egg yolk, vanilla, flour and salt; mix well.

2. Spread into a greased 13-in. x 9-in. x 2-in. baking pan. Bake at 350° for 20-25 minutes or until golden brown. Melt chocolate in a heavy saucepan over low heat, stirring constantly. Spread over hot bars. Sprinkle immediately with nuts. Cool in pan on a wire rack. Cut into 1-1/4-in. squares.

Yield: 4-1/2 dozen.

Lime Cooler Bars

Dorothy Anderson
Ottawa, Kansas

My family says this is one of their favorites. I guarantee it will get thumbs-up approval from your gang, too. Lime juice puts a tangy twist on these tantalizing bars, offering a burst of citrus flavor in every mouth-watering bite.

2-1/2 cups all-purpose flour, *divided*
1/2 cup confectioners' sugar
3/4 cup cold butter
4 eggs
2 cups sugar
1/3 cup lime juice
1/2 teaspoon grated lime peel
1/2 teaspoon baking powder
Additional confectioners' sugar

1. In a bowl, combine 2 cups flour and confectioners' sugar; cut in butter until mixture resembles coarse crumbs. Pat into a greased 13-in. x 9-in. x 2-in. baking pan. Bake at 350° for 20 minutes or until lightly browned.

2. In a bowl, whisk the eggs, sugar, lime juice and peel until frothy. Combine the baking powder and remaining flour; whisk in egg mixture. Pour over hot crust.

3. Bake 20-25 minutes longer or until light golden brown. Cool in pan on a wire rack. Dust with confectioners' sugar. Cut into bars.

Yield: 3 dozen.

Spicy Butter Thins

Elsie Vince, Peoria, Arizona

I spotted this recipe in a newspaper when teaching in California more than 20 years ago. Even today, my son says these are his all-time favorite treat.

- 3/4 cup all-purpose flour
- 1/4 cup sugar
- 1 teaspoon ground cinnamon
- 1 teaspoon instant coffee granules
- 1/2 teaspoon ground ginger
- 1/2 cup butter
- 1 cup butterscotch chips, *divided*
- 1 egg
- 1/2 cup chopped salted peanuts

1. In a bowl, combine the first five ingredients; set aside. In a heavy saucepan over low heat, melt butter and 2/3 cup butterscotch chips. Remove from the heat. Stir in the dry ingredients and egg; mix well.

2. Spread into an ungreased 15-in. x 10-in. x 1-in. baking pan. Sprinkle with peanuts and remaining chips. Bake at 300° for 25-30 minutes or until lightly browned. Immediately cut into bars and remove from pan. Cool on wire racks. Store in an airtight container.

Yield: about 3 dozen.

Chocolate Coconut Bars

Sharon Skildum
Maple Grove, Minnesota

A middle layer of coconut makes these sweet chocolaty treats taste similar to a Mounds candy bar! If time is short, don't wait for the bars to cool—just lay on several thin milk chocolate bars right after you take the pan from the oven and spread them as they melt.

- 2 cups graham cracker crumbs
- 1/2 cup butter, melted
- 1/4 cup sugar
- 2 cups flaked coconut
- 1 can (14 ounces) sweetened condensed milk
- 1/2 cup chopped pecans
- 1 plain chocolate candy bar (7 ounces)
- 2 tablespoons creamy peanut butter

1. Combine the crumbs, butter and sugar. Press into a greased 13-in. x 9-in. x 2-in. baking pan. Bake at 350° for 10 minutes.

2. Meanwhile, in a bowl, combine coconut, milk and pecans; spread over the crust. Bake at 350° for 15 minutes. Cool in pan on a wire rack.

3. In a small saucepan, melt candy bar and peanut butter over low heat; spread over cooled bars. Let stand until frosting is set. Cut into bars.

Yield: about 3 dozen.

Editor's Note: Reduced-fat or generic brands of peanut butter are not recommended for this recipe.

Black-Bottom Banana Bars

Rene Wright
Ferryville, Wisconsin

These bars stay very moist, and their rich banana and chocolate flavor is even better the second day. My mother-in-law gave me this recipe, and it's a big favorite with both my husband and sons.

1/2 cup butter, softened
1 cup sugar
1 egg
1 teaspoon vanilla extract
1-1/2 cups mashed ripe bananas (about 3 medium)
1-1/2 cups all-purpose flour
1 teaspoon baking powder
1 teaspoon baking soda
1/2 teaspoon salt
1/4 cup baking cocoa

1. In a mixing bowl, cream butter and sugar. Add egg and vanilla; beat until thoroughly combined. Blend in the bananas. Combine the flour, baking powder, baking soda and salt; add to creamed mixture and mix well.

2. Divide batter in half. Add cocoa to half; spread into a greased 13-in. x 9-in. x 2-in. baking pan. Spoon remaining batter on top and swirl with a knife. Bake at 350° for 25 minutes or until a toothpick inserted near the center comes out clean. Cool in pan on a wire rack. Cut into bars.

Yield: 2-1/2 to 3 dozen.

Dreamy Fudge Bar Cookies

This good-looking, great-tasting bar cookie classic has a hint of almond flavoring.

Loretta Coverdell, Amanda, Ohio

1 cup shortening
2 cups packed brown sugar
2 eggs
2-1/2 cups all-purpose flour
1 teaspoon baking soda
Dash salt
3 cups rolled oats

CHOCOLATE FILLING:
2 cups (12 ounces) semisweet chocolate chips
1 can (14 ounces) sweetened condensed milk
1 tablespoon butter
1 cup chopped walnuts
1/4 to 1/2 teaspoon almond extract

1. In a mixing bowl, cream shortening and sugar. Add eggs, one at a time, beating well after each addition. Combine flour, soda, salt and oats; stir into creamed mixture; set aside.

2. For filling, combine chips, milk and butter in a saucepan. Heat over low heat until chips are melted, stirring until smooth. Cool slightly. Stir in walnuts and extract. Press two-thirds of oat mixture into bottom of a greased 15-in. x 10-in. x 1-in. baking pan. Cover with filling and sprinkle remaining oat mixture on top. Flatten slightly.

3. Bake at 350° for 20 minutes or until set. Cool in pan on a wire rack. Cut into bars.

Yield: about 3 dozen.

Cherry Cocoa Shortbread Squares

Bettie Martin
Oneida, Wisconsin

Whenever there is a potluck at work or a family gathering, I'm asked to bring these delectable bars. I found the recipe years ago and have made it countless times since.

> 1/2 cup plus 2 tablespoons butter, softened, *divided*
> 1/4 cup sugar
>   1 cup all-purpose flour
>   2 tablespoons baking cocoa
>   2 cups confectioners' sugar
>   2 tablespoons milk
> 1/2 teaspoon vanilla extract
>   18 maraschino cherries, halved

GLAZE:
>   1 square (1 ounce) unsweetened chocolate
> 1-1/2 teaspoons butter

1. In a mixing bowl, cream 1/2 cup butter and sugar. Beat in flour and cocoa (mixture will be crumbly). Spread into a greased 9-in. square baking pan. Bake at 350° for 15 minutes or until surface is set. Cool in pan on a wire rack for 15 minutes.

2. Meanwhile, in a mixing bowl, combine confectioners' sugar and remaining butter; beat in milk and vanilla until smooth. Spread over crust. Pat the cherries dry with a paper towel; arrange over the frosting and press down gently.

3. In a microwave-safe bowl, melt the chocolate and butter; stir until smooth. Drizzle over the cherries. Refrigerate until the glaze has set. Cut into squares.

Yield: 3 dozen.

Strawberry Jam Bars

Patricia Olson, Barstow, California

There's a golden crust nicely seasoned with nutmeg, allspice and honey on these sweet bars. The recipe was given to me by an aunt.

> 1/2 cup butter, softened
> 3/4 cup sugar
>   1 egg
>   1 tablespoon honey
> 1-1/4 cups all-purpose flour
> 1/4 teaspoon baking powder
> 1/8 teaspoon ground allspice
> 1/8 teaspoon ground nutmeg
> 2/3 cup strawberry jam
> 1/2 cup chopped walnuts

1. In a mixing bowl, cream butter and sugar. Beat in egg and honey. Combine the flour, baking powder, allspice and nutmeg; gradually add to creamed mixture.

2. Divide dough in half; spread half into a lightly greased 9-in. square baking pan. Spread with jam. Drop remaining dough by teaspoonfuls over jam.

3. Sprinkle with walnuts. Bake at 350° for 25-30 minutes or until top is golden brown. Cool in pan on a wire rack. Cut into bars.

Yield: 16 bars.

Dream Bars

These bar cookies are a family favorite and excellent travelers. Wonderfully moist and chewy, they're definite winners with the men and kids.

Hillary Lawson
Plummer, Idaho

CRUST:
- 1 cup all-purpose flour
- 1/2 cup packed brown sugar
- 1/2 cup cold butter

FILLING:
- 2 eggs, lightly beaten
- 1 cup packed brown sugar
- 1 teaspoon vanilla extract
- 2 tablespoons all-purpose flour
- 1/2 teaspoon salt
- 1 cup flaked coconut
- 1 cup chopped walnuts

1. In a small bowl, combine flour and brown sugar; cut in butter until crumbly. Pat into a 13-in. x 9-in. x 2-in. baking pan. Bake at 350° for 10 minutes.

2. Meanwhile, in a mixing bowl, beat eggs and brown sugar; stir in vanilla. Combine flour and salt; add to egg mixture. Fold in coconut and walnuts. Spread over baked crust.

3. Bake 20-25 minutes longer or until golden brown. Cool in pan on a wire rack. Cut into bars.

Yield: 32 servings.

Lemon Graham Squares

Janis Plourde
Smooth Rock Falls, Ontario

My Aunt Jackie brought these lemon bars to every family gathering. They're my favorite lemon dessert. The crispy top and bottom give them a nice texture.

- 1 can (14 ounces) sweetened condensed milk
- 1/2 cup lemon juice
- 1-1/2 cups graham cracker crumbs (about 24 squares)
- 3/4 cup all-purpose flour
- 1/3 cup packed brown sugar
- 1/2 teaspoon baking powder
- Dash salt
- 1/2 cup butter, melted

1. In a bowl, combine the milk and lemon juice; mix well and set aside. In another bowl, combine the cracker crumbs, flour, brown sugar, baking powder and salt. Stir in butter until crumbly.

2. Press half of the crumb mixture into a greased 9-in. square baking dish. Pour lemon mixture over crust; sprinkle with remaining crumbs. Bake at 375° for 20-25 minutes or until lightly browned. Cool in pan on a wire rack. Cut into bars.

Yield: 3 dozen.

Coconut Pecan Bars

Susan Hamilton, Fulton, Missouri

With their a butterscotch flavor, these tasty bars have always been welcomed with open arms by my family. Since they're simple to make, kids can have fun pitching in.

1 cup butter, softened
2 cups packed brown sugar
2 eggs
2 teaspoons vanilla extract
2 cups all-purpose flour
1 teaspoon salt
1 teaspoon baking powder
1-1/2 cups flaked coconut
1 cup chopped pecans
Confectioners' sugar

1. In a mixing bowl, cream butter and brown sugar. Add eggs, one at a time, beating well after each addition. Beat in vanilla. Combine flour, salt and baking powder; gradually add to the creamed mixture. Stir in coconut and pecans (batter will be thick).

2. Spread into a greased 15-in. x 10-in. x 1-in. baking pan. Bake at 350° for 20-25 minutes or until a toothpick inserted near the center comes out clean. Cool in pan on a wire rack. Dust with confectioners' sugar, then cut into bars.

Yield: 4 dozen.

Raspberry Walnut Shortbread

Pat Habiger
Spearville, Kansas

A sweet raspberry filling is sandwiched between a crispy crust and a crunchy brown sugar topping in these satisfying snack bars.

1-1/4 cups plus 2 tablespoons all-purpose flour, *divided*
1/2 cup sugar
1/2 cup cold butter
1/2 cup raspberry jam
2 eggs
1/2 cup packed brown sugar
1 teaspoon vanilla extract
1/8 teaspoon baking soda
1 cup finely chopped walnuts

1. In a small bowl, combine 1-1/4 cups flour and sugar; cut in the butter until crumbly. Press into a greased 9-in. square baking pan. Bake at 350° for 20-25 minutes or until edges are lightly browned. Place on a wire rack. Spread jam over hot crust.

2. In a mixing bowl, beat eggs, brown sugar and vanilla. Combine baking soda and remaining flour; stir into the egg mixture just until combined. Fold in walnuts. Spoon over jam; spread evenly.

3. Bake 17-20 minutes longer or until golden brown and set. Cool in pan on a wire rack. Cut into bars.

Yield: 16 servings.

Chewy Peanut Bars

Diane Eitreim
Garretson, South Dakota

Kids will gobble up these chewy peanut-packed treats made with two kinds of crunchy cereal. The sweet coating contrasts nicely with the salty nuts to make these bars a surefire favorite.

- 5 cups cornflakes
- 3 cups crisp rice cereal
- 1 cup dry roasted peanuts
- 1 cup flaked coconut
- 1 cup light corn syrup
- 1/2 cup butter
- 1/2 cup half-and-half cream
- 1/2 cup sugar

1. In a large bowl, combine the first four ingredients; set aside. In a heavy saucepan, combine corn syrup, butter, cream and sugar; cook and stir over medium heat until sugar is dissolved. Cook until a candy thermometer reads 234° (soft-ball stage).

2. Pour over cereal mixture and toss to coat. Pat into a greased 13-in. x 9-in. x 2-in. baking pan. Cool before cutting.

Yield: 2 dozen.

Frosted Cinnamon Zucchini Bars

Bonita Holzbacher, Batesville, Indiana

I figure you can never have enough recipes calling for zucchini! These cake-like bars with a cinnamon-flavored frosting are unbelievably good.

- 3/4 cup butter, softened
- 1/2 cup sugar
- 1/2 cup packed brown sugar
- 2 eggs
- 1 teaspoon vanilla extract
- 1-3/4 cups all-purpose flour
- 1-1/2 teaspoons baking powder
- 2 cups shredded zucchini
- 1 cup flaked coconut
- 3/4 cup chopped walnuts

FROSTING:
- 2 cups confectioners' sugar
- 1 teaspoon ground cinnamon
- 2 tablespoons butter, melted
- 1 teaspoon vanilla extract
- 2 to 3 tablespoons milk

1. In a mixing bowl, cream butter and sugars. Add the eggs, one at a time, beating well after each addition. Beat in vanilla. Combine flour and baking powder; gradually add to the creamed mixture. Stir in zucchini, coconut and nuts.

2. Spread into a greased 15-in. x 10-in. x 1-in. baking pan. Bake at 350° for 25-30 minutes or until a toothpick inserted near the center comes out clean. Cool in pan on a wire rack.

3. In a bowl, combine sugar and cinnamon. Stir in butter, vanilla and enough milk until frosting achieves spreading consistency. Frost cooled bars. Cut into bars.

Yield: about 5 dozen.

Pineapple Coconut Squares

Elaine Anderson
Aliquippa, Pennsylvania

I don't remember where I got this recipe, but I'm glad I have it, since my family enjoys it so much.

- 2 tablespoons butter, melted
- 3 tablespoons sugar
- 1 egg
- 1 cup all-purpose flour
- 1 teaspoon baking powder
- 2 cans (8 ounces *each*) unsweetened crushed pineapple, drained

TOPPING:
- 1 tablespoon butter, melted
- 1 cup sugar
- 2 eggs
- 2 cups flaked coconut

1. In a mixing bowl, beat butter and sugar. Beat in egg. Combine flour and baking powder; stir into egg mixture. Press into a 9-in. square baking pan coated with nonstick cooking spray. Spread the pineapple over crust; set aside.

2. For topping, in a mixing bowl, beat butter and sugar. Beat in eggs. Stir in coconut. Spread over pineapple. Bake at 325° for 35-40 minutes or until golden brown. Cool in pan on a wire rack. Cut into bars.

Yield: 16 servings.

Almond Toffee Shortbread

Darlene Brenden, Salem, Oregon

The topping for these yummy shortbread squares tastes like a chewy toffee bar. If you can't find the toffee bits, buy Heath candy bars and chop them up.

- 1 cup whole blanched almonds, toasted
- 3/4 cup confectioners' sugar, *divided*
- 1 cup butter, softened
- 1/4 teaspoon almond extract
- 1-3/4 cups all-purpose flour
- 1/4 teaspoon salt
- 1 package English toffee bits (10 ounces) *or* almond brickle chips (7-1/2 ounces)
- 3/4 cup light corn syrup
- 3/4 cup sliced almonds, *divided*
- 3/4 cup flaked coconut, *divided*

1. In a food processor or blender, place the whole almonds and 1/4 cup confectioners' sugar. Cover and process until the nuts are finely ground; set aside.

2. In a mixing bowl, cream butter and remaining sugar until light and fluffy. Beat in extract. Combine flour, salt and ground almond mixture; gradually add to creamed mixture. Press into a greased 15-in. x 10-in. x 1-in. baking pan. Bake at 350° for 20 minutes.

3. Meanwhile, combine toffee bits and corn syrup in a heavy saucepan. Cook and stir over medium heat until toffee is melted. Remove from the heat; stir in 1/2 cup sliced almonds and 1/2 cup coconut. Carefully spread over hot crust. Sprinkle with remaining almonds and coconut.

4. Bake 15 minutes longer or until golden brown and bubbly. Cool on a wire rack. Cut into squares.

Yield: about 8 dozen.

Chewy Pecan Bars

Jeanne Gerlach, Frisco, Colorado

A friend from Texas gave me this recipe years ago. Because it's so easy to make, I've relied on it quite often.

1/4 cup butter, melted
4 eggs
2 cups packed brown sugar
2 teaspoons vanilla extract
2/3 cup all-purpose flour
1/4 teaspoon baking soda
1/4 teaspoon salt
2 cups chopped pecans
Confectioners' sugar

1. Spread butter evenly in an ungreased 13-in. x 9-in. x 2-in. baking pan. In a mixing bowl, beat eggs, brown sugar and vanilla. Combine flour, baking soda and salt; gradually add to egg mixture. Stir in pecans.

2. Spread into prepared pan. Bake at 350° for 30-35 minutes or until browned. Dust with confectioners' sugar. Cool on a wire rack. Cut into bars.

Yield: 3 dozen.

Spice Bars

Brooke Pike
Pierre, South Dakota

These bars smell so good while they are baking—the spicy aroma brings everyone to the kitchen in a hurry!

6 tablespoons buttermilk
1/3 cup packed brown sugar
1/4 cup molasses
3 tablespoons butter, melted
1 egg
1 teaspoon vanilla extract
1-1/4 cups all-purpose flour
3/4 teaspoon ground cinnamon, *divided*
1-1/4 teaspoons Chinese five spice powder
1/2 teaspoon baking powder
1/4 teaspoon baking soda
1/4 teaspoon salt
1/3 cup raisins
1 tablespoon confectioners' sugar

1. In a mixing bowl, combine the buttermilk, brown sugar, molasses, butter, egg and vanilla; mix well. Combine flour, 1/2 teaspoon cinnamon, five spice powder, baking powder, baking soda and salt; add to the buttermilk mixture and beat until smooth. Stir in raisins.

2. Pour into a 9-in. square baking pan coated with nonstick cooking spray. Bake at 350° for 18-20 minutes or until a toothpick inserted near the center comes out clean. Cool in pan on a wire rack. Combine confectioners' sugar and remaining cinnamon; sprinkle over bars. Cut into bars.

Yield: 1 dozen.

Pumpkin Spice Cookies, p. 232

Peanut Butter Caramel Bars, p. 222

Mint Candy Cookies, p. 222

Spiced Cookie Strips, p. 231

Shortcut Creations

Make fabulous cookies without all the mixing and measuring. These cookies all start with a convenience product like cake mixes, refrigerated cookie dough or store-bought cookies. Just add a few items to quickly create rave-winning homemade delights.

Mint Candy Cookies

Christina Hitchcock
Blakely, Pennsylvania

Because you start with a store-bought cookie mix, it takes no time at all to make these minty treats. I usually drizzle melted chocolate chips over the cookie tops, but pink candy coating looks lovely for Valentine's Day.

- 1 package (17-1/2 ounces) sugar cookie mix
- 40 to 45 mint Andes Candies
- 6 ounces pink candy coating disks

Heart-shaped decorating sprinkles, optional

1. Prepare the cookie dough according to package directions. Cover and chill for 15-20 minutes or until easy to handle.

2. Pat a scant tablespoonful of dough in a thin layer around each mint candy. Place 2 in. apart on ungreased baking sheets. Bake at 375° for 7-9 minutes or until set. Cool for 1 minute before removing from pans to wire racks to cool completely.

3. In a microwave-safe bowl, melt candy coating; stir until smooth. Drizzle over cookies. Top with decorating sprinkles if desired.

Yield: about 3-1/2 dozen.

Editor's Note: White candy coating tinted with red food coloring may be substituted for the pink candy coating.

Peanut Butter Caramel Bars

(Pictured on page 221)
Lee Ann Karnowski, Stevens Point, Wisconsin

When my husband, Bob, and our three sons sit down to dinner, they ask, "What's for dessert?" I have a happy group of guys when I report that these rich bars are on the menu. They're chock-full of yummy ingredients.

- 1 package (18-1/4 ounces) yellow cake mix
- 1/2 cup butter, softened
- 1 egg
- 20 miniature peanut butter cups, chopped
- 2 tablespoons cornstarch
- 1 jar (12-1/4 ounces) caramel ice cream topping
- 1/4 cup peanut butter
- 1/2 cup salted peanuts

TOPPING:
- 1 can (16 ounces) milk chocolate frosting
- 1/2 cup chopped salted peanuts

1. In a mixing bowl, combine the dry cake mix, butter and egg; beat until no longer crumbly, about 3 minutes. Stir in the peanut butter cups. Press into a greased 13-in. x 9-in. x 2-in. baking pan. Bake at 350° for 18-22 minutes or until lightly browned.

2. Meanwhile, in a saucepan, combine cornstarch, caramel topping and peanut butter until smooth. Cook over low heat, stirring occasionally, until mixture comes to a boil, about 25 minutes. Cook and stir 1-2 minutes longer. Remove from the heat; stir in peanuts. Spread evenly over warm crust. Bake 6-7 minutes longer or until almost set. Cool completely on a wire rack.

3. Spread with frosting; sprinkle with peanuts. Refrigerate for at least 1 hour before cutting. Store in the refrigerator.

Yield: about 3 dozen.

Editor's Note: Reduced-fat or generic brands of peanut butter are not recommended for this recipe.

Lemon-Lime Crackle Cookies

Ada Merwin, Waterford, Michigan

You can taste the spirit of Christmases past in these chewy old-time cookies with their crackle tops and lemony flavor. They're a luscious addition to cookie exchanges.

- 1/2 cup flaked coconut
- 2 teaspoons grated lemon peel
- 2 teaspoons grated lime peel
- 2 cups whipped topping
- 2 eggs
- 2 tablespoons whipped topping mix
- 1 teaspoon lemon juice
- 1 package (18-1/4 ounces) lemon cake mix

Confectioners' sugar

1. In a blender or food processor, combine the coconut, lemon peel and lime peel. Cover and process until finely chopped, about 30 seconds; set aside. In a mixing bowl, combine whipped topping, eggs, dry whipped topping mix and lemon juice. Add the dry cake mix and coconut mixture; mix well.

2. Drop by tablespoonfuls into a bowl of confectioner's sugar. Shape into balls. Place 2 in. apart on greased baking sheets. Bake at 350° for 10-12 minutes or until the edges are golden brown. Remove to wire racks to cool completely.

Yield: about 3 dozen.

Editor's Note: This recipe was tested with Dream Whip topping.

Chewy Date Nut Bars

Linda Hutmacher
Teutopolis, Illinois

You'll need just six ingredients, including a convenient boxed cake mix, to bake up these chewy bars. They are my husband's favorite snack, and he loves to take them to work. I often whip up a batch for bake sales or to share with my co-workers at our local car dealership.

- 1 package (18-1/4 ounces) yellow cake mix
- 3/4 cup packed brown sugar
- 3/4 cup butter, melted
- 2 eggs
- 2 cups chopped dates
- 2 cups chopped walnuts

1. In a mixing bowl, combine dry cake mix and brown sugar. Add butter and eggs; beat on medium speed for 2 minutes. Combine the dates and walnuts; stir into batter (the batter will be stiff).

2. Spread into a greased 13-in. x 9-in. x 2-in. baking pan. Bake at 350° for 35-45 minutes or until edges are golden brown. Cool on a wire rack for 10 minutes. Run a knife around sides of pan to loosen; cool completely before cutting.

Yield: 3 dozen.

Pecan Lemon Bars

June Trom, Blooming Prairie, Minnesota

I take advantage of convenient refrigerated cookie dough to make these divine lemon squares. All 27 of my grandchildren love their sweet and tangy flavor.

- 1 tube (18 ounces) refrigerated sugar cookie dough
- 1 cup chopped pecans, *divided*
- 1/3 cup corn syrup
- 1/4 cup lemon juice
- 1 egg, beaten
- 1 tablespoon butter, melted
- 1 tablespoon grated lemon peel
- 1/2 cup sugar
- 5 teaspoons all-purpose flour

Confectioners' sugar

1. Cut dough into 1/2-in. slices; press into an ungreased 13-in. x 9-in. x 2-in. baking pan. Sprinkle with 1/2 cup pecans; press firmly into crust. Bake at 375° for 10-12 minutes or until light golden brown.

2. Reduce heat to 350°. In a bowl, combine the corn syrup, lemon juice, egg, butter and lemon peel. Combine sugar, flour and remaining pecans; stir into the lemon mixture until blended. Pour over the crust. Bake for 18-20 minutes or until golden brown. Cool on a wire rack. Dust with confectioners' sugar. Cut into bars.

Yield: 2 to 2-1/2 dozen.

Fire Truck Cookies

Rhonda Walsh
Cleveland, Tennessee

Along with eight other day school teachers, we created this snack for a fire safety program at the school.

- 16 whole graham crackers (4-3/4 inches x 2-1/2 inches)
- 1 cup vanilla frosting

Red paste *or* liquid food coloring

- 32 chocolate cream-filled sandwich cookies

Black shoestring licorice

- 16 red gumdrops

1. With a serrated knife, cut the top left- or right-hand corner off of each graham cracker at a 45° angle. Tint frosting red; frost crackers. Place two sandwich cookies on each for wheels.

2. For each truck, cut licorice into two 2-1/2-in. pieces, five 1/2-in. pieces and two 1-1/2-in. pieces. Place the large pieces parallel to each other above wheels, with the small pieces between to form a ladder. Place the medium pieces at cut edge, forming a windshield. Add a gumdrop for light.

Yield: 16 cookies.

Chocolate Peanut Butter Grahams

Geraldine Sliva
Elgin, Illinois

Because so many people seem to love the combination of chocolate and peanut butter, I came up with this no-bake cookie recipe.

- 1 jar (18 ounces) peanut butter
- 1 package (16 ounces) graham crackers, broken into rectangles
- 1-1/2 pounds milk chocolate candy coating

1. Spread a rounded teaspoonful of peanut butter on one side of half of the graham crackers. Top with remaining crackers.

2. In a heavy saucepan over low heat, melt candy coating; stir until smooth. Dip cookies in coating to completely cover; allow excess to drip off. Place on waxed paper-lined baking sheets; let stand until set. Store in an airtight container in a cool, dry place.

Yield: 5 dozen.

Coconut Chip Cookies

Flora Alers, Clinton, Maryland

A package of cake mix is transformed into a big batch of tasty cookies that are filled with coconut, nuts and chocolate chips. With just six ingredients, this recipe can be whipped up in a jiffy.

- 1 package (18-1/4 ounces) white cake mix
- 2 eggs
- 1/3 cup vegetable oil
- 1 cup flaked coconut
- 1/2 cup semisweet chocolate chips
- 1/4 cup chopped macadamia nuts *or* almonds

1. In a mixing bowl, beat dry cake mix, eggs and oil (batter will be very stiff). Stir in coconut, chips and nuts.

2. Roll into 1-in. balls. Place on lightly greased baking sheets. Bake at 350° for 10 minutes or until a slight indentation remains when lightly touched. Cool for 2 minutes before removing to wire racks.

Yield: 3-1/2 dozen.

Citrus Cookies

Taste of Home Test Kitchen
Greendale, Wisconsin

Dress up convenient refrigerated cookie dough to create these sweet summery treats. The orange and lemon cookies taste like the sunny citrus slices they resemble.

> 1 tube (18 ounces) refrigerated sugar cookie dough
> 2 teaspoons grated orange peel
> 2 teaspoons orange extract

Orange and yellow paste food coloring

> 2 teaspoons grated lemon peel
> 2 teaspoons lemon extract

Granulated sugar

> 1/2 cup vanilla frosting

Orange and yellow colored sugar

1. Divide cookie dough in half. Place one half in a bowl. Add the orange peel, orange extract and orange food coloring; mix well. Add lemon peel, lemon extract and yellow food coloring to the remaining dough; mix well. Cover and refrigerate for 2 hours or until firm.

2. Roll dough into 1-in. balls. Place 2 in. apart on ungreased baking sheets. Coat the bottom of a glass with nonstick cooking spray, then dip in granulated sugar. Flatten dough balls, redipping glass in sugar as needed. Bake at 375° for 8-10 minutes or until edges are golden brown. Remove to wire racks to cool completely.

3. Cut a small hole in the corner of a small plastic bag; add frosting. Pipe circle of frosting on cookie tops; dip in colored sugar. Pipe lines of frosting for citrus sections.

Yield: about 2 dozen.

Strawberry Cookies

My family finds these fruity cookies to be a light treat in summer. I sometimes use lemon cake mix in place of the strawberry.

Nancy Shelton, Boaz, Kentucky

> 1 package (18-1/4 ounces) strawberry cake mix
> 1 egg, lightly beaten
> 1 carton (8 ounces) frozen whipped topping, thawed
> 2 cups confectioners' sugar

1. In a mixing bowl, combine the dry cake mix, egg and whipped topping until well combined. Place confectioners' sugar in a shallow dish.

2. Drop dough by tablespoonfuls into sugar; turn to coat. Place 2 in. apart on greased baking sheets. Bake at 350° for 10-12 minutes or until lightly browned around the edges. Remove to wire racks to cool.

Yield: about 5 dozen.

Easy Macaroons

Judy Farlow, Boise, Idaho

My family likes macaroons, so when they raved about this easy-to-make pastel version, I knew I had a keeper.

- 1 pint lemon *or* orange sherbet
- 2 tablespoons almond extract
- 1 package (18-1/4 ounces) white cake mix
- 6 cups flaked coconut

1. In a mixing bowl, beat sherbet and almond extract until sherbet is slightly softened. Gradually add dry cake mix. Stir in coconut.

2. Drop by rounded teaspoonfuls 2 in. apart onto greased baking sheets. Bake at 350° for 12-15 minutes or until edges are lightly browned. Remove to wire racks to cool.

Yield: about 10-1/2 dozen.

Gingerbread Cookie Wreath

Kelly Loudon
Olathe, Kansas

Here's a fun way to add a musical note to a celebration. You get a jump on the preparation by using packaged gingerbread mix.

- 1 package (14-1/2 ounces) gingerbread cake/cookie mix *or* 2 cups gingerbread cookie dough of your choice
- 1/2 pound white candy coating, melted
- 1/4 cup green colored sugar
- 15 red-hot candies

1. Prepare mix according to package directions for cookies. Set aside 1/4 cup dough. On a greased baking sheet, roll out remaining dough into a 9-1/2-in. circle. With a sharp knife, cut a 4-in. circle from the center of the 9-1/2-in. circle. Remove 4-in. circle; add to reserved dough. Bake 9-1/2-in. ring at 375° for 12-15 minutes or until edges are firm (do not overbake). Cool for 1 minute before removing to a wire rack.

2. Roll out reserved dough to 1/2-in. thickness. Cut out 5 musical notes with a floured 4-in. musical note cutter and 10 holly leaves with a floured 1-1/2-in. leaf cutter. Place 2 in. apart on a greased baking sheet. Bake at 375° for 10-12 minutes or until edges are firm. Remove to a wire rack to cool.

3. Dip holly leaves halfway in candy coating; sprinkle with green sugar. Place on a ring as shown in photo. Cut a small hole in the corner of pastry or plastic bag; insert round tip #3. Fill with remaining candy coating. Squeeze a small amount on the back of cookies; attach to wreath. Pipe around edges of notes. Pipe small dots of coating above holly leaves to attach candies. Allow coating to set completely, about 30 minutes.

Yield: 1 wreath.

Peanutty Chocolate Cookies

Brenda Jackson, Garden City, Kansas

Whenever I take these cookies, I'm always asked for the recipe. To dress them up, I reserve some chocolate and nuts to press into each cookie before baking.

- 1 cup chunky peanut butter
- 2 tablespoons vegetable oil
- 2 eggs
- 1 package fudge brownie mix (13-inch x 9-inch pan size)
- 1/2 cup water
- 12 ounces milk chocolate candy bars, coarsely chopped
- 1/2 cup unsalted peanuts

1. In a large mixing bowl, cream peanut butter and oil. Beat in eggs just until combined. Stir in brownie mix and water. Fold in the chopped candy bars and peanuts.

2. Drop by heaping tablespoonfuls 2 in. apart onto greased baking sheets. Bake at 350° for 12-14 minutes or until lightly browned. Remove to wire racks to cool.

Yield: about 3-1/2 dozen.

Editor's Note: Reduced-fat or generic brands of peanut butter are not recommended for this recipe.

German Chocolate Cookies

Leslie Henke
Louisville, Colorado

A handy boxed cake mix hurries along the preparation of these chewy cookies studded with chips and raisins. I make them for our family reunion each year, and they always get rave reviews.

- 1 package (18-1/4 ounces) German chocolate cake mix
- 2 eggs
- 1/2 cup butter, melted
- 1/2 cup quick-cooking oats
- 1 cup (6 ounces) semisweet chocolate chips
- 1/2 cup raisins

1. In a mixing bowl, combine dry cake mix, eggs, butter and oats; mix well. Stir in the chocolate chips and raisins.

2. Drop by heaping tablespoonfuls 2 in. apart onto ungreased baking sheets. Bake at 350° for 9-11 minutes or until set. Cool for 5 minutes before removing to wire racks.

Yield: about 3-1/2 dozen.

Double Chip Biscotti

Taste of Home Test Kitchen
Greendale, Wisconsin

Refrigerated cookie dough gives you a head start on making biscotti from scratch. For true chocolate lovers, substitute chocolate chips for the vanilla.

- 1 tube (18 ounces) refrigerated chocolate chip cookie dough
- 1/2 cup vanilla *or* white chips
- 1/2 cup coarsely chopped macadamia nuts

1. In a medium bowl, combine the dough, chips and nuts; knead until well combined. Divide dough in half. On greased baking sheets, shape each piece into a 13-in. x 2-1/2-in. log. Bake at 375° for 12-14 minutes or until golden brown.

2. Remove from oven; cut diagonally with a serrated knife into 1-in. slices, separating each piece about 1/4 in. after cutting. Bake 5-6 minutes longer or until firm. Cool for 2 minutes before removing to wire racks.

Yield: about 2 dozen.

Soft Raisin Cookies

Ray Amet, Kansas City, Missouri

- 1 package (9 ounces) yellow cake mix
- 1 cup quick-cooking oats
- 6 tablespoons unsweetened applesauce
- 1/4 cup egg substitute
- 2 tablespoons butter, melted
- 1/2 teaspoon apple pie spice
- 1/2 cup raisins

I modified a recipe for cake mix cookies to make it healthier. My family likes my version, with its mild spice flavor and touch of sweetness from raisins, even better than the original.

1. In a mixing bowl, combine the dry cake mix, oats, applesauce, egg substitute, butter and apple pie spice; beat until blended. Stir in raisins.

2. Drop by tablespoonfuls 2 in. apart onto baking sheets coated with nonstick cooking spray. Bake at 375° for 10-12 minutes or until the edges are lightly browned. Cool for 5 minutes before removing to wire racks.

Yield: 2 dozen.

Peanut Butter Cookie Cups

Kristi Tackett
Banner, Kentucky

I'm a busy schoolteacher and pastor's wife who always looks for shortcuts. I wouldn't dare show my face at a church dinner or bake sale without these tempting peanut butter treats. They're quick and easy to make and always a hit.

1 package (17-1/2 ounces) peanut butter cookie mix

36 miniature peanut butter cups, unwrapped

1. Prepare cookie mix according to package directions. Roll the dough into 1-in. balls. Place in greased miniature muffin cups. Press dough evenly onto bottom and up sides of each cup. Bake at 350° for 11-13 minutes or until set.

2. Immediately place a peanut butter cup in each cup; press down gently. Cool for 10 minutes; carefully remove from pans.

Yield: 3 dozen.

Editor's Note: 2-1/4 cups peanut butter cookie dough of your choice can be substituted for the mix.

Mint Sandwich Cookies

Melissa Thompson, Anderson, Ohio

Canned frosting, peppermint extract and chocolate candy coating quickly turn crackers into these wonderful little no-bake cookies.

1 can (16 ounces) vanilla frosting

1/2 teaspoon peppermint extract

3 to 5 drops green food coloring, optional

72 butter-flavored crackers

1 pound dark chocolate candy coating, coarsely chopped

1. In a bowl, combine the frosting, extract and food coloring if desired. Spread over half of the crackers; top with remaining crackers.

2. Place candy coating in a microwave-safe bowl. Microwave on high for 1-2 minutes or until smooth. Dip the cookies in coating. Place on waxed paper until chocolate is completely set. Store in an airtight container at room temperature.

Yield: 3 dozen.

Spiced Cookie Strips

(Pictured on page 221)
Taste of Home Test Kitchen
Greendale, Wisconsin

Convenient refrigerated sugar cookie dough and a few spices from your cupboard are all you need to bake a batch of these yummy cookie strips. Your family will want to gobble them up right out of the oven. They're that good!

1 tube (18 ounces) refrigerated sugar cookie dough
2 tablespoons all-purpose flour
2 tablespoons butter, melted
1/2 teaspoon ground nutmeg
1/4 teaspoon ground cinnamon
1/4 teaspoon ground cloves

1. Remove cookie dough from package and coat with flour. Shake excess flour onto work surface. Roll out dough on floured surface into a 12-in. x 8-in. rectangle. Using a pizza cutter or sharp knife, cut rectangle in half lengthwise. Cut widthwise into 1-in. strips. Carefully transfer strips to two ungreased baking sheets.

2. Combine butter and spices; brush over strips. Bake at 425° for 10-12 minutes or until edges are golden brown. Cool for 2 minutes before removing to wire racks.

Yield: 2 dozen.

Easy Chocolate Caramel Cookies

Melanie Steele
Plano, Texas

I rely on a cake mix and chocolate-covered caramels to fix these popular cookies. They are very quick to prepare, yet they taste so good when served fresh from the oven. People are surprised to bite into this crisp cookie and find a gooey caramel center.

1 package (18-1/4 ounces) devil's food cake mix
1 egg
1/4 cup water
3 tablespoons vegetable oil
38 Rolo candies
Chopped hazelnuts

1. In a bowl, combine the dry cake mix, egg, water and oil; mix well. Roll rounded teaspoonfuls of dough into balls. Press a candy into each; reshape balls. Dip tops in hazelnuts.

2. Place on ungreased baking sheets. Bake at 350° for 8-10 minutes or until tops are cracked. Cool for 2 minutes before removing to wire racks.

Yield: 3 dozen.

Editor's Note: If the dough is sticky, spray hands lightly with nonstick cooking spray before rolling into balls.

Pumpkin Spice Cookies

These big, soft spice cookies have a sweet frosting that makes them an extra special treat. Enjoy!

(Pictured on page 220)
Taste of Home Test Kitchen
Greendale, Wisconsin

1 package (18-1/4 ounces) yellow cake mix
1/2 cup quick-cooking oats
2 to 2-1/2 teaspoons pumpkin pie spice
1 egg
1 can (15 ounces) solid-pack pumpkin
2 tablespoons canola oil
3 cups confectioners' sugar
1 teaspoon grated orange peel
3 to 4 tablespoons orange juice

1. In a bowl, combine the dry cake mix, oats and pumpkin pie spice. In another bowl, beat the egg, pumpkin and oil; stir into dry ingredients just until moistened.

2. Drop by 2 tablespoonfuls onto baking sheets coated with nonstick cooking spray; flatten with the back of a spoon. Bake at 350° for 18-20 minutes or until edges are golden brown. Remove to wire racks to cool.

3. In a bowl, combine confectioners' sugar, orange peel and enough orange juice to achieve spreading consistency. Frost cooled cookies.

Yield: 32 cookies.

Cookies in a Jiffy

Clara Hielkema
Wyoming, Michigan

You'll be amazed and delighted with how quickly you can whip up a batch of these homemade cookies.

1 package (9 ounces) yellow cake mix
2/3 cup quick-cooking oats
1/2 cup butter, melted
1 egg
1/2 cup red and green Holiday M&M's *or* butterscotch chips

1. In a mixing bowl, beat the first four ingredients. Stir in the M&M's or chips.

2. Drop by tablespoonfuls 2 in. apart onto ungreased baking sheets. Bake at 375° for 10-12 minutes or until lightly browned. Immediately remove to wire racks to cool.

Yield: 2 dozen.

Very Chocolaty PB Brownies

Marcella Cremer
Decatur, Illinois

I came up with these fudgy peanut butter brownies when I ran out of ingredients I needed for my usual recipe. They take less than 10 minutes to mix up.

- 1 package (17-1/2 ounces) peanut butter cookie mix
- 1/2 cup baking cocoa
- 2/3 cup chocolate syrup
- 1/4 cup butter, melted
- 1 egg
- 1/2 cup chopped walnuts *or* peanuts

FROSTING:
- 2 cups plus 2 tablespoons confectioners' sugar
- 1/2 cup chocolate syrup
- 1/4 cup baking cocoa
- 1/4 cup butter, melted
- 1/2 teaspoon vanilla extract

1. In a mixing bowl, combine cookie mix and cocoa. Add chocolate syrup, butter and egg; beat until combined. Stir in nuts.

2. Spread into a greased 13-in. x 9-in. x 2-in. baking pan. Bake at 350° for 28-32 minutes or until a toothpick inserted near the center comes out clean. Cool on a wire rack.

3. Meanwhile, combine the frosting ingredients in a bowl; stir until smooth. Spread over brownies. Cut into squares.

Yield: 2 dozen.

Editor's Note: This recipe was tested with Betty Crocker peanut butter cookie mix.

Quick Chocolate Sandwich Cookies

Mary Rempel, Altona, Manitoba

These cookies freeze well, so it's easy to keep some on hand for last-minute munching. In summer, I often make them larger to use for ice cream sandwiches.

- 2 packages (18-1/4 ounces *each*) devil's food cake mix
- 1 cup vegetable oil
- 4 eggs

FILLING:
- 1 package (8 ounces) cream cheese, softened
- 1/4 cup butter, softened
- 2-1/2 cups confectioners' sugar
- 1 teaspoon vanilla extract

1. In a mixing bowl, combine the cake mixes, oil and eggs; mix well. Roll into 1-in. balls. Place 2 in. apart on ungreased baking sheets. Do not flatten. Bake at 350° for 8-10 minutes or until set. Cool for 5 minutes before removing to wire racks (cookies will flatten as the cool).

2. In a small mixing bowl, beat cream cheese and butter. Add sugar and vanilla; beat until smooth. Spread on the bottom of half of the cookies; top with remaining cookies. Store in the refrigerator.

Yield: about 6 dozen.

Mexican Cookies

Kathy Ybarra
Rock Springs, Wyoming

Add a sweet treat to a meal of tacos, enchiladas or fajitas with this easy-to-make dessert.

- 4 flour tortillas (6 inches)
- 1/2 cup semisweet chocolate chips
- 3/4 teaspoon shortening
- 1/4 cup confectioners' sugar
- 1/4 teaspoon ground cinnamon

1. Cut each tortilla into eight wedges; place on ungreased baking sheets. Bake at 400° for 10-12 minutes or until lightly browned.

2. Meanwhile, in a microwave or heavy saucepan, melt chocolate chips and shortening. Stir until smooth; keep warm. In a large resealable plastic bag, combine confectioners' sugar and cinnamon. Add tortilla wedges a few at a time; shake to coat. Place on waxed paper-lined baking sheets. Drizzle with melted chocolate. Refrigerate until serving.

Yield: 32 cookies.

Pecan-Topped Sugar Cookies

Betty Lech, St. Charles, Illinois

This recipe dresses up refrigerated cookie dough with cream cheese and coconut. Folks love the almond flavor.

- 1 can (8 ounces) almond paste
- 1 package (3 ounces) cream cheese, softened
- 1/4 cup flaked coconut
- 1 tube (18 ounces) refrigerated sugar cookie dough
- 1 cup pecan halves

1. In a mixing bowl, beat almond paste and cream cheese. Add coconut; mix well. Cut cookie dough into 1/2-in. slices; divide each slice into four portions.

2. Roll into balls. Place 2 in. apart on greased baking sheets. Shape 1/2 teaspoonfuls of almond mixture into balls; place one on each ball of dough. Lightly press pecans into tops.

3. Bake at 350° for 10-12 minutes or until lightly browned. Remove to wire racks to cool.

Yield: about 3-1/2 dozen.

Lemon Crisp Cookies

Julia Livingston, Frostproof, Florida

Lemon Crisp Cookies are a snap to make using a boxed cake mix. The sunny yellow color and big lemon flavor are sure to bring smiles to your family.

- 1 package (18-1/4 ounces) lemon cake mix
- 1 cup crisp rice cereal
- 1/2 cup butter, melted
- 1 egg, beaten
- 1 teaspoon grated lemon peel

1. In a large bowl, combine all ingredients until well mixed (dough will be crumbly).

2. Roll into 1-in. balls. Place 2 in. apart on ungreased baking sheets. Bake at 350° for 10-12 minutes or until set. Cool for 1 minute before removing to a wire rack.

Yield: about 4 dozen.

Chocolate Chip Cheese Bars

Teri Lindquist
Gurnee, Illinois

This is my most requested dessert recipe. Everyone loves these yummy bars with their soft cream cheese filling. And they couldn't be easier to make!

- 1 tube (18 ounces) refrigerated chocolate chip cookie dough
- 1 package (8 ounces) cream cheese, softened
- 1/2 cup sugar
- 1 egg

1. Cut cookie dough in half. For crust, press half of the dough onto the bottom of a greased 8-in. square baking dish.

2. In a mixing bowl, beat cream cheese, sugar and egg until smooth. Spread over crust. Crumble remaining dough over top. Bake at 350° for 35-40 minutes or until a toothpick inserted near the center comes out clean. Cool on a wire rack. Refrigerate leftovers.

Yield: 12-16 servings.

Editor's Note: 2 cups of your favorite chocolate chip cookie dough can be substituted for the refrigerated dough.

Brownie Crackles

Ellen Govertsen, Wheaton, Illinois

Chocolate chips and a fudge brownie mix create the rich flavor in these sweet cookies. Rolling the dough in powdered sugar gives them their inviting crackled appearance.

- 1 package fudge brownie mix (13-inch x 9-inch pan size)
- 1 cup all-purpose flour
- 1 egg
- 1/2 cup water
- 1/4 cup vegetable oil
- 1 cup (6 ounces) semisweet chocolate chips

Confectioners' sugar

1. In a mixing bowl, combine brownie mix, flour, egg, water and oil; mix well. Stir in chocolate chips. Place confectioners' sugar in a shallow dish. Drop dough by tablespoonfuls into sugar; roll to coat.

2. Place 2 in. apart on greased baking sheets. Bake at 350° for 8-10 minutes or until set. Remove to wire racks to cool.

Yield: 4-1/2 dozen.

Dipped Peanut Butter Sandwich Cookies

Jackie Howell
Gordo, Alabama

This is a tempting treat you'll love to give. The recipe is almost too simple to believe!

- 1/2 cup creamy peanut butter
- 1 sleeve (4 ounces) round butter-flavored crackers
- 1 cup white, semisweet, *or* milk chocolate chips
- 1 tablespoon shortening

1. Spread peanut butter on half of the crackers; top with remaining crackers to make sandwiches. Refrigerate.

2. In a small heavy saucepan or microwave, melt chocolate chips and shortening, stirring until smooth. Dip sandwiches and place on waxed paper until chocolate hardens.

Yield: 9 servings.

Easy Gingerbread Cutouts

Sandy McKenzie
Braham, Minnesota

I rely on this tried-and-true recipe during the holidays. The cream cheese frosting complements the cookies' gingery flavor and sets up nicely for easy packaging and stacking.

- 1 package (18-1/4 ounces) spice cake mix
- 3/4 cup all-purpose flour
- 2 eggs
- 1/3 cup vegetable oil
- 1/3 cup molasses
- 2 teaspoons ground ginger
- 3/4 cup canned cream cheese frosting, warmed slightly

Red-hot candies

1. In a mixing bowl, combine dry cake mix, flour, eggs, oil, molasses and ginger; mix well. Refrigerate for 30 minutes or until easy to handle.

2. On a floured surface, roll out dough to 1/8-in. thickness. Cut with a floured 5-in. cookie cutters.

3. Place 3 in. apart on ungreased baking sheets. Bake at 375° for 7-10 minutes or until edges are firm and bottom is lightly browned. Remove to wire racks to cool.

4. Decorate with cream cheese frosting as desired. Use red-hots for eyes, nose and buttons.

Yield: 2-1/2 dozen.

Making Cutout Cookies

1. For easier handling, chill dough before rolling out. Lightly flour the surface and the rolling pin. Roll out dough as evenly as possible to the recommended thickness.

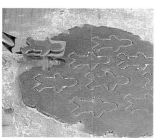

2. Dip the cutter in flour, then press into the dough. With a large metal spatula or pancake turner, move cookies to baking sheet.

3. Bake according to recipe directions. Remove cookies from the baking sheet to a wire rack, being careful to support the entire cookie. Cool completely before frosting and/or storing.

Double Frosted Brownies

Jean Kolessar
Orland Park, Illinois

I stir up moist brownies from a boxed mix, then I dress them up with two kinds of frosting. The two-tones treats have a luscious look and sweet taste.

        1 package fudge brownie
          mix (13-inch x 9-inch pan
          size)
    1/2 cup butter, softened
    1-1/2 cups confectioners' sugar
        2 tablespoons instant vanilla
          pudding mix
        2 to 3 tablespoons milk
        1 can (16 ounces) chocolate
          fudge frosting

1. Prepare brownie mix according to package directions. Spread the batter into a greased 13-in. x 9-in. x 2-in. baking pan. Bake at 350° for 25-30 minutes or until a toothpick inserted 2 in. from side of pan comes out clean. Cool completely on a wire rack.

2. In a mixing bowl, beat butter, sugar and pudding mix until blended. Add enough milk to achieve spreading consistency. Frost brownies. Cover and refrigerate for 30 minutes. Spread with fudge frosting. Cut into bars. Store in the refrigerator.

Yield: 3 dozen.

Chocolate Peanut Butter Cookies

Mary Pulyer, Port St. Lucie, Florida

It's a snap to make a batch of tasty cookies using this recipe, which starts with a basic boxed cake mix. My husband and son gobble them up.

        1 package (18-3/4 ounces)
          devil's food cake mix
        2 eggs
    1/3 cup vegetable oil
        1 package (10 ounces)
          peanut butter chips

1. In a mixing bowl, beat cake mix, eggs and oil (batter will be very stiff). Stir in chips.

2. Roll into 1-in. balls. Place on lightly greased baking sheets; flatten slightly. Bake at 350° for 10 minutes or until a slight indentation remains when lightly touched. Cool for 2 minutes before removing to wire racks.

Yield: 4 dozen.

Editor's Note: Reduced-fat or generic brands of peanut butter are not recommended for this recipe.

Cranberry Crispies

LaVern Kraft, Lytton, Iowa

At holiday rush time, you can't go wrong with these simple cookies. They're a snap to stir up with a boxed quick bread mix, and they bake up crisp and delicious.

- 1 package (15.6 ounces) cranberry quick bread mix
- 1/2 cup butter, melted
- 1/2 cup finely chopped walnuts
- 1 egg
- 1/2 cup dried cranberries

1. In a bowl, combine the bread mix, butter, walnuts and egg; mix well. Stir in cranberries.

2. Roll into 1-1/4-in. balls. Place 3 in. apart on ungreased baking sheets. Flatten to 1/8-in. thickness with a glass dipped in sugar. Bake at 350° for 10-12 minutes or until light golden brown. Remove to wire racks to cool.

Yield: 2-1/2 dozen.

Christmas Eve Mice

Margene Pons
West Valley City, Utah

Assembling these merry mice is so much fun that the kids will definitely want to help. My daughter gave me the recipe, along with a warning— your guests just might think these treats are too cute to eat!

- 24 double-stuffed cream-filled chocolate sandwich cookies
- 1 cup (6 ounces) semisweet chocolate chips
- 2 teaspoons shortening
- 24 red maraschino cherries with stems, well drained
- 24 milk chocolate kisses
- 48 sliced almonds
- 1 small tube green decorative icing gel
- 1 small tube red decorative icing gel

1. Carefully twist cookies apart; set aside the halves with cream filling. Save plain halves for another use.

2. In a microwave or saucepan, melt chocolate chips and shortening; stirring until smooth. Holding each cherry by the stem, dip in the melted chocolate, then press onto the bottom of a chocolate kiss. Place on the cream filling of cookie, with cherry stem extending beyond cookie edge.

3. For ears, place the slivered almonds between the cherry and the kiss. Refrigerate until set. With green gel, pipe holly leaves on the cream. With red gel, pipe holly berries between leaves and pipe eyes on each chocolate kiss. Store in an airtight container at room temperature.

Yield: 2 dozen.

Butterscotch Pecan Cookies

No one will guess these buttery treats start with a simple cake mix and a box of instant pudding!

Betty Janway, Ruston, Louisiana

- 1 package (18-1/4 ounces) butter recipe cake mix
- 1 package (3.4 ounces) instant butterscotch pudding mix
- 1/4 cup all-purpose flour
- 3/4 cup vegetable oil
- 1 egg
- 1 cup chopped pecans

1. In mixing bowl, combine the first five ingredients; mix well. Stir in pecans (the dough will be crumbly).

2. Roll tablespoonfuls into balls; place 2 in. apart on greased baking sheets. Bake at 350° for 10-12 minutes or until golden brown. Cool for 2 minutes before removing to wire racks.

Yield: 4 dozen.

Editor's Note: This recipe was tested with Pillsbury brand butter recipe cake mix.

Quick Ghost Cookies

Denise Smith
Lusk, Wyoming

I spruce up store-bought cookies for the holiday. These are a real hit with "goblins" of all ages.

- 1 pound white candy coating, cut into chunks
- 1 package (1 pound) Nutter Butter peanut butter cookies

Mini semisweet chocolate chips

1. In a small, heavy saucepan or microwave, melt the candy coating, stirring occasionally. Dip cookies into coating, covering completely. Place on waxed paper.

2. Brush ends with a pastry brush dipped in coating where fingers touched cookies. While coating is still warm, place two chips on each cookie for eyes. Let stand until set. Store in an airtight container.

Yield: about 3 dozen.

No-Fuss Strawberry Bars

Karen Mead
Pittsburgh, Pennsylvania

I bake for a group of seniors every week, and this is one of the goodies they request most. I always keep the ingredients on hand for last-minute baking emergencies. Give these bars your own twist by replacing the strawberry jam with the fruit jam of your choice.

- 1/2 cup butter, softened
- 1/2 cup packed brown sugar
- 1 egg
- 1 package (18-1/4 ounces) white cake mix
- 1 cup finely crushed cornflakes
- 1 cup strawberry jam *or* preserves

1. In a mixing bowl, cream butter and brown sugar until smooth. Add egg; mix well. Gradually add dry cake mix and cornflakes. Set aside 1-1/2 cups for topping. Press remaining dough into a greased 13-in. x 9-in. x 2-in. baking pan.

2. Carefully spread jam over crust. Sprinkle with reserved dough; gently press down. Bake at 350° for 30 minutes or until golden brown. Cool completely on a wire rack. Cut into bars.

Yield: 2 dozen.

Fun Marshmallow Bars

These colorful kid-tested treats go fast at bake sales. A cake mix really cuts your prep time.

Debbie Brunssen, Randolph, Nebraska

- 1 package (18-1/4 ounces) devil's food cake mix
- 1/4 cup butter, melted
- 1/4 cup water
- 1 egg
- 3 cups miniature marshmallows
- 1 cup milk chocolate M&M's
- 1/2 cup chopped peanuts

1. In a mixing bowl, combine dry cake mix, butter, water and egg; mix well. Press into a greased 13-in. x 9-in. x 2-in. baking pan. Bake at 375° for 20-22 minutes or until a toothpick inserted near center comes out clean.

2. Sprinkle with marshmallows, M&M's and peanuts. Bake 2-3 minutes longer or until the marshmallows begin to melt. Cool on a wire rack before cutting.

Yield: 3-1/2 dozen.

Macaroon Bars

Carolyn Kyzer
Alexander, Arkansas

Guests will never recognize the refrigerated crescent roll dough that goes into these almond-flavored bars. You can easily assemble these chewy coconut treats in no time at all.

- 3-1/4 cups flaked coconut, *divided*
- 1 can (14 ounces) sweetened condensed milk
- 1 teaspoon almond extract
- 1 tube (8 ounces) refrigerated crescent rolls

1. Sprinkle 1-1/2 cups coconut into a well-greased 13-in. x 9-in. x 2-in. baking pan. Combine milk and extract; drizzle half over the coconut. Unroll crescent dough; arrange in a single layer over coconut. Drizzle with remaining coconut.

2. Bake at 350° for 30-35 minutes or until golden brown. Cool completely on a wire rack before cutting. Store in the refrigerator.

Yield: 3 dozen.

Orange Crispy Cookies

Barbara Wentzel, Fort Bragg, California

A boxed cake mix brings these cookies together in a snap. Big on orange flavor but short on kitchen time, this crowd-pleaser is the solution to your bake sale needs.

- 1 package (18-1/4 ounces) white cake mix
- 1/2 cup butter, melted
- 1 egg, beaten
- 2 teaspoons grated orange peel
- 2 teaspoons orange extract
- 1 cup crisp rice cereal
- 1 cup chopped walnuts, optional

1. In a mixing bowl, combine the first five ingredients; mix well. Stir in cereal and walnuts if desired.

2. Roll into 1-in. balls. Place 2 in. apart on ungreased baking sheets. Bake at 350° for 12-14 minutes or until lightly browned. Cool for 1 minute before removing to wire racks.

Yield: about 4 dozen.

Brickle Cookies

Robert Moon, Tampa, Florida

The only problem with these cookies is that once you eat one, you want more. This makes a small batch so you won't have too many around to tempt you.

1 package (9 ounces) yellow cake mix
1/4 cup vegetable oil
1 egg, lightly beaten
1/2 teaspoon vanilla extract
1/2 cup chopped pecans
1/2 cup almond brickle chips *or* English toffee bits

1. In a mixing bowl, combine the dry cake mix, vegetable oil, egg and vanilla; mix well. Stir in pecans. Refrigerate for 1 hour or until firm enough to handle.

2. Roll into 1-in. balls; dip top of each ball into toffee bits and set 2 in. apart on greased baking sheets. Bake at 350° for 10-12 minutes or until golden brown. Cool for 3 minutes before removing to wire racks.

Yield: about 1-1/2 dozen.

Chocolate Chip Mint Cookies

Patricia Kaseta
Brockton, Massachusetts

I jazz up a packaged cookie mix, then let Junior Mints melt on top of the warm treats to create an easy frosting. These delicious cookies are requested at every gathering.

1 package (17-1/2 ounces) chocolate chip cookie mix
3 tablespoons water
1 egg
1/4 cup vegetable oil
1/2 cup semisweet chocolate chips
1/2 cup vanilla *or* white chips
1/2 cup chopped walnuts
1 package (5-1/2 ounces) Junior Mints

1. In a mixing bowl, combine cookie mix, water, egg and oil; mix well. Stir in the chips and nuts.

2. Drop by tablespoonfuls 2 in. apart onto ungreased baking sheets. Bake at 350° for 7-9 minutes or until edges are golden brown.

3. Remove from the oven; place one candy on each cookie. Remove to wire racks. When candy is melted, spread over cookie. Cool completely.

Yield: 4 dozen.

Chocolate Meringue Stars, p. 247

Christmas Cookie Ornaments, p. 262

Painted Holiday Delights, p. 249

Christmas Wreaths, p. 248

Christmas Classics

Cookies at Christmas are a holiday tradition—for gift giving, cookie exchanges or as a special treat for family and guests. The variety of festive cookies featured here are sure to create a dazzling assortment on your cookie trays.

Snowflake and Icicle Cookies

Taste of Home Test Kitchen
Greendale, Wisconsin

Bring some of winter's wonder indoors with shaped butter cookies that get their sparkle from edible glitter. These cookie ornaments are great favors for your trim-a-tree party guests.

1 cup butter, softened
1 cup confectioners' sugar
1 egg
1 teaspoon vanilla extract
1/2 to 1 teaspoon almond
　　extract
2-1/2 cups all-purpose flour
1/2 teaspoon salt

GLAZE:
1-1/2 cups confectioners' sugar
1 tablespoon light corn
　　syrup
1/4 teaspoon vanilla extract
2 to 3 tablespoons water
White edible glitter *or* coarse
　　sugar
Ribbon

1. In a large mixing bowl, cream the butter and sugar. Beat in the egg and extracts until light and fluffy. Combine flour and salt; gradually add to the creamed mixture. Divide dough in half. Place one portion in a bowl; shape the other portion into a 5-in. log. Cover both and refrigerate for 1-2 hours or until easy to handle.

2. For snowflakes: Divide dough from bowl in half. On a lightly floured surface, roll out one portion to 1/8-in. thickness. (Refrigerate other portion until ready to use.) Cut nine medium snowflakes and six large snowflakes with cookie cutters.

3. Carefully place 1 in. apart on ungreased baking sheets. Using small decorating cutters, cut out desired shapes to create designs in snowflakes. Use a toothpick to help remove the cutouts. Cut six small snowflakes and place 1 in. apart on another baking sheet. With a plastic straw, poke a hole in the top of each cookie.

4. Bake medium and large snowflakes at 375° for 6-1/2 to 7 minutes and small snowflakes for 6 minutes or until bottoms are lightly browned. Remove to wire racks to cool.

5. For icicles: Cut the log into 1/4-in. slices; roll each into a 9-in. rope, tapering from the center to each end. Fold each rope in half; twist Pinching the ends to a point. Place 2 in. apart on ungreased baking sheets.

6. Bake at 375° for 8-10 minutes or until lightly browned. Immediately poke a hole in the top of each icicle with a plastic straw. Remove to wire racks to cool.

7. For glaze, combine sugar, corn syrup and vanilla in a bowl. Gradually add enough water to make a this glaze. Brush over snowflakes and icicles; sprinkle with glitter or sugar. Let stand for at least 5 minutes or until set. Thread ribbon through the hole in the icicles and small snowflakes and through a cutout in the medium and large snowflakes.

Yield: about 20 icicles and 21 snowflakes.

Chocolate Meringue Stars

(Pictured on page 244)
Edna F. Lee, Greeley, Colorado

These light, delicate chewy cookies sure make for merry munching. Their big chocolate flavor makes it difficult to keep the kids away from them long enough to get any on the cookie tray.

    3 **egg whites**
3/4 **teaspoon vanilla extract**
3/4 **cup sugar**
1/4 **cup baking cocoa**

GLAZE:
    3 **squares (1 ounce *each*)**
       semisweet chocolate
    1 **tablespoon shortening**

1. In a mixing bowl, beat egg whites and vanilla on medium speed until soft peaks form. Gradually add the sugar, about 2 tablespoons at a time, beating on high until stiff peaks form. Gently fold in the cocoa. Place in a pastry bag with a large open star tip (#8b).

2. Line baking sheets with ungreased parchment paper. Pipe stars, about 1-1/4-in. diameter, onto parchment paper, or drop by rounded teaspoonfuls. Bake at 300° for 30-35 minutes or until lightly browned. Remove from parchment paper; cool on wire racks.

3. In a microwave or heavy saucepan, melt chocolate and shortening; stir until smooth. Dip the cookies halfway into glaze; place on waxed paper until set.

Yield: about 4 dozen.

Eggnog Logs

Kim Jordan
Dunsmuir, California

These cute little logs are a tasty addition to a cookie tray.

    1 **cup butter, softened**
3/4 **cup sugar**
1-1/4 **teaspoons ground nutmeg**
    1 **egg**
    2 **teaspoons vanilla extract**
1/2 **to 1 teaspoon rum extract**
    3 **cups all-purpose flour**

FROSTING:
1/4 **cup butter, softened**
    3 **cups confectioners' sugar,**
       divided
    1 **teaspoon vanilla extract**
1/2 **to 1 teaspoon rum extract**
    2 **tablespoons half-and-half**
       cream
Ground nutmeg

1. In a mixing bowl, cream butter and sugar. Add the nutmeg, egg and extracts; mix thoroughly. Stir in flour. If necessary, refrigerate dough for easier handling.

2. On a lightly floured surface, shape dough into 1/2-in.-diameter rolls; cut each into 3-in.-long pieces. Place 2 in. apart on ungreased baking sheets. Bake at 350° for 15 minutes or until lightly browned. Remove to wire racks to cool.

3. For frosting, cream butter until light and fluffy. Add 2 cups sugar and extracts; mix well. Beat in cream and remaining sugar. Frost cookies. With tines of a small fork, make lines down frosting to simulate bark. Sprinkle with nutmeg.

Yield: 4-1/2 dozen.

Christmas Wreaths

(Pictured on page 245)
Taste of Home Test Kitchen
Greendale, Wisconsin

Cornflakes take the place of traditional rice cereal in these sweet no-bake treats. Dressed up with green food coloring and red candies, they look nice on cookie platters and dessert buffets.

20 large marshmallows
2 tablespoons butter, cubed
Green food coloring
3 cups cornflakes
72 miniature red M&M baking bits

1. In a microwave-safe bowl, combine the marshmallows and butter. Microwave, uncovered, on high for 1 minute or until butter is melted and marshmallows are puffed. Add food coloring; mix well. Stir in the cornflakes.

2. Shape mixture into 3-in. wreaths on a waxed paper-lined baking sheet. Immediately press M&M's in three clusters of three for berries. Let stand until set.

Yield: 8 wreaths.

Peppermint Biscotti

Paula Marchesi
Lenhartsville, Pennsylvania

Dipped in melted chocolate and rolled in crushed peppermint candy, this flavorful biscotti is a favorite. It's one of the many sweets I make for Christmas.

3/4 cup butter, softened
3/4 cup sugar
3 eggs
2 teaspoons peppermint extract
3-1/4 cups all-purpose flour
1 teaspoon baking powder
1/4 teaspoon salt
1 cup crushed peppermint candy

FROSTING:
2 cups (12 ounces) semisweet chocolate chips
2 tablespoons shortening
1/2 cup crushed peppermint candy

1. In a large mixing bowl, cream butter and sugar. Add eggs, one at a time, beating well after each addition. Beat in extract. Combine the flour, baking soda and salt; stir in peppermint candy. Gradually add to creamed mixture, beating until blended (dough will be stiff).

2. Divide dough in half. On an ungreased baking sheet, roll each portion into a 12-in. x 2-1/2-in. rectangle. Bake at 350° for 25-30 minutes or until golden brown. Carefully remove to wire racks; cool for 15 minutes.

3. Transfer to a cutting board; cut diagonally with a sharp knife into 1/2-in. slices. Place cut side down on ungreased baking sheets. Bake for 12-15 minutes or until firm. Remove to wire racks to cool.

4. In a microwave-safe bowl, melt chocolate chips and shortening; stir until smooth. Dip one end of each cookie in chocolate; roll in candy. Place on waxed paper until set. Store in an airtight container.

Yield: about 3-1/2 dozen.

Painted Holiday Delights

Judy Degenstein
Ottawa, Kansas

These soft sandwich cookies are eye-catching, thanks to the holiday designs you paint on with food coloring.

    2 cups all-purpose flour
  1/2 cup sugar
  1/2 cup confectioners' sugar
    2 teaspoons ground
        cinnamon
  3/4 teaspoon baking powder
  1/4 teaspoon salt
  1/2 cup cold butter
    1 egg
  1/4 cup orange juice

FILLING:
    1 package (8 ounces) cream
        cheese, softened
    3 tablespoons
        confectioners' sugar
    3 tablespoons strawberry
        preserves

GLAZE:
    1 cup confectioners' sugar
  1/4 teaspoon vanilla extract
    1 to 2 tablespoons milk
Assorted food coloring

1. In a bowl, combine the first six ingredients. Cut in butter until mixture resembles coarse crumbs. Combine egg and orange juice; stir into crumb mixture just until moistened. Shape into a ball; cover and chill for 1-2 hours or until easy to handle.

2. On a floured surface, roll out dough to 1/8-in. thickness. Cut with a floured 2-in. round cookie cutter.

3. Place 1 in. apart on ungreased baking sheets. Bake at 375° for 8-10 minutes or until lightly browned. Remove to wire racks to cool.

4. Combine filling ingredients; spread on the bottom of half of cookies. Top with remaining cookies.

5. For glaze, combine sugar, vanilla and enough milk to achieve desired consistency. Spread over tops of cookies; let stand until set. Using a small new paintbrush and food coloring, paint holiday designs on cookie tops. Store in the refrigerator.

Yield: about 2 dozen.

Chocolate Shortbread

Katherine Both, Rocky Mountain House, Alberta

This chocolate-flavored shortbread only requires a few ingredients, which are always in my pantry. They are a popular choice to make when the occasion calls for a cookie.

    1 cup butter, softened
  1/3 cup unsweetened cocoa
  2/3 cup confectioners' sugar
Dash salt
1-1/2 cups all-purpose flour

1. In a large mixing bowl, cream butter until light and fluffy. Blend in remaining ingredients. Cover and refrigerate for 1 hour.

2. Drop by rounded teaspoonfuls 2 in. apart on greased baking sheets. Bake at 300° for about 20 minutes or until the cookies are set. Remove to wire racks to cool.

Yield: about 4 dozen cookies.

Chocolate Reindeer

Lisa Rupple
Keenesburg, Colorado

These cute cutout reindeer really fly off the plate when my brother's around. They're his favorite! The subtle chocolate color and taste make them a nice alternative to plain vanilla sugar cookies.

1 cup butter, softened
1 cup sugar
1/2 cup packed brown sugar
1 egg
1 teaspoon vanilla extract
2-3/4 cups all-purpose flour
1/2 cup baking cocoa
1 teaspoon baking soda
44 red-hot candies

ICING (optional)
1-1/2 cups confectioners' sugar
2 to 3 tablespoons milk

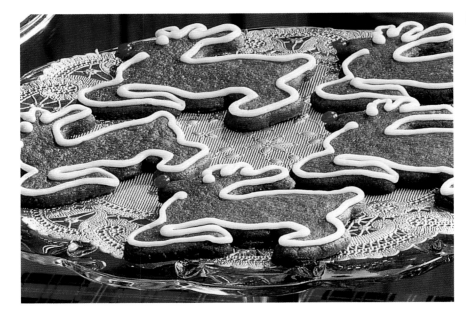

1. In a mixing bowl, cream butter and sugars until fluffy. Beat in egg and vanilla. Combine flour, cocoa and baking soda; add to creamed mixture and mix well. Cover and refrigerate for at least 2 hours.

2. On a lightly floured surface, roll dough to 1/8-in. thickness. Cut with a floured reindeer-shaped cookie cutter. Place 2 in. apart on greased baking sheets. Bake at 375° for 8-9 minutes. Immediately press a red-hot onto each nose. Cool for 2-3 minutes before removing to wire racks.

3. If desired, combine confectioners' sugar and milk until smooth. Cut a small hole in the corner of a heavy-duty resealable plastic bag; fill with icing. Pipe around edges of cookies and add a dot for eye.

Yield: about 3-1/2 dozen.

Cranberry Nut Swirls

Carla Hodenfield, Mandan, North Dakota

When we want to "pull a fast one" on the guys in our family, who claim they don't like cranberries in any shape or form, we make this recipe. Everyone, including the guys, enjoys these cookies.

1/2 cup butter, softened
3/4 cup sugar
1 egg
1 teaspoon vanilla extract
1-1/2 cups all-purpose flour
1/4 teaspoon baking powder
1/4 teaspoon salt
1/2 cup finely ground cranberries
1/2 cup finely chopped walnuts
1 tablespoon grated orange peel
3 tablespoons brown sugar
2 teaspoons milk

1. In a large mixing bowl, combine first four ingredients. Beat until light and fluffy, scraping the bowl occasionally. Combine dry ingredients; add to the creamed mixture. Cover and refrigerate at least 1 hour.

2. In a small bowl, combine the cranberries, walnuts and orange peel; set aside. On a lightly floured surface, roll dough into a 10-in. square. Combine brown sugar and milk; spread over dough. Sprinkle with the cranberry mixture, to within a 1/2 in. of edges; roll up tightly, jelly-roll style. Wrap in plastic wrap. Refrigerate for several hours or overnight.

3. Unwrap dough. Cut roll into 1/4-in. slices and place on well-greased baking sheets. Bake at 375° for 14-15 minutes or until edges are light brown. Remove to wire racks to cool.

Yield: about 3-1/2 dozen.

Sweetheart Cookies

Pamela Esposito, Smithville, New Jersey

These rounds filled with fruit preserves were blue-ribbon winners at the county fair two years running. A family favorite, they never last past December 25!

3/4 cup butter, softened
1/2 cup sugar
1 egg yolk
1-1/2 cups all-purpose flour
2 tablespoons raspberry *or* strawberry preserves
Confectioners' sugar, optional

1. In a mixing bowl, cream butter and sugar. Add egg yolk; mix well. Stir in the flour by hand. On a lightly floured surface, gently knead dough for 2-3 minutes or until thoroughly combined.

2. Roll into 1-in. balls. Place 2 in. apart on greased baking sheets. Using the end of a wooden spoon handle, make an indention in the center of each. Fill each with 1/4 teaspoon preserves. Bake at 350° for 13-15 minutes or until edges are lightly browned. Remove to wire racks. Dust warm cookies with confectioners' sugar if desired. Cool.

Yield: about 2 dozen.

Raspberry Ribbons

Patsy Wolfenden
Golden, British Columbia

I make these attractive, buttery cookies to serve at our remote guest lodge, and all the girls in the kitchen are addicted to them!

1 cup butter, softened
1/2 cup sugar
1 egg
1 teaspoon vanilla extract
2-1/4 cups all-purpose flour
1/2 teaspoon baking powder
1/4 teaspoon salt
1/2 cup raspberry jam

GLAZE:
1 cup confectioners' sugar
2 tablespoons evaporated milk
1/2 teaspoon vanilla extract

1. In a mixing bowl, cream butter and sugar. Beat in egg and vanilla. Combine the flour, baking powder and salt; gradually add to creamed mixture and mix well.

2. Divide dough into four portions; shape each into a 10-in. x 2-1/2-in. log. Place 4 in. apart on greased or foil-lined baking sheets. Make a 1/2-in. depression down the center of each log. Bake at 350° for 10 minutes.

3. Fill depressions with jam. Bake 10-15 minutes longer or until lightly browned. Cool for 2 minutes. Remove to a cutting board; cut into 3/4-in. slices. Place on wire racks.

4. In a small bowl, combine glaze ingredients until smooth. Drizzle over warm cookies. Cool completely.

Yield: about 5 dozen.

Cherry Macaroons

Sherma Talbot, Salt Lake City, Utah

I received this recipe along with its ingredients at my bridal shower. Now these are a favorite of our sons.

1-1/3 cups shortening
1-1/2 cups sugar
   2 eggs
   1 teaspoon almond extract
3-1/2 cups all-purpose flour
   2 teaspoons baking powder
   2 teaspoons baking soda
   1 teaspoon salt
1-1/2 cups flaked coconut
   1 cup maraschino cherries, chopped

1. In a mixing bowl, cream shortening and sugar. Add eggs and extract; mix well. Combine flour, baking powder, baking soda and salt; gradually add to creamed mixture. Stir in the coconut and cherries (dough will be very stiff).

2. Drop by rounded teaspoonfuls 2 in apart onto greased baking sheets. Bake at 375° for 10-12 minutes or until lightly browned. Cool on wire racks.

Yield: about 6 dozen.

Surprise Package Cookies

Lorraine Meyer
Bend, Oregon

Each of these buttery cookies has a chocolate mint candy inside. They're my very favorite cookie and are always part of our Christmas cookie selection.

   1 cup butter, softened
   1 cup sugar
1/2 cup packed brown sugar
   2 eggs
   1 teaspoon vanilla extract
   3 cups all-purpose flour
   1 teaspoon baking powder
1/2 teaspoon salt
 65 mint Andes candies

1. In a mixing bowl, cream the butter and sugars. Add the eggs, one at a time, beating well after each addition. Beat in vanilla. Combine the flour, baking powder and salt; gradually add to creamed mixture. Cover and refrigerate for 2 hours or until easy to handle.

2. With floured hands, shape a tablespoonful of dough around 42 candies, forming rectangular cookies. Place 2 in. apart on greased baking sheets. Bake at 375° for 10-12 minutes or until edges are golden brown. Remove to wire racks to cool.

3. In a microwave or heavy saucepan, melt the remaining candies; drizzle over cookies.

Yield: 3-1/2 dozen.

Holly Wreaths

Dee Lein
Longmont, Colorado

I've never come across another spritz cookie like this—one calling for cream cheese as an ingredient. That helps to keep these wreaths moist a long time, while also adding a delicious flavor.

1 cup butter, softened
1 package (3 ounces) cream cheese, softened
1/2 cup sugar
1 teaspoon vanilla extract
2 cups all-purpose flour
Green cherries, cut into thin slices
Cinnamon red-hot candies
Frosting and decorator gel

1. In a mixing bowl, cream butter and cream cheese. Add sugar; blend well. Stir in vanilla. Gradually beat in flour.

2. Using a cookie press fitted with star tip, form dough into 2-1/2-in. wreaths on ungreased baking sheets. Bake at 375° for 10-12 minutes or until set (do not brown). Remove to wire racks to cool.

3. Decorate wreaths with green cherry "leaves" and cinnamon candy "berries" attached with a drop of frosting. Add bows with decorator gel.

Yield: about 3 dozen.

Pfeffernuesse

Betty Hawkshaw
Alexandria, Virginia

These mild spice cookies, perfect for dunking, come from an old family recipe. This German cookie sometimes has black pepper in the dough for an added zip.

1 cup butter, softened
1 cup sugar
2 eggs
1/2 cup light corn syrup
1/2 cup molasses
1/3 cup water
6-2/3 cups all-purpose flour
1/4 cup crushed aniseed
1 teaspoon baking soda
1 teaspoon ground cinnamon
1/2 teaspoon ground nutmeg
1/4 teaspoon ground cloves
1/4 teaspoon ground allspice
Confectioners' sugar

1. In a mixing bowl, cream the butter and sugar. Add the eggs, one at a time, beating well after each addition. In a bowl, combine corn syrup, molasses and water; set aside. Combine the flour, aniseed, baking soda and spices; add to creamed mixture alternately with molasses mixture. Cover and refrigerate overnight.

2. Roll into 1-in. balls. Place 2 in. apart on greased baking sheets. Bake at 400° for 11-12 minutes or until golden brown. Roll the warm cookies in confectioners' sugar. Cool on wire racks.

Yield: 8 dozen.

Peanut Butter Cutout Cookies

Cindi Bauer
Marshfield, Wisconsin

Here's a nice change of pace from the more traditional sugar cutouts. And children will find that these peanut butter versions are just as much fun to decorate with frosting, sprinkles and a dash of Yuletide imagination.

> 1 cup creamy peanut butter
> 3/4 cup sugar
> 3/4 cup packed brown sugar
> 2 eggs
> 1/3 cup milk
> 1 teaspoon vanilla extract
> 2-1/2 cups all-purpose flour
> 1/2 teaspoon baking powder
> 1/2 teaspoon baking soda

Vanilla frosting

Red, green, yellow and blue gel food coloring

Assorted colored sprinkles

1. In a large mixing bowl, cream peanut butter and sugars. Beat in the eggs, milk and vanilla. Combine the flour, baking powder and baking soda; add to creamed mixture and mix well. Cover and refrigerate for 2 hours or until easy to handle.

2. On a lightly floured surface, roll out dough to 1/4-in. thickness. Cut with floured 2-in. to 4-in. cookie cutters.

3. Place 2 in. apart in ungreased baking sheets. Bake at 375° for 7-9 minutes or until edges are browned. Cool for 1 minute before removing to wire racks. Frost and decorate as desired.

Yield: about 4-1/2 dozen.

Editor's Note: Reduced-fat or generic brands of peanut butter are not recommended for this recipe.

Italian Christmas Cookies

Doris Marshall, Strasburg, Pennsylvania

A single batch of these mouth-watering cookies is never enough. I usually make one to give away and two more to keep at home.

> 1 cup butter, softened
> 2 cups sugar
> 3 eggs
> 1 carton (15 ounces) ricotta cheese
> 2 teaspoons vanilla extract
> 4 cups all-purpose flour
> 1 teaspoon salt
> 1 teaspoon baking soda

FROSTING:
> 1/4 cup butter, softened
> 3 to 4 cups confectioners' sugar
> 1/2 teaspoon vanilla extract
> 3 to 4 tablespoons milk

Colored sprinkles

1. In a mixing bowl, cream butter and sugar. Add the eggs, one at a time, beating well after each addition. Beat in ricotta and vanilla. Combine flour, salt and baking soda; gradually add to creamed mixture.

2. Drop by rounded teaspoonfuls 2 in. apart onto greased baking sheets. Bake at 350° for 10-12 minutes or until lightly browned. Remove to wire racks to cool.

3. In a mixing bowl, cream butter, sugar and vanilla. Add enough milk until frosting reaches spreading consistency. Frost cooled cookies and immediately decorate with sprinkles. Store in the refrigerator.

Yield: 8-1/2 dozen.

Peppermint Kisses

Lynn Bernstetter
Lake Elmo, Minnesota

These are fun, refreshing and low in fat! I pipe the airy meringue batter, but if your prefer you can drop it from a tablespoon.

- 2 egg whites
- 1/8 teaspoon salt
- 1/8 teaspoon cream of tartar
- 1/2 cup sugar
- 2 peppermint candy canes (one green, one red), crushed

1. In a mixing bowl, beat the egg whites, salt and cream of tartar; on medium speed until soft peaks form. Add sugar, 1 tablespoon at a time, beating on high until stiff, glossy peaks form.

2. Spoon meringue into a pastry bag or a resealable plastic bag. If using a plastic bag, cut a 1-in. hole in a corner. On ungreased foil-lined baking sheets, pipe meringue into 1-1/2-in.-high mounds, forming a kiss shape. Sprinkle half with red crushed candy cane and half with green crushed candy cane.

3. Bake at 225° for 1-1/2 to 2 hours or until dry but not brown. Cool; remove from foil. Store in an airtight container.

Yield: 3 dozen.

Chocolate Mint Creams

Beverly Fehner
Gladstone, Missouri

This recipe came from an old family friend and is always high on everyone's cookie request list. I make at least six batches for Noel nibbling and also give some away as gifts.

- 1 cup butter, softened
- 1-1/2 cups confectioners' sugar
- 2 squares (1 ounce *each*) unsweetened chocolate, melted and cooled
- 1 egg
- 1 teaspoon vanilla extract
- 2-1/2 cups all-purpose flour
- 1 teaspoon baking soda
- 1 teaspoon cream of tartar
- 1/4 teaspoon salt

FROSTING:
- 1/4 cup butter, softened
- 2 cups confectioners' sugar
- 2 tablespoons milk
- 1/2 teaspoon peppermint extract

Green food coloring, optional

1. In a large mixing bowl, cream butter and confectioners' sugar. Add the chocolate, egg and vanilla; mix well. Combine dry ingredients; gradually add to the creamed mixture, beating well. Shape the dough into a 2-in. diameter roll; wrap in plastic wrap. Refrigerate for 1 hour or until firm.

2. Unwrap dough and cut into 1/8-in. slices. Place 2 in. apart on ungreased baking sheets. Bake at 400° for 7-8 minutes or until edges are firm. Remove to wire racks to cool.

3. In a small mixing bowl, combine frosting ingredients. Frost cookies. Store in airtight containers.

Yield: about 6 dozen.

Decorating Cookies with Royal Icing

1. Cut a small hole in the corner of a pastry or plastic bag. Insert a round tip; fill bag with icing. Hold bag at a 45° angle to the cookie, and pipe a bead of icing around the edge.

2. Thin remaining icing so that it will flow smoothly. Fill another bag with thinned icing. Starting in the middle, fill in the cookie with the thinned icing, letting icing flow up to the outline. Let cookies dry overnight.

3. With a new small paintbrush, paint designs on the cookies with liquid food coloring.

Holiday Biscotti

Libia Foglesong
San Bruno, California

A twice-baked Italian cookie, biscotti makes a wonderful "dunker." A pretty way to present a batch is on a Christmasy plate arranged in wagon-wheel fashion.

1/2 cup butter, softened
1 cup sugar
3 eggs
2 teaspoons vanilla extract
1 teaspoon orange extract
3 cups all-purpose flour
2 teaspoons baking powder
1/2 teaspoon salt
2/3 cup dried cranberries, coarsely chopped
2/3 cup pistachios, coarsely chopped
2 tablespoons grated orange peel

1. In a mixing bowl, cream the butter and sugar. Add the eggs, one at a time, beating well after each addition. Stir in extracts. Combine flour, baking powder and salt; gradually add to creamed mixture and mix well (dough will be sticky). Stir in cranberries, pistachios and orange peel. Cover and chill for 30 minutes.

2. Divide dough in half. On a floured surface, shape each half into a loaf 1-1/2 to 2-in. diameter. Place on an ungreased baking sheet. Bake at 350° for 30-35 minutes.

3. Cool for 5 minutes. Cut diagonally into 3/4-in.-thick slices. Place slices, cut side down, on an ungreased baking sheet. Bake for 9-10 minutes. Turn slices over. Bake 10 minutes longer or until golden brown. Remove to wire racks to cool. Store in an airtight container.

Yield: 2 dozen.

Holiday Ginger Cutouts

Joanne MacVey
Blue Grass, Iowa

Looking to get a little creative with your cookie decorating? Paint your own masterpiece on a ginger cookie canvas!

1 cup shortening
1 cup sugar
1 egg
1 cup molasses
2 tablespoons white vinegar
4-1/2 cups all-purpose flour
2 teaspoons ground ginger
1-1/2 teaspoons baking soda
1 teaspoon ground cinnamon
3/4 teaspoon ground cloves
1/2 teaspoon salt

ICING:
4 cups confectioners' sugar
2 tablespoons meringue powder
1/2 cup warm water
Assorted colors of liquid food coloring
Round pastry tip #2, #3 or #4

1. In a mixing bowl, cream shortening and sugar. Add the egg, molasses and vinegar; mix well. Combine dry ingredients; add to creamed mixture and mix well. Cover and refrigerate for 3 hours or overnight.

2. On a lightly floured surface, roll out dough to 1/8-in. thickness and cut into desired shapes.

3. Place 1 in. apart on lightly greased baking sheets. Bake at 350° for 7-9 minutes or until set. Remove to wire racks to cool.

4. For icing, sift confectioners' sugar and meringue powder into a large mixing bowl. Add water; beat on low speed until blended. Beat on high for 5-6 minutes or until soft peaks form. Place a damp paper towel over bowl and cover tightly until ready to use.

5. Cut a small hole in the corner of a pastry or plastic bag; insert round tip. Fill bag with 1 cup icing. Outline each cookie with icing.

6. Tint remaining icing with food coloring if desired. Add water, a few drops at a time, until mixture is thin enough to flow smoothly. Prepare additional pastry or plastic bags with thinned icing. Fill in cookies, letting icing flow up to the outline.

7. Let cookies dry at room temperature overnight. With food coloring and small new paintbrush, paint designs on dry icing. Store cookies in airtight containers.

Yield: about 6 dozen.

Editor's Note: Meringue powder can be ordered by mail from Wilton Indutries, Inc. Call 1-800/794-5866 or visit www.wilton.com

Cardamom Almond Biscotti

Verna Eberhart
Watertown, South Dakota

These crunchy cookie slices are requested often during the holidays, particularly by my husband. He likes to dunk them in coffee.

1 cup butter, softened
1-3/4 cups sugar
2 eggs
2 teaspoons almond extract
5-1/4 cups all-purpose flour
1 teaspoon baking soda
1 teaspoon salt
1 teaspoon ground cardamom
1 cup (8 ounces) sour cream
1 cup chopped almonds

1. In a large mixing bowl, cream butter and sugar until light and fluffy. Add eggs, one at a time, beating well after each addition. Beat in extract. Combine the flour, baking soda, salt and cardamom; add to the creamed mixture alternately with sour cream. Fold in almonds.

2. Divide dough into fourths. On two greased baking sheets, shape each portion into a 15-in. log (two logs per pan). Bake at 350° for 30 minutes or until lightly browned and firm to the touch.

3. Transfer to a cutting board; cut at a 45° angle with a sharp knife into 1/2-in. slices. Place cut side down on greased baking sheets. Bake for 5-6 minutes on each side or until lightly browned. Remove to wire racks to cool. Store in airtight containers.

Yield: about 7 dozen.

Peanut Butter Kiss Cookies

Dee Davis, Sun City, Arizona

These are great for little ones, and they keep adults guessing as to how they can be made with only five ingredients.

1 cup peanut butter
1 cup sugar
1 egg
1 teaspoon vanilla extract
24 milk chocolate kisses

1. In a mixing bowl, cream peanut butter and sugar. Add the egg and vanilla; beat until blended.

2. Roll into 1-1/4-in. balls. Place 2 in. apart on ungreased baking sheets. Bake at 350° for 10-12 minutes or until tops are slightly cracked. Remove from the oven and immediately press one chocolate kiss into the center of each cookie. Cool for 5 minutes before removing to wire racks.

Yield: 2 dozen.

Editor's Note: Reduced-fat or generic brands of peanut butter are not recommended for this recipe.

Rosettes

Iola Egle, McCook, Nebraska

Dipping the edges of these traditional favorites in icing defines their lacy pattern. These are best when made shortly before they are served.

2 eggs
2 teaspoons sugar
1 cup milk
1 tablespoon vanilla extract
1 cup all-purpose flour
1/4 teaspoon salt
Oil for deep-fat frying

ICING:
2 cups confectioners' sugar
1 teaspoon vanilla extract
1 to 3 tablespoons water

1. In a mixing bowl, beat eggs and sugar; stir in milk and vanilla. Combine flour and salt; add to batter and beat until smooth.

2. Heat 2-1/2 in. of oil to 365° in a deep-fat fryer or electric skillet. Place rosette iron in hot oil, then dip in batter, three-fourths up on sides of iron (do not let batter run over top of iron). Immediately place into hot oil; loosen rosette with fork and remove iron. Fry 1-2 minutes per side or until golden. Remove to a wire rack covered with paper towel. Repeat with remaining batter.

3. For icing, combine the sugar, vanilla and enough water to achieve a dipping consistency. Dip edges of rosettes into icing; dry on wire racks.

Yield: 4-5 dozen.

Christmas Sandwich Cremes

Janice Poechman
Walkerton, Ontario

These melt-in-your-mouth sandwich cookies have a scrumptious filling. I helped my sister make these in high school when she needed a project in her home economics class. "She got an A+!"

1 cup butter, softened
1/3 cup heavy whipping cream
2 cups all-purpose flour
Sugar

FILLING:
1/2 cup butter, softened
1-1/2 cups confectioners' sugar
2 teaspoons vanilla extract
Food coloring

1. In a large mixing bowl, combine the butter, cream and flour. Cover and refrigerate for 2 hours or until dough is easy to handle.

2. Divide into thirds; let one portion stand at room temperature for 15 minutes (keep remaining dough refrigerated until ready to roll out). On a floured surface, roll out dough to 1/8-in. thickness. Cut with a floured 1-1/2-in.-round cookie cutter. Place cutouts in a shallow dish filled with sugar; turn to coat.

3. Place 2 in. apart on ungreased baking sheets. Prick with a fork several times. Bake at 375° for 7-9 minutes or until set. Remove to wire racks to cool completely.

4. For filling, in a mixing bowl, cream butter and sugar. Add vanilla. Tint with food coloring. Spread about 1 teaspoon of filling over half of the cookies; top with remaining cookies.

Yield: 4 dozen.

Eggnog Snickerdoodles

Darlene Brenden, Salem, Oregon

It simply wouldn't be Christmas without these melt-in-your-mouth cookies on my platter! They have a lovely eggnog flavor and look great with their crunchy tops.

1/2 cup butter, softened
1/2 cup shortening
1-3/4 cups sugar, *divided*
2 eggs
1/4 to 1/2 teaspoon rum extract
2-3/4 cups all-purpose flour
2 teaspoons cream of tartar
1 teaspoon baking soda
1/4 teaspoon salt
2 teaspoons ground nutmeg

1. In a mixing bowl, cream butter, shortening and 1-1/2 cups sugar. Beat in eggs and extract. Combine the flour, cream of tartar, baking soda and salt; gradually add to creamed mixture. In a shallow bowl, combine the nutmeg and remaining sugar.

2. Roll dough into 1-in. balls; roll in sugar mixture. Place 2 in. apart on ungreased baking sheets. Bake at 400° for 10-12 minutes or until lightly browned. Remove to wire racks to cool.

Yield: 6-1/2 dozen.

Frosted Ginger Creams

Shirley Clark
Columbia, Missouri

I have many recipes featuring ginger, but these soft cookies are real gems.

1/4 cup shortening
1/2 cup sugar
1 egg
1/3 cup molasses
2 cups all-purpose flour
1 teaspoon ground ginger
1/2 teaspoon baking soda
1/2 teaspoon salt
1/2 teaspoon ground cinnamon
1/2 teaspoon ground cloves
1/3 cup water

FROSTING:
1-1/2 ounces cream cheese, softened
3 tablespoons butter, softened
1 cup plus 3 tablespoons confectioners' sugar
1/2 teaspoon vanilla extract
1 to 2 teaspoons lemon juice

1. In a large mixing bowl cream shortening and sugar. Beat in egg and molasses. Combine the flour, ginger, baking soda, salt, cinnamon and cloves; gradually add to creamed mixture alternately with water (dough will be soft).

2. Drop by heaping teaspoonfuls 2 in. apart onto greased baking sheets. Bake at 400° for 7-8 minutes or until tops are cracked. Remove to wire racks to cool.

3. In a small mixing bowl, beat cream cheese, butter and confectioners' sugar until light and fluffy. Beat in vanilla and enough lemon juice to achieve spreading consistency. Frost cookies. Store in the refrigerator.

Yield: about 4 dozen.

Fennel Tea Cookies

Susan Beck
Napa, California

These tender, buttery tea cookies have a lovely fennel flavor and add a touch of elegance to any holiday cookie tray. Rolled in confectioners' sugar, they look like snowballs!

- 1 tablespoon fennel seed, crushed
- 2 tablespoons boiling water
- 3/4 cup butter, softened
- 2/3 cup packed brown sugar
- 1 egg
- 2 cups all-purpose flour
- 1/2 teaspoon baking soda

Confectioners' sugar

1. In a small bowl, soak fennel seed in boiling water; set aside. In a mixing bowl, cream butter and brown sugar. Beat in egg. Drain fennel seed. Combine the flour, baking soda and fennel seed; gradually add to creamed mixture.

2. Roll into 1-in. balls; place 2 in. apart on ungreased baking sheets. Bake at 350° for 10-12 minutes or until lightly browned. Roll warm cookies in confectioners' sugar. Cool on wire racks.

Yield: 3 dozen.

Jam-Filled Wreaths

Monica Wilson, Pomona, New York

I make these beautiful wreath-shaped cookies with jewel-red centers every Christmas. The dusting of powdered sugar gives them a snowy look. My mother cut the recipe out of a newspaper some 30 years ago.

- 3/4 cup butter, softened
- 1 cup sugar
- 2 eggs
- 1-1/2 cups all-purpose flour
- 1 teaspoon baking powder
- 1 teaspoon ground cinnamon
- 1/2 teaspoon ground allspice
- 1 cup quick-cooking oats
- 3/4 cup finely chopped nuts
- 1 jar (18 ounces) seedless raspberry jam

Confectioners' sugar

1. In a mixing bowl, cream butter and sugar. Add the eggs, one at a time, beating well after each addition. Combine the flour, baking powder, cinnamon and allspice; add to the creamed mixture. Stir in oats and nuts; mix well. Refrigerate for 3 hours or until dough is easy to handle.

2. On a floured surface, roll out half of the dough to 1/8-in. thickness. Cut with a floured 2-1/2-in.-round cookie cutter. Repeat with remaining dough, using a 2-1/2-in. doughnut cutter, so the center is cut out of each cookie.

3. Place 2 in. apart on lightly greased baking sheets. Bake at 400° for 6-8 minutes or until lightly browned. Cool on wire racks.

4. Spread 1 teaspoon jam over solid cookies. Place cookies with centers cut out over jam, forming a sandwich. Dust with confectioners' sugar. Fill centers with additional jam if desired.

Yield: 2-1/2 dozen.

Caramel Heavenlies

Dawn Burns
Troy, Ohio

My mom made these dressy, sweet cookies for cookie exchanges when I was a little girl, letting me sprinkle on the almonds and coconut.

- 12 graham crackers (4-3/4 inches x 2-1/2 inches)
- 2 cups miniature marshmallows
- 3/4 cup butter
- 3/4 cup packed brown sugar
- 1 teaspoon ground cinnamon
- 1 teaspoon vanilla extract
- 1 cup sliced almonds
- 1 cup flaked coconut

1. Line a 15-in. x 10-in. x 1-in. baking pan with foil. Place graham crackers in pan; cover with marshmallows. In a saucepan, cook and stir butter, brown sugar and cinnamon over medium heat until the butter is melted and sugar is dissolved. Remove from the heat; stir in vanilla.

2. Spoon over the marshmallows. Sprinkle with almonds and coconut. Bake at 350° for 14-16 minutes or until browned. Cool completely. Cut into 2-in. squares, then cut each square in half to form triangles.

Yield: about 6 dozen.

Christmas Cookie Ornaments

(Pictured on page 245)
Taste of Home Test Kitchen, Greendale, Wisconsin

These cookies can be baked, then frozen undecorated. So on a fall weekend, bake up as many batches as you need, cool and freeze. Then later you can just defrost them and decorate.

- 1/2 cup butter, softened
- 1/3 cup shortening
- 1 cup sugar
- 1/4 cup honey
- 1 egg
- 1/2 teaspoon vanilla extract
- 3 cups all-purpose flour
- 1/4 teaspoon salt

FROSTING:
- 6-2/3 cups confectioners' sugar
- 1/2 cup water
- 1 tablespoon light corn syrup
- 1 teaspoon vanilla extract
- Assorted liquid *or* paste food coloring

1. In a mixing bowl, cream the butter, shortening and sugar. Beat in the honey, egg and vanilla. Gradually add the flour and salt.

2. Turn dough onto a floured surface and roll dough to 1/8-in. thickness. Cut into shapes using floured cookie cutters. Place cutouts 2 in. apart on ungreased baking sheets.

3. Using a plastic straw, make a hole in the top of each cookie. Remove the center circle of dough. Bake at 350° for 6 minutes or until edges are lightly browned. Remove to wire racks to cool.

4. For frosting, combine the confectioners' sugar, water, corn syrup and vanilla. Beat until smooth. Tint the frosting with liquid or paste food coloring in desired colors.

5. Place each color of frosting in a pastry or plastic bag. Cut a small hole in the tip of each bag. Spread and pipe frosting onto cookies as desired.

6. If desired, create stitch marks on a stocking or veins on holly leaves by dipping a toothpick in food coloring and painting on the lines.

7. For hanging loops, cut forty 8-inch strips of 1/8-inch-wide ribbon. Thread a ribbon strip through the hole in each cookie and tie the ends into a bow.

Yield: 40 (3-inch) cookies.

Peppermint Pinwheels

Marcia Hostetter, Canton, New York

Put a spin on your holidays with these bright swirls! This recipe makes rich-tasting cookies with a minty flavor that sometimes surprises people.

- 3/4 cup butter, softened
- 3/4 cup sugar
- 1 egg yolk
- 1 teaspoon vanilla extract
- 2 cups all-purpose flour
- 1/2 teaspoon baking powder
- 1/2 teaspoon salt
- 1/2 teaspoon peppermint extract
- 1/4 teaspoon red liquid food coloring

1. In a mixing bowl, cream butter and sugar. Beat in egg yolk and vanilla. Combine the flour, baking powder and salt; gradually add to creamed mixture and mix well. Divide dough in half; add extract and red food coloring to one portion.

2. Roll out each portion of dough between waxed paper into a 16-in. x 10-in. rectangle. Remove waxed paper. Place red rectangle over plain rectangle. Roll up tightly jelly-roll style, starting with a long side. Wrap in plastic wrap. Refrigerate overnight or until firm.

3. Unwrap the dough and cut into 1/4-in. slices. Place 2 in. apart on lightly greased baking sheets. Bake at 350° for 12-14 minutes or until set. Cool for 2 minutes before removing to wire racks.

Yield: about 4 dozen.

Candy Cane Cookies

Taste of Home Test Kitchen
Greendale, Wisconsin

Guests will have a merry time munching these mild mint cookies. The cute crunchy candy canes are easy to form once you color the dough—just roll into ropes and twist together.

- 1/2 cup butter, softened
- 1/2 cup shortening
- 1 cup sugar
- 1/4 cup confectioners' sugar
- 1/2 cup milk
- 1 egg
- 1 teaspoon peppermint extract
- 1 teaspoon vanilla extract
- 3-1/2 cups all-purpose flour
- 1/4 teaspoon salt
- Green and red food coloring

1. In a bowl, cream butter, shortening and sugars. Beat in milk, egg and extracts. Gradually add flour and salt. Set aside half of the dough. Divide remaining dough in half; add the green food coloring to one portion and red food coloring to the other. Wrap each dough separately in plastic wrap. Refrigerate for 1 hour or until easy to handle.

2. Roll 1/2 teaspoonfuls of each color of dough into 3-in. ropes. Place each green rope next to a white rope; press together gently and twist. Repeat with red ropes and remaining white ropes.

3. Place 2 in. apart on ungreased baking sheets. Curve one end, forming a cane. Bake at 350° for 11-13 minutes or until set. Cool for 2 minutes; carefully remove to wire racks.

Yield: about 6 dozen.

Two-Tone Christmas Cookies

Marie Capobianco, Portsmouth, Rhode Island

I dreamed up this recipe using two of my favorite flavors, pistachio and raspberry. These pink and green cookies are tasty and eye-catching, too. They're perfect for formal or informal gatherings, and everybody likes them.

1 cup butter, softened
1-1/2 cups sugar
2 egg yolks
2 teaspoons vanilla extract
1 teaspoon almond extract
3-1/2 cups all-purpose flour
1 teaspoon salt
1 teaspoon baking powder
1/2 teaspoon baking soda
9 drops green food coloring
1 tablespoon milk
1/3 cup chopped pistachios
9 drops red food coloring
3 tablespoons seedless raspberry preserves
2 cups (12 ounces) semisweet chocolate chips, melted
Additional chopped pistachios

1. In a mixing bowl, cream butter and sugar. Beat in egg yolks and extracts. Combine the flour, salt, baking powder and baking soda; gradually add to creamed mixture. Divide dough in half. Stir green food coloring, milk and nuts into one portion; mix well. Add red food coloring and jam to the other half.

2. Shape each portion between two pieces of waxed paper into an 8-in. x 6-in. rectangle. Cut in half lengthwise. Place one green rectangle on a piece of plastic wrap. Top with pink rectangle; press together lightly. Repeat. Wrap each in plastic wrap and refrigerate overnight.

3. Unwrap the dough and cut in half lengthwise. Return one rectangle to the refrigerator. Cut the remaining rectangle into 1/8-in. slices. Place 1 in. apart on ungreased baking sheets. Bake at 375° for 7-9 minutes or until set. Remove to wire racks to cool. Repeat with the remaining dough. Drizzle the cooled cookies with melted chocolate. Sprinkle with additional pistachios.

Yield: 6-1/2 dozen.

Nutmeg Sugar Crisps

Kristi Thorpe
Portland, Oregon

My grandma shared her recipe for these old-fashioned sugar cookies with the unexpected taste of nutmeg. They are light, crunchy and so delicious.

1 cup butter, softened
3/4 cup sugar
1/2 cup confectioners' sugar
1 egg
1 teaspoon vanilla extract
2-1/2 cups all-purpose flour
1/2 teaspoon baking soda
1/2 teaspoon cream of tartar
1/4 to 1/2 teaspoon ground nutmeg
1/8 teaspoon salt

1. In a mixing bowl, cream butter and sugars. Beat in egg and vanilla; mix well. Combine the flour, baking soda, cream of tartar, nutmeg and salt; add to the creamed mixture and mix well. Refrigerate for 1 hour.

2. Roll into 3/4-in. balls. Place the balls 2 in. apart on greased baking sheets. Flatten with a glass dipped in sugar. Bake at 350° for 10-12 minutes or until lightly browned. Remove to wire racks to cool.

Yield: about 6 dozen.

Merigue Kisses

Tami Henke
Lockport, Illinois

There's a nice surprise of chocolate inside these frothy kisses. They're my husband's top choice each Christmas.

3 egg whites
1 teaspoon vanilla extract
1/4 teaspoon cream of tartar
Dash salt
1 cup sugar
Red and green food coloring, optional
44 chocolate kisses

1. In a mixing bowl, beat egg whites, vanilla, cream of tartar and salt; on medium speed until soft peaks form. Gradually add sugar, two tablespoons at a time, beating on high until stiff peaks form, about 5-8 minutes. If desired, divide batter in half and fold in red and green food coloring.

2. Drop by rounded tablespoonfuls 1-1/2 in. apart onto lightly greased baking sheets. Press a chocolate kiss into the center of each cookie and cover it with meringue using a knife.

3. Bake at 275° for 30-35 minutes or until firm to the touch. Immediately remove to a wire rack to cool. Store in an airtight container.

Yield: 44 cookies.

Fruitcake Cookies

Dorcas Wright, Guelph, Ontario

My old-fashioned goodies are fun, colorful and chewy without being sticky. They are bite-size fruitcake treats.

1/2 cup butter, softened
1/2 cup shortening
1/2 cup sugar
1/2 cup packed brown sugar
1 egg
1 teaspoon vanilla extract
1 cup all-purpose flour
1/2 teaspoon baking soda
1/2 teaspoon salt
2 cups old-fashioned oats
1 cup flaked coconut
1/2 cup chopped dates
1/2 cup *each* chopped red and green candied cherries
1/2 cup chopped candied pineapple

1. In a mixing bowl, cream butter, shortening and sugars. Add egg and vanilla; mix well. Combine flour, baking soda, salt and oats; add to creamed mixture and mix well. Stir in the coconut, dates, cherries and pineapple.

2. Shape into 1-in. balls; place 1 in. apart on greased baking sheets. Bake at 325° for 15 minutes or until lightly browned. Cool on wire racks.

Yield: 5-6 dozen.

Pumpkin Pecan Tassies

Pat Habiger
Spearville, Kansas

These delicious mini tarts are lovely for Christmas or to serve at a tea. They're worth the extra time it takes to make them.

1/2 cup butter, softened
1 package (3 ounces) cream cheese, softened
1 cup all-purpose flour

FILLING:
3/4 cup packed brown sugar, *divided*
1/4 cup canned pumpkin
4 teaspoons plus 1 tablespoon butter, melted, *divided*
1 egg yolk
1 tablespoon half-and-half cream
1 teaspoon vanilla extract
1/4 teaspoon rum extract
1/8 teaspoon ground cinnamon
1/8 teaspoon ground nutmeg
1/2 cup chopped pecans

1. In a small mixing bowl, cream butter and cream cheese. Beat in flour. Shape into 24 balls. With floured fingers, press onto the bottom and up the sides of greased miniature muffin cups. Bake at 325° for 8-10 minutes or until edges are lightly browned.

2. Meanwhile, in a bowl, combine 1/2 cup brown sugar, pumpkin, 4 teaspoons butter, egg yolk, cream, extracts, cinnamon and nutmeg. Spoon into warm cups. Combine the pecans and remaining brown sugar and butter; sprinkle over filling.

3. Bake 23-27 minutes longer or until set and edges are golden brown. Cool for 10 minutes before removing to wire racks.

Yield: 2 dozen.

Greek Holiday Cookies

Nicole Moskou, New York, New York

In Greece, these buttery golden twists are a traditional treat for Easter and other celebrations. One side of my family is Greek, and I enjoy making foods that keep me in touch with my heritage.

1-1/2 cups butter, softened
1-1/4 cups sugar
4 eggs
2 tablespoons orange juice
3 teaspoons vanilla extract
5-1/4 cups all-purpose flour
1-1/2 teaspoons baking powder
3/4 teaspoon baking soda

1. In a large mixing bowl, cream butter and sugar. Add 2 eggs; beat well. Beat in orange juice and vanilla. Combine the flour, baking powder and baking soda; gradually add to creamed mixture. Cover and refrigerate for 1 hour or until easy to handle.

2. Roll dough into 1-1/4-in. balls. Shape each into a 6-in. rope; fold in half and twist twice. Place 2 in. apart on ungreased baking sheets.

3. In a small bowl, beat remaining eggs; brush over dough. Bake at 350° for 7-12 minutes or until edges are golden brown. Remove to wire racks.

Yield: about 6-1/2 dozen.

Finnish Christmas Cookies

Judith Outlaw, Portland, Oregon

My friend bakes these cookies at Christmas. They're popular at cookie exchanges, but her husband urges her not to trade any of them!

2 cups butter, softened
1 cup sugar
4 cups all-purpose flour
1 egg, beaten
2/3 cup finely chopped almonds
Colored sugar, optional

1. In a mixing bowl, cream butter and sugar until fluffy. Beat in flour. Cover and refrigerate for 1 hour.

2. Roll out onto a well-floured surface to 1/4-in. thickness. Brush lightly with egg. Sprinkle with almonds and sugar if desired. Using a fluted pastry cutter or knife, cut into 2-in. x 1-in. strips.

3. Place 1 in. apart on ungreased baking sheets. Bake at 350° for 10-12 minute or until lightly browned. Remove to wire racks to cool.

Yield: about 6 dozen.

Gingerbread Snowflakes

Shelly Rynearson
Dousman, Wisconsin

Cutting my favorite gingerbread cookie dough into snowflake shapes and decorating them with white icing was ideal for my theme get-together. I save these crunchy treats to enjoy on the way home from our Christmas tree outing.

1 cup butter, softened
1 cup sugar
1 cup molasses
1/4 cup water
5 cups all-purpose flour
2-1/2 teaspoons ground ginger
1-1/2 teaspoons baking soda
1-1/2 teaspoons ground cinnamon
1/2 teaspoon ground allspice
1/4 teaspoon salt

FROSTING:
3-3/4 cups (1 pound) confectioners' sugar
1/4 cup water
1-1/2 teaspoons light corn syrup
1/2 teaspoon vanilla extract

1. In a mixing bowl, cream butter and sugar. Beat in molasses and water. Combine the flour, ginger, baking soda, cinnamon, allspice and salt; gradually add to creamed mixture. Cover and refrigerate for 1 hour or until easy to handle.

2. On a lightly floured surface, roll out dough to 1/4-in. thickness. Cut with floured 2-1/2-in. cookie cutters.

3. Place 2 in. apart on ungreased baking sheets. Bake at 350° for 10-12 minutes or until edges are firm. Remove to wire racks to cool.

4. In a small mixing bowl, combine frosting ingredients; beat until smooth. Transfer to a plastic bag. Cut a small hole in a corner of the bag; pipe frosting onto cookies.

Yield: about 5 dozen.

Lemon Butter Cookies, p. 270

Dutch Treats, p. 277

Kipplens, p. 286

Chocolate Chip Cookie Pops, p. 280

Big Batch Bonanza

Need a batch of cookies for a bake sale, potluck or class trip? Start with any one of these tempting recipes. Each one makes at least 10 dozen cookies!

Lemon Butter Cookies

Judy McCreight
Springfield, Illinois

These tender cutout cookies have a slight lemon flavor that makes them stand out from the rest. They're very easy to roll out compared to other sugar cookies I've worked with. I know you'll enjoy them as much as we do.

   1 cup butter, softened
   2 cups sugar
   2 eggs, beaten
 1/4 cup milk
   2 teaspoons lemon extract
 1/2 teaspoon salt
4-1/2 cups all-purpose flour
   2 teaspoons baking powder
 1/4 teaspoon baking soda
Colored sugar, optional

1. In a mixing bowl, cream butter and sugar. Add eggs, milk and extract. Combine dry ingredients; gradually add to creamed mixture. Cover and chill for 2 hours.

2. Roll out on a lightly floured surface to 1/8-in. thickness. Cut with a floured 2-in. cookie cutter. Place 2 in. apart on ungreased baking sheets. Sprinkle with colored sugar if desired.

3. Bake at 350° for 8-9 minutes or until the edges just begin to brown. Remove to wire racks to cool.

Yield: about 13 dozen.

Chunky Oatmeal Cookies

Donna Borth, Lowell, Michigan

Adults and kids alike love these morsels dotted with M&Ms. I made these flourless cookies to serve at a housewarming party and they were a hit.

  12 eggs
   1 package (32 ounces) brown sugar
   4 cups sugar
   2 cups butter, softened
  18 cups old-fashioned oats
   3 jars (1 pound *each*) peanut butter
 1/4 cup ground cinnamon
 1/4 cup vanilla extract
   8 teaspoons baking soda
   3 cups (18 ounces) semisweet chocolate chips
   1 package (16 ounces) M&M's

1. In a mixing bowl, combine eggs and sugars. Add butter; mix well. Add oats. Add the peanut butter, cinnamon, vanilla and baking soda; mix well. Stir in chocolate chips and M&M's.

2. Drop by rounded tablespoonfuls 2 in. apart onto ungreased baking sheets. Flatten if desired. Bake at 350° for 12-14 minutes or until set. Remove to wire racks to cool.

Yield: 24 dozen.

Editor's Note: This recipe does not use flour. Reduced-fat or generic brands of peanut butter are not recommended for this recipe.

Soft Gingersnaps

Shawn Barto, Clermont, Florida

Loaded with molasses and plenty of spices, these cookies deliver the old-fashioned flavor everyone loves.

1-1/2 cups butter, softened
2 cups sugar
2 eggs
1/2 cup molasses
4-1/2 cups all-purpose flour
3 teaspoons baking soda
2 teaspoons ground cinnamon
1 teaspoon ground ginger
1 teaspoon ground cloves
1/2 teaspoon salt
1/2 teaspoon ground nutmeg
Additional sugar

1. In a mixing bowl, cream the butter and sugar. Add the eggs, one at a time, beating well after each addition. Beat in molasses. Combine the flour, baking soda, cinnamon, ginger, cloves, salt and nutmeg; gradually add to creamed mixture. Refrigerate for 1 hour or until dough is easy to handle.

2. Roll into 1-in. balls; roll in additional sugar. Place 2 in. apart on ungreased baking sheets. Bake at 350° for 8-12 minutes or until puffy and lightly browned. Cool for 1 minute before removing to wire racks.

Yield: 11 dozen.

German Chocolate Toffee Cookies

Joyce Robb
Dillon, Montana

When I first shared these crisp cookies with folks at the hospital where I work as a cook, everyone's palate was pleased! German sweet chocolate gives these cookies a unique twist.

1 cup butter, softened
1 cup shortening
2-1/2 cups sugar
1/2 cup packed brown sugar
1 package (4 ounces) German sweet chocolate, melted
4 eggs
2 teaspoons water
2 teaspoons vanilla extract
6-1/2 cups all-purpose flour
2 teaspoons baking soda
1-1/2 teaspoons salt
1-1/2 cups English toffee bits *or* almond brickle chips
1-1/2 cups chopped walnuts

1. In a mixing bowl, cream the butter, shortening and sugar. Beat in the chocolate. Add eggs, one at a time, beating well after each addition. Beat in water and vanilla. Combine flour, baking soda and salt; gradually add to the creamed mixture. Stir in toffee bits and walnuts.

2. Drop by tablespoonfuls 2 in. apart onto greased baking sheets. Bake at 350° for 12-15 minutes or until golden brown. Remove to wire racks to cool completely.

Yield: 13 dozen.

Bushel of Cookies

Martha Schwartz, Jackson, Ohio

This recipe turns out what seems like a bushelful of cookies—that's probably how it got its name. The flavor of the raisins and pecans comes through in every bite, and the butterscotch chips add a delicious taste.

- 2 pounds raisins
- 1 pound pecans
- 5 cups butter, softened
- 11 cups sugar
- 12 eggs
- 1 cup maple syrup
- 1 quart milk
- 1/4 cup vanilla extract
- 12 cups quick-cooking oats
- 21 cups all-purpose flour
- 2 teaspoons salt
- 1/4 cup baking powder
- 1/4 cup baking soda
- 2 packages (10 to 11 ounces *each*) butterscotch chips

1. Grind or finely chop raisins and pecans; set aside. In a mixing bowl, cream butter and sugar. Add eggs, a few at a time, mixing well after each addition. Add syrup, milk and vanilla; mix well. Stir in the oats, raisins and pecans. Combine the flour, salt, baking powder and baking soda; stir into oat mixture. Fold in chips. Cover and chill for 2 hours.

2. Drop by rounded tablespoonfuls 2 in. apart onto greased baking sheets. Bake at 350° for 13-15 minutes or until set. Remove to wire racks to cool.

Yield: 24 dozen.

Black Walnut Cookies

Doug Black
Conover, North Carolina

Black walnuts have a more distinctive flavor than the traditional English walnuts. Since black walnuts have a short shelf life, it's best to store them in the freezer.

- 1 cup butter, softened
- 2 cups packed brown sugar
- 2 eggs
- 1 teaspoon vanilla extract
- 3-1/2 cups all-purpose flour
- 1 teaspoon baking soda
- 1/4 teaspoon salt
- 2 cups chopped black walnuts, *divided*

1. In a mixing bowl, cream the butter and brown sugar. Beat in eggs and vanilla. Combine flour, baking soda and salt; gradually add to the creamed mixture. Stir in 1-1/4 cups of walnuts. Finely chop the remaining nuts.

2. Shape dough into two 15-in. logs. Roll logs in chopped nuts, pressing gently. Wrap each in plastic wrap. Refrigerate for 2 hours or until firm.

3. Unwrap and cut into 1/4-in. slices. Place 2 in. apart on greased baking sheets. Bake at 350° for 8-11 minutes. Remove to wire racks to cool.

Yield: 10 dozen.

Pumpkin Chip Cookies

Tami Burroughs
Salem, Oregon

These golden cake-like cookies are my favorite, especially around the holidays. They disappear quickly from my dessert trays. The subtle pumpkin and cinnamon flavors pair nicely with chocolate chips.

1-1/2 cups butter, softened
    2 cups packed brown sugar
    1 cup sugar
    1 can (15 ounces) solid-pack pumpkin
    1 egg
    1 teaspoon vanilla extract
    4 cups all-purpose flour
    2 cups quick-cooking oats
    2 teaspoons baking soda
    2 teaspoons ground cinnamon
    1 teaspoon salt
    2 cups (12 ounces) semisweet chocolate chips

1. In a large mixing bowl, cream butter and sugars. Beat in the pumpkin, egg and vanilla. Combine the flour, oats, baking soda, cinnamon and salt; gradually add to creamed mixture. Stir in chocolate chips.

2. Drop by tablespoonfuls 2 in. apart onto ungreased baking sheets. Bake at 350° for 10-12 minutes or until lightly browned. Remove to wire racks to cool.

Yield: 10 dozen.

Double-Chip Cookies

Diana Dube, Rockland, Maine

These buttery cookies are packed with vanilla and peanut butter chips plus walnuts. I'm never left with any to take home after a potluck dinner.

    2 cups butter, softened
1-1/2 cups sugar
1-1/2 cups packed brown sugar
    4 eggs
    3 teaspoons vanilla extract
    5 cups all-purpose flour
    3 teaspoons baking soda
    1 teaspoon salt
    3 cups chopped walnuts
    1 package (10 to 12 ounces) vanilla *or* white chips
    1 package (10 ounces) peanut butter chips

1. In a large mixing bowl, cream butter and sugars. Add eggs, one at a time, beating well after each addition. Beat in vanilla. Combine the flour, baking soda and salt; gradually add to the creamed mixture. Stir in walnuts and chips.

2. Drop by rounded tablespoonfuls 2 in. apart onto ungreased baking sheets. Bake at 350° for 10-12 minutes or until golden brown. Remove to wire racks to cool.

Yield: about 10 dozen.

Grossmutter's Peppernuts

Marilyn Kutzli
Clinton, Iowa

Before Christmas, my grandmother would bake peppernuts and store them until the "big day." When we'd come home from school, the whole house would smell like anise and we knew the holiday season was about to begin.

- 3 eggs
- 2 cups sugar
- 2-3/4 cups all-purpose flour
- 1 teaspoon anise extract *or* crushed anise seed

1. In a large mixing bowl, beat eggs and sugar at medium speed for 15 minutes. Reduce speed and slowly add flour and anise. Mix until well combined. On a lightly floured surface, shape dough into ropes about 1/2 in. in diameter. Cover and refrigerate for 1 hour.

2. Slice ropes into 1/2-in. lengths. Place on greased baking sheets. Bake at 350° for 6-8 minutes or until set. Cookies will harden upon standing. When cool, store in airtight containers; they are best if allowed to age before serving.

Yield: 30 dozen.

Cookies for a Crowd

Mary Green, Mishicot, Wisconsin

I'm a cook at a 4-H camp. Our campers go wild over these crisp cookies with an excellent peanutty flavor.

- 4 cups shortening
- 4 cups packed brown sugar
- 4 cups sugar
- 8 eggs
- 4 cups peanut butter
- 4 teaspoons vanilla extract
- 10 cups all-purpose flour
- 4 teaspoons baking soda
- 4 teaspoons salt
- 1 cup chopped salted peanuts, optional

1. Cream shortening and sugars. Add eggs, peanut butter and vanilla; mix well. Combine flour, baking soda and salt; gradually add to creamed mixture well. Stir in peanuts if desired.

2. Drop by rounded teaspoonfuls 2 in. apart onto ungreased baking sheets. Flatten with a fork if desired. Bake at 350° for 10-12 minutes or until set. Remove to wire racks to cool.

Yield: about 20 dozen.

Editor's Note: Reduced-fat or generic brands of peanut butter are not recommended for this recipe.

Grandma's Oatmeal Cookies

Mary Ann Konechne
Kimball, South Dakota

This recipe—a favorite of my husband's—goes back to my great-grandmother. At Christmastime, we use colored sugar for a festive touch.

2 cups sugar
1-1/2 cups shortening
4 eggs
4 teaspoons water
4 cups all-purpose flour
2 teaspoons baking soda
1/2 teaspoon salt
2 teaspoons ground cinnamon
4 cups quick-cooking oats
2 cups chopped raisins
1 cup chopped walnuts
Additional granulated sugar *or* colored sugar

1. In a large mixing bowl, cream sugar and shortening. Add eggs, one at a time, beating well after each addition. Beat in water. Combine the flour, baking soda and salt; gradually add to creamed mixture. Stir in oats, raisins and walnuts.

2. On a surface sprinkled with additional sugar or colored sugar, roll out dough to 1/4-in. thickness. Cut with desired cutters. Place on greased baking sheets. Bake at 350° for 12-15 minutes or until set. Remove to wire racks to cool.

Yield: 12 dozen.

Whole Wheat Toffee Sandies

Alice Kahnk
Kennard, Nebraska

Crisp and loaded with goodies, these are my husband's favorite cookies. I used to bake them in large batches when our four sons still lived at home. Now I whip them up for our grandchildren.

1 cup butter, softened
1 cup sugar
1 cup confectioners' sugar
1 cup vegetable oil
2 eggs
1 teaspoon almond extract
3-1/2 cups all-purpose flour
1 cup whole wheat flour
1 teaspoon baking soda
1 teaspoon cream of tartar
1 teaspoon salt
2 cups chopped almonds
1 package (6 ounces) English toffee bits
Additional sugar

1. In a mixing bowl, cream butter and sugars. Add oil, eggs and extract; mix well. Combine flours, baking soda, cream of tartar and salt; gradually add to creamed mixture. Stir in almonds and toffee bits.

2. Roll into 1-in. balls; roll in sugar. Place on ungreased baking sheets and flatten with a fork. Bake at 350° for 12-14 minutes or until lightly browned. Remove to wire racks to cool.

Yield: about 12 dozen.

Jumbo Raisin Cookies

Becky Melander
Clinton Township, Michigan

When I was growing up, my mother would make these soft and spicy raisin cookies once a month. Since the recipe makes a huge batch, she would freeze some to snack on later.

- 2 cups water
- 4 cups raisins
- 1 cup butter, softened
- 1 cup shortening
- 4 cups sugar
- 6 eggs
- 2 teaspoons vanilla extract
- 8 cups all-purpose flour
- 4 teaspoons baking soda
- 4 teaspoons baking powder
- 4 teaspoons salt
- 1 tablespoon ground cinnamon
- 1 teaspoon ground nutmeg
- 1/2 teaspoon ground allspice
- 2 cups (12 ounces) semisweet chocolate chips

1. In a saucepan, combine the water and raisins. Bring to a boil. Remove from the heat; cool to room temperature (do not drain).

2. In a large mixing bowl, cream butter, shortening and sugar. Add eggs, one at a time, beating well after each addition. Beat in vanilla. Combine the dry ingredients; gradually add to the creamed mixture. Stir in chocolate chips and raisins with any liquid.

3. Drop by heaping tablespoonfuls 2 in. apart onto greased baking sheets. Bake at 350° for 12-15 minutes or until golden brown. Remove to wire racks to cool completely.

Yield: 13 dozen.

Cherry Christmas Slices

Katie Koziolek
Hartland, Minnesota

You'll especially appreciate this recipe around the hurried holidays because the dough can be frozen for up to 2 months. So when planning your holiday cookie baking spree, be sure to include these.

- 1 cup butter, softened
- 1 cup confectioners' sugar
- 1 egg
- 1 teaspoon vanilla extract
- 2-1/4 cups all-purpose flour
- 2 cups red and green candied cherries, halved
- 1 cup pecan halves

1. In a mixing bowl, cream the butter and sugar. Add egg and vanilla; beat until fluffy. Add flour; mix well. Stir in cherries and pecans. Cover and refrigerate for 1 hour. Shape dough into three 10-in. rolls; wrap in plastic wrap and place in a freezer bag. Freeze up to 2 months or until ready to bake.

2. To bake, unwrap and cut frozen rolls into 1/8-in. slices. Place 1 in. apart on ungreased baking sheets. Bake at 325° for 10-12 minutes or until edges are golden brown. Remove to wire racks to cool.

Yield: about 11 dozen.

Dutch Treats

Ava Rexrode
Blue Grass, Virginia

I was born and raised in Holland, where we used almond paste quite often in our baking. I created this recipe to capture the outstanding flavors of home.

1 cup butter, softened
2 packages (3 ounces *each*) cream cheese, softened
2 cups all-purpose flour

FILLING:
3 eggs
1 cup sugar
1 can (8 ounces) almond paste, cut into cubes
Sliced almonds

1. In a mixing bowl, cream butter and cream cheese. Gradually add the flour. Cover and refrigerate for 1 hour or until easy to handle.

2. Roll into 1-in. balls. Press dough onto the bottom and up the sides of ungreased miniature muffin cups; set aside.

3. For filling, beat eggs in a mixing bowl until light and fluffy. Add sugar; mix well. Beat in the almond paste. Spoon a rounded teaspoonful into each cup; top each with three almond slices.

4. Bake at 325° for 25-30 minutes or until lightly browned and filling is set. Cool for 10 minutes before removing to wire racks.

Yield: about 10 dozen.

Ginger Poppy Seed Cookies

Mary Priesgen, Theresa, Wisconsin

Poppy seed and ginger pair up nicely in these popular treats. The refrigerated dough slices easily and bakes quickly.

3 cups butter, softened
1-1/2 cups sugar
1-1/2 cups packed brown sugar
3 eggs
2 teaspoons vanilla extract
7-1/2 cups all-purpose flour
1/2 cup poppy seeds
4 teaspoons ground cinnamon
2 teaspoons ground ginger
1-1/2 teaspoons baking soda
3/4 teaspoon salt

1. In a large mixing bowl, cream the butter and sugars. Add eggs and vanilla. Combine the remaining ingredients; add to creamed mixture. Shape into four 13-in. rolls. Wrap each in plastic wrap. Refrigerate for 2 hours or overnight.

2. Unwrap dough and cut into 1/4-in. slices. Place 2 in. apart on ungreased baking sheets. Bake at 375° for 9-11 minutes or until edges are golden brown. Remove to wire racks to cool.

Yield: about 17 dozen.

Orange Slice Cookies

Britt Strain
Idaho Falls, Idaho

Soft candy orange slices are a refreshing addition to these crispy vanilla chip cookies. To quickly cut the orange candy, use scissors, rinsing the blades with cold water occasionally to reduce sticking.

> 1 cup candy orange slices
> 1-1/2 cups sugar, *divided*
> 1 cup butter, softened
> 1-1/2 cups packed brown sugar
> 2 eggs
> 2 teaspoons vanilla extract
> 4 cups all-purpose flour
> 2 teaspoons baking soda
> 1 teaspoon salt
> 1 package (10 to 12 ounces) vanilla chips *or* white chips
> 1 cup chopped pecans

1. Cut each orange slice into eight pieces. Roll in 1/4 cup sugar; set aside. In a mixing bowl, cream the butter, shortening, brown sugar and remaining sugar. Add eggs, one at a time, beating well after each addition. Beat in vanilla. Combine the flour, baking soda and salt; gradually add to creamed mixture. Stir in chips, pecans and orange slice pieces.

2. Roll into 1-in. balls. Place 2 in. apart on ungreased baking sheets. Bake at 375° for 10-12 minutes or until golden brown. Remove to wire racks to cool completely.

Yield: about 10 dozen.

Cinnamon Almond Strips

When I was young, I could hardly wait for the holidays because I knew these rich cookies would make an appearance on the cookie tray. Now I make them for holidays throughout the year.

Fred Grover
Lake Havasu City, Arizona

> 1-1/2 cups butter, softened
> 1 cup sugar
> 3 eggs, *separated*
> 3 cups all-purpose flour
>
> **TOPPING:**
> 1-1/2 cups sugar
> 1 cup finely chopped almonds
> 1-1/2 teaspoons ground cinnamon

1. In a mixing bowl, cream butter and sugar. Beat in egg yolks; mix well. Gradually add flour.

2. Using a cookie press fitted with a bar disk, press dough into long strips onto ungreased baking sheets. Beat egg whites until stiff; brush over dough. Combine topping ingredients; sprinkle over strips. Cut each strip into 2-in. pieces (there is no need to separate the pieces).

3. Bake at 350° for 8-10 minutes or until edges are firm (do not brown). Cut into pieces again if necessary. Remove to wire racks to cool.

Yield: about 10 dozen.

Sponge Cake Cookies

Terry Carpenter, Vineland, New Jersey

My heart's warmed by these cookies because the recipe comes from my grandmother. No wedding, shower or holiday gathering went by without our caring matriarch or her pretty little treats.

1 cup butter, softened
1-1/2 cups sugar
8 eggs
2 tablespoons lemon extract
4 cups all-purpose flour
1/4 cup baking powder
FROSTING:
1/2 cup butter, softened
3-3/4 cups confectioners' sugar
1 teaspoon lemon extract
1/8 teaspoon salt
3 to 4 tablespoons milk
Food coloring, optional
4 cups flaked coconut, optional

1. In a mixing bowl, cream the butter and sugar. Add the eggs, one at a time, beating well after each addition. Beat in extract. Combine flour and baking powder; gradually add to the creamed mixture.

2. Drop by teaspoonfuls 3 in. apart onto ungreased baking sheets. Bake at 400° for 6-8 minutes or until the edges are lightly browned. Remove to wire racks to cool.

3. In a mixing bowl, cream butter, sugar, extract and salt. Add enough milk to achieve spreading consistency. Tint with food coloring if desired. Frost cooled cookies. Sprinkle with coconut if desired.

Yield: 11 dozen.

Lemon-Butter Spritz Cookies

Paula Pelis
Lenhartsville, Pennsylvania

This recipe makes a lot of terrific cookies! Using a cookie press may be too difficult for children to master. Instead, have them help sprinkle the cookies with colored sugar before baking.

2 cups butter, softened
1-1/4 cups sugar
2 eggs
Grated peel of 1 lemon
2 teaspoons lemon juice
1 teaspoon vanilla extract
5-1/4 cups all-purpose flour
1/4 teaspoon salt
Colored sugar

1. In a large mixing bowl, cream butter and sugar. Add the eggs, lemon peel, lemon juice and vanilla; mix well. Stir together flour and salt; gradually add to creamed mixture.

2. Using a cookie press fitted with the disk of your choice, press dough 2 in. apart onto ungreased baking sheets. Sprinkle with colored sugar. Bake at 400° for 8-10 minutes or until lightly brown around the edges. Remove to wire racks to cool.

Yield: about 12 dozen.

Brown Sugar Crinkles

Donna Frame
Montgomery Village, Maryland

The addition of brown sugar makes these deliciously different from traditional sugar cookies. They're attractive and simple to make. The recipe can be easily cut in half.

      1 cup butter, softened
      1 cup shortening
      3 cups sugar
1-1/2 cups packed brown sugar
      6 eggs
      1 tablespoon vanilla extract
      6 cups all-purpose flour
      1 tablespoon baking soda
1-1/2 teaspoons salt

1. In a mixing bowl, cream butter, shortening and sugars. Add eggs, one at a time, beating well after each addition. Beat in vanilla. Combine flour, baking soda and salt; gradually add to the creamed mixture (the dough will be soft).

2. Drop by rounded teaspoonfuls 2 in. apart onto ungreased baking sheets. Flatten with a glass dipped in sugar. Bake at 350° for 10-12 minutes or until lightly browned. Cool for 2 minutes before removing to wire racks completely.

Yield: about 13 dozen.

Chocolate Chip Cookie Pops

Silretta Graves
Park Forest, Illinois

My family prefers milk chocolate to dark or semisweet chocolate, so I created this recipe. Baking the pops on a stick makes them fun, but the cookies are just as delicious by themselves.

      2 cups butter, softened
1-1/2 cups sugar
1-1/2 cups packed brown sugar
      3 eggs
      1 tablespoon vanilla extract
4-3/4 cups all-purpose flour
1-1/2 teaspoons baking soda
      1 teaspoon salt
      3 cups milk chocolate chips
      2 cups chopped pecans
     12 dozen wooden craft *or* Popsicle sticks, optional

1. In a large mixing bowl, cream the butter and sugars. Add eggs, one at a time, beating well after each addition. Beat in vanilla. Combine flour, baking soda and salt; gradually add to creamed mixture. Transfer to a larger bowl if necessary. Stir in chips and pecans.

2. Drop by rounded teaspoonful 3 in. apart onto ungreased baking sheets. Insert a wooden stick into each cookie if desired. Bake at 375° for 10-12 minutes or until lightly browned. Cool for 1-2 minutes before removing to wire racks.

Yield: about 12 dozen.

Chocolate Topped Peanut Butter Spritz

Dolores Deegan
Pottstown, Pennsylvania

Peanut butter sets these delicious cookies apart from other spritz. The chocolate drizzle makes them extra special.

1 cup butter, softened
1 cup peanut butter
1 cup granulated sugar
1 cup brown sugar
2 eggs
2 cups all-purpose flour
1 teaspoon baking soda
1/2 teaspoon salt

CHOCOLATE TOPPING:
1-1/2 cups semisweet chocolate chips
1 tablespoons shortening
Chopped peanuts

1. In a large bowl, cream together butter, peanut butter and sugars. Beat in eggs until fluffy. Combine flour, baking soda and salt; gradually add to creamed mixture; blend well. Cover and refrigerate for 15 minutes.

2. Using a cookie press fitted with a zigzag disk, press dough into long strips onto ungreased baking sheets. Cut each strip into 2-in. pieces (there is no need to separate the pieces). Bake at 350° for 6-8 minutes or until set (do not brown). Remove to wire racks to cool.

3. In a microwave or saucepan, melt chocolate and shortening, stirring until smooth. Cut a small hole in the corner of pastry or plastic bag. Fill with chocolate mixture. Pipe a strip of chocolate down center of each cookie. Sprinkle with chopped peanuts.

Yield: 16 dozen.

Editor's Note: Reduced-fat or generic brands of peanut butter are not recommended for this recipe.

Mom's Cherry Date Cookies

Hope Huggins, Santa Cruz, California

My mother made these festive drop cookies as far back as I can remember—80 years at least. We called them "the Christmas cookies," maybe because they're so full of fruit and nuts.

1 cup shortening
1-1/2 cups packed brown sugar
3 eggs
2-1/2 cups all-purpose flour
1 teaspoon baking soda
1 teaspoon ground cinnamon
1/2 teaspoon salt
3 tablespoons hot water
1 cup chopped walnuts
1/2 cup chopped dates
1/2 cup quartered maraschino cherries

1. In a mixing bowl, cream shortening and brown sugar. Add eggs, one at a time, beating well after each addition. Combine the flour, baking soda, cinnamon and salt; add to creamed mixture alternately with water. Stir in walnuts, dates and cherries.

2. Drop by rounded teaspoonfuls 2 in. apart onto ungreased baking sheets. Bake at 375° for 8-9 minutes or until golden brown. Remove to wire racks to cool.

Yield: 10-1/2 dozen.

Editor's Note: To make 5 dozen larger cookies, drop dough by rounded tablespoonfuls 3 in. apart onto ungreased baking sheets. Bake for 9-10 minutes.

Jeweled Cookies

Ruth Ann Stelfox
Raymond, Alberta

Candied fruits give a stained-glass look to these cookies. They're like shortbread, but dressed up.

 1 pound butter, softened
2-1/2 cups sugar
 3 eggs
 5 cups all-purpose flour
 1 teaspoon baking soda
1-1/2 cups raisins
 1 cup coarsely chopped walnuts
 1/2 cup *each* chopped red and green candied cherries
 1/2 cup chopped candied pineapple

1. In a mixing bowl, cream butter and sugar. Add eggs, one at a time, beating well after each. Combine flour and baking soda; add to creamed mixture. Stir in raisins, nuts, cherries and pineapple; mix well. Shape into 2-in. rolls; wrap in waxed paper or foil. Freeze at least 2 hours.

2. Cut into 1/4-in. slices; place 1 in. apart on greased baking sheets. Bake at 350° for 8-10 minutes or until lightly browned. Remove to wire racks to cool completely.

Yield: 12-14 dozen.

Big-Batch Butterscotch Cookies

JoAnne Riechman, McComb, Ohio

My mom and I perfected this recipe years ago. The rich butterscotch flavor earns us rave review when we bring these crowd-pleasing cookies to gatherings.

1-1/2 cups butter, softened
 3 cups packed brown sugar
 3 eggs
 1 tablespoon vanilla extract
5-1/4 cups all-purpose flour
 1 tablespoon baking powder
1-1/2 teaspoons baking soda
 1/2 teaspoon cream of tartar

1. In a large mixing bowl, cream the butter and brown sugar. Add eggs, one at a time, beating well after each addition. Beat in vanilla. Transfer to a larger bowl if necessary. Combine flour, baking powder, baking soda and cream of tartar; gradually add to the creamed mixture.

2. Drop by level tablespoonfuls 2 in. apart onto ungreased baking sheets. Bake at 350° for 10-12 minutes or until golden brown. Remove to wire racks to cool.

Yield: about 20 dozen.

Soft Apple Butter Delights

Shirley Harter, Greenfield, Indiana

I won first place at a local apple bake-off with this original recipe. I especially like to take these hearty cookies to gatherings in fall.

- 1 cup butter, softened
- 2 cups packed brown sugar
- 2 eggs
- 1/2 cup brewed coffee, room temperature
- 3-1/2 cups all-purpose flour
- 1 teaspoon baking soda
- 1 teaspoon salt
- 1 teaspoon ground nutmeg
- 2 cups apple butter
- 1 cup chopped walnuts

1. In a large mixing bowl, cream the butter and brown sugar. Add eggs, one at a time, beating well after each addition. Beat in coffee. Combine flour, baking soda, salt and nutmeg; gradually add to the creamed mixture. Stir in apple butter and walnuts (dough will be soft). Cover and chill for 1 hour.

2. Drop by teaspoonfuls 2 in. apart onto lightly greased baking sheets. Bake at 400° for 10-12 minutes or until edges are firm. Remove to wire racks to cool.

Yield: 10 dozen.

Editor's Note: This recipe was tested with commercially prepared apple butter.

Eggnog Cookies

Myra Innes
Auburn, Kansas

This cookie's flavor fits right into the holiday spirit.

- 1 cup butter, softened
- 2 cups sugar
- 1 cup eggnog
- 1 teaspoon baking soda
- 1/2 teaspoon ground nutmeg
- 5-1/2 cups all-purpose flour
- 1 egg white, lightly beaten
- Colored sugar

1. In a mixing bowl, cream the butter and sugar. Beat in eggnog, baking soda and nutmeg. Gradually add flour and mix well. Cover and chill for 1 hour.

2. On a lightly floured surface, roll out half of dough to 1/8-in. thickness. Cut into desired shapes; place 2 in. apart on ungreased baking sheets. Repeat with the remaining dough. Brush with the egg white; sprinkle with the colored sugar.

3. Bake at 350° for 6-8 minutes or until edges are lightly browned. Remove to wire racks to cool.

Yield: about 16 dozen.

Editor's Note: This recipe was tested with commercially prepared eggnog.

Big Batch Cookies

Diana Dube, Rockland, Maine

It's nice to offer a little homemade taste when feeding a hungry horde. These cookies also freeze well, so you can make them when time allows.

> 2 cups butter, softened
> 1-1/2 cups sugar
> 1-1/2 cups packed brown sugar
> 4 eggs, lightly beaten
> 1 tablespoon vanilla extract
> 5 cups all-purpose flour
> 1 tablespoon baking soda
> 1 teaspoon salt
> 1 pound (3-3/4 cups) chopped walnuts
> 2 packages (10 ounces *each*) peanut butter chips

1. In a large mixing bowl, cream butter and sugars. Add eggs and vanilla; mix well. Combine flour, baking soda and salt; add to creamed mixture and mix well. Fold in the nuts and chips.

2. Drop by rounded teaspoonfuls onto ungreased baking sheets. Bake at 350° for 10-12 minutes or until lightly browned. Remove to wire racks to cool completely.

Yield: 12 dozen.

Mint Morsels

Adina Skilbred
Prairie du Sac, Wisconsin

Is it a cookie or a candy? No matter which answer folks choose, they find these minty morsels yummy.

> 1/3 cup shortening
> 1/3 cup butter, softened
> 3/4 cup sugar
> 1 egg
> 1 tablespoon milk
> 1 teaspoon vanilla extract
> 1-3/4 cups all-purpose flour
> 1/3 cup baking cocoa
> 1-1/2 teaspoons baking powder
> 1/4 teaspoon salt
> 1/8 teaspoon ground cinnamon

PEPPERMINT LAYER:
> 4 cups confectioners' sugar
> 6 tablespoons corn syrup
> 6 tablespoons butter, melted
> 2 to 3 teaspoons peppermint extract

CHOCOLATE COATING:
> 2 packages (11-1/2 ounces *each*) milk chocolate chips
> 1/4 cup shortening

1. In a mixing bowl, cream shortening, butter and sugar. Add egg, milk and vanilla; mix well. Combine flour, cocoa, baking powder, salt and cinnamon; add to creamed mixture and mix well. Cover and refrigerate for 8 hours or overnight.

2. On a lightly floured surface, roll dough to 1/8-in. thickness. Cut with a 1-1/2-in.-round cookie cutter. Place 2 in. apart on ungreased baking sheets. Bake at 375° for 6-8 minutes or until set. Cool for 2 minutes; remove to wire racks to cool completely.

3. Combine peppermint layer ingredients; mix well. Knead for 1 minute or until smooth. Shape into 120 balls, 1/2 in. each. Place a ball on each cookie and flatten to cover cookie. Place on waxed paper-lined baking sheets; refrigerate for 30 minutes. In a microwave, melt the chips and shortening. Spread about 1 teaspoonful over each cookie. Chill until firm.

Yield: about 10 dozen.

Italian Holiday Cookies

Sue Seymour
Valatie, New York

Many of our holiday traditions center around the foods my mother made while I was growing up. These cookies, which we called "Strufoli," bring back wonderful memories.

- 1 tablespoon sugar
- 1 teaspoon grated lemon peel
- 1 teaspoon vanilla extract
- 1/2 teaspoon salt
- 4 eggs
- 2-1/2 cups all-purpose flour
- Vegetable oil for deep-fat frying
- 1 cup honey
- Candy sprinkles

1. In a mixing bowl, combine sugar, lemon peel, vanilla and salt. Add eggs and 2 cups flour; mix well. Turn onto a floured board and knead in remaining flour (dough will be soft).

2. With a floured knife or scissors, cut into 20 pieces. With hands, roll each piece into pencil shapes. Cut the "pencils" into 1/2-in. pieces. In an electric skillet or deep-fat fryer, heat oil to 375°. Fry pieces, a few at a time, for 2 minutes per side or until golden brown. Drain on paper towels. Place in a large bowl.

3. Heat honey to boiling; pour over cookies and mix well. With a slotted spoon, spoon onto a serving platter and slowly mound into a tree shape if desired. Decorate with candy sprinkles. Cool completely.

Yield: about 15 dozen.

Michigan Cherry Drops

Carol Blue, Barnesville, Pennsylvania

I usually double this recipe so that I have plenty to share during the holidays. Pretty pink cookies such as these are a wonderful treat.

- 1 cup butter, softened
- 1 cup sugar
- 1/2 cup packed brown sugar
- 4 eggs
- 1-1/2 teaspoons vanilla extract
- 4 cups all-purpose flour
- 1 teaspoon salt
- 1 teaspoon ground cinnamon
- 1/2 teaspoon ground nutmeg
- 3-1/2 cups chopped walnuts
- 3 cups chopped maraschino cherries
- 2-2/3 cups raisins

1. In a large mixing bowl, cream the butter and sugars. Add eggs, one at a time, beating well after each addition. Beat in vanilla. Combine flour, salt, cinnamon and nutmeg; gradually add to creamed mixture. Transfer to a large bowl if necessary. Stir in walnuts, cherries and raisins.

2. Drop by tablespoonfuls 2 in. apart onto ungreased baking sheets. Bake at 350° for 16-18 minutes or until lightly browned. Remove to wire racks to cool. Store in an airtight container.

Yield: about 14 dozen.

Kipplens

Susan Bohannon
Kokomo, Indiana

My Great-Aunt Hilda makes this recipe every Christmas, and everybody just raves about it! Kipplens taste a lot like Mexican wedding cakes, but I like them better.

    2 cups butter, softened
    1 cup sugar
    5 cups all-purpose flour
    2 teaspoons vanilla extract
    2 cups chopped pecans
    1/4 teaspoon salt
Confectioners' sugar

1. In a mixing bowl, cream butter and sugar; add flour, vanilla, pecans and salt. Mix well.

2. Roll dough into 1-in. balls and place on ungreased baking sheets. Bake at 325° for 17-20 minutes or until lightly browned. Remove to wire racks. Cool cookies slightly before rolling them in confectioners' sugar.

Yield: 12 dozen.

Oatmeal Molasses Crisps

Jori Schellenberger, Everett, Washington

The cooking in Amish and Mennonite homes is guaranteed delicious. So when I found this recipe in an Amish family cookbook, I knew I had to try it. It's become a favorite.

2-1/2 cups butter, softened
    5 cups sugar
    4 eggs
    1/3 cup dark molasses
    1 tablespoon vanilla extract
4-1/3 cups all-purpose flour
    4 teaspoons baking powder
    3 teaspoons ground cinnamon
    2 teaspoons salt
    1 teaspoon baking soda
4-3/4 cups old-fashioned oats
    2 cups finely chopped pecans

1. In a large mixing bowl, cream butter and sugar. Add eggs, one at a time, beating well after each addition. Beat in molasses and vanilla. Combine the flour, baking powder, cinnamon, salt and baking soda; gradually add to the creamed mixture. Transfer to a larger bowl if necessary. Stir in oats and pecans.

2. Drop by tablespoonfuls 2 in. apart onto greased baking sheets. Bake at 375° for 8-10 minutes or until edges are firm. Cool for 3 minutes before removing to wire racks.

Yield: 15 dozen.

Buttery Yeast Spritz

Janet Stucky, Sterling, Illinois

Yeast may be an unusual ingredient for cookies, but the buttery flavor is fabulous. These were my mother's favorite cookies...now I make them for my children and grandchildren.

- 1 package (1/4 ounce) active dry yeast
- 2 tablespoons warm water (110° to 115°)
- 2 cups butter, softened
- 1 cup sugar
- 2 egg yolks
- 4 cups all-purpose flour

1. In a bowl, dissolve yeast in warm water; set aside. In a mixing bowl, cream butter and sugar. Beat in egg yolks and yeast mixture. Gradually add flour.

2. Using a cookie press fitted with disk of your choice, press dough into desired shapes 1 in. apart onto ungreased baking sheets. Bake at 400° for 7-9 minutes or until lightly browned. Remove to wire racks to cool.

Yield: 13 dozen.

Spice Cookies With Pumpkin Dip

Kelly McNeal
Derby, Kansas

My husband and two kids are sure to eat the first dozen of these cookies, warm from the oven, before the next tray is even done. A co-worker gave me the recipe for the pumpkin dip, which everyone loves with the cookies.

- 1-1/2 cups butter, softened
- 2 cups sugar
- 2 eggs
- 1/2 cup molasses
- 4 cups all-purpose flour
- 4 teaspoons baking soda
- 2 teaspoons ground cinnamon
- 1 teaspoon *each* ground ginger and cloves
- 1 teaspoon salt

PUMPKIN DIP:
- 1 package (8 ounces) cream cheese, softened
- 2 cups pumpkin pie filling
- 2 cups confectioners' sugar
- 1/2 to 1 teaspoon ground cinnamon
- 1/4 to 1/2 teaspoon ground ginger

1. In a mixing bowl, cream the butter and sugar. Add the eggs, one at a time, beating well after each addition. Add molasses; mix well. Combine flour, baking soda, cinnamon, ginger, cloves and salt; add to creamed mixture and mix well. Cover and refrigerate overnight.

2. Shape into 1/2-in. balls; roll in sugar. Place 2 in. apart on ungreased baking sheets. Bake at 375° for 6 minutes or until edges begin to brown. Cool for 2 minutes before removing to a wire racks.

3. For dip, beat cream cheese in a mixing bowl until smooth. Add pumpkin pie filling; beat well. Add sugar, cinnamon and ginger; beat until smooth. Serve with cookies. Store leftover dip in the refrigerator.

Yield: about 20 dozen (3 cups dip).

Toffee Chip Cookies

Kay Frances Ronnenkamp
Albion, Nebraska

These cookies combine several mouth-watering flavors. The generous size of the batch gives me plenty of scrumptious cookies to have on hand and extras to send to our sons at college.

- 1 cup butter, softened
- 1/2 cup vegetable oil
- 1 cup sugar
- 1 cup packed brown sugar
- 1 teaspoon vanilla extract
- 2 eggs
- 3-1/2 cups all-purpose flour
- 1 teaspoon cream of tartar
- 1 teaspoon baking soda
- 1 teaspoon salt
- 3 cups crisp rice cereal
- 1 cup quick-cooking oats
- 1 cup flaked coconut
- 1 cup chopped pecans
- 1 cup English toffee bits *or* almond brickle chips

1. In a large mixing bowl, cream butter, oil, sugars and vanilla. Add eggs, one at a time, beating well after each addition. Combine the flour, cream of tartar, baking soda and salt; add to creamed mixture. Stir in remaining ingredients.

2. Drop by tablespoonfuls 2 in. apart onto ungreased baking sheets. Bake at 350° for 10-12 minutes or until lightly browned. Remove to wire racks to cool.

Yield: 12 dozen.

Valentine Butter Cookies

Eleanor Slimak
Chicago, Illinois

Melt in your mouth is what these buttery cookies do!

- 2 cups butter, softened
- 2 cups sugar
- 3 eggs
- 1 tablespoon vanilla extract
- 6 cups all-purpose flour
- 2 teaspoons baking powder
- Red decorator's sugar, optional

1. In a mixing bowl, cream butter and sugar. Add eggs and vanilla; mix well. Combine flour and baking powder; gradually add to creamed mixture and mix well.

2. Using a cookie press fitted with the heart disk, press dough 2 in. apart onto ungreased baking sheets. Decorate with sugar if desired. Bake at 350° for 10-12 minutes or until set (do not brown). Remove to wire racks to cool completely.

Yield: 18-19 dozen.

Whipped Shortbread

Jane Ficiur
Bow Island, Alberta

This version of shortbread is fragile, but not too sweet and melts in your mouth. Mostly I make it for the holidays...but I'll also prepare it year-round for wedding showers and ladies teas.

3 cups butter, softened
1-1/2 cups confectioners' sugar, sifted
4-1/2 cups all-purpose flour
1-1/2 cups cornstarch
Nonpareils *and/or* halved candied cherries

1. Using a heavy-duty mixer, beat butter on medium speed until light and fluffy. Gradually add dry ingredients, beating constantly until well blended. Dust hands lightly with additional cornstarch.

2. Roll dough into 1-in. balls, dip in nonpareils and place on ungreased baking sheet. Press balls lightly with a floured fork. To decorate with cherries, place balls on baking sheet and press lightly with fork. Top each with a cherry half.

3. Bake at 300° for 20-22 minutes or until cookie is set but not browned. Remove to wire racks to cool.

Yield: 16-18 dozen.

Nut-Filled Horns

Penny Field, Waynesboro, Virginia

"Simply the best" is what most folks say after sampling these rich, flaky cookies. It's a thrill to share them with friends and family.

2 cups butter, softened
2 packages (8 ounces *each*) cream cheese, softened
2 egg yolks
4-1/2 cups all-purpose flour
2 teaspoons baking powder

FILLING:
4 cups finely chopped walnuts
1-1/2 to 2 cups sugar
6 tablespoons evaporated milk
1-1/2 teaspoons vanilla extract

1. In a large mixing bowl, cream the butter and cream cheese. Add egg yolks. Combine flour and baking powder; gradually add to the creamed mixture. Cover and refrigerate overnight.

2. In a bowl, combine filling ingredients (mixture will be thick). Divide dough into fourths (dough will be sticky). On a well-sugared surface, roll out each portion into a 12-in. x 10-in. rectangle. Cut into 2-in. squares. Place about 1 teaspoon filling in the center of each square. Fold over two opposite corners; seal tightly.

3. Place 2 in. apart on ungreased baking sheets. Bake at 350° for 15-18 minutes or until lightly browned. Remove to wire racks to cool.

Yield: 10 dozen.

General Recipe Index

Chocolate Coconut Neapolitans, 89
Chocolate Mint Creams, 255
Chocolate Peppermint Pinwheels, 101
Chocolate Pinwheels, 95
Cranberry Nut Swirls, 250
Cream Cheese-Filled Cookies, 97
Cute Kitty Cookies, 105
Date Swirl Cookies, 103
Double Butterscotch Cookies, 101
Double Peanut Butter Cookies, 88
Fruit 'n' Nut Cookies, 104
Ginger Poppy Seed Cookies, 277
Ginger Thins, 100
Hazelnut Shortbread, 92
Honey Spice Cookies, 92
Icebox Cookies, 19
Icebox Sugar Cookies, 99
Jeweled Cookies, 282
Lemon Pecan Slices, 96
Lemon Refrigerator Cookies, 16
Mom's Coconut Cookies, 95
Orange Pecan Cookies, 103
Owl Cookies, 99
Pastelitos De Boda, 96
Peanut Butter Pinwheels, 90
Pecan Rounds, 100
Peppermint Candy Cookies, 94
Peppermint Cookies, 97
Peppermint Pinwheels, 263
Peppermint Wafers, 21
Raspberry Nut Pinwheels, 13
Raspberry Swirls, 98
Rolled Oat Cookies, 91
Sesame Coconut Cookies, 104
Strawberry-Nut Pinwheel Cookies, 88
Toffee Cranberry Crisps, 38
Two-Tone Butter Cookies, 102
Two-Tone Christmas Cookies, 264
Watermelon Slice Cookies, 91

RHUBARB
Rhubarb Custard Bars, 198
Rhubarb Dream Bars, 202
Rhubarb-Filled Cookies, 58

SANDWICH COOKIES
Almond Jelly Cookies, 159
Apricot-Filled Cookies, 165
Austrian Nut Cookies, 146
Caramel Creams, 164
Cherry-Filled Cookies, 148
Cherry-Filled Heart Cookies, 162
Chocolate Almond Cookies, 167
Chocolate Mint Cookies, 160
Chocolate Peanut Butter Sandwich
    Cookies, 156
Chocolaty Double Crunchers, 163
Christmas Sandwich Cremes, 259
Dipped Peanut Butter Sandwich
    Cookies, 236
Dipped Sandwich Cookies, 157

Fruit-Filled Spritz Cookies, 160
Jam-Filled Wreaths, 261
Lacy Oat Sandwich Wafers, 161
Lemon-Cream Sandwich Cookies, 158
Linzer Heart Cookies, 157
Maple Sandwich Cookies, 163
Mint Sandwich Cookies, 230
Oatmeal Sandwich Cookies, 156
Old-Fashioned Raisin Cookies, 153
Old-Fashioned Whoopie Pies, 161
Painted Holiday Delights, 249
Pumpkin Whoopie Pies, 167
Quick Chocolate Sandwich
    Cookies, 233
Rainbow Cookies, 166
S'more Sandwich Cookies, 158
Strawberry Sandwich Cookies, 159
Surprise Sugar Stars, 148
Toffee Sandwich Cookies, 164

SESAME SEEDS
Apricot Sesame Cookies, 119
Fruit 'n' Nut Bars, 201
Sesame Coconut Cookies, 104
Sesame Seed Cookies, 52
Watermelon Slice Cookies, 91

SHAPED COOKIES
Almond Kiss Cookies, 125
Almond-Tipped Shortbread
    Fingers, 110
Angel Wings, 131
Apricot Cheese Crescents, 120
Apricot Pecan Tassies, 114
Apricot Sesame Cookies, 119
Beary Cute Cookies, 116
Braided Sweetheart Cookies, 109
Brickle Cookies, 243
Butter Cookies, 124
Butterfinger Cookies, 20
Butterscotch Pecan Cookies, 240
Butterscotch Snickerdoodles, 129
Buttery Almond Cookies, 133
Buttery Yeast Spritz, 287
Candy Cane Cookies, 263
Caramel Heavenlies, 262
Caramel Pecan Treasures, 118
Cardamom Almond Biscotti, 258
Cardamom Cookies, 111
Cherry Snowballs, 11
Chocolate Cappuccino Cookies, 129
Chocolate Caramel Cookies, 130
Chocolate Chip Butter Cookies, 29
Chocolate-Covered Cherry
    Cookies, 122
Chocolate-Filled Poppy Seed
    Cookies, 123
Chocolate Jubilees, 18
Chocolate Macadamia Meltaways, 115
Chocolate Malted Cookies, 30

Chocolate Meringue Stars, 247
Chocolate Mint Crisps, 125
Chocolate Peanut Butter Cookies, 238
Chocolate Pecan Thumbprints, 128
Chocolate Puddles, 124
Chocolate Snowballs, 34
Chocolate Thumbprint Cookies, 119
Chocolate Topped Peanut Butter
    Spritz, 281
Cinnamon Almond Crescents, 128
Cinnamon Almond Strips, 278
Cinnamon Crackle Cookies, 127
Citrus Cookies, 226
Cocoa Surprise Cookies, 44
Coconut Chip Cookies, 225
Coconut Washboards, 15
Coffee Bonbons, 131
Cookie Jar Gingersnaps, 11
Cookie Sticks, 30
Cranberry Crispies, 239
Cream Cheese Bells, 114
Cream Filberts, 130
Crinkle-Top Chocolate Cookies, 38
Crisp 'n' Chewy Cookies, 41
Crisp Lemon Sugar Cookies, 23
Crispy Oat Cookies, 121
Crispy Scotchies, 39
Double Chip Biscotti, 229
Double Chocolate Biscotti, 48
Double Chocolate Chip Cookies, 35
Double Chocolate Sprinkle Cookies, 13
Dutch Treats, 277
Easy Chocolate Caramel Cookies, 231
Eggnog Logs, 247
Eggnog Snickerdoodles, 260
Farm Mouse Cookies, 112
Favorite Molasses Cookies, 127
Fennel Tea Cookies, 261
Festive Shortbread Logs, 116
Frosted Cocoa Cookies, 126
Frosted Snowmen, 115
Fruitcake Cookies, 265
Golden Raisin Cookies, 22
Greek Holiday Cookies, 266
Grossmutter's Peppernuts, 274
Hazelnut Shortbread, 92
Holiday Biscotti, 256
Holly Wreaths, 253
Honey-Peanut Butter Cookies, 126
Italian Holiday Cookies, 285
Kipplens, 286
Lemon-Butter Spritz Cookies, 279
Lemon Crisp Cookies, 235
Lemon-Lime Crackle Cookies, 223
Lo-Cal Molasses Cookies, 117
Malted Milk Cookies, 22
Meringue Bunnies, 109
Mexican Wedding Cakes, 117
Mint Candy Cookies, 222
Mocha Crackle Cookies, 24
Monster Cookies, 28

Alphabetical Recipe Index

A

B

C